Kraków,
Warsaw &
Gdańsk

CONTENTS

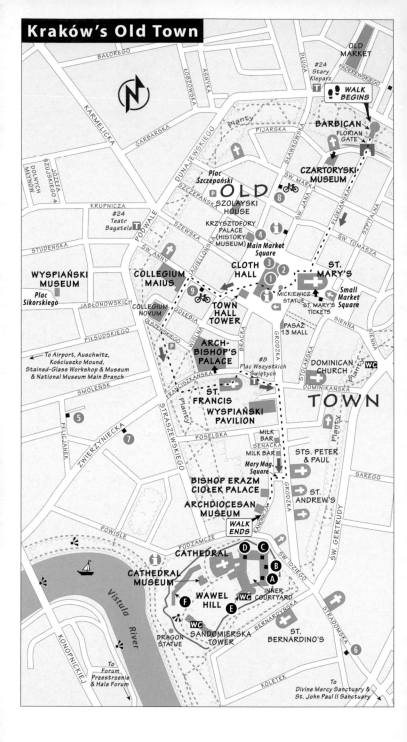

Kraków's Old Town

OLD MARKET

BAŁOREGO

DŁUGA

PADEREWSKIEGO

ŁOBZOWSKA

ASNYKA

GARBARSKA

PIJARSKA

#24 Stary Kleparz

WALK BEGINS

BARBICAN

FLORIAN GATE

KARMELICKA

SŁAWKOWSKA

CZARTORYSKI MUSEUM

JÓZEFA ŚLUSKIEGO 4

DOLNYCH MŁYNÓW

KRUPNICZA

SZCZEPAŃSKA

Plac Szczepański

OLD

SZOLAYSKI HOUSE

SW. MARKA

FLORIAŃSKA

SW. JANA

#24 Teatr Bagatela

PODWALE

SZEWSKA

KRZYSZTOFORY PALACE (HISTORY MUSEUM)

4

Main Market Square

SW. TOMASZA

STUDENSKA

SW. ANNY

AGIELLOŃSKA

CLOTH HALL

3

2

1

ST. MARY'S

WYSPIAŃSKI MUSEUM

COLLEGIUM MAIUS

9

Small Market Square

Plac Sikorskiego

JABŁONOWSKICH

COLLEGIUM NOVUM

GOŁĘBIA

TOWN HALL TOWER

MICKIEWICZ STATUE

ST. MARY'S TICKETS

SIENNA

SIENNA

PIŁSUDSKIEGO

OLSZEWSKIEGO

WIŚLNA

BRACKA

PASAŻ 13 MALL

SMOLEŃSK

← To Airport, Auschwitz, Kościuszko Mound, Stained-Glass Workshop & Museum & National Museum Main Branch

ARCH-BISHOP'S PALACE

GRODZKA

#8 Plac Wszystkich Świętych

DOMINICAN CHURCH

WC

SZPITALNA

5

FELICJANEK

ZWIERZYNIECKA

7

STRASZEWSKIEGO

FRANCISZKAŃSKA

ST. FRANCIS

WYSPIAŃSKI PAVILION

POSELSKA

DOMINIKAŃSKA

TOWN

SZTOLARSKA

MILK BAR

SENACKA

MILK BAR

Mary Mag. Square

STS. PETER & PAUL

SAREGO

BISHOP ERAZM CIOŁEK PALACE

GRODZKA

ST. ANDREW'S

ARCHDIOCESAN MUSEUM

WALK ENDS

KANONICZA

SW. GERTRUDY

POWIŚLE

PODZAMCZE

CATHEDRAL

D

C

B

A

CATHEDRAL MUSEUM

INNER COURTYARD

BERNARDYŃSKA

STRADOMSKA

F

WAWEL HILL

WC

E

ST. BERNARDINO'S

Vistula River

WC

SANDOMIERSKA TOWER

DRAGON STATUE

6

KONOPNICKIEJ

To Forum Przestrzenie & Hala Forum

KOLETEK

To Divine Mercy Sanctuary & St. John Paul II Sanctuary

Sights & Services

1. Gallery of 19th-Century Polish Art (Entrance)
2. Rynek Underground Museum (Entrance)
3. Rynek Underground Museum (Tickets)
4. Museum of Kraków Visitors Center & Ticket Office
5. Massolit Books
6. Frania Café/Laundry
7. Betty Clean Laundry
8. Kraków Bike Tours
9. Bike Rental

Wawel Castle Sights

A. Royal State Rooms
B. Royal Private Apartments
C. Crown Treasury & Armory
D. Art of the Orient
E. Lost Wawel
F. Wawel Recovered

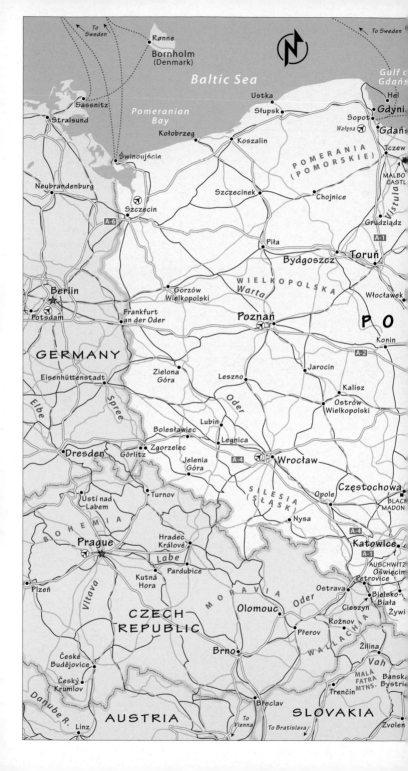

INTRODUCTION

This Snapshot guide, excerpted from my guidebook *Rick Steves Central Europe*, introduces you to a trio of grand Polish cities: historic Kraków, thriving Warsaw, and gorgeous Gdańsk. Covering the best of Poland, this book offers an enjoyable cross-section of this proud nation.

Poland's historical capital, Kraków, clusters around one of Europe's biggest and most inviting market squares. Explore Kraków's picture-perfect Old Town—filled with museums, restaurants, university life, and Old World charm—and head to the Kazimierz neighborhood to learn about Poland's Jewish story. Side-trip to the world's most powerful memorial to the victims of the Holocaust at the former Auschwitz-Birkenau concentration camp.

For a look at today's Poland, visit Warsaw—leveled in World War II, rebuilt soon after, and now rapidly gentrifying. Stroll through Warsaw's reconstructed Old Town, promenade along newly spiffed-up boulevards, gape up at the communist-style Palace of Culture and Science, and dip into engaging museums on WWII history, native son Fryderyk Chopin, Polish painters, and much more.

On the Baltic Coast, Gdańsk offers a vibrantly colorful main drag fronted by opulent old Hanseatic facades, plus inspiring tales from the toppling of communism at the shipyard where the Solidarity trade union was born. Nearby in Pomerania is a pair of medieval red-brick sights: the imposing Gothic headquarters of the Teutonic Knights, Malbork Castle; and the appealing, gingerbread-scented town of Toruń.

To help you have the best trip possible, I've included the following topics in this book:

- **Planning Your Time,** with advice on how to make the most of your limited time
- **Orientation,** including tourist information offices (abbreviated as TI), tips on public transportation, local tour options, and helpful hints
- **Sights,** with ratings and strategies for meaningful and efficient visits
- **Sleeping** and **Eating,** with good-value recommendations in every price range
- **Connections,** with tips on trains, buses, and boats

And near the end of this book, **Practicalities** has information on money, staying connected, hotel reservations, transportation, and other helpful advice.

To travel smartly, read this little book in its entirety before you go. It's my hope that this guide will make your trip more meaningful and rewarding. Traveling like a temporary local, you'll get the absolute most out of every mile, minute, and dollar.

Szczęśliwej podróży—Happy travels!

Rick Steves

POLAND
Polska

POLAND

Polska

Poland is a land of surprises. Some travelers may still imagine this place as a backwards, impoverished land of rusting factories, smoggy cities, and gloomy citizens—only to be left speechless when they step into Kraków's vibrant main square, Gdańsk's colorful Royal Way, or Warsaw's trendy hipster zones. Today's Poland has a vibrant urbanity, an enticing food and design culture, dynamic history, and kindhearted locals.

The Poles are a proud people—as moved by their spectacular failures as by their successes. Their quiet elegance has been tempered by generations of abuse by foreign powers.

In a way, there are two Polands: lively, cosmopolitan urban centers; and countless tiny farm villages in the countryside. A societal tension exists between city-dwelling progressives and what they call the "simple people" of Poland: salt-of-the-earth Poles descended from generations of farmers, who still live an uncomplicated, agrarian lifestyle and tend to be politically conservative and staunchly Euroskeptic.

Poland is arguably Europe's most devoutly Catholic country. Even compared to other nominally Catholic countries, travelers are

struck by how the Poles' faith pervades their lives and worldviews. This is probably because the Catholic faith has united and sustained the Poles through many tough times. Squeezed between Protestant Germany (Prussia) and Eastern Orthodox Russia, Poland wasn't even a country for generations (during the Partitions, 1795-1918)—but its Catholicism helped keep its spirit alive. Then, under communism, Poles found their religion a source of both strength and rebellion—they could express dissent against the atheistic regime by going to church. Be sure to step into some serene church interiors. These aren't museums—you'll almost certainly see locals engrossed

in prayer. (Visit with respect: Maintain silence, and if you want to take pictures, do so discreetly.)

Much of Poland's story is a Jewish story. Starting in the Middle Ages, Poland was a magnet for Jewish refugees because of its relatively welcoming policies. "Relatively" is the operative word. Polish history is rife with pogroms and other acts of violence, and Jewish people were forbidden from owning land; that's why they settled mostly in cities.

Jewish cultural life in Poland blossomed in the early 20th century. Before World War II, 80 percent of Europe's Jews lived in this country. Warsaw was the world's second-largest Jewish city (after New York), with 380,000 Jews (out of a total population of 1.2 million). But the Holocaust (and a later Soviet policy of sending "troublemaking" Jews to Israel) decimated the Jewish population.

This tragic chapter, combined with postwar border shifts and population movements, made Poland one of Europe's most ethnically homogeneous countries. Today, 97 percent of citizens are ethnic Poles; only a few thousand Polish Jews remain, along with small minorities of Ukrainians and Germans.

Poland has long been staunchly pro-America. Of course, their big neighbors (Russia and Germany) have been their historic enemies. And when Hitler invaded in 1939, the Poles felt let down by their supposed European friends (France and Britain), who declared war on Germany but provided virtually no military support to the Polish resistance. America, meanwhile, is seen as the big ally from across the ocean—and the home of the largest population of Poles outside of Poland.

Poles may strike some visitors as brusque. Among older generations, this may be a holdover from challenging communist times.

And it may help to know that, because of the plainspoken cadence of Polish, Poles speaking English sometimes sound more impatient or gruff than they realize. Part of the Poles' charm is that they're not as slick and self-assured as many Europeans: They're kind, soft-spoken, and quite shy. On a recent train trip in Poland, I offered my seatmate a snack—and spent the rest of the trip enjoying a delightful conversation with a new friend.

HELPFUL HINTS

Price Ranges: Many hotels and restaurants in Poland fall in this book's lower price ranges (**$** and **$$**). This is a reflection not of quality but of the value of Poland compared to other destinations in Central Europe. A **$$** hotel or restaurant in Poland can often meet or exceed the caliber of a **$$$$** place in Prague or Vienna. Don't be put off by seemingly low prices: Even elegant choices don't break the bank here, and frugal travelers can order high on the menu.

Restroom Signage: To confuse tourists, the Poles have devised a secret way of marking their WCs. You'll see doors marked with *męska* (men) and *damska* (women)—but even more often, you'll simply see a triangle (for men) or a circle (for women).

Train Tickets: It's easiest to buy train tickets online at www.intercity.pl; while not particularly user-friendly, it's in English and workable with a little patience (it helps to create a log-in). Tickets are emailed, and you can simply show them on your phone to the conductor. At train stations, you'll see both ticket machines and staffed windows *(kasy)*. These may be marked (sometimes only in Polish) for domestic tickets, international tickets, and so on; ask to make sure you're in the right line. Leave plenty of time to buy your ticket.

Train Station Lingo: "PKP" is the abbreviation for Polish National Railways ("PKS" is for buses). In larger towns with several train stations, you'll normally use the one called Główny (meaning "Main"—except in Warsaw, where it's *Centralna*). *Dworzec główny* means "main train station." Most stations have several platforms *(peron)*, each of which has two tracks *(tor)*. Departures are generally listed by the *peron*, so keep your eye on both tracks for your train. Arrivals are *przyjazdy,* and departures are *odjazdy.* Left-luggage counters or lockers are marked *przechowalnia bagażu.* On arriving at a station, to get

Poland Almanac

Official Name: Rzeczpospolita Polska (Republic of Poland), or Polska for short.

Snapshot History: This thousand-year-old country has been dominated by foreign powers for much of the past two centuries, finally achieving true independence (from the Soviet Union) in 1989.

People: As of mid-2023, this stands at over 41 million people (slightly less than California)—which includes at least 1.5 million recent arrivals from Ukraine who may not become permanent residents. Four out of every five Poles are practicing Catholics.

Latitude and Longitude: 52°N and 20°E (similar latitude to Berlin, London, and Edmonton, Alberta).

Area: 121,000 square miles, the same as New Mexico.

Geography: Because of its overall flatness, Poland has been a corridor for invading armies since its infancy. The Vistula River (650 miles) runs south-to-north up the middle of the country, passing through Kraków and Warsaw, and emptying into the Baltic Sea at Gdańsk. Poland's climate is generally cool and rainy—40,000 storks love it.

Biggest Cities: Warsaw (the capital, 1.8 million), Kraków (800,000), and Łódź (660,000).

Economy: The gross domestic product is $1.1 trillion, with a GDP per capita of $29,500. The 1990s saw an aggressive and successful transition from state-run socialism to privately owned capitalism.

Currency: 1 złoty (zł, or PLN) = 100 groszy (gr) = about 25 cents; 4 zł = about $1.

Government: Poland's mostly figurehead president selects the prime minister and cabinet, with legislators' approval. They govern along with a two-house legislature (Sejm and Senat) of 560 seats. Prime Minister Mateusz Morawiecki represents the majority political party, the right-wing Law and Justice (Prawo i Sprawiedliwość, or PiS for short). President Andrzej Duda, formerly of PiS (but currently a conservative-leaning independent), was narrowly reelected to a second five-year term in 2020.

Flag: The upper half is white, and the lower half is red—the traditional colors of Poland. Poetic Poles claim the white represents honor, and the red represents the blood spilled by the Poles to protect that honor. The flag sometimes includes a coat of arms with a crowned eagle (representing Polish sovereignty). Under Soviet rule, the crown was removed from the emblem, and the eagle's talons were trimmed. On regaining its independence, Poland coronated its eagle once more.

POLAND

into town, follow signs for *wyjście* (sometimes followed by *do centrum* or *do miasta*).

Transit Route Planner: For a good public transit route planner for most Polish cities, try https://jakdojade.pl. You can also buy transit tickets on the Jakdojade app.

Easter Revelry: This is a major holiday in Poland, rivaling Christmas in importance. Expect most businesses to close from Friday or Saturday through Monday (which is also a national holiday). If you're in town for Easter, take part in some of the special traditions: All week, churches feature specially decorated chapels and altars. On Saturday, Poles bring lovingly decorated baskets of food to be blessed at church (Święconka). On Easter Sunday, Poles attend Mass and celebrate with an hours-long breakfast (the sour soup *żurek* is one of many traditional dishes). Monday is Śmigus-Dyngus, when people throw water at their loved ones (no joke).

Busy May: May 1 is May Day and May 3 is Constitution Day; this usually causes virtually the entire country to close down for a week. Later in the month, younger kids get out of school, so families go on vacation (Kraków is one of the most popular domestic destinations).

POLISH HISTORY

Poland is flat. Glancing at a topographical map of Europe, it's easy to see the Poles' historical dilemma: The path of least resistance from northern Europe to Russia leads right through Poland. Over the years, many invaders—from Genghis Khan to Napoleon to Hitler—have taken advantage of this fact. The country has been called "God's playground" for the many wars that have rumbled through its territory. Poland has been invaded by Soviets, Nazis, French, Austrians, Russians, Prussians, Swedes, Teutonic Knights, Tatars, Bohemians, Magyars—and, about 1,300 years ago, Poles.

Medieval Greatness

The first Poles were the Polonians ("people of the plains"), a Slavic band that arrived here in the eighth century. In 966, Mieszko I, duke of the Polonian tribe, adopted Christianity and founded the Piast dynasty, which would last for more than 400 years. Centuries before Germany, Italy, or Spain first united, Poland was born.

Poland struggled against two different invaders in the 13th

Top 10 Dates That Changed Poland

AD 966: The Polish king Mieszko I is baptized a Christian, symbolically uniting the Polish people and founding the nation.

1385: The Polish queen Jadwiga marries a Lithuanian duke, starting the two-century reign of the Jagiełło family.

1410: Poland defeats the Teutonic Knights at the Battle of Grunwald, part of a golden age of territorial expansion and cultural achievement.

1572: The last Jagiellonian king dies, soon replaced by bickering nobles and foreign kings. Poland declines.

1795: In the last of three Partitions, the country is divvied up by its more-powerful neighbors: Russia, Prussia, and Austria.

1918: Following World War I, Poland finally reclaims its land and sovereignty.

1939: The Free City of Danzig (today's Gdańsk) is invaded by Nazi Germany, starting World War II. At war's end, the country is "liberated" (i.e., occupied) by the Soviet Union. After the war, Poland's borders and population shift significantly westward.

1980: Lech Wałęsa and the Solidarity trade union lead a successful strike, demanding more freedom from the communist regime.

1989: Poland gains independence under its first president—Lech Wałęsa. Fifteen years later, Poland joins the European Union.

2010: President Lech Kaczyński and 95 other high-level government officials are killed in a plane crash in Smoleńsk, Russia.

century: the Tatars (Mongols who ravaged the south) and the Teutonic Knights (Germans who conquered the north). But despite these challenges, Poland persevered. The last king of the Piast dynasty was also the greatest: Kazimierz the Great, who famously "found a Poland made of wood and left one made of brick and stone," and helped bring Poland (and its then-capital, Kraków) to international prominence. The progressive Kazimierz also invited Europe's much-persecuted Jews to settle here, establishing Poland as a relative haven for the Jewish people, which it would remain until the Nazis arrived.

Kazimierz the Great died at the end of the 14th century without a male heir. His grand-niece, Princess Jadwiga, became "king" (the Poles weren't ready for a "queen") and married Lithuanian prince Władysław Jagiełło, uniting their countries against a common enemy, the Teutonic Knights. Their marriage marked the beginning of the Jagiellonian dynasty and set the stage for Poland's golden age.

During this time, Poland expanded its territory, the Polish nobility began to acquire more political influence, Italy's Renaissance (and its architectural styles) became popular, and the Toruń-born astronomer Nicholas Copernicus shook up the scientific world with his bold new heliocentric theory. Up on the Baltic coast, the port city of Danzig (today's Gdańsk) took advantage of its Hanseatic League trading partnership to become one of Europe's most prosperous cities.

Foreign Kings and Partitions

When the Jagiellonians died out in 1572, political power shifted to the nobility. Poland became a republic of nobles governed by its wealthiest 10 percent—the *szlachta*, who elected a series of foreign kings. In the 16th and 17th centuries, with its territory spanning from the Baltic Sea to the Black Sea, the Polish-Lithuanian Commonwealth was the largest state in Europe.

But over time, many of the elected kings made selfish or poor diplomatic decisions and squandered the country's resources. To make matters worse, the nobles' parliament (Sejm) introduced the concept of *liberum veto* (literally "I freely forbid"), whereby any measure could be vetoed by a single member. This policy, which effectively demanded unanimous approval for any law to be passed, paralyzed the Sejm's already-waning power.

Sensing the Commonwealth's weakness, in the mid-17th century forces from Sweden rampaged through Polish and Lithuanian lands in the devastating "Swedish Deluge." While Poland eventually reclaimed its territory, a third of its population was dead. The Commonwealth continued to import self-serving foreign kings, including Saxony's Augustus the Strong and his son, who drained Polish wealth to finance vanity projects in their hometown of Dresden.

By the late 18th century, the Commonwealth was floundering...and surrounded by three land-hungry empires (Russia, Prussia, and Austria). The Poles were unaware that these neighbors had entered into an agreement now dubbed the "Alliance of the Three Black Eagles" (all three of those countries, coincidentally, had that same symbol); they began to circle Poland's white eagle. Stanisław August Poniatowski, elected king with Russian support in 1764, would be Poland's last.

Over the course of less than 25 years, Russia, Prussia, and Austria divided Polish territory among themselves in a series of three Partitions. In 1772 and again in 1790, Poland was forced into ceding large chunks of land to its neighbors. Desperate to reform their government, Poles enacted Europe's first democratic constitution (and the world's second, after the US Constitution) on May 3, 1791—still celebrated as a national holiday. This visionary document protected the peasants, dispensed with both *liberum veto* and the election of the king, and set up something resembling a modern nation. But the constitution alarmed Poland's neighbors, who swept in soon after with the third and final Partition in 1795. "Poland" disappeared from Europe's maps, not to return until 1918.

Even though Poland was gone, the Poles wouldn't go quietly. As the Partitions were taking place, Polish soldier Tadeusz Kościuszko (also a hero of the American Revolution) returned home to lead an unsuccessful military resistance against the Russians in 1794.

Napoleon offered a brief glimmer of hope to the Poles in the early 19th century, when he marched eastward through Europe and set up the semi-independent "Duchy of Warsaw" in Polish lands. But that fleeting taste of freedom lasted only eight years, until Napoleon's defeat at Waterloo. The Congress of Vienna, which again redistributed Polish territory to Prussia, Russia, and Austria, is sometimes called (by Poles) the "Fourth Partition." In a classic case of "my enemy's enemy is my friend," the Poles still have great affection for Napoleon for how fiercely he fought against their mutual foes.

The Napoleonic connection also established France as a safe haven for refugee Poles. After another failed uprising against Russia in 1830, many of Poland's top artists and writers fled to Paris—including pianist Fryderyk Chopin and Romantic poet Adam Mickiewicz (whose statue adorns Kraków's main square and Warsaw's Royal Way). These Polish artists tried to preserve the nation's spirit with music and words; those who remained in Poland continued to fight with swords and fists. By the end of the 19th century, the image of the Pole as a tireless, idealistic insurgent emerged. During this time, some Romantics—with typically melodramatic flair—dubbed Poland "the Christ of nations" for the way it was misunderstood and persecuted by the world, despite its nobility.

Poles didn't just flock to France during the Partitions. Untold numbers of Polish people uprooted their lives to pursue a better future in the New World. About 10 million Americans have Polish ancestry, and most of them came stateside from the mid-19th to early 20th century. Because the sophisticated and educated tended to remain in Poland, these new arrivals were mostly poor farmers who were (at first) unschooled and didn't speak English, placing them on a bottom rung of American society. It was during this time that the tradition of insulting "Polack jokes" emerged. Some claim these originated in Chicago, which was both a national trendsetter in humor and a magnet for Polish immigrants. Others suggest that German immigrants to America imported cruel

POLAND

stereotypes of their Polish neighbors from the Old World. Either way, the jokes became more vicious through the 20th century, until the Polish government actually lobbied the US State Department to put a stop to them.

As the map of Europe was redrawn following World War I, Poland emerged as a reborn nation, under the war hero-turned-head of state, Marshal Józef Piłsudski. The newly reformed "Second Polish Republic," which patched together the bits and pieces of territory that had been under foreign rule for decades, enjoyed a diverse ethnic mix—including Germans, Russians, Ukrainians, Lithuanians, and an enormous Jewish minority. A third of Poland spoke no Polish.

This interwar period was particularly good to Poland's Jews. They were, for the first time, legally protected citizens of Poland, with full voting rights. Cities like Warsaw, Kraków, and Wilno (today's Vilnius, Lithuania)—where Jews made up a quarter to a third of the population—saw the blossoming of a rich Jewish culture.

Meanwhile, the historic Baltic port city of Gdańsk—which was bicultural (German and Polish)—was granted the special "Free City of Danzig" status to avoid dealing with the prickly issue of whether to assign it to Germany or Poland. But the peace was not to last.

World War II
On September 1, 1939, Adolf Hitler began World War II by attacking Danzig to bring it into the German fold. Before the month was out, Hitler's forces had overrun Poland, and the Soviets had taken over a swath of eastern Poland (today part of Ukraine, Belarus, and Lithuania).

In their *Drang nach Osten* ("March to the East"), the Nazis considered the Poles *slawische Untermenschen*, "Slavic sub-humans" who were useful only for manual labor. Poland was also home to a huge population of Jewish people. Nazi Germany annexed Polish regions that it claimed historic ties to, while the rest (including "Warschau" and "Krakau") became a puppet state ruled by the *Generalgouvernement* and Hitler's handpicked governor, Hans Frank. The Nazis considered this area *Lebensraum*—"living space" that wasn't nice enough to actually incorporate into Germany but served perfectly as extra territory for building things that Germans didn't want in their backyards...such as notorious death camps, including Auschwitz-Birkenau.

The Poles anxiously awaited the promised military aid of France and Britain; when help failed to arrive, they took matters into their own hands, forming a ragtag "Polish Home Army" and staging incredibly courageous but lopsided battles against their powerful German overlords (such as the Warsaw Uprising). Throughout the spring of 1945, as the Nazis retreated from their failed invasion of the Soviet Union, the Red Army gradually "liberated" the rubble of Poland from Nazi oppression—guaranteeing it another four decades of oppression under another regime.

During World War II, occupied Poland had the strictest laws in the Nazi realm: Along with Serbia, this was the only place where, if you were caught trying to help Jews escape, your entire family could be executed. And yet, many Poles risked their lives to help escapees. Of course, many other Poles looked the other way, and some willingly participated in Nazi atrocities. Poland (whose current government would rather forget some of this nuance) is still coming to grips with its role in the Holocaust.

But there's no denying that Poland was horrifically scarred by World War II. With six million deaths over six years—including both Polish Jews and ethnic Poles—Poland suffered the worst per-capita losses of any nation. By the war's end, one out of every five Polish citizens was dead—and 90 percent of those killed were civilians. While the human and infrastructure loss of World War II was incalculable, that war's cultural losses were also devastating—for example, some 60,000 paintings were lost.

At the war's end, the victorious Allies shifted Poland's borders significantly westward—folding historically German areas into Polish territory and appropriating previously Polish areas for the USSR. This prompted a massive movement of populations—which today we'd decry as "ethnic cleansing"—as Germans were forcibly removed from western Poland, and Poles from newly Soviet territory were transplanted to Poland proper. Entire cities were repopulated (such as the formerly German metropolis of Breslau, which was renamed Wrocław and filled with refugee Poles from Lwów, now Lviv, in Ukraine). After millions died in the war, millions more were displaced from their ancestral homes. When the dust settled, Poland was almost exclusively populated by Poles.

Saddle on a Cow: Poland Under Communism

Poland suffered horribly under the communists. A postwar intimidation regime was designed to frighten people "on board" and coincided with government seizure of private property, rationing, and food shortages. The country enjoyed a relatively open society under Premier Władysław Gomułka in the 1960s, but the impractical, centrally planned economy began to unravel in the 1970s. Stores were marked by long lines stretching around the block.

The little absurdities of communist life—which today seem almost comical—made every day a struggle. For years, every elderly woman in Poland had hair the same strange magenta color. There was only one color of dye available, so if you had dyed hair, the

POLAND

The Heritage of Communism

While communism is an ugly memory for most Poles, those who were teenagers when it ended—with only gauzy memories of communist times and no experience grappling with its adult realities—have some nostalgia. A friend who was 13 in 1989 recalled those days this way:

"My childhood is filled with happy memories. Under communism, life was family-oriented. Careers didn't matter. There was no way to get rich, no reason to rush, so we had time. People always had time.

"But there were also shortages. We stood in line not knowing what would be for sale. We'd buy whatever shoes were available and then trade for the right size. At grocery stores, vinegar and mustard were always on the shelf, along with plastic cheese to make it seem less empty. We had to carry ration coupons, which we'd present when buying a staple that was in short supply. We didn't necessarily buy what we needed—just anything that could be bartered  on the black market. I remember my mother and father had to 'organize' for special events...somehow find a good sausage and some Coca-Cola.

"Instead of a tidy roll of toilet paper, bathrooms came with a wad of old newspapers. Sometimes my uncle would bring us several toilet paper rolls, held together with a string— the best gift anyone could give.

"Boys in my neighborhood collected pop cans. Cans from other countries represented a world of opportunities beyond our borders. Parents could buy these cans on the black market, and the few families who were allowed to travel returned home with a treasure trove of cans. One boy up the street from me went to Italy and proudly brought home a Pepsi can. Everyone wanted to see this huge status symbol. But a month later, communism ended, you could buy whatever you wanted, and everyone's can collections were worthless.

"We had real chocolate only for Christmas. The rest of the year, we got something called 'chocolate-like product,' which was sweet, dark, and smelled vaguely of chocolate. And we had oranges from Cuba for Christmas, too. Everybody was excited when the newspapers announced, 'The boat with the oranges from Cuba is just five days away.' The smell of Christmas was so special: chocolate and oranges. Now we have that smell every day. Still, my happiest Christmases were under communism."

choice was simple: Let your hair grow out (and look clownishly half red and half white), or line up and go red.

During these difficult times, the Poles often rose up—staging major protests in 1956, 1968, 1970, and 1976. Stalin famously noted that introducing communism to the Poles was like putting a saddle on a cow.

When an anticommunist Polish cardinal named Karol Wojtyła (later known as St. John Paul II) was elected pope in 1978, then visited his homeland in 1979, it was a sign to his compatriots that change was in the air. In 1980, Lech Wałęsa, an electrician at the shipyards in Gdańsk, became the leader of the Solidarity movement, the first workers' union in communist Eastern Europe. After an initial 18-day strike at the Gdańsk shipyards, the communist regime gave in, legalizing Solidarity.

But the union grew too powerful, and the communists felt their control slipping away. On Sunday, December 13, 1981, Poland's head of state, General Wojciech Jaruzelski, appeared on national television to declare martial law in order to "forestall Soviet intervention." (Whether the Soviets actually would have invaded remains a hotly debated issue.) Tanks ominously rolled through the streets of Poland on that snowy December morning, and the Poles were terrified.

Martial law lasted until 1983. Each Pole has chilling memories of this frightening time. During riots, the people would flock into churches—the only place they could be safe from the ZOMO (riot police). People would go for their evening walks during the 19:30 government-sanctioned national news as a sign of protest. But Solidarity struggled on, going underground and becoming a united movement of all demographics, 10 million members strong (more than a quarter of the population).

In July 1989, the ruling Communist Party agreed to hold open elections (reserving 65 percent of representatives for themselves). Their goal was to appease Solidarity, but the plan backfired: Communists didn't win a single contested seat. These elections helped spark the chain reaction across Eastern Europe that eventually tore down the Iron Curtain. Lech Wałęsa became Poland's first postcommunist president.

Poland in the 21st Century

When 10 new countries joined the European Union in May 2004,

Poland was the most ambivalent of the bunch. After centuries of being under other empires' authority, the Poles were hardly eager to relinquish some of their hard-fought autonomy to Brussels. Many Poles thought that EU membership would make things worse (higher prices, a loss of traditional lifestyles) before they got better. But most people agreed that their country had to join to thrive in today's Europe.

The most obvious initial impact of EU membership was the droves of job-seeking young Poles who migrated to other EU countries (mostly the UK, Ireland, and Sweden, which were the first to waive visa requirements for Eastern European workers). Many found employment at hotels and restaurants. In the mid-aughts, visitors to London and Dublin noticed a surprising language barrier at hotel front desks, and Polish-language expat newspapers joined British gossip rags on newsstands. Those who remained in Poland were concerned about the "brain drain" of bright young people flocking out of their country. But with the 2008 economic crisis, quite a few Polish expats returned home. Britain's departure from the EU (2020's Brexit) slammed the door shut on that already-waning British-Polish connection—though a large number of Polish expats remain in the UK.

Poland is by far the most populous of the Central European EU members, with over 41 million people (about the same as Spain, or about half the size of Germany). This makes Poland the sixth largest of the 26 EU member states—giving it serious political clout, which it has already asserted...sometimes to the dismay of the EU's more established powers.

On the American political spectrum, Poland may be the most conservative country in Europe. This is partly due to the outsize influence of Catholicism on political discourse, and partly because Poles are phobic when it comes to "big government"—after being subjugated and manipulated by so many foreign oppressors over the centuries.

Since the early 2000s, the country's right wing has been represented by a pair of twin brothers, Lech and Jarosław Kaczyński. (The Kaczyński brothers were child actors who appeared in several popular movies together.) Their conservative Law and Justice Party (PiS for short) is pro-tax cuts, fiercely Euroskeptic (anti-EU), and very Catholic. In the 2005 presidential election, Lech Kaczyński emerged as the victor, then took the controversial step of appointing his identical twin brother Jarosław as Poland's prime minister.

The political pendulum swung back toward the left in October 2007, when the Kaczyński brothers' main political rival, the pro-EU Donald Tusk, led his Civic Platform Party to victory in the parliamentary elections. The name Kaczyński loosely means "duck"—so the Poles quipped that they were led by "Donald and the Ducks."

Tragically, the levity wasn't to last. On April 10, 2010, a plane carrying President Lech Kaczyński and a large contingent of Poland's leaders crashed in a thick fog near the city of Smoleńsk, Russia. All 96 people on board—including top government, military, and business officials, high-ranking clergy, and others—were killed, plunging the nation into a period of stunned mourning. Poles wondered why, yet again, an unprecedented tragedy had befallen their nation. (Ironically, the group's trip was intended to put a painful chapter of Poland's history to rest: a commemoration of the Polish officers and enlisted men killed in the Soviet massacre at Katyń.)

Over the last decade, the political pendulum has just kept on swinging, as key governmental posts have gone back and forth between the two dominant parties—the Civic Platform (which controlled parliament 2007-2015) and Law and Justice (2015-present).

Since taking power, Law and Justice—chaired by Jarosław Kaczyński—has come under fire for policies that many observers consider borderline-authoritarian (in the vein of Viktor Orbán's Fidesz in Hungary, or Donald Trump in the US). They've packed the ostensibly autonomous Constitutional Tribunal with party loyalists; purged opposition Supreme Court judges, civil servants, and military leaders; levied fines against critical news coverage in a manner that threatens freedom of the press; and removed the director of the Museum of the Second World War in Gdańsk—deeming the exhibit "not Polish enough" and installing a new director who altered many of the exhibits. Because of these and other concerns, in late 2017, the EU initiated Article 7 of the EU Treaty for the first time—stripping Poland of some of its voting rights within the EU.

And yet, at the same time, Donald Tusk—Poland's former prime minister and most high-profile left-leaning politician—has become a major player in the EU government, serving two terms as the president of the European Council (2014-2019). It remains to be seen where the Polish political pendulum swings next. But one thing is clear: The Poles are making their presence felt in European politics.

Invasion of Ukraine

When Vladimir Putin's Russia invaded Ukraine in February 2022, millions of Ukrainians fled to neighboring countries—and more than eight million of them crossed the border into Poland. Even a year and a half later, an estimated 1.5 million Ukrainians were still in Poland.

However, this was not a chaotic "refugee crisis," with sprawl-

POLAND

Bar Mleczny (Milk Bar)

When you see a "bar" in Poland, it doesn't mean alcohol—it means cheap grub. Eating at a *bar mleczny* (bar MLECH-neh) is an essential Polish sightseeing experience. These cafete-
rias, which you'll see all over the country, are a remarkably affordable way to get a good meal...and, with the right atti-
tude, a fun cultural experience.

In the communist era, the government subsidized milk bars, allowing workers to enjoy a meal out. The name comes from the cheese cutlets that were sold here, back in a time when good meat was rare. The
tradition (and name) continues today, as milk-bar prices re-
main astoundingly low: a filling meal for under $10. And, while communist-era fare could be gross, today's milk-bar cuisine is typically great.

Milk bars usually offer many of the traditional tastes listed in the "Polish food" section. Common items are soups (such as *żurek* and *barszcz*), a variety of cabbage-based salads, *kotlet* (fried pork chops), pierogi (similar to ravioli, with various fillings), and *naleśniki* (pancakes). You'll see glasses of juice, as well as bottles of water and Coke.

There are two broad categories of milk bars: updated, modern cafeterias that cater to tourists (English menus), add some modern twists to their traditional fare, and charge about 50 percent more; and time-machine dives that haven't changed for decades. At truly traditional milk bars, the service is aimed at locals, which means limited English and a confusing ordering system.

Every milk bar is a little different, but here's the general procedure: Head to the counter, wait to be acknowledged, and point to what you want. Handy vocabulary: *to* (sounds like "toe") means "this"; *i* (pronounced "ee") means "and."

If the milk-bar server asks you any questions, you have three options: Nod stupidly until they just give you something, repeat one of the things they just said (assuming they've asked you to choose between two options, like meat or cheese in your pierogi), or hope that a kindly English-speaking Pole in line will leap to your rescue. If nothing else, ordering at a milk bar is an adventure in gestures. Smiling seems to slightly extend the patience of milk-bar staffers.

Once your tray is all loaded up, pay the cashier, do a dou-
ble-take when you realize how cheap your bill is, then find a table. After the meal, bus your own dishes to the little window.

ing tent cities and desperately miserable people camped out in squalor at borders, as we saw with Syrian refugees in southeastern Europe in the fall of 2015. Rather, Poland absorbed these new arrivals smoothly, with locals opening up their homes to take in strangers in need. Across the political divide, Poles were united on the importance of helping their neighbors. People here justifiably feel great pride in how their country rose to the occasion when faced with an unprecedented humanitarian crisis.

The resolution of this latest chapter of Poland's story is not yet known. As the war in Ukraine drags on, more refugees are deciding to—at least for now—make new lives, putting down roots in Poland.

As time wears on, popular opinion is mixed. When I traveled around Poland in 2022 and 2023, most Poles I spoke with were proud of what they'd done for the Ukrainians. But some did raise concerns, including worry that this influx from a foreign (albeit similar) culture might lead to unwanted cultural shifts in the greater society. Others groused that generous policies designed to help the new arrivals (for example, free passage on public transportation) were not sustainable long-term. A few also noted that Ukraine has never formally apologized for WWII-era atrocities against the Poles (the so-called "Volhynian Slaughter," in which tens of thousands of Polish civilians were ethnically cleansed by Ukrainian partisans in Nazi-occupied territory).

Still others pointed out that Poland lost approximately as many people when the country joined the EU and bright young workers moved to other European lands to find better employment. When viewing things from a historical perspective, Poland is simply replenishing its population.

Poland's tourism industry also took a hit with the war, as many international visitors stayed away—perhaps not realizing that, as a member of NATO and the EU, Poland is in an entirely different geopolitical situation than Ukraine, at far lower risk of invasion. As Poles who work in tourism are still waiting to recoup their losses from the double-whammy of the Covid-19 pandemic and the Ukraine war, it's clear to any visitor that the country is a safe, fascinating, rewarding place to visit.

POLISH FOOD

Polish food is hearty and tasty—most classic dishes were created to provide calories for working fields and farms. Because Poland is north of the Carpathian Mountains, its weather tends to be chilly, limiting the kinds of fruits and vegetables that flourish here. As in other northern European countries (such as Ukraine, Russia, or Scandinavia), dominant staples include potatoes, dill, berries, beets, and rye. Much of what you might think of as "Jewish cuisine"

POLAND

turns up on Polish menus (gefilte fish, potato pancakes, chicken soup, and so forth)—which makes sense, given that Poles and Jews lived in the same area for centuries.

For such a big country, you'll find that menus are quite similar nationwide. Any regional variations were papered over during the communist period, when "Polish cuisine" was legally standardized. (Restaurants—which were rare—were obligated to meticulously follow recipes from one official, government-issued cookbook.) Over the last generation, some of this regional variation is beginning to return—especially in Gdańsk on the Baltic coast, with access to more seafood and influence from Scandinavian chefs—but you'll still find a lot of consistency from place to place.

Polish soups are a highlight; they claim to have more than 200 types. The most typical are *żurek* and *barszcz*. *Żurek* (often translated as "sour soup" on menus) is a thickened, light-colored soup made from a sourdough or rye base, usually containing a hard-boiled egg and pieces of *kiełbasa* (sausage).

Barszcz, better known to Americans as borscht, is a savory beet soup that you'll see in several varieties: *Barszcz czerwony* (red borscht) is a thin, flavorful broth with a deep red color, sometimes containing dumplings *(uszkami)* or a hard-boiled egg. *Barszcz ukraiński* (Ukrainian borscht) is thicker, with cream and vegetables (usually cabbage, beans, and carrots). Confusingly, there's another type of "borscht" that has no beets at all: *barszcz biały* ("white borscht"), which is very similar to the sour soup *żurek*.

In summer, try the "Polish gazpacho"—*chłodnik*, a savory cream soup with beets, onions, and radishes that's served cold. I had never met a Polish soup I didn't like...until I was introduced to *flaki* (sometimes *flaczki*)—tripe soup.

Another Polish dish that may be familiar is pierogi. These ravioli-like dumplings come with various fillings. The most traditional are minced meat, sauerkraut, mushroom, cheese, and blueberry; many restaurants also experiment with more exotic fillings. Pierogi are often served with specks of fatty bacon to add flavor. Pierogi are a budget traveler's dream: Restaurants serving them are everywhere, and they're generally cheap, tasty, and very filling.

Bigos is a rich and delicious sauerkraut stew cooked with meat, mushrooms, and whatever's in the pantry. It's sort of the Polish version of chili—it's a beloved comfort food, especially in the cold of winter, and everyone has their own recipe. *Gołąbki* is a dish of cabbage leaves stuffed with minced meat and rice in a tomato or mushroom sauce. *Kotlet schabowy* (fried pork chop) is another favorite.

Kaczka (duck) is popular, as is freshwater fish: Look for *pstrąg* (trout) and *węgorz* (eel). Carp *(karp)* is also common, especially at Christmas. Traditionally, people would bring home a live carp before the holiday, then keep it in the bathtub until it was time to eat. One Polish friend explained that she came to think of the carp as a family pet; at Christmas, her parents told her it had swum away, down the drain...at exactly the same time they were sitting down for a fish dinner. (She became a vegetarian for 20 years, and still won't touch carp. She terms this affliction "carp-al trauma syndrome.") On the Baltic Coast (such as in Gdańsk), you'll also see *łosoś* (salmon), *śledź* (herring), and *dorsz* (cod).

Poles eat lots of potatoes, which are served with nearly every meal. Look for *placki ziemniaczane*—potato pancakes.

Some dreary old foods are newly hip in today's Poland. Herring-and-vodka bars are trendy. The Polish street food *zapiekanka*—a toasted baguette with melted cheese, rubbery mushrooms from a can, and a drizzle of ersatz ketchup—began life as a "hardship food" under communism, as a pale imitation of pizza. These days it has been reborn as a street-food staple; *zapiekanka* vendors top them with a world of creative flavors. The bagel-like bread rings you'll see sold on the street, *obwarzanki* (singular *obwarzanek*), are also cheap, and usually fresh and tasty. And, as throughout Europe, gourmet hamburgers are in—including a trend for vegan burgers.

Poland has good pastries—look for a *cukiernia* (pastry shop). The classic Polish treat is *pączki*, glazed jelly doughnuts. They can have different fillings, but most typical is a wild-rose jam.

Szarlotka is apple cake—sometimes made with chunks of apples (especially in season), sometimes with apple filling. *Sernik* is cheesecake, *makowiec* is a poppy-seed roll, and *winebreda* is like a Danish. *Napoleonka* is a French-style treat with layers of crispy wafers and custard. A *mazurek* could be vaguely compared to a "dessert pizza"—a dense, sweet flatbread smothered with even sweeter spreads (often chocolate or caramel) and other toppings. The yeast or sponge cake called *babka* literally means "grandma"—it's named for the Bundt-pan shape, which resembles a traditional woman's skirt. A *babeczka* ("little grandma") is a smaller version, like a cupcake.

Lody (ice cream) is popular. The tall, skinny cones of soft-serve ice cream are called *świderki*, sometimes translated as "American ice cream." The most beloved traditional candy is *ptasie mleczko* (birds' milk), which is semisour marshmallow covered with chocolate. E. Wedel is the country's top brand of chocolate, with outlets in all the big cities.

Thirsty? *Woda* is water, *woda mineralna* is bottled water

POLAND

Poland's "Other" Cuisines: Georgian and Ukrainian

With the influx of war refugees from Ukraine—many of whom have decided to put down roots in their adopted homeland—Poland's culinary scene is also evolving. In addition to tradi-

tional Polish fare, travelers can look for restaurants serving two other cuisines: Georgian and Ukrainian.

Keep an eye out for **Georgian** restaurants and bakeries (look for *gruzińska*). Through-out the former USSR—includ-ing in Ukraine—food from Georgia, the former Soviet satellite in the Caucasus, is a beloved, flavorful change of pace from the dominant local fare. (Compare it to Mexican cuisine in the US, or Indian food in Britain.) Even before the arrival of Ukrainian refugees, Georgian food was catching on in Po-land—and now that trend is accelerating.

Georgian food is utterly delicious, with a more vibrant and varied flavor profile than most Polish cooking. Herbs, spic-es, walnuts, and plums are major ingredients. Popular items include *khachapuri* (hot bread filled with cheese and other fill-ings, somewhat like a calzone, sometimes topped with a fried egg), *chinkhali* or *khinkali* (a hearty filled dumpling gathered into a thick, doughy "handle" and dipped into sauces), *khar-cho* (a spicy broth with lots of meat and onions), *satsivi* (diced chicken in a spicy yellow sauce), and Georgian-style salad—typically tomato, cucumber, onion, and herbs, mixed up with a walnut paste. Because this cuisine is relatively new even for Poles, many Georgian restaurants have enticing and educa-tional picture menus. If you have yet to try a Georgian meal... do it here.

Ukrainian cuisine has many similarities to Poland's own cooking, but with a regional spin: Staples include "Ukraini-an-style" borscht, a red beet stew thick with vegetables and beans; the pierogi-like *varenyky;* and cabbage rolls (like a Pol-ish *gołąbki*) called *holubtsi*. Other mainstays are the filled rolls called *pyrizhky;* the polenta-like cornmeal dish *banosh,* with meat and other flavorings mixed in; and *syrnyky,* deep-fried cheese-curd pancakes with berry sauce. Rye, which thrives in the Ukrainian climate, is a dominant flavor. Some Ukrainian restaurants also feature Georgian dishes, thanks to that cui-sine's popularity there.

As you consider where to eat, consider going beyond Polish fare—and the ubiquitous Italian places—to try some of these unique cuisines that you may not find back home.

(*gazowana* is with gas, *niegazowana* is without), *kawa* is coffee, *herbata* is tea, *sok* is juice, and *mleko* is milk. Żywiec, Okocim, and Lech are the best-known brands of *piwo* (beer).

Wódka (vodka) is a Polish staple—the word means, roughly, "precious little water." Poles take vodka seriously and control its production assiduously. Its ingredients are domestically grown, and pure vodka contains some combination of just six ingredients: potatoes, rye, wheat, barley, oats, and the wheat-rye hybrid triticale. Quality vodkas have different flavor profiles depending on how the distiller has blended these ingredients; for example, potato gives an oily consistency, rye is sweeter and warming, and wheat is also sweet but lighter—ideal for summery mixed drinks.

Żubrówka, the most famous brand of vodka, comes with a blade of grass from the bison reserves in eastern Poland (look for the bison on the label). The bison "flavor" the grass...then the grass flavors the vodka. Poles often mix Żubrówka with apple juice, and call this cocktail *szarlotka* ("apple cake").

Traditionally, vodka is shot rather than sipped, and it's chased not by another drink but by salty, greasy food: pickles, lard, herring, potato pancakes, or steak tartare (but never just bread, which soaks up the spirit and keeps it in the stomach). For "Cheers!" say, "*Na zdrowie!*" (nah ZDROH-vyeh).

Other distillates are also popular, both traditional (Polish gins, whiskeys, and aqua vita, here called *okowita*) and more creative options—hipster-run artisanal distilleries are popping up all over. *Nalewka,* essentially a fruit-infused brandy (like a cordial), is typically made by macerating fruit with sugar, then pouring over vodka or firewater; it's often aged, and can be used for medicinal purposes. The sour cherry version, *wiśniówka,* is newly trendy—you'll see little pubs selling it all over Poland. Another "health" drink is the brandy called Krupnik: Poles swear that if you're getting a cold, mixing a slug of Krupnik with hot water and a squeeze of lemon will fix you right up.

Unusual nonalcoholic drinks to try if you have the chance are *kwas* (a cold, fizzy, Ukrainian-style beverage made from day-old rye bread) and *kompot* (a hot drink made from stewed berries). Poles are unusually fond of carrot juice (often cut with fruit juice); Kubuś is the most popular brand.

"Bon appétit" is "*Smacznego*" (smatch-NEH-goh). To pay, ask for the *rachunek* (rah-KHOO-nehk).

POLISH LANGUAGE

Polish is closely related to its neighboring Slavic languages (Slovak and Czech), with the biggest difference being that Polish has lots of fricatives (hissing sounds—"sh" and "ch"—often in close proximity).

Polish intimidates Americans with long, difficult-to-pronounce words. But if you take your time and sound things out, you'll develop an ear for it. One rule of thumb that helps: The stress is generally on the next-to-last syllable.

Polish has some letters that don't appear in English, and some letters and combinations are pronounced differently than in English:

ć, ci, and **cz** all sound like "ch" as in "church"

ś, si, and **sz** all sound like "sh" as in "short"

ż, ź, zi, and **rz** all sound like "zh" as in "leisure"

dż and **dź** both sound like the "dj" sound in "jeans"

ń and **ni** sound like "ny" as in "canyon"

ę and **ą** are pronounced nasally, as in French: "e*n*" and "a*n*"

c sounds like "ts" as in "cats"

ch sounds like "kh" as in the Scottish "loch"

j sounds like "y" as in "yellow"

w sounds like "v" as in "Victor"

ł sounds like "w" as in "with"

So to Poles, "Lech Wałęsa" isn't pronounced "lehk wah-LEH-sah," as Americans tend to say—but "lehkh vah-WEHN-sah."

The Polish people you meet will be impressed and flattered if you take the time to learn a little of their language. To get started, check out the selection of Polish survival phrases on the following pages.

As you're tracking down addresses, these words will help: *miasto* (mee-AH-stoh, town), *plac* (plahts, square), *rynek* (REE-ne-hk, big market square), *ulica* (OO-leet-sah, road), *aleja* (ah-LAY-yah, avenue), and *most* (mohst, bridge). And that long word you see everywhere—*zapraszamy*—means "welcome."

Polish Survival Phrases

Keep in mind a few Polish pronunciation tips: w sounds like "v," ł sounds like "w," ch is a back-of-your-throat "kh" sound (as in the Scottish "loch"), and rz sounds like the "zh" sound in "pleasure." The vowels with a tail (ą and ę) have a slight nasal "n" sound at the end, similar to French.

Hello. (formal) / Goodbye.	Dzień dobry. / Do widzenia. jehn **doh**-brih / doh veed-**zay**-nyah
Hi. / Bye. (informal)	Cześć. cheshch
Do you speak English? (asked of a man)	Czy Pan mówi po angielsku? chih pahn **moo**-vee poh ahn-**gyehl**-skoo
Do you speak English? (asked of a woman)	Czy Pani mówi po angielsku? chih **pah**-nee **moo**-vee poh ahn-**gyehl**-skoo
Yes. / No.	Tak. / Nie. tahk / nyeh
I (don't) understand.	(Nie) rozumiem. (nyeh) roh-**zoo**-myehm
Please. / You're welcome. / Can I help you?	Proszę. **proh**-sheh
Thank you (very much).	Dziękuję (bardzo). jehn-**koo**-yeh (**bard**-zoh)
Excuse me. / I'm sorry.	Przepraszam. psheh-**prah**-shahm
No problem.	Żaden problem. **zhah**-dehn **proh**-blehm
Good.	Dobrze. **dohb**-zheh
one / two / three	jeden / dwa / trzy **yeh**-dehn / dvah / tzhih
hundred / thousand	sto / tysiąc stoh / **tih**-shants
How much?	Ile? **ee**-leh
local currency	złoty (zł) **zwoh**-tih
Is it free?	Czy to jest za darmo? chih toh yehst zah **dar**-moh
Is it included?	Czy jest to wliczone? chih yehst toh vlee-**choh**-neh
Where can I find / buy...?	Gdzie mogę dostać / kupić...? guh-**dyeh moh**-geh **doh**-statch / **koo**-peech
I'd like... (said by a man)	Chciałbym... **khchaw**-beem
I'd like... (said by a woman)	Chciałabym... **khchah**-wah-beem
...a room.	...pokój. **poh**-kooey
...a ticket to _____.	...bilet do _____. **bee**-leht doh _____
Where is...?	Gdzie jest...? guh-**dyeh** yehst
...the train station	...dworzec kolejowy **dvoh**-zhehts koh-leh-**yoh**-vih
...the bus station	...dworzec autobusowy **dvoh**-zhehts ow-toh-boos-**oh**-vih
...the tourist information office	...informacja turystyczna een-for-**maht**-syah too-ris-**titch**-nah
...the toilet	...toaleta toh-ah-**leh**-tah
men / women	męska / damska **mehn**-skah / **dahm**-skah
left / right / straight	lewo / prawo / prosto **leh**-voh / **prah**-voh / **proh**-stoh
At what time...?	O której godzinie...? oh kuh-**too**-ray gohd-**zhee**-nyeh
...does this open / close	...będzie otwarte / zamknięte **bend**-zheh oht-**vahr**-teh / zahm-**knyehn**-teh
today / tomorrow	dzisiaj / jutro jee-shī / **yoo**-troh

In a Polish Restaurant

I'd like to reserve... (said by a man)	Chciałbym zarezerwować... **khchaw**-beem zah-reh-zehr-**voh**-vahch
I'd like to reserve... (said by a woman)	Chciałabym zarezerwować... **khchah**-wah-beem zah-reh-zehr-**voh**-vahch
We'd like...	Chcielibyśmy... **khchehl**-ee-bish-mih
...a table for one person / two people.	...stolik na jedną osobę / dwie osoby. **stoh**-leek nah **yehd**-now oh-**soh**-beh / dvyeh oh-**soh**-bih
The menu (in English), please.	Menu (po angielsku), proszę. **meh**-noo (poh ahn-**gyehl**-skoo) **proh**-sheh
service (not) included	usługa (nie) wliczona oos-**woo**-gah (nyeh) **vlee**-choh-nah
cover charge	wstęp vstenp
"to go"	na wynos nah **vih**-nohs
with / without	z / bez z / behz
and / or	i / lub ee / loob
milk bar (cheap cafeteria)	bar mleczny bar **mletch**-nih
fixed-price meal (of the day)	zestaw (dnia) **zehs**-tahv (dih-**nyah**)
specialty of the house	specjalność zakładu speht-**syahl**-nohshch zah-**kwah**-doo
daily special	danie dnia **dah**-nyeh dih-**nyah**
breakfast / lunch / dinner	śniadanie / obiad / kolacja shnyah-**dahn**-yeh / **oh**-bee-aht / koh-**laht**-syah
appetizers	przystawki pshih-**stahv**-kee
bread / cheese / sandwich	chleb / ser / kanapka khlehb / sehr / kah-**nahp**-kah
soup / salad	zupa / sałatka **zoo**-pah / sah-**waht**-kah
meat / poultry	mięso / drób **myehn**-soh / droob
fish / seafood	ryba / owoce morza **rih**-bah / oh-**voht**-seh **moh**-zhah
fruit / vegetables	owoce / warzywa oh-**voht**-seh / vah-**zhih**-vah
dessert	deser **deh**-sehr
(tap) water	woda (z kranu) **voh**-dah (**skrah**-noo)
mineral water	woda mineralna **voh**-dah mee-neh-**rahl**-nah
carbonated / not carbonated	gazowana / niegazowana gah-zoh-**vah**-nah / **nyeh**-gah-zoh-vah-nah
milk	mleko **mleh**-koh
(orange) juice	sok (pomarańczowy) sohk (poh-mah-rayn-**choh**-vih)
coffee / tea	kawa / herbata **kah**-vah / hehr-**bah**-tah
wine / beer / vodka	wino / piwo / wódka **vee**-noh / **pee**-voh / **vood**-kah
red / white	czerwone / białe chehr-**voh**-neh / bee-**ah**-weh
glass / bottle	szklanka / butelka **shklahn**-kah / boo-**tehl**-kah
Cheers!	Na zdrowie! nah **zdroh**-vyeh
More. / Another.	Więcej. / Inny. **vyehnt**-say / **een**-neh
The same.	Taki sam. **tah**-kee sahm
the bill / I'll pay.	rachunek / Ja płacę. rah-**khoo**-nehk / yah **pwaht**-seh
tip	napiwek nah-**pee**-vehk
Delicious!	Pyszne! **pish**-neh

KRAKÓW

Kraków is easily Poland's best destination: a beautiful, user-friendly, old-fashioned city buzzing with history, enjoyable sights, tourists, and college students. Even though the country's capital moved from here to Warsaw more than 400 years ago, Kraków remains Poland's cultural and intellectual center. Increasingly (and justifiably) popular, Kraków is giving Prague a run for its money on the "must visit" tourist route.

What's so special about it? First off, Kraków is simply charming; more than any town in Europe, it seems made for aimless strolling. And its historic walls and former moat corral an unusually full range of activities and interests: bustling university life, thought-provoking museums, breathtaking churches that evoke a powerful faith (and include many sights relating to Poland's favorite son, St. John Paul II), sprawling parks that invite you to relax, vivid artifacts of Poland's Jewish heritage, and a burgeoning foodie and nightlife scene. Nearby, there are compelling side trips to the most notorious Holocaust site anywhere (Auschwitz-Birkenau), a communist planned workers town (Nowa Huta), and a mine filled with salty statues (Wieliczka). With so many opportunities to learn, to have fun, or to do both at once, it's no surprise that Kraków has become a world-class destination.

PLANNING YOUR TIME

Don't skimp on your time in Kraków. It takes a minimum of two days to experience the city, and a third (or even a fourth) day lets you dig in and consider a world of fascinating side trips.

Almost everyone coming to Kraków also visits the Auschwitz-Birkenau Concentration Camp Memorial—and should. As it's about an hour and a half away, this demands the better part of a day. Visiting Auschwitz requires a reservation, which you need to book long in advance (see the next chapter).

If you have only two full days (the "express plan"), start off with my self-guided walk through the Old Town and a quick stroll up to Wawel Castle, then head over to the Schindler's Factory Museum and wind down your day in Kazimierz. Your second day is for side-tripping to Auschwitz. This plan gives you a once-over-lightly look at Kraków but leaves almost no time for entering the sights.

More time buys you the chance to relax, enjoy, and linger: Tackle the Old Town and Wawel Castle on the first day, Kazimierz and museums of your choice on the second day, and Auschwitz (and other side trips) with additional days. If you have a special interest, you could side-trip to the St. John Paul II pilgrimage sites on the outskirts of town, or to the communist architecture of the Nowa Huta suburb. Wieliczka Salt Mine is another crowd-pleasing, half-day option.

Regardless of how long you stay, your evening choices are many and varied: Savor the Main Market Square over dinner or a drink, take in a jazz show, do a pub crawl through the city's many youthful bars and clubs (best in Kazimierz), or enjoy traditional Jewish music and cuisine (also in Kazimierz).

Orientation to Kraków

Kraków (Poles say KROCK-oof, but you can say KRACK-cow; it's sometimes spelled "Cracow" in English) is mercifully compact, flat, and easy to navigate. While it's Poland's second-biggest city (with 780,000 people), the tourist's Kraków feels small—from the main square, you can walk to just about everything of interest in less than 15 minutes. Just to the south is Poland's primary waterway, the Vistula River (Wisła, VEES-wah).

Most sights—and almost all recommended hotels and restaurants—are in the **Old Town** (Stare Miasto, STAH-reh mee-AH-stoh), which is surrounded by a greenbelt called the Planty (PLAHN-tee). In the center of the Old Town lies the Main Market Square (Rynek Główny, REE-nehk GWOHV-neh)—it's such an important landmark, I call it simply "the Square." At the Old Town's northeast corner, just outside the ring road, is the main train station. And at the southern end of the Old Town, on the riverbank, is the hill called **Wawel** (VAH-vehl)—with a historic castle, museums, and Poland's national church.

About a 20-minute walk (or quick tram/taxi ride) southeast of the Square is the neighborhood called **Kazimierz** (kah-ZHEE-mehzh)—with Jewish landmarks and Holocaust sites (including the Schindler's Factory Museum) and the city's best food and nightlife area.

A few more attractions are just beyond the core, including the St. John Paul II pilgrimage sites (in the Łagiewniki neighborhood), the communist-planned town of Nowa Huta, Wieliczka Salt Mine, and the Kościuszko Mound.

The southern mountains are not far away, and Kraków fills a shallow, bowl-shaped valley ringed by hills—which means the city has a tendency to trap fog and, sometimes, smog.

TOURIST INFORMATION

Kraków has many helpful TIs, called InfoKraków (https://infokrakow.pl). Four branches are in or near the Old Town (most are open daily 9:00-17:00, but some have slight variations):

• In the **Planty** park, between the main train station and Main Market Square (open later in July-Sept—until 19:00, in a round kiosk at Ulica Szpitalna 25, +48 533 818 291)

• On **Ulica Św. Jana,** just north of the Main Market Square (specializes in concert tickets, daily year-round 9:00-17:00, at #2, +48 533 826 409)

• In the **Cloth Hall** right on the Main Market Square (at #1/3, +48 530 290 661)

• Just west of **Wawel Hill** (also covers the entire region, Powiśle 11, +48 533 826 031)

Other TI branches are in **Kazimierz** (Ulica Józefa 7, +48 533 834 969) and the **airport** (daily 9:00-19:00, +48 533 825 344). There's a "TI" marked inside the **Wyspiański Pavilion,** but it's really more of a gift shop (called "Kraków Story") that can answer a few questions. Note that the TIs sell tickets for only one tour company, Kraków Booking; for additional options, see "Tours in Kraków," later, and look around online.

Sightseeing Pass: The TI's **Kraków Tourist Card** includes admission to 40 city museums (basically everything except the Wawel Hill sights and Wieliczka Salt Mine)—but unless you're sightseeing like mad, it's unlikely you'd save money with the card. Given how walkable Kraków is, the version that does not include public transit is a better value than the one that does.

Warning: Many private travel agencies, room-booking services, and tour operators masquerade as TIs, with deceptive *i* signs. If I haven't listed them in this section, they're not a real TI.

Museum of Kraków (Muzeum Krakowa) Visitors Center: Facing the Main Market Square is an information office and ticket desk for the Museum of Kraków, where you can prebook tickets for the popular Schindler's Factory Museum and Rynek Underground Museum. If you've arrived in town to find online tickets already sold out, additional tickets often become available here for

KRAKÓW

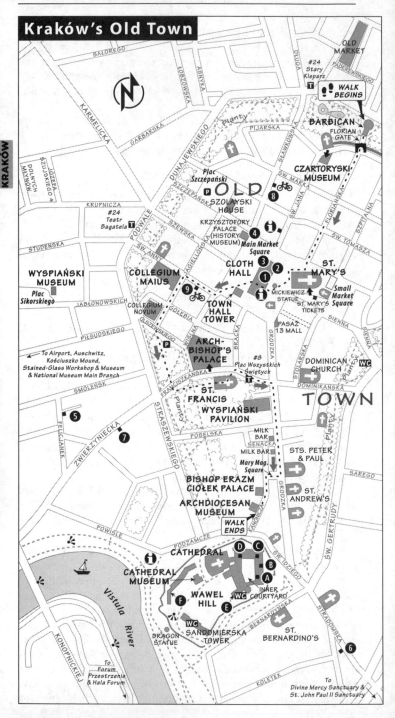

Kraków's Old Town

BALDREGO

KARMELICKA

JÓZEFA
SZUJSKIEGO
DOLNYCH
MŁYNÓW

KRUPNICZA

STUDENSKA

WYSPIAŃSKI
MUSEUM

Plac
Sikorskiego

JABŁONOWSKICH

PIŁSUDSKIEGO

SMOLENSK

ZWIERZYNIECKA

FELICJANEK

KONOPNICKIEJ

POWIŚLE

Vistula
River

To
Forum
Przestrzenie
& Hala Forum

GARBARSKA

DUNAJEWSKIEGO

PODWALE

SZEWSKA

SW. ANNY

JAGIELLOŃSKA

COLLEGIUM
MAIUS

COLLEGIUM
NOVUM

GOŁĘBIA

OLSZEWSKIEGO

WIŚLNA

FRANCISZKAŃSKA

STRASZEWSKIEGO

BRACKA

Planty

PIJARSKA

Plac
Szczepański

SZCZEPAŃSKA

SZOŁAYSKI
HOUSE

KRZYSZTOFORY
PALACE
(HISTORY
MUSEUM)

OLD

Main Market
Square

CLOTH
HALL

TOWN
HALL
TOWER

ARCH-
BISHOP'S
PALACE

ST.
FRANCIS

WYSPIAŃSKI
PAVILION

POSELSKA

MILK
BAR
SENACKA

MILK BAR

Mary Mag.
Square

BISHOP ERAZM
CIOŁEK PALACE

ARCHDIOCESAN
MUSEUM

WALK
ENDS

PODZAMCZE

CATHEDRAL

CATHEDRAL
MUSEUM

WAWEL
HILL

DRAGON
STATUE

SANDOMIERSKA
TOWER

SŁAWKOWSKA

SW. MARKA

SW. JANA

SW. TOMASZA

FLORIAŃSKA

MIKIEWICZ
STATUE

ST. MARY'S
TICKETS

PASAŻ
13 MALL

GRODZKA

#8
Plac Wszystkich
Świętych

ST. MARY'S

Small
Market
Square

SIENNA

DOMINICAN
CHURCH

WC

DOMINIKAŃSKA

TOWN

STOLARSKA

Planty

INNER
COURTYARD

WC

WC

ŚW. IDZIEGO

STS. PETER
& PAUL

ST.
ANDREW'S

SW. GERTRUDY

SAREGO

STRADOMSKA

ST.
BERNARDINO'S

6

KOLETEK

To
Divine Mercy Sanctuary &
St. John Paul II Sanctuary

OLD
MARKET

DŁUGA

PADEREWSKIEGO

#24
Stary
Kleparz

T

WALK
BEGINS

BARBICAN

FLORIAN
GATE

CZARTORYSKI
MUSEUM

8

#24
Teatr
Bagatela

T

To Airport, Auschwitz,
Kościuszko Mound,
Stained-Glass Workshop & Museum
& National Museum Main Branch

5

7

9

4

3 2

1

N

To
Forum
Przestrzenie
& Hala Forum

KOBZYŃSKA

ASNYKA

BASZTOWA

D C

B

A

F

E

BERNARDYŃSKA

KRAKÓW

Sights & Services

1 Gallery of 19th-Century Polish Art (Entrance)

2 Rynek Underground Museum (Entrance)

3 Rynek Underground Museum (Tickets)

4 Museum of Kraków Visitors Center & Ticket Office

5 Massolit Books

6 Frania Café/Laundry

7 Betty Clean Laundry

8 Kraków Bike Tours

9 Bike Rental

Wawel Castle Sights

A Royal State Rooms

B Royal Private Apartments

C Crown Treasury & Armory

D Art of the Orient

E Lost Wawel

F Wawel Recovered

KRAKÓW

> # Don't Miss Out!
> ## Book Key Sights in Advance
>
> A few popular Kraków attractions can fill up at busy times, and it pays to reserve ahead. If you're going to **Auschwitz,** book as far in advance as possible—ideally three months ahead (details in the next chapter). In Kraków, **Schindler's Factory Museum** also sells out well in advance. Especially during busy times, it's also smart to book several days ahead for **Wieliczka Salt Mine** and the **Rynek Underground Museum.** All can be prebooked online. Or, for the Schindler and Rynek sights, you can book in person at the Museum of Kraków ticket office right on the Main Market Square (see "Tourist Information"); if you arrive in town without a reservation, swing by that office to see what's available.
>
> What constitutes **"busy times"?** It's crowded all summer long, and weekends anytime. Things reach a peak during Poland's long summer holiday weekends (Labor Day and Constitution Day, May 1-3; Corpus Christi, usually in late May or early June; and Assumption, Aug 15). If coming at these times, anticipate crowds and book well ahead.

the following day, as unused slots bought up by big tour operators are returned and resold (daily 10:00-19:00, at #35 at the Square's northwest corner—see map on page 38, +48 12 426 5060). This location also has a town history exhibit.

ARRIVAL IN KRAKÓW
By Train

Kraków's main train station (called "Kraków Główny," KROCK-oof GWOHV-neh) sits just northeast of the Old Town, adjoining the sprawling Galeria Krakowska shopping mall. The station and the mall face a broad plaza (Plac Dworcowy) across the ring road from the Planty park and Old Town. My recommended Old Town hotels are within about a 15-to-20-minute walk, or a quick taxi ride. (If you're staying in the Old Town, the tram doesn't save you much time; for those staying in Kazimierz—a 30-minute walk away—the tram is worthwhile.)

The main concourse has all of the amenities: ATMs, lockers (under the big schedule board between the ticket windows), WCs, and a handy Biedronka minisupermarket. From this area, five numbered escalators lead up to the train platforms. If you need to buy tickets, tucked under the escalators is a long row of numbered ticket windows (some for domestic tickets only, others for domestic and international—check signs before you line up). In the middle of the ticket windows (between #11 and #12) is the PKP Passenger Service Center, which is more likely to have staff who speak English. There are ticket machines around this area, or you can buy most tickets online (www.intercity.pl).

Getting Between the Station and Downtown: The easiest option is to take a **taxi;** they wait in the parking lot on the station's rooftop—go up the stairs or elevator from your platform (15-20 zł into town; for a fair rate, be sure to take a taxi marked with a company name and telephone number). Or order an **Uber,** which is often cheaper (see "Getting Around Kraków," later).

If you prefer to walk or take a tram, you'll be funneled through the Galeria Krakowska shopping mall. Begin by following *Exit to the City* signs. Once inside the mall, continue straight ahead. To **walk,** follow *Old Town* signs, which eventually route you to the left. You'll pop out at a big plaza where you'll continue straight, taking the broad ramp down into a pedestrian underpass beneath the ring road, emerging into the Planty. The Main Market Square is straight ahead (look for the twin spires of St. Mary's Church).

If you'd rather take a **tram,** continue straight ahead through the mall, following signs for *Exit Pawia street.* Emerging here, you'll see the Dworzec Główny Zachód tram stop; tram #3 in the direction of Nowy Bieżanów stops at the eastern edge of the Old Town (Poczta Główna stop) before continuing to Kazimierz (Miodowa stop).

There is a **shortcut** to avoid going through the sprawling and sometimes congested mall: The modern train station is attached to the old station (the yellow building facing the big plaza, now hosting art exhibitions) by a sidewalk under a green canopy. This can save you a little walking (and a lot of shopping temptations). It's tricky to find from inside the station: Go behind the Biedronka supermarket, near track 1, and exit toward Lubicz street. Walk up the ramp and follow the green canopy to the plaza.

To get **from town to the station** (or to the bus station behind it), head to the northeast corner of the Planty, take the underpass beneath the ring road, walk across the plaza and into the Galeria Krakowska mall, and once inside, follow signs to *Railway Station* and *Station Hall.*

By Bus

The bus station is directly behind the main train station. When arriving by bus, first head into the train station, then continue through it, following the directions given earlier for arrival by train.

To get *to* the bus station from the Old Town (for example, to catch a bus to Auschwitz), walk all the way through to the far end of the train station area (past platform 5, exit marked for *Bus Station*). The bus terminal (marked *Dworzec Autobusowy*) is upstairs. Inside are the standard amenities (lockers and WCs), domestic and international ticket windows, and an electronic board showing

KRAKÓW

Kraków: A Snapshot History

Kraków grew wealthy from trade in the late 10th and early 11th centuries. Traders who passed through were required to stop here and sell their wares at a reduced cost. Local merchants resold those goods with big price hikes...and Kraków thrived. In 1038, it became Poland's capital.

Tatars invaded in 1241, leaving the city in ruins. Krakovians rebuilt their streets in a near-perfect grid, unlike the narrow, maze-like lanes of most medieval towns. The destruction also paved the way for the spectacular Main Market Square—still Kraków's best feature.

King Kazimierz the Great sparked Kraków's golden age in the 14th century (see the sidebar, later). In 1364, he established the university that still defines the city (and counts Copernicus and St. John Paul II among its alumni).

But Kraków's power waned as Poland's political center shifted to Warsaw. In 1596, the capital officially moved north. And with the Partitions of the late 18th century, Poland disappeared from the map and Kraków became a provincial backwater of Vienna.

After Napoleon briefly reshuffled Europe in the early 19th century, Kraków was granted the status of a relatively independent city-state for about 30 years. The Free City of Kraków, a tiny sliver wedged between three of Europe's mightiest empires, enjoyed an economic boom that saw the creation of the Planty park, the arrival of gas lighting and trams, and the construction of upscale suburbs outside the Old Town. Only after the unsuccessful Kraków Uprising of 1846 was the city forcefully brought back into the Austrian fold. But despite Kraków's reduced prominence, Austria's comparatively liberal climate allowed the city to become a haven for intellectuals and progressives (including a young rev-

the next several departures. Some bus departures, marked on the board with a *G*, leave from the upper *(gorna)* stalls, which you can see out the window. Other bus departures, marked with a *D*, leave from the lower *(dolna)* stalls in the garage beneath your feet; to find these, use the stairs or the elevator right in the middle of the bus terminal. Because the bus station area can be challenging to navigate, leave yourself plenty of time before departure.

By Car

Centrum signs lead you into the Old Town—you'll know you're there when you hit the ring road that surrounds the Planty park. Parking garages surround the Old Town. Your hotelier can advise you on directions and parking.

By Plane

The modern **John Paul II Kraków-Balice Airport** is about 10 miles

KRAKÓW

olutionary thinker from Russia named Vladimir Lenin).

The Nazis overran Poland in September 1939, installing the *Generalgouvernement,* a ruling body headed by Hans Frank. Germany wanted to quickly develop "Krakau" into their Polish capital. They renamed the Main Market Square "Adolf-Hitler-Platz," tore down statues of Polish figures (including the Adam Mickiewicz statue that dominates the Main Market Square today), and invested heavily in construction and industrialization (opening the door for Oskar Schindler to take over a factory from its Jewish owners). The German "New Order" included seizing businesses, rationing, and a strict curfew for Poles and Jews alike. A set of "Jewish laws" targeted, then decimated, Poland's huge Jewish population.

Kraków's cityscape emerged from World War II virtually unscathed. But when the communists took over, they decided to give intellectual (and potentially dissident) Kraków an injection of Soviet values. They built Nowa Huta, an enormous steelworks and planned town for workers, on the outskirts, dooming Kraków to decades of smog.

St. John Paul II was born (as Karol Wojtyła) in nearby Wadowice and served as archbishop of Kraków before being called to Rome. Today, the hometown boy-turned-saint draws lots of pilgrims and is, for many, a big part of the city's attraction. Saintly ties aside, Kraków might be the most Catholic town in Europe's most Catholic country; be sure to visit a few of its many churches.

In recent years, the city's Kazimierz district has come back to life—both with Jewish-themed cultural sights and with lively bars, food trucks, and restaurants. This mingling of the historic with the contemporary typifies a city that always has been Poland's heartbeat.

west of the center (code: KRK, www.krakowairport.pl). The easiest way downtown is to hop on the slick and speedy **train** (follow *Kolej do Centrum* signs up the ramp, then across the sky bridge to the parking garage; 17 zł, 1-2/hour, 18 minutes to Kraków's main train station—see arrival instructions earlier, under "By Train"). There's also a **taxi** stand in front of the terminal; the official rate for the 30-minute ride into town should be about 110 zł. You can also order an Uber (typically cheaper than a taxi) or arrange a taxi transfer in advance (such as with recommended driver Andrew Durman, listed under "Tours in Kraków," later).

Many budget flights—including some on Wizz Air and Ryanair—use the **International Airport Katowice in Pyrzowice** (Międzynarodowy Port Lotniczy Katowice w Pyrzowicach, code: KTW, www.katowice-airport.com). This airport is about 18 miles from the city of Katowice, which is about 50 miles west of Kraków. Direct buses run sporadically between Katowice Airport and Kraków's main train station area (60 zł, trip takes 1.75 hours, generally scheduled to meet incoming flights, www.matuszek.com. pl). You can also take the bus from Katowice Airport to Katowice's train station (hourly, 50 minutes), then take the train to Kraków (hourly, 1.5 hours). Wizz Air's website (www.wizzair.com) is useful for figuring out your connection.

HELPFUL HINTS

Exchange Rate: 1 złoty (zł, or PLN) = about 25 cents; 4 zł = about $1.

Book Ahead: In Kraków, you're wise to book in advance your visits to the popular Schindler's Factory Museum, Wieliczka Salt Mine, and Rynek Underground Museum (see details in each listing)—and you definitely need to book well ahead for a visit to Auschwitz (see next chapter). That and perhaps a fancy dinner and any tour you hope to take is all you need to concern yourself with in advance.

Sightseeing Tips: Aside from the churches, most major sights are managed by one of three organizations: the **National Museum in Kraków,** mainly art collections (www.mnk.pl); **Museum of Kraków/Muzeum Krakowa,** mainly historical exhibits (including Schindler's Factory and Rynek Underground Museum, www.muzeumkrakowa.pl); and the many underwhelming sights at **Wawel Castle** (www.wawel.krakow.pl). All three organizations tend to tinker with hours, closed days, and free days. Before heading out, check the "Kraków at a Glance" sidebar, later, and confirm with the websites above.

Many sights are **closed** on Monday, but others remain open: Wieliczka Salt Mine, all the churches, Jagiellonian University Museum, Jewish-themed sights in Kazimierz, and a few of the sights at Wawel Castle (morning only). On Tuesday, the Wawel Castle sights close early, but the cathedral remains open. On Saturday, most of Kazimierz's Jewish-themed sights are closed. On Sunday, churches have limited hours for sightseers (for example, Wawel Cathedral opens at 12:30).

Also be aware of days that certain sights are **free:** On Tuesday, the National Museum branches (including the Czartoryski Museum, Wyspiański Museum, and Gallery of 19th-Century Polish Art in the Cloth Hall) are free, but some are open limited hours; the Rynek Underground Museum is also free (but open shorter hours and crowded). On Monday, the Schindler's Factory Museum is free, open only in the morning, and extremely crowded.

Bookstore: For an impressive selection of new and used English books, try **Massolit Books,** just west of the Old Town. They also have a café with drinks and light snacks, and a good children's section (daily 10:00-20:00, Ulica Felicjanek 4, +48 12 432 4150, www.massolit.com).

Laundry: The inviting **Frania Café,** a short walk from Wawel Castle (on the way to Kazimierz), is a café/pub with washers and dryers (pay more for full service), relaxing ambience, a full bar serving espresso drinks and laundry-themed hard drinks, an enticing menu, long hours, and a friendly staff (daily 7:30-22:00, Stradomska 19, +48 783 945 021, www. pralniasamoobslugowa.pl).

Betty Clean is a full-service laundry that's slightly closer to the Old Town, but expensive (priced per item not per load, takes 24 hours—or pay extra for express service, Mon-Fri 8:00-18:00, Sat 10:00-14:00, closed Sun, just outside the Planty park at Ulica Zwierzyniecka 6, +48 12 423 0848).

For locations, see the "Kraków's Old Town" map.

GETTING AROUND KRAKÓW

Kraków's top sights and best hotels are easily accessible by foot. You'll need wheels only if you're going to outlying areas (Kazimierz, Nowa Huta, John Paul II pilgrimage sites, and so on).

By Public Transit

Trams and buses zip around Kraków's urban sprawl. The same tickets work system-wide and are based on how long the ride takes: 4 zł/20 minutes *(20-minutowy)*, 6 zł/1 hour *(60-minutowy)*. You can also get tickets good for 24 hours (17 zł), 48 hours (35 zł), and 72 hours (50 zł). Buy tickets at kiosks, at the machines you'll see at bigger stops, or on board (look for a machine; if not, buy your ticket from the driver). Some machines take credit cards, others only cash. You can also buy tickets on the Jakdojade app, which works in other Polish cities as well. Always validate a single-ride ticket when you board the bus or tram. For a good route planner, see Jakdojade.pl.

Tram #3 is particularly handy. It goes from the side of the train station (Dworzec Główny Zachód) to the ring road in front of the station (Dworzec Główny), then stops at the eastern edge of the Old Town (Poczta Główna, at the main post office) before continuing to Kazimierz (Miodowa is at the north end, near Ulica Szeroka; Św. Wawrzyńca is at the south end, near the old tram depot) and Podgórze, near the Schindler's Factory Museum (Plac Bohaterow Getta). **Tram #24** is also useful: It stops at the western edge of the Old Town (Teatr Bagatela), then loops around the northern edge to stop near the Barbican (Stary Kleparz) before meeting up with tram #3 in front of the train station (Dworzec Główny) and continuing on to Kazimierz and Podgórze (same stops as listed above).

By Taxi or Uber

Only take cabs that are clearly marked with a company logo and telephone number. Legitimate Kraków taxis start at 9 zł and charge about 3 zł per kilometer—or more at night—while unofficial taxis charge whatever they like. Rides generally cost around 20-25 zł but can take longer than you'd expect: Due to the Old Town's many traffic restrictions and pedestrian zones, a "short ride across town" may require looping all the way around the ring road. You're more likely to get the fair metered rate by calling a cab, rather than taking one waiting at tourist spots. Well-established companies include **iCar** (+48 12 653 55 55), **Megataxi** (+48 12 19625), **Radio Taxi** (+48 12 19191), and **Barbakan** (+48 12 19661).

Uber is typically cheaper than Kraków's official taxis (though prices can spike during busy "surge" periods). Be aware that, while some taxi companies are allowed to pick up and drop off within Kraków's highly restricted Old Town, Ubers generally can't—so you may need to walk to the ring road. In my experience, Polish Uber drivers (and their cars) are a bit less polished and professional than those back home—but they're cheap, usually friendly, and handy.

By Bike

The riverfront bike path is enticing on a nice day; the Planty park, while inviting, can be a bit crowded for biking. **KRK Bike Rental** is very central and affordably rents a variety of bikes, from city touring bikes to electric models (daily 9:00-21:00, less in bad weather, closed Nov-March, Ulica Św. Anny 4, +48 509 267 733, www.krkbikerental.pl).

Tours in Kraków

Local Guides

I've enjoyed working with several wonderful Kraków guides. Prices are standard and affordable (500 zł/half-day, 900 zł/day), and some of them have cars for day-tripping into the countryside for an extra charge.

Tomasz Klimek (+48 605 231 923, tomasz.klimek@interia.pl) and his business partner **Monika Prylinska** (+48 693 648 528, monikaprylinska@gmail.com) are both top-notch guides; together they run Kraków Urban Tours (see later), but you can also hire them one-on-one (500 zł/half-day, 900 zł/day, slightly more with a car).

Two other great guides are **Anna Bakowska** (+48 604 151 293, leadertour@wp.pl) and **Marta Chmielowska** (+48 603 668 008, martachm7@gmail.com).

I wouldn't bother hiring a guide for the trip to Auschwitz—

only official Auschwitz guides can legally give tours on-site, so you'll wind up joining one of the tours once there; instead, it's a better value to hire a driver (like Andrew or Chester, listed next).

Drivers

Since Kraków is such a useful home base for day trips, it can be handy to splurge on a private driver for door-to-door service. **Andrew (Andrzej) Durman,** a Pole who lived in Chicago and speaks fluent English, is a gregarious driver, translator, miracle worker, and all-around great guy. While not a licensed tour guide, Andrew is an eager conversationalist and loves to provide lively commentary while you roll. Although you can hire Andrew for a simple airport transfer or an Auschwitz day trip, he also enjoys tackling more ambitious itineraries, from helping you explore your Polish ancestry to taking you on multiday journeys around Poland and beyond. These prices are transportation only for up to 4 people: 600 zł to Auschwitz, 350 zł to Wieliczka Salt Mine, 120 zł for transfer from Kraków-Balice Airport, or 800 zł for an all-day trip into the countryside—such as into the High Tatras or to track down your Polish roots near Kraków (more to cover gas costs for trips longer than 100 km one-way; long-distance transfers for up to 4 people to Prague, Budapest, Vienna, or Berlin for 2,500 zł—or 300 zł extra if he makes longer stops en route or picks you up there; all prices higher for bigger van, +48 602 243 306, andrew@tour-service.pl). If he's busy, Andrew may send you with one of his English-speaking colleagues, such as Karol or Stefan.

Local guide Marta Chmielowska's husband, **Czesław** (a.k.a. Chester), can also drive you to nearby locations (650 zł for all-day trip to Auschwitz, 400 zł to Wieliczka Salt Mine, or a very long day combining Wieliczka and Auschwitz for 1,000 zł; 2,400 zł for a transfer to Prague; to book, see Marta's contact information, earlier).

Kraków Urban Tours

This company, run by recommended guides Tomasz and Monika (who also guide tours for me in Europe), works hard to put travelers in touch with genuine cultural experiences that many tourists miss. In addition to a variety of local walking tours—including a "Greatest Hits" Old Town walk (€50) and a food tour (€90)—they've curated some special experiences that offer more cultural intimacy. For example, their pierogi-making class begins at the Kleparz farmers market, where you'll personally shop for the ingredients, then heads to a local home (rather than a classroom or restaurant) to make pierogi just like Babcia used to make (€70/person for a 4-plus-hour experience). They also have tours to Nowa Huta to learn about the communist period; all-day trips into the mountains around Zakopane; a "Made in Kraków" shopping tour

Kraków at a Glance

▲▲▲**Main Market Square** Stunning heart of Kraków and a people magnet any time of day; the centerpiece Cloth Hall features souvenirs and museum upstairs. See page 58.

▲▲**St. Mary's Church** Landmark church with extraordinary wood-carved Gothic altarpiece. **Hours:** Mon-Sat 11:30-17:45, Sun from 14:00. See page 55.

▲▲**St. Francis Basilica** Lovely Gothic church with some of Poland's best Art Nouveau. **Hours:** Mon-Sat 10:00-16:00, Sun 13:00-15:30; open longer hours for services and prayer. See page 64.

▲▲**Wawel Cathedral** Poland's national church, with tons of tombs, a crypt, and a climbable tower. **Hours:** Mon-Sat 9:00-17:00, Sun from 12:30; Nov-March daily until 16:00; cathedral museum closed Sun off-season; tower climb in summer only. See page 70.

▲▲**Wawel Castle Grounds** Historic hilltop with views, castle, cathedral, courtyard with chakras, and a passel of museums. **Hours:** Grounds open daily 6:00 until dusk, but some museums closed Mon. See page 75.

▲▲**Gallery of 19th-Century Polish Art** Worthwhile collection of paintings by should-be-famous artists, upstairs in the Cloth Hall. **Hours:** Tue-Sun 10:00-18:00, closed Mon. See page 80.

▲▲**Czartoryski Museum** Eclectic collection of historic bric-a-brac and art, including Leonardo's stunning *Lady with an Ermine*. **Hours:** Tue-Sun 10:00-18:00, closed Mon. See page 84.

▲▲**Stanisław Wyspiański Museum** Small but delightful collection of the great Młoda Polska (Art Nouveau) master. **Hours:** Tue and Fri-Sun 10:00-17:00, closed Mon and Wed-Thu. See page 88.

that helps you find locally made, meaningful items to take home; an innovative pinhole photography tour; and a handmade souvenir workshop with proceeds that support local homelessness-relief charities. You can either join a scheduled tour with other travelers or (for a higher cost) book a private experience. It's fun to peruse their offerings (+48 665 015 665, www.krakowurbantours.com, info@krakowurbantours.com).

Walking Tours

A variety of interchangeable companies run daily city walking tours in English in summer. Most do a three-hour tour of the Old

▲▲**Rynek Underground Museum** Exhibit on medieval Kraków filling excavated cellars beneath the Main Market Square. **Hours:** Mon & Wed-Thu 10:00-19:00 (closed second Mon of each month), Tue until 14:00, Fri-Sun until 20:00. See page 90.

▲▲**Wieliczka Salt Mine** Medieval salt mine on the outskirts of the city (and time-consuming to visit) featuring an underground world of salty caverns and hand-hewn salt sculptures. **Hours:** Tours at the top of each hour, daily 8:00-18:00, shorter hours off-season. See page 120.

▲▲**Schindler's Factory Museum** Building where Oskar Schindler saved over 1,000 Jewish workers, now an engaging exhibit about Kraków's WWII experience. **Hours:** Mon 10:00-14:00, Tue-Sun until 18:00 (closed first Tue of the month). See page 108.

▲▲**Old Jewish Cemetery** Poignant burial site in Kazimierz, with graves from 1552 to 1800. **Hours:** Sun-Fri 9:00-16:00, sometimes until 18:00 May-Sept, closes earlier in winter and by sundown on Fri, closed Sat. See page 97.

▲**New Jewish Cemetery** Graveyard with tombs from after 1800, partly restored after Nazi desecration. **Hours:** Sun-Fri 8:00-16:00, closed Sat. See page 105.

▲**Pharmacy Under the Eagle** Small but evocative, with interactive exhibits about the Holocaust in Kraków. **Hours:** Wed-Sun 10:00-17:00; closed Mon-Tue. See page 107.

▲**Stained-Glass Workshop and Museum** Stained-glass factory offering tours and hands-on classes. **Hours:** Tours Tue-Sat at 12:00 and 15:00, classes by appointment. See page 94.

Town as well as a three-hour tour of Kazimierz, the Jewish district (expect to pay about 70 zł per tour). Guide quality can be variable and the scene is continually evolving; it's best to pick up local fliers (the TI works exclusively with one company, Kraków Booking, but hotel reception desks generally have more options), then choose the one that fits your interests and schedule. For a more established outfit, consider Kraków Urban Tours, earlier. You'll also see ads for "free" tours—which are not really free (the guide gets paid only if you tip generously).

Food Tours

Kraków Urban Tours, described earlier, offers casual evening food walks that basically assemble a full meal with a little sightseeing thrown in (at 18:00, €90, 3 hours, www.krakowurbantours.com, info@krakowurbantours.com).

Another fine choice is **Eat Polska,** which smartly connects food to culture and history, making the experience equal parts informative and delicious (about €80 for a food tour or a vodka tasting with hearty food pairings, get details and book at www.eatpolska.com).

Crazy Guides

This irreverent company offers tours to the communist suburb of Nowa Huta and other outlying sights. For details, see page 124.

Bike Tours

Kraków Bike Tours is a well-established operation that runs daily four-hour bike tours in English, with 25 stops in the Old Town, Kazimierz, and Podgórze (€24, you can pay extra to use an electric bike, July-Sept daily at 10:00 and 15:00, spring and fall only 1/day at 10:00, confirm details and prebook online, office in the courtyard at Sławkowska 11, +48 510 394 657, www.krakowbiketour.com).

Bus Tours to Auschwitz or Wieliczka

As Kraków is so easily enjoyed on foot, taking a bus tour doesn't make much sense in town. But they can be handy for reaching outlying sights. Various tour companies run itineraries to Auschwitz (6 hours), Wieliczka Salt Mine (4 hours), and other regional side trips (each itinerary around 140-170 zł).

Given the difficulty of reserving your own appointment at Auschwitz (explained in the next chapter), one of these bus tours—which include a guided tour of the camp—may be your most convenient option. **See Kraków** (www.seekrakow.com) and **Discover Cracow** (www.discovercracow.com) typically use smaller 19-seat minibuses. They sometimes offer hotel pickup, which seems convenient, but you'll waste a lot of time driving around the city to other hotels. **Kraków Booking** (which has a monopoly at the TI; www.krakowbooking.com) and **Cracow City Tours** (www.cracowcitytours.com) use larger 50-seat buses with a central pickup point near the Old Town.

At any company, the on-bus guiding is hit-or-miss but largely irrelevant since you'll be handed off to an official Auschwitz guide once at the camp. Note that the many tour offices and faux-TIs you'll see around town simply sell tickets for these companies. If you waited too long to reserve at Auschwitz and are desperate to get in at short notice, try dropping into various agencies around town to see if anyone has space.

Buggy Tours

You'll see (and hear) horse-drawn buggies that trot around Kraków from the Main Market Square. The going rate is a hefty 300 zł for a 30-minute tour to the castle and back (though prices can be soft when it's not too busy). After dark, they're lit up like fanciful Cinderella coaches—a memorable scene, all lined up in front of St. Mary's Church.

Golf-Cart Tours

Several outfits around town (including on the Square) offer tours on a golf cart with recorded commentary. Given the limits on car traffic in the old center, this can be a handy way to connect the sights for those with limited mobility. Generally, you'll pay about 250 zł for a 30-minute tour around the Old Town; to extend the trip to Kazimierz, it's 500 zł; and adding the Podgórze former Jewish ghetto and Schindler's Factory costs a total of 750 zł (these prices are for the entire golf cart, up to 5 people). Prices tend to be soft—try haggling.

Kraków's Royal Way Walk

This self-guided walk is designed to link up most of Kraków's major sights (see the map on page 38). Much of the walk follows a route called the "Royal Way" because the king used to follow this same path when he returned to Kraków after a journey. After the capital moved to Warsaw, most kings still used Wawel Cathedral for important events. In fact, from 1320 to 1795, nearly every Polish king traversed Kraków's Royal Way at least twice: on the day he was crowned and on the day he was buried. You could sprint through this walk in about an hour and a half (less than a mile altogether), but it's much more fun if you take it like the kings did...slowly.

• *Begin just outside the main gate (the Florian Gate) at the north end of the Old Town. Face the tall, rectangular tower marking the town entrance.*

▲City Walls and Barbican (Barbakan)

Tatars—those battle-hardened invaders from Central Asia—destroyed Kraków in 1241. To better defend their rebuilt city, Krakovians built this **wall**. The original rampart had 47 watchtowers and eight gates. (You'll find a bronze model of the wall just to the right of the tower.)

Now turn around. The big, round defensive fort standing outside the wall is the **Barbican,** built to provide extra fortification to weak sections—namely, the gates. Imagine how it looked in 1500,

KRAKÓW

when the Barbican stood outside the town moat with a long bridge leading to the Florian Gate—the city's main entryway. Today, you can pay a small fee to scramble along the passages and fortifications of the Barbican, though there's little to see inside, other than a small but good exhibit giving you a sense of how the walls were designed. The same ticket also lets you climb up onto the surviving stretch of Old Town walls flanking the Florian Gate (entry from inside walls).

• *The greenbelt within which the Barbican sits is called the...*

▲▲Planty

By the 19th century, Kraków's no-longer-necessary city wall had fallen into disrepair. As the Austrian authorities were doing all over their empire, they decided

to tear down what remained, fill in the moat, and plant trees. (The name comes not from the English "plant" but from the Polish *plantovac,* or "flat"—because they flattened out this area to create it.) Today, the Planty is a beautiful park that stretches 2.5 miles around the entire perimeter of Kraków's Old Town. To give your Kraków visit an extra dimension, consider a quick bike ride around the Planty (best early in the morning, when it's less crowded) with a side trip along the parklike riverbank near Wawel Castle; you'll see bike-rental places around the Old Town (including KRK Bike Rental, mentioned in "Getting Around Kraków," earlier).

Circle around the left side of the Barbican. On your left, keep an eye out for a unique monument depicting an elderly, bearded man in the corner of a huge frame. This honors **Jan Matejko,** arguably Poland's most beloved painter, who specialized in giant-scale epic historical scenes several times larger than this frame. We'll hear Matejko's name many more times on this walk.

As you continue around the Barbican, look down to see the much lower ground level around its base—making it easy to imagine that the Planty was once anything but flat.

• *Across the busy street from the Barbican, standing in the middle of the long park, is the...*

Grunwald Monument

This memorial honors one of the most important battles in the history of a nation that has seen more than its share: the Battle of Grunwald on July 15, 1410, when Polish and Lithuanian forces banded together to finally defeat the Teutonic Knights, who had been running roughshod over the lands along the Baltic. Lying dramatically slain at the base of this monument, like a toppled Goliath, is the defeated Grand Master of the Teutonic Knights— German crusaders who had originally been brought to Poland as mercenaries. It's easy to see this vanquished statue as a thinly veiled metaphor for one of Poland's powerful, often domineering neighbors. When the Nazis took power here, this statue was one of the first things they tore down. When they left, it was one of the first things the Poles put back up.

• *If you'd like to see a slice of Krakovian life, side-trip one block to the left of the monument, to the local farmers market. It hides a block behind the busy ring road.*

The Old Market (Stary Kleparz)

The colorful Old Market offers a refreshing dash of Kraków that has nothing to do with history or tourism. It's just lots of hard-scrabble people selling what they grow or knit, and lots of others buying. Wander around as if on a cultural scavenger hunt. Find the freshest doughnuts *(pączki)*, the most popular bakery, the villager selling slippers she knitted, the smelliest smoked-fish stand, and the old man with the smoked cheese (Mon-Sat 7:00-18:00—but busiest and most interesting in the morning, closed Sun).

• *Now retrace your steps to the Barbican and enter the Old Town by walking through the...*

Florian Gate (Brama Floriańska)

As you approach the gate, look up at the **crowned white eagle,** representing courage and freedom—the historic symbol of the Polish people.

Inside the gate, notice the little chapel on the right with a replica of the famous **Black Madonna of Częstochowa,** the most important religious symbol among Polish Catholics. The original, located in Częstochowa (70 miles north of Kraków), is an Eastern Orthodox-style icon of mysterious origin with several mystical legends attached to it. After the icon's believed role in protecting a monastery from

Swedish invaders in the mid-17th century, it was named "Queen and Protector of Poland."

Once through the gate, look back at it. High above is **St. Florian,** patron of the fire brigade. As fire was a big concern for a wooden city of the 15th century, Florian gets a place of honor.

You'll often see traditionally clad **musicians** near the gate, performing their lilting folk melodies for tips.

• *You're standing at the head of Kraków's historic (and now touristic) gamut...*

▲Floriańska Street (Ulica Floriańska)

In good weather, hanging on the inside of the city wall in both directions is a makeshift **art gallery,** where—traditionally—starv-

ing students hawk the works they've painted at the Academy of Fine Arts (across the busy street from the Barbican). The entrance to get on top of the wall—covered by the Barbican ticket—is at the left end of this gallery. If you detoured just a little farther along the wall, to the brick skybridge, you'd reach the entrance to the **Czartoryski Museum,** an eclectic collection of artifacts, including a famous portrait (no, not *that* one) by Leonardo da Vinci...see page 84).

Now begin strolling down **Floriańska street** (floh-ree-AHN-skah). Notice that all over town, storefronts advertising themselves as "tourist information" offices are actually tourist sales agencies (see a list of legitimate TIs on page 37). Along with the fast-food joints, also notice some uniquely Polish snacks: The various pizza and kebab windows also sell *zapiekanka*—a toasted baguette with toppings, similar to a French bread pizza. Or, for an even quicker bite, buy an *obwarzanek* (ring-shaped, bagel-like roll, typically fresh) from a street vendor; many still use their old-fashioned blue carts. Pijana Wiśnia (on the right at #36) sells the sour-cherry liqueur called *wiśniówka;* while this is a very old drink, it's newly

trendy—you'll see shops like this one all over Poland.

About halfway down the first block, on the left (at #45, round green sign), look for **Jama Michalika** ("Michael's Cave"). Around the turn of the 20th century, this dark, atmospheric café was a hangout of the *Młoda Polska* (Young Poland) movement—the Polish answer to Art Nouveau. The walls are papered with sketches from poor artists—local bohemians who couldn't pay their tabs. Today, it hosts a folk troupe that performs traditional music and dance with dinner many evenings (see listing under "Entertainment in Kraków"). Poke around inside this circa-1900 time warp and appreciate this unique art gallery. (For a real time warp, notice the smokers in their own hazy room up front.)

Tourist-clogged Floriańska has more than its share of tacky amusements: wax museum, "Beer House," Thai spa, "I Heart Kraków" shop, and Candy Cat bulk-candy store. But there are some real family-run businesses mixed in: For example, about a block farther down, at #20 (on the right), **Staropolskie Trunki** ("Old Polish Drinks") offers an education in vodka, with a long bar and countless vodkas and liquors—all open and ready to be tasted. They don't carry any big brand names; these are all locally made. They can help you navigate your options—let them know if you like sweet, dry, and so on (four tastes for 25 zł with an explanation from the bartender, daily 10:00-late).

• *Continue into the Main Market Square, where you'll run into...*

▲▲St. Mary's Church (Kościół Mariacki)

A church has stood on this spot for 800 years. The original church was destroyed by the first Tatar invasion in 1241, but all subsequent versions—including the current one—have been built on the same foundation. You can look down the sides to see how the Main Market Square has risen about seven feet over the centuries.

How many church towers does St. Mary's have? Technically, the answer is one. The shorter tower belongs to the church; the taller one is a municipal watchtower, from which you'll hear a bugler playing the hourly *hejnał* song. According to Kraków's favorite legend, during that first Tatar invasion, a town watchman saw the enemy approaching and sounded the alarm. Before he could finish the tune, an arrow pierced his throat—which is why, even today, the *hejnał* stops suddenly partway through. Today's buglers—12 in all—are firemen first, musicians second. Each one works a 24-hour shift up there, playing the

hejnał four times on the hour—with one bugle call for each direction. (It's even broadcast on national Polish radio at noon.) While you're in Kraków, you'll certainly hear one of these tiny, hourly, broken performances.

To see one of the most finely crafted Gothic altarpieces any-where, it's worth paying admission to enter the church. The front door is open 14 hours a day and is free to those who come to pray, but tourists use the door around the right side (buy your ticket across the little square from this door). The panels of the altarpiece are opened with fanfare each day at 11:50.

Cost and Hours: 15 zł, Mon-Sat 11:30-17:45, Sun from 14:00.

Visiting the Church: Inside, you're struck by the lavish decor. This was the church of the everyday townspeople, built out of a spirit of competition with the royal high church at Wawel Castle.

At the altar is one of the best medieval **woodcarvings** in ex-istence—the exquisite, three-part altarpiece by German Veit Stoss

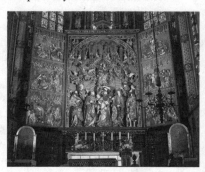

(Wit Stwosz in Polish). Carved over 12 years and completed in 1489, it's packed with emo-tion rare in Gothic art. Get as close as you can and study the remarkable details. Stoss used oak for the structural parts and linden trunks for the fig-ures. The open altar depicts the Dormition (death—or, if split-ting theological hairs, heavenly sleep) of the Virgin. The artist catches the apostles around Mary, reacting in the seconds after she collapses. Mary is depicted in three stages: At the bottom, her body goes limp in the arms of her panicking followers. In the middle, her soul—radiating beams of light—is being escorted to heaven by Jesus. And, at the very top (in the cupola above the frame), Mary sits upon a heavenly throne as she's crowned by Jesus. The six scenes on the sides are the Annunciation, birth of Jesus, visit by the Three Magi, Jesus' Resurrection, his Ascension, and Mary becoming the mother of the apostles at Pentecost.

When the Nazis invaded Poland, they made a list of artistic masterpieces they planned to plunder and take home to Germa-ny—and this altarpiece was on it. It was dismantled and taken to Nürnberg, where it was hidden away in a cellar and managed to survive that city's destruction. After the war, it was returned here and painstakingly reassembled.

There's more to St. Mary's than the altar. While you're ad-miring this church's art, notice the flowery Neo-Gothic painting covering the choir walls. Stare up into the starry, starry blue ceil-ing. As you wander around, consider that the church was renovated a century ago by three Polish geniuses from two very different artistic generations: the venerable positivist Jan Matejko and his Art Nouveau students, Stanisław Wyspiański and Józef Mehoffer

Kazimierz the Great (1333-1370)

Out of the many centuries of Polish kings, only one earned the nickname "great," and he's the only one worth remembering: Kazimierz the Great.

K. the G., who ruled Poland from Kraków in the 14th century, was one of those larger-than-life medieval kings who left his mark on all fronts—from war to diplomacy, art patronage to womanizing. His scribes bragged that Kazimierz "found a Poland made of wood, and left one made of brick and stone." He put Kraków on the map as a major European capital. He founded many villages (some of which still bear his name—including one that's an important neighborhood of Kraków) and replaced wooden structures with stone ones (such as Kraków's Cloth Hall). Kazimierz also established the Kraków Academy (today's Jagiellonian University), the second-oldest university in Central Europe. And to protect all of these new building projects, he heavily fortified Poland by building a series of imposing forts and walls around its perimeter. If you have a 50 zł note, take a look at it: That's Kazimierz the Great on the front, and on the back you'll see his capital, Cracovia, and the most important town he founded, Casmirus.

Most of all, Kazimierz is remembered as a progressive, tolerant king. In the 14th century, other nations were deporting—or even interning—their Jewish subjects, who were commonly scapegoated for anything that went wrong. But the enlightened Kazimierz created policies that granted Jews more opportunities (often related to banking and trade) and allowed them a chance for higher social standing—establishing the country as a safe haven for Jews in Europe.

Kazimierz the Great was the last of Poland's long-lived Piast dynasty. Although he left no male heir—at least, no legitimate one—Kazimierz's advances set the stage for Poland's golden age (14th-16th century). After his death, Poland united with Lithuania (against the common threat of the Teutonic Knights), the Jagiellonian dynasty was born, and Poland became one of Europe's mightiest medieval powers.

(we'll learn more about these two later on our walk). The huge silver bird under the organ loft in back is that symbol of Poland, the crowned white eagle.

Tower Climb: For the best view in town, you can climb 271 steep, claustrophobic stairs to the top of the taller tower to visit the *hejnał* fireman (20 zł, pay at the ticket office for the church, departs at :05 and :30 past each hour; May-Sept Tue-Sat 10:00-17:30, Sun from 13:00, closed Mon; on good-weather days in shoulder season, open only Thu-Sat; closed off-season and in bad weather).

• *Leaving the church, notice the neck clamps dangling from the exterior walls near the side door. If you were leaving Mass in centuries past, there would be criminals chained here for public humiliation. You'd spit on them before turning right and stepping into one of the biggest market squares anywhere.*

▲▲▲Main Market Square (Rynek Główny), a.k.a. "The Square"

Kraków's marvelous Square, one of Europe's most gasp-worthy public spaces, bustles with street musicians, colorful flower stalls, cotton-candy vendors, loiter-ing teenagers, the local break-dancing troupe, businesspeople commuting by foot, gawking tourists, soap-balloon-blowers, and the lusty coos of pigeons. The Square is where Kraków lives. It's often filled with vari-ous special events, markets, and festivals. The biggest are the sea-sonal markets around Easter and

Christmas, but you're likely to stumble on something special going on just about any time of year (especially June through Aug).

The Square was established in the 13th century, when the city had to be rebuilt after being flattened by the Tatars. At the time, it was the biggest square in medieval Europe. It was illegal to sell anything on the street, so everything had to be sold here on the Main Market Square. It was divided into smaller markets, such as the butcher stalls, the ironworkers' tents, and the still-standing Cloth Hall (described later).

Notice the modern **fountain** with the glass pyramid at this end of the Square. A major excavation of the surrounding area created a museum of Kraków's medieval history that literally sprawls beneath the Square (for more on the recommended **Rynek Underground Museum,** see page 90).

The statue in the middle of the Square is a traditional meeting place for Krakovians. It depicts Romantic poet **Adam Mickiewicz** (1789-1855), who's considered the "Polish Shakespeare." His epic masterpiece, *Pan Tadeusz,* is still regarded as one of the greatest works in Polish literature. A wistful, nostalgic tale of Polish-Lith-uanian nobility, *Pan Tadeusz* stirred patriotism in a Poland that had been dismantled by surrounding empires through a series of three Partitions.

The Square is so beautiful partly because the Old Town was spared the bombs of World War II. The Nazis considered Kraków a city with Germanic roots and wanted it saved. But they were quick to destroy any symbols of Polish culture or pride. The statue

The Młoda Polska (Young Poland) Art Movement

Polish art in the late 19th century was ruled by positivism, a school with a very literal, straightforward focus on Polish history. But when the next generation of Kraków's artists came

into their own in the early 1900s, they decided that the old school was exactly that. Though moved by the same spirit and goals as the previous generation—evoking Polish patriotism at a time when their country was being occupied—these new artists used very different methods. They were inspired by a renewed appreciation of folklore and peasant life. Rather than being earnest and literal (an 18th-century Polish war hero on horseback), the new art was playful and highly symbolic (the artist frolicking in a magical garden in the idyllic Polish countryside). This movement became known as Młoda Polska (Young Poland)—Art Nouveau with a Polish accent.

Stanisław Wyspiański (vees-PAYN-skee, 1869-1907) was the leader of Młoda Polska. He produced beautiful artwork, from simple drawings to the stirring stained-glass images in Kraków's St. Francis Basilica. Wyspiański was an expert at capturing human faces with realistic detail, emotion, and personality. The versatile Wyspiański was also an accomplished stage designer and writer. His patriotic play *The Wedding*—about the nuptials of a big-city artist and a peasant girl—is regarded as one of Poland's finest dramas. In Kraków, you can tour the Wyspiański Museum and see his works in St. Francis Basilica and other churches; he's also well represented in Warsaw's National Museum.

Józef Mehoffer (may-HOH-fehr), Wyspiański's good friend and rival, was another great Młoda Polska artist. Mehoffer's style is more expressionistic and abstract than Wyspiański's, often creating an otherworldly effect. See Mehoffer's work in Kraków's St. Francis Basilica and at the artist's former residence (see the Józef Mehoffer House), and in Warsaw at the National Museum.

Other names to look for include **Jacek Malczewski** (mahl-CHEHV-skee), who specialized in self-portraits, and **Olga Boznańska** (bohz-NAHN-skah), the movement's only prominent female artist. Both are featured in Warsaw's National Museum; Malczewski's works also appear in Kraków's Gallery of 19th-Century Polish Art.

of Adam Mickiewicz, for example, was pulled down immediately after occupation.

At the far end of the Square, you'll see the tiny, cubical, copper-domed **Church of St. Adalbert,** one of the oldest churches in Kraków (10th century). This Romanesque structure predates the Square. Like St. Mary's (described earlier), it seems to be at an angle because it's aligned east-west, as was the custom when it was built. (In other words, the churches aren't crooked—the Square is. Any other "crooked" building you see around town predates the 13th-century grid created during the rebuilding of Kraków.)

Drinks are reasonably priced at cafés on the Square (figure 15-20 zł for a coffee, soft drink, beer, or wine; and about 30 zł for a fancier cocktail). Find a spot where you like the view and the chairs, then sit and sip. Order a coffee, Polish *piwo* (beer, such as Żywiec, Okocim, or Lech), or a shot of *wódka* (Żubrówka is a quality brand; for more on Polish drinks, see page 29). For a higher vantage point, the Cloth Hall's **Café Szał terrace**—overlooking the Square and St. Mary's Church—offers one of the best views in town (daily, enter through Gallery of 19th-Century Polish Art entrance).

As the Square buzzes around you, imagine this place before 1989. There were no outdoor cafés, no touristy souvenir stands, and no salespeople hawking cotton candy or neon-lit whirligigs. The communist government shut down all but a handful of the businesses. They didn't want people to congregate here—they should be at home, because "a rested worker is a productive worker." The buildings were covered with soot from the nearby Lenin Steelworks in Nowa Huta. The communists denied the pollution, and when the student "Green Brigades" staged a demonstration in this Square to raise awareness in the 1970s, they were immediately arrested. How things have changed.

• *The huge, yellow building right in the middle of the Square is the...*

▲▲Cloth Hall (Sukiennice)

In the Middle Ages, this was the place where cloth sellers had their market stalls. Kazimierz the Great turned the Cloth Hall into a permanent structure in the 14th century. In 1555, it burned down and was replaced by the current building. The crowned letter *S* (at the top of the gable above the entryway) stands for King Sigismund the Old, who commissioned this version of the hall. As Sigismund fancied all things Italian (including women—

he married an Italian princess), this structure is in the Italianate Renaissance style. Sigismund kicked off a nationwide trend, and you'll still see Renaissance-style buildings like this one all over the country, making the style typically Polish. We'll see more works by Sigismund's imported Italian architects at Wawel Castle.

The Cloth Hall is still a functioning market—selling mostly souvenirs, including wood carvings, chess sets, jewelry (especially amber), painted boxes, and trinkets. Cloth Hall prices are slightly inflated, but still cheap by American standards. You're paying a little extra for the convenience and the atmosphere, but you'll see locals buying gifts here, too.

Pay WCs are at each end of the Cloth Hall. The upstairs of the Cloth Hall is home to the excellent **Gallery of 19th-Century Polish Art** (enter behind the statue of Adam; for a self-guided tour, see page 81).

• *Browse through the Cloth Hall passageway. As you emerge into the sleepier half of the Square, the big tower on your left is the...*

Town Hall Tower

This is all that remains of a town hall building from the 14th century—when Kraków was the powerful capital of Poland. (To visualize the intact structure, look for the bronze model to the right of the stairs.) After the 18th-century Partitions of Poland, Kraków's prominence took a nosedive. As the town's importance crumbled, so did its town hall. It was cheaper to tear down the building than to repair it, and all that was left standing was this nearly 200-foot-tall tower. In summer, you can climb the tower, stopping along the way to poke around an exhibit on Kraków history, but the views from up top are disappointing (18 zł, free on Mon, open March-Oct Mon 11:00-15:00, Tue-Sun until 18:00, likely closed off-season).

Nearby: The **gigantic head** at the base of the Town Hall Tower is a sculpture by contemporary artist Igor Mitoraj, who studied here in Kraków. Typical of Mitoraj's works, the head is an empty shell that appears to be wrapped in cloth. While some locals enjoy having a work by their fellow Krakovian in such a prominent place, others disapprove of its sharp contrast with the Square's genteel Old World ambience. Tourists enjoy playing peek-a-boo with the head's eyes.

• *When you're finished on the Square, we'll head toward Wawel Hill. The official Royal Way makes a beeline for the castle, but we'll take a scenic detour to see some less touristy back streets, visit Kraków's historic university and one of its best churches, and go for a quick walk through the Planty park.*

Exit the square at the corner nearest the Town Hall Tower—basically, in the direction the giant head is looking—then turn right along Ulica Św. Anny. After one block, turn left onto Jagiellońska street. Enter the courtyard of the big, red-brick building on your right.

Jagiellonian University and the Collegium Maius

Kraków had the second university in Central Europe (founded in 1364, after Prague's). Over the centuries, Jagiellonian U. has boasted such illustrious grads as Copernicus and St. John Paul II. And today, the city's character is still defined largely by its huge student population (numbering around 150,000). Many of the university buildings fill the area to the west of the Old Town, so  you'll see more students (and fewer tourist traps) in this part of town than elsewhere.

This building—called the Collegium Maius—is the historic heart of Kraków's university culture. It dates from the 15th century. In the Middle Ages, professors were completely devoted to their scholarly pursuits. They were unmarried and lived, ate, and slept here in an almost monastic environment. They taught downstairs and lived upstairs. In many ways, this building feels more like a monastery than a university. While this courtyard is the most interesting part, you can also tour the interior. The courtyard also hosts free temporary exhibits; look for posters.

The university also comes with some chilling history. On November 6, 1939, the occupying Nazis called all professors together for a meeting. With 183 gathered unknowingly in a hall, they were unceremoniously loaded into trucks and sent to concentration camps, where many were killed. Hitler knew: If you want to decapitate a culture, you kill its intelligentsia.

Before you leave, if you're a fan of rich, thick hot chocolate, enjoy a cup at **Kawiarnia U Pęcherza** (down the stairs near the entrance)—widely regarded as the best in town.

If it's open, head down the *sgraffito*-lined passage on the side of the courtyard (it's on your left as you enter the courtyard). You'll emerge into the **Professors' Garden,** a tranquil space filled with red brick, ivy, stony statues, and inviting benches (open daily 9:00-18:30 or until dusk, closed off-season).

• *Exit the garden through the fancy gate and turn right on Jagiellońska. Spot any students? You'll follow this for two more blocks, passing the much larger and newer, but still red-brick,* **Collegium Novum** *building—the modern administrative headquarters of Jag U., built in the late 19th century to commemorate the 500th anniversary of the building we just left.*

Jagiellońska dead-ends at a dynamic statue on a pillar. Turn left into the inviting **Planty**—*the ring park we saw at the start of this walk. You'll stroll about five minutes through the Planty—dodging bikes and hearing the rattle of trams through the trees—with the Old Town buildings on your left and the ring road through the park on your right. When you reach a street with tram tracks, cross it and turn left. Pause in the park just before the church and take note of the light-yellow building on the left (across the street), with a picture of St. John Paul II smiling down from above the stone doorway.*

Archbishop's Palace

This building was St. John Paul II's residence when he was the archbishop of Kraków. And even after he became pope, it remained his home-away-from-Rome for visits to his hometown. After a long day of saying formal Mass during his visits to Kraków, he'd wind up here. Weary as he was, before going to bed he'd stand in the window above the entrance for hours, chatting casually with the people assembled below—about religion, but also about sports, current events, and whatever was on their minds.

In 2005, when the pope's health deteriorated, this street filled with his supporters, even though he was in Rome. For days, somber locals focused their vigil on this same window, their eyes fixed on a black crucifix that had been placed here. At 21:37 on the night of April 2, 2005, the pope passed away in Rome. Ten thousand Krakovians were on this street, under this window, listening to a Mass broadcast on loudspeakers from the church. When the priest announced the pope's death, every single person simultaneously fell to their knees in silence. For the next several days, thousands of the faith-

ful continued to stand on this street, staring intently at the window where they last saw the man they considered to be the greatest Pole.
• *Now go through the back door of one of Kraków's finest churches...*

▲▲St. Francis Basilica (Bazylika Św. Franciszka)

This beautiful Gothic church, which was St. John Paul II's home church while he was archbishop of Kraków, features some of Po-

land's best Art Nouveau in situ (in the setting for which it was intended). After an 1850 fire, it was redecorated by the two leading members of the Młoda Polska (Young Poland) movement: Stanisław Wyspiański and Józef Mehoffer. The glorious decorations inside this church are the result of their great rivalry run amok.

Cost and Hours: Free; open for visitors Mon-Sat 10:00-16:00, Sun 13:00-15:30; longer hours for services and prayer.

Visiting the Basilica: Step through the door and let your eyes adjust to the low light. Take a few steps up the nave, pausing at the third pew on the left. On the back of this pew, notice the **silver plate** labeled "Jan Paweł II"—marking JPII's favorite place to pray when he lived in the Archbishop's Palace across the street. Just beyond, on the left, you'll see a painting of Poland's premier pontiff.

Now walk another 20 feet down the nave and notice the painting on the right, with an orange-and-blue background. This depicts **St. Maksymilian Kolbe,** the Catholic priest who sacrificed his own life to save a fellow inmate at Auschwitz in 1941 (notice the *16670*—his concentration camp number—etched into the background; read his story on page 161). Kolbe is particularly beloved here, as he actually served at this church.

Now turn around and look up above the door you entered. There, in all its glory, is the stained-glass window titled *God the Father Let It Be,* created by the great Art Nouveau artist Stanisław Wyspiański—and regarded by some as his finest masterpiece. (For more on Wyspiański, see page 59.) The colors beneath the Creator change from yellows and oranges (fire) to soothing blues (water), depending on the light. Wyspiański was supposedly inspired by Michelangelo's vision of God in the Sistine Chapel, though he used a street beggar to model God's specific features. Wyspiański also painted the delightful floral stained-glass windows that line the nave, high up—fitting for a church dedicated to a saint so famous for his spiritual connection to nature.

Now turn back around to face the main altar and head into the **chapel** on the left. This important chapel houses a replica of the Shroud of Turin—which, since it touched the original shroud, is also considered a holy relic (displayed along the left side of the chapel). At the main altar in this chapel, notice the plaques honoring Michał Tomaszek and Zbigniew Strzałkowski. These two Polish priests traveled to Peru as missionaries. There, they (along with an Italian priest) were murdered by communist guerrillas calling themselves the Shining Path. Today, they are considered martyrs.

Before leaving this chapel, look high on the walls at the glorious Stations of the Cross. These were painted by **Józef Mehoffer**—
a friend and rival of Wyspiański—as a response to Wyspiański's work.

Now head back into the nave, turn left, and walk toward the main altar. (If a service is going on, you may not be able to get very far—just look from here.) On the walls, notice Wyspiański's gorgeous Art Nouveau floral patterns.

Up in the apse, take a moment to appreciate the Wyspiański-designed **stained-glass windows** flanking the high altar. On the right is St. Francis, the church's namesake, holding up his hands to show the stigmata on his palms. On the left is the Blessed Salomea—a medieval Polish woman who became queen of Hungary but later returned to Poland and entered a convent after her husband's death. Notice she's dropping a crown—repudiating the earthly world and giving herself over to the simple, stop-and-smell-God's-roses lifestyle of St. Francis. Salomea (who's buried in a side chapel) founded this church. Notice also the Mucha-like paintings by Wyspiański on the pilasters between the windows... yet one more sumptuous Art Nouveau detail in this church that's so rich with them.

• *Head back outside. If no services are going on, you can slip out the side door, to the left of the altar. Otherwise, head back out the way you came and hook right. Either way, you're heading to the right along Franciszkańska street. After passing a few monuments and a tram stop, turn right down busy...*

Grodzka Street

Now you're back on the Royal Way proper. At the corner of Grodzka street stands the modern, copper-colored **Wyspiański Pavilion.**

Karol Wojtyła (1920-2005): The Greatest Pole

The man who became St. John Paul II began his life as Karol Wojtyła, born to a military officer and his wife in the town of Wadowice near Kraków on May 18, 1920. Karol's mother died when he was only nine years old, and his older brother was gone just a few years later. At age 18, Karol moved with his father to Kraków to study philosophy and drama at Jagiellonian University.

Young Karol was gregarious and athletic—an avid skier, hiker, swimmer, and soccer goalie—but his real passion was acting. During the Nazi occupation in World War II, he worked in a quarry to avoid being sent to a labor camp in Germany. In defiance of the Nazis, he secretly studied theology and appeared in illegal underground theatrical productions. When the war ended, he resumed his studies, now at the theology faculty.

After graduating in 1947, Wojtyła swiftly rose through the ranks of the Catholic Church hierarchy. By 1964, he was archbishop of Kraków, and just three years later, he became the youngest cardinal ever. Throughout the 1960s, he fought an ongoing battle with the regime when they refused to allow the construction of a church in the Kraków suburb of Nowa Huta. After years of saying Mass for huge crowds in open fields, Wojtyła finally convinced the communists to allow the construction of the Lord's Ark Church in 1977. A year later, Karol Wojtyła was called to the papacy—the first non-Italian pope in more than four centuries. In 1979, he paid a visit to his native Poland. In a series of cautiously provocative speeches, he demonstrated to his countrymen the potential for mass opposition to communism.

Imagine you're Polish in the 1970s. Your country was devastated by World War II and has struggled under an oppressive regime ever since. Food shortages are epidemic. Lines stretch around the block even to buy a measly scrap of bread. Life is bleak, oppressive, and hopeless. Then someone who speaks your language—someone you've admired your entire life, and one of the only people you've seen successfully stand up to the regime—becomes one of the world's most influential people. A Pole like

Step inside (daily 9:00-20:00) to see three recent stained-glass windows based on designs Wyspiański once submitted for a contest to redecorate Wawel Cathedral. Although these designs were rejected back then, they were finally realized on the hundredth anniversary of his death (in 2007). Visible from inside the building during the day, and gloriously illuminated to be seen outside the building at night, they represent three Polish historical figures: the gaunt St. Stanisław (Poland's first saint), the skeletal Kazimierz the Great (in the middle), and the swooning King Henry the Pious.

you is the leader of a billion Catholics. He makes you believe that the impossible can happen. He says to you again and again: *"Nie lękajcie się"*—"Have no fear." And you begin to believe it.

From his bully pulpit, the pope had a knack for cleverly challenging the communists—just firmly enough to get his point across but stopping short of jeopardizing the stature of the Church in Poland. Gentle but pointed wordplay was his specialty. The inspirational role he played in the lives of Lech Wałęsa and the other leaders of Solidarity emboldened them to rise up; it's no coincidence that the first successful trade union strikes in the Soviet Bloc took place shortly after John Paul II became pope. Many people (including Mikhail Gorbachev) credited John Paul II for the collapse of Eastern European communism.

Even as John Paul II's easy charisma attracted new worshippers to the Church (especially young people), his conservatism on issues such as birth control, homosexuality, and female priests pushed away many Catholics. Under his watch, the Church struggled with pedophilia scandals. Many still fault him for turning a blind eye and not putting a stop to these abuses much earlier. By the end of his papacy, John Paul II's failing health and conservatism had caused him to lose stature in worldwide public opinion.

And yet, approval of the pope never waned in Poland. His compatriots—even the relatively few atheists and agnostics—saw John Paul II both as the greatest hero of their people...and as a member of the family, like a kindly grandfather. When Pope John Paul II died on April 2, 2005, the mourning in his homeland was particularly deep and sustained. Musical performances of all kinds were canceled, and the irreverent MTV-style music channel simply went off the air out of respect.

A speedy nine years after his death, Karol Wojtyła became St. John Paul II in April 2014. Out of 265 popes, few have been given the title "great," but there's already talk in Rome of increasing their ranks. Someday soon we may speak of this man as "St. John Paul the Great." His fellow Poles already do.

If you're not churched out, you can dip into the **Dominican Church**—just a block away, to your left (described later).

Now continue down Grodzka street. This lively thoroughfare, connecting the Square with Wawel, is teeming with shops—and some of Kraków's best restaurants (see "Eating in Kraków," later). Survey your options now and choose (and maybe reserve) your favorite for dinner tonight. This street is also characterized by its fine arcades over the sidewalks. While this might seem like a charming Renaissance feature, the arcades were actually added by the Nazis after they invaded in 1939; they wanted to convert Kraków into a city befitting its status as the capital of their Polish puppet state.

This is also a good street to find some of Kraków's **milk bars.** The most traditional one is about two blocks down, on the right (at #45), with a simple *Bar Mleczny* sign. These government-subsidized cafeterias are the locals' choice for a quick, cheap, filling, lowbrow lunch. Prices are deliriously cheap (soup costs about a dollar), and the food isn't bad.

• *One more block ahead, the small square on your right is...*

Mary Magdalene Square (Plac Św. Marii Magdaleny)

This square offers a great visual example of Kraków's deeply religious character. In the Middle Ages, Kraków was known as "Little Rome" for its many churches. Today, there are 142 churches and monasteries within the city limits (32 in the Old Town alone)—more per square mile than anywhere outside of Rome. You can see several of them from this spot: The nearest, with the picturesque white facade and row of saints out front, is the Roman-style **Church of Saints Peter and Paul** (Poland's first Baroque church, and a popular tourist concert venue). The statues lining this church's facade are the 11 apostles (minus Judas), plus Mary Magdalene, the square's namesake. The next church to the right, with the twin towers, is the Romanesque **St. Andrew's** (now with a Baroque interior). Dating from the rough-and-tumble 11th century, it was designed to double as a place of last refuge—notice the arrow slits around the impassable lower floor. According to legend, a spring inside this church provided water to citizens who holed up here during the Tatar invasions. The church was spared, but that didn't save the rest of Kraków from being overrun by marauding armies. Imagine this stone fortress of God being the only building standing amid a smoldering and flattened Kraków after the 13th-century destruction.

If you look farther down the street, you can see three more churches. And even the square next to you used to be a church, too—it burned in 1855, and only its footprint survives.

• *Go through the square and turn left down...*

Kanonicza Street (Ulica Kanonicza)

With so many churches around here, the clergy had to live somewhere. Many lived on this well-preserved street—supposedly the oldest street in Kraków. As you walk, look for the cardinal hats over three different doorways. The **Hotel Copernicus,** on the left at #16, is named for a famous guest who stayed here five centuries ago. Directly across the street at #17, the **Bishop Erazm Ciołek**

Palace hosts a good exhibit of medieval art and Orthodox icons. Next door, the yellow house at #19 is where Karol Wojtyła lived for 10 years after World War II—long before he became St. John Paul II. Today, this building houses the **Archdiocesan Museum,** which is the top spot in the Old Town to learn about Kraków's favorite son. Both of these sights are described later, under "Sights in Kraków."

• *This marks the end of Kanonicza street—and the end of our self-guided walk. But there's still much more to see. Across the busy street, a ramp leads up to the most important piece of ground in all of Poland: Wawel.*

Sights in and near the Old Town

WAWEL HILL

Wawel (VAH-vehl), a symbol of Polish royalty and independence, is sacred territory to every Polish person. A castle has stood here since

the beginning of Poland's recorded history. Today, Wawel—awash in tourists —is the most visited sight in the country. Crowds and an overly complex admissions system for the hill's many historic sights can be exasperating. Thankfully, a stroll through the cathedral and around the castle grounds—with the help of the following commentary—is enough. I've described these sights in the order of a handy self-guided walk. The many museums on Wawel (all described in this section) are mildly interesting but can be skipped (grounds open daily from 6:00 until dusk, inner courtyard closes 30 minutes earlier). In May and June, it's mobbed with students, as it's a required field trip for Polish schoolkids.

Wawel Sights: The sights you'll enter at Wawel are divided into two institutions, cathedral and castle, each with separate tickets. Tickets for the castle sights are sold at two points (at the long line at the top of the ramp; or with no line at the top of the hill, across the central square). To enter the most important sight—the cathedral—buy your ticket at the office across from the cathedral entrance.

• *From Kanonicza street—where my self-guided Old Town walk ends—head up the long ramp to the castle entry.*

Entry Ramp

Huffing up this ramp, it's easy to imagine how this location—rising above the otherwise flat plains around Kraków—was both strategic and easy to defend. When Kraków was part of the Habsburg Empire in the 19th century, the Austrians turned this castle complex into a fortress, destroying much of its delicate beauty. When Poland regained its independence after World·War I, the castle was returned to its former glory. The bricks you see on your left as you climb the ramp bear the names of Poles from around the world who donated to the cause.

The jaunty equestrian statue ahead is **Tadeusz Kościuszko** (1746-1817). If that name seems familiar, it's because Kościuszko was a hero of the American Revolution and helped design West Point. When he returned to his native Poland, he fought bravely but unsuccessfully against the Russians (during the Partitions that would divide Poland's territory among three neighboring powers). Kościuszko also gave his name to several American towns, a county in Indiana, a brand of mustard from Illinois, and the tallest mountain in Australia.

• *Hiking through the Heraldic Gate next to Kościuszko, you pass the ticket office (if you'll be going into the museums, use the other ticket office, with shorter lines, on the top of the hill. As you crest the hill and pass through the stone gate, on your left is...*

▲▲Wawel Cathedral

Poland's national church is its Westminster Abbey. While the history buried here is pretty murky to most Americans, to Poles, this church is *the* national mausoleum. It holds the tombs of nearly all of Poland's most important rulers and greatest historical figures.

Cost and Hours: 22 zł ticket includes cathedral entry, tower climb, crypt, royal tombs, the John Paul II Wawel Cathedral Museum, and the Archdiocesan Museum not far away (described later). Buy this ticket at the house across from the cathedral entry—marked *KASA*—where you can also rent an audioguide. The cathedral is open Mon-Sat 9:00-17:00, Sun from 12:30 (except the cathedral museum is closed Sun off-season), Nov-March daily until 16:00 (+48 12 429 9516, www.katedra-wawelska.pl).

Cathedral Exterior

Before entering, go around to the far side of the cathedral to take in its profile. This uniquely eclectic church is the product of centuries of haphazard additions—it's surrounded by some 17 chapels and towers that were grafted on to the original, Romanesque, 12th-century core. (The white base of the nearest tower is original. Anything at Wawel that's made of white limestone like this was probably part of the earliest Romanesque structures.) In a sense, when you're looking at the cathedral, you're barely seeing the "cathedral" at all—just these many addenda. To give you a sense of the historical sweep, scan the chapels from left to right: 14th-century Gothic, 12th-century Romanesque (the base of the tower), 17th-century Baroque (the inside is Baroque, though the exterior is a copy of its Renaissance neighbor), 16th-century Renaissance, and 18th- and 19th-century Neoclassical. (This variety in styles is even more evident in the chapels' interiors, which we'll see soon.)

Pay attention to the two particularly interesting domed chapels to the right of the tall tower. The gold one is the Sigismund Chapel, housing memorials to the Jagiellonian kings—including Sigismund the Old, who was responsible for Kraków's Renaissance renovation in the 16th century. The Jagiellonian Dynasty was a high point in Polish history. During that golden 16th century, Poland was triple the size it is today, stretching all the way to the Ottoman Empire and the Black Sea. Poles consider the Sigismund Chapel, made with 80 pounds of gold, to be the finest Renaissance chapel north of the Alps. The copper-domed chapel next to it, home to the Swedish Vasa dynasty, resembles its neighbor (but it's a copy built 150 years later, and without all that gold).

Go back around and face the church's **front entry** for more architectonic extravagance. The tallest tower, called the Sigismund Tower, has a clock with only an hour hand. Climbing a few steps into the entry, you see Gothic chapels (with pointy windows) flanking the door, a Renaissance ceiling, lavish Baroque decoration over the door, and some big bones (a simple whale rib and two vertebrae). In the Middle Ages, these were thought to have been the bones of the mythic Wawel dragon and put here as an oddity to be viewed by the public. (Back

then, there were no museums, so unusual items like these were used to lure people to the church.) The door is the original from the 14th century, with fine wrought-iron work. The K with the crown stands for Kazimierz the Great. The black marble frame is made of Kraków stone from nearby quarries.

KRAKÓW

Cathedral Interior

The cathedral interior is slathered in Baroque memorials and tombs, decorated with tapestries, and soaked in Polish history. The ensemble was designed to help keep Polish identity strong through the ages. It has…and it still does.

After you step inside, you'll follow the one-way, clockwise route that leads you through the choir, then around the back of the apse, then back to the entry.

At the entry, look straight ahead to see the silver tomb under a **canopy,** inspired by the one in St. Peter's Basilica at the Vatican. It contains the remains of the first Polish saint, Stanisław (from the 11th century). In front of the canopy, look for a metallic reliquary that's shaped like a book with its pages being ruffled by the wind (labeled, in Latin, *Sanctus Johannes Paulus II*). The glass capsule in the reliquary holds a drop of St. John Paul II's blood. It takes this shape because of what believers consider a highly significant moment during his memorial service: Before a crowd of thousands on St. Peter's Square in Rome, a book was placed on John Paul II's simple wooden coffin. As the service processed, its pages were ruffled back and forth by the wind, until they were finally slammed shut…as if the Holy Spirit were "closing the book" on his life.

Go behind this canopy into the ornately carved **choir** area. For 200 years, the colorful chair to the right of the high altar has been the seat of Kraków's archbishops, including Karol Wojtyła, who served here for 14 years before becoming pope. It's also here that Polish royal coronations took place.

Now you'll continue into the left aisle. Straight ahead is the entrance to the **Sigismund Tower;** to ascend it, you'll climb 70 claustrophobic wooden stairs to the 11-ton Sigismund Bell and pleasant views of the steeples and spires of Kraków.

Before moving on, there's another small sight back toward where you entered the church: Look for the low-profile staircase and descend into the little **crypt** (with a rare purely Romanesque interior), which houses the remains of Adam Mickiewicz, the Romantic poet whose statue dominates the Main Market Square; and another beloved Romantic poet and playwright, Juliusz Słowacki. You'll also find a white marble monument to Fryderyk Chopin (who's buried in Paris), put here on the 200th anniversary of his birth in 2010.

Now continue around the apse (behind the main altar). After looping around to the right, as you head back up the far aisle, look for the red-marble tomb (on the right) of The Great One—**Kazimierz,** of course. Look for *Kazimierz III Wielki.* At his feet you can see a little animal that was originally intended to be a lion, but because local craftspeople lacked a model, it wound up looking more like a beaver with a lion's mane. This is an allusion to a famous saying about Kazimierz, the nation-builder: He found a Poland made of wood, and left one made of brick and stone. The belt Kazimierz wears represents the fortifications he built in a ring around his Polish realm.

You may notice that there's one VIP (Very Important Pole) who's missing...Karol Wojtyła, a.k.a. John Paul II. Even so, a few more steps toward the entrance, on the left, is the **Chapel of St. John Paul II.** The late pontiff left no specific requests for his body, and the Vatican controversially (to Poles, at least) chose to entomb him in Vatican City, instead of sending him back home to Wawel. While Karol Wojtyła's remains are in St. Peter's Basilica, this chapel was recently converted to honor him—with a plaque in the floor and an altar with his picture. Someday, Poles hope, he may be moved here (but, the Vatican says, don't hold your breath).

Back out in the main church, about 10 steps farther on the right, is the white sarcophagus of **St. Jadwiga** (with a dog at her feet). This 14th-century "king" of Poland advanced the fortunes of her realm by partnering with the king of Lithuania. The resulting Jagiellonian dynasty fought off the Teutonic Knights, helped Christianize Lithuania, and oversaw a high-water mark in Polish history. (Despite the queen's many contributions, the sexism of the age meant that she was considered a "king" rather than a "queen.") She was sainted by Pope John Paul II in 1997.

Across from Jadwiga, peek into the gorgeous 16th-century **Sigismund Chapel,** with its silver altar (this is the gold-roofed chapel you just saw from outside). Locals consider this the "Pearl of the Polish Renaissance" and the finest Renaissance structure outside Italy.

Next, look into the **Vasa Chapel** (past the side door, also on the left): Remember that its exterior matches the restrained, Renaissance style of the Sigismund Chapel, but the interior is clearly Baroque, slathered with gold and silver—quite a contrast.

To the left of the main door, take a look at the Gothic **Holy Cross Chapel,** with its seemingly Orthodox-style 14th-century frescoes.

In the back corner of the church—on the other side of the main door—is the entrance through the Czartoryski Chapel to the **royal tombs.** (You'll exit outside the church, so be sure you're done in here first.) Once downstairs, the first big room, an original Romanesque space called St. Leonard's Crypt, houses Poland's greatest war heroes: Kościuszko (of American Revolution fame), Jan III Sobieski (who successfully defended Vienna from the Ottomans; he's in the simple black coffin with the gold inscription *J III S*), Sikorski, Poniatowski, and so on. Poles consider this room highly significant as the place where St. John Paul II celebrated his first Mass after becoming a priest (in November 1946).

Then you'll wander through several rooms of second-tier Polish kings, queens, and their kids. Head down more stairs into a stark corridor, where you'll run into the plaque honoring the Polish victims of the Katyń massacre in the USSR during World War II. Stepping into the next room, you'll see the tomb of President Lech Kaczyński and his wife Helena, who were among the 96 Polish politicians killed in a tragic 2010 plane crash at Smoleńsk, where the diplomats had planned to attend a ceremony memorializing the Katyń massacre. Up a few stairs is the final grave, belonging to Marshal Józef Piłsudski, the WWI hero who later seized power and was the de facto ruler of Poland from 1926 to 1935. His tomb was moved here so the rowdy soldiers who came to pay their respects wouldn't disturb the others.

• *Exit near the Kaczyński tomb. To visit the cathedral's museum (covered by the same ticket), cross the little square and head up the stairs next to the statue of St. John Paul II.*

John Paul II Wawel Cathedral Museum

This small museum fills four rooms with artifacts relating to both the cathedral and St. John Paul II. Downstairs is the Royal Room, with vestments, swords, regalia, coronation robes, and items that were once buried with the kings, as well as early treasury items (from the 11th through 16th century). Upstairs is the "Papal Room" with items from St. John Paul II's life: his armchair, vestments, caps, shoes, and miter (pointy pope hat), plus souvenirs from his travels. (If you're into  papal memorabilia, the collection at the nearby Archdiocesan Museum—covered by the same ticket and described later—is better.) The adjoining room holds a later treasury collection (17th through 20th century).

Cost and Hours: Same ticket and hours as the cathedral (see earlier), except the museum is closed Sun off-season.

• *When you're finished with the cathedral sights, stroll around the...*

▲▲Wawel Castle Grounds

In the rest of the castle, you'll uncover more fragments of Kraków's history and have the opportunity to visit several museums. I con-

sider the museums skip-pable, but if you want to visit them, buy tickets before you enter the inner courtyard. Read the descriptions on page 78 to decide which, if any, museums appeal to you.

❍ Self-Guided Tour: This guided stroll, which doesn't enter any of the admission-charging attractions, is plenty for most visitors.

• *For a historical orientation, stand with the cathedral to your back, and survey the empty field between here and the castle walls.*

Gothic Church Ruins: This hilltop has seen lots of changes over the years. Kazimierz the Great turned a small fortress into a mighty Gothic castle in the 14th century. But that original fortress burned to the ground in 1499, and ever since, Wawel has been in flux. For example, in the grassy field, notice the foundations of two Gothic churches that were destroyed when the Austrians took over Wawel in the 19th century and needed a parade ground for their troops. (They built the red-brick hospital building beyond the field, now used by the Wawel administration.)

• *Facing the cathedral, look right to find a grand green-and-pink entry-way. Go through here and into the palace's dramatically Renaissance-style...*

Inner Courtyard: If this space seems to have echoes of Florence, that's because it was designed and built by young Florentines after Kazimierz's original castle burned down. As with the Cloth Hall, recall that Sigismund the Old married an Italian princess (Bona Sforza, from the famous Milanese family). Along with his bride, he imported Italian architecture, fashion (low-cut dresses), and food (tomatoes and potatoes, which had arrived in Italy from the New World).

The courtyard has three distinct levels: The ground floor housed the private apartments of the higher nobility (governors and castle administrators), the middle level held the private apartments of the king, and the top floor—much taller, to allow more light to fill its large spaces—were the public state rooms of the king. (They have the opposite problem in Italy, where the goal is shade rather than sunshine, so the lower floors are taller—the reverse of what you see here.)

The wing to the right of where you entered is fascist in style (notice the column-like grooves around the windows). It was built as the headquarters of the noto-rious Nazi governor of German-occupied Poland, Hans Frank. (He was tried and executed in Nürnberg after the war.)

At the right end of the courtyard is a false wall, de-signed to create a pleasant Re-naissance symmetry, and also to give the illusion that the castle is bigger than it is. Looking through the windows, notice that there's nothing but air on the other side. When foreign dignitaries visited, these windows could be covered to complete the illusion. The entrances to most Wawel museums are around this courtyard, and some believe that you'll find something even more special: chakra.

Adherents to the Hindu concept of **chakra** believe that a powerful energy field connects all living things. Some believe that, mirroring the seven chakra points on the body (from head to groin), there are seven points on the surface of the earth where this energy is most concentrated: Delhi, Delphi, Jerusalem, Mecca, Rome, Velehrad...and Wawel Hill—specifically over there in the corner (immediately to your left as you enter the courtyard—the stretches of wall flanking the door to the baggage-check room, and all the way to the door in the corner). Look for peaceful people (here or elsewhere on the castle grounds) with their eyes closed. One thing's for sure: They're not thinking of Kazimierz the Great. The smudge marks on the wall are from people pressing up against this corner, trying to absorb some good vibes from this chakra spot.

The Wawel administration seems creeped out by all this. They've done what they can to discourage this ritual (such as put-ting up information boards right where the power is supposedly most focused), but believers still gravitate from far and wide to hug the wall. Give it a try...and let the chakra be with you. (Just for fun, ask a Wawel tour guide about the chakra, and watch her squirm—they're forbidden to talk about it.)

• *If you want to visit some of the* **castle museums** *(you can enter most of them from this courtyard), you'll first need to buy tickets elsewhere. Stick with me for a little longer to finish our tour of the grounds, and we'll wind up near a ticket office.*

Head slightly downhill through the square, across to the gap in the buildings beyond the field, to the...

Viewpoint over the Vistula: Belly up to the wall and enjoy the panorama over the **Vistula River** and Kraków's outskirts. The "Polish Mississippi"—which runs its entire course in Polish lands—is the nation's artery for trade and cultural connection. It stretches 650 miles from the foothills of the Tatra Mountains in southern Poland, through many of the country's major cities (Kraków, Warsaw, Toruń), before emptying into the Baltic Sea in Gdańsk.

From this viewpoint, you can see some unusual landmarks, including the odd wavy-roofed building just across the river (which houses the Manggha Japanese art gallery) and the biggest conference center in Poland (to the left of the wavy building). A bit farther to the left is an eyesore of a communist concrete hotel, now home to a very cool summertime "beach bar" with a Ferris wheel (the Forum Przestrzenie, described on page 136). To the right, the suspiciously symmetrical little bulge that tops the highest hill on the horizon is the artificial Kościuszko Mound (described later). And on a particularly crisp day, far in the distance (beyond the wavy building), you can see the Tatra Mountains marking the border of Slovakia.

Now look directly below you, along the riverbank (to the left), to find a fire-belching monument to the **dragon** that was instrumental in the founding of Kraków. Once upon a time, a prince named Krak founded a town on Wawel Hill. It was the perfect location—except for the fire-breathing dragon that lived in the caves under the hill and terrorized the town. Prince Krak had to feed the dragon all of the town's livestock to keep the monster from going after the townspeople. But Krak, with the help of a clever shoemaker, came up with a plan. They stuffed a sheep's skin with sulfur and left it outside the dragon's cave. The dragon swallowed it and, before long, developed a terrible case of heartburn. To put the fire out, the dragon started drinking water from the Vistula. He kept drinking and drinking until he finally exploded. The town was saved, and Kraków thrived. Today, visitors enjoy watching the dragon blow fire into the air (about every four minutes; can vary from a big plume to a tiny puff).

If you'd like a higher viewpoint on the riverfront, you can pay a few złoty to climb 137 stairs to the top of **Sandomierska Tower** (at the far end of the hill, past the visitors center, no elevator; open only in summer). But I'd skip it—the view from up top is only through small windows.

• *Our Wawel tour is finished. If you'd like to explore some of the museums, you can buy your tickets in the nearby visitors center (head back into the main Wawel complex—with the empty field—and turn right); here you'll also find WCs, a café, and a gift shop. Or you can head to the riverfront park: Walk downhill (through the Dragon's Den, or use the main ramp and circle around the base of the hill) to reach the embankment—a delightful place to simply stroll and relax, with beautiful views back on the castle complex.*

Wawel Castle Museums

Wawel Castle offers a dizzying array of museums, exhibits, and attractions, all covered by separate tickets. Visitors stand before a long, pointlessly complicated menu of options, puzzling over how to spend their time and money. But here's the good news: Most, arguably all, of the Wawel Castle sights are skippable. While some of the castle's fine artifacts and pretty rooms are appealing to Poles, most casual visitors find that the best visit is simply to enjoy the cathedral and the castle grounds (following my self-guided tour, earlier). But in case you'd like to dig deeper, here's the scoop.

Tickets: Each sight has its own ticket (prices listed later); English descriptions are posted, and you can rent an audioguide for 12 zł that covers a few of the sights. Sort through your choices and buy tickets at the visitors center at the far corner of the castle grounds (across the field from the cathedral, in the big red-brick building). You can't buy tickets at the door of any sight, so choose and buy your tickets here at the start of your visit. The number of tickets per sight are limited and come with an assigned entry time (though ticket-checkers tend to be pretty flexible). It's possible to reserve ahead online or by phone (see the official website for details)...but I wouldn't bother. Frankly, if they're sold out, you're not missing much.

Hours: The hours of the various exhibits change frequently and there can be exceptions from sight to sight; for the latest, see www.wawel.krakow.pl. But in general, most of these sights should be open Tue 9:30-14:00, Wed-Sun until 17:00. Most sights are closed Mondays, but some are open and free Monday mornings until 13:00 (these rotate every few months).

Sights: Unless you're a Poland completist, the only Wawel attraction really worth considering is the first one.

To see the **Royal State Rooms** (Komnaty Królewskie), costing 35 zł and worth ▲, you climb up to the top floor and wander through some halls with antique furniture to reach the Throne Room, with 30 carved heads in the ceiling. According to legend, one of these heads got mouthy when the king was trying to pass

judgment—so its mouth has been covered to keep it quiet. Continue into some of the palace's finest rooms, with 16th-century Brussels tapestries (140 of the original 300 survive), remarkably decorated wooden ceilings, and gorgeous leather-tooled walls. Wandering these halls with their period furnishings, you get a feeling for the 16th- and 17th-century glory days of Poland, when it was a leading power in Central Europe. The Senate Room, with its throne and elaborate tapestries, is the climax.

The **Royal Private Apartments** (Prywatne Apartamenty Królewskie) are similar to the State Rooms and essentially redundant. Touring these, you'll see a columned hall, some Meissen porcelain, and a variety of artwork (30 zł).

The **Crown Treasury** (Skarbiec Koronny) shows off an impressive collection of regalia: giant banners (some dating back to the 16th century); swords, scepters, helmets, shields, and kingly chain mail; exquisite items gifted to Jan III Sobieski in thanks for defeating the Ottomans in the 1683 Battle of Vienna (including a sumptuous mantle from King Louis XIV and a comically oversized coronation sword from the pope); a rustic table loaded down with gold, silver, and enamel tankards; and lots of other fancy items once belonging to Polish royals (35 zł).

The **Armory** (Zbrojownia) is a decent collection of swords, saddles, and shields; ornately decorated muskets, crossbows, and axes; and cannons (20 zł).

The small **Art of the Orient** (Sztuka Wschodu) exhibit displays Ottoman swords, carpets, banners, vases, and other items dating from Jan III Sobieski's victory in the Battle of Vienna (20 zł).

The **Lost Wawel** (Wawel Zaginiony) exhibit traces the history of the hill and its various churches and castles. You'll see a model of the entire castle complex in the 18th century (pre-Austrian razing) then walk through scarcely explained excavations of a 10th-century church. On the way, you'll see models of the cathedral at various stages, and a display of tiles from 16th-century stoves that once heated the place (15 zł).

The **Wawel Recovered** (Wawel Odzyskany) exhibit is a more modern look at the evolution of this hilltop—with more models and reconstructions than actual foundations (15 zł).

There are also **temporary exhibits,** a separate ticket to walk along the castle's **first-floor galleries,** access to the **Royal Gardens** on the hillsides below the castle, and likely even more by the time you read this.

Eating: Various light eateries circle the castle courtyard, but if you just want a drink, it's hard to beat the cheap self-service snack bar next to the Lost Wawel entrance, with fine views across to the cathedral.

KRAKÓW'S ART MUSEUMS

Kraków's National Museum (Muzeum Narodowe) is made up of a series of small but interesting art collections scattered through-out the city (http://mnk.pl). These are some of the most engaging sights in town; you can find details on current exhibitions at the National Museum website. An 80 zł **combo-ticket,** called a *karnet,* covers the permanent collections in all of these museums (good for your entire stay)—worth considering if you'll be visiting more than three of them. National Museum branches are usually free to enter one day a week—likely Tuesday, but check the website.

▲▲Gallery of 19th-Century Polish Art (Galeria Sztuki Polskiej XIX Wieku)

This small and surprisingly enjoyable collection of works by obscure Polish artists fills the upper level of the Cloth Hall. While you

probably won't recognize any of the Polish names in here—and this collection isn't quite as im-pressive as Warsaw's National Gallery—many of these paint-ings are just plain delightful. It's worth a visit to see some Polish canvases in their native land and to enjoy views over the Square from the hall's upper terraces.

Cost and Hours: 32 zł, free on Tue; open Tue-Sun 10:00-18:00, closed Mon; entrance on side of Cloth Hall facing Adam Mickiewicz statue, +48 12 424 4600.

Background: During the 19th century—when every piece of art in this museum was created—there was no "Poland." The country had been split up among its powerful neighbors in a se-ries of three Partitions and would not appear again on the map of Europe until after World War I. Meanwhile, the 19th century was a period of national revival throughout Europe, when vari-ous previously marginalized ethnic groups began to take pride in what made them different from their neighbors. So the artists you see represented here were grappling with trying to forge a national identity at a time when they didn't even have a country. You'll sense a pessimism that comes from people who feel abused by foreign powers, mingled with a resolute spirit of national pride.

❍ Self-Guided Tour: The collection fills just four rooms: two small rooms in the center and two big halls on either side. On a quick visit, focus on the highlights in the big halls I mention here.

Entering the Cloth Hall, buy your ticket and head up the stairs (or use the elevator). The obligatory coat check is on floor 1, and the museum is on floor 2. Between them, peek out onto the inviting **café terrace** for a fine view of the Square and St. Mary's (then return here after your museum visit for a scenic drink.)

The first two small rooms contain little of interest. You enter **Room I** (Bacciarelli Room), with works from the Enlightenment; straight ahead is **Room II** (Michałowski Room), featuring Romantic works from 1822 to 1863. The larger, twin halls on either side merit a linger.

Siemiradzki Room (Room III, on the right): This features art of the Academy—that is, "conformist" art embraced by the art critics of the day. Entering the room, turn right and survey the canvases counterclockwise. The space is dominated by the works of Jan Matejko, a remarkably productive painter who specialized in epic historical scenes that also commented on his own era.

• *Circling the room, look for these paintings.*

Jan Matejko, *Wenyhora:* The first big canvas (immediately on your right as you enter, next to the door) is Matejko's depiction of Wenyhora, a late-18th-century Ukrainian soothsayer who, according to legend, foretold Poland's hardships—the three Partitions, Poland's pact with Napoleon, and its difficulties regaining nationhood. Like many Poles of the era, Matejko was preoccupied with Poland's tragic fate, imbuing this scene with an air of inevitable tragedy.

Jacek Malcezewski, *Death of Ellenai:* A similar gloominess is reflected in this canvas. The main characters in a Polish Romantic poem, Ellenai and Anhelli, have been exiled to a remote cabin in Siberia (in Russia, one of the great powers occupying Poland). Just when they think things can't get worse...Ellenai dies. Anhelli sits immobilized by grief.

• *A few canvases down, dominating the right side of the hall, is...*

Jan Matejko, *Tadeusz Kościuszko at Racławice:* One of the heroes of the American Revolution, now back in his native Poland fighting the Russians, doffs his hat after his unlikely victory at the Battle at Racławice. In this battle (which ultimately had little bearing on Russia's drive to overtake Poland), a ragtag army of Polish peasants defeated the Russian forces. Kościuszko is clad in an

American uniform, indicating Matejko's respect for the American ideals of democracy and self-determination.

• *Dominating the far wall is...*

Henryk Siemiradzki, *Nero's Torches:* On the left, Roman citizens eagerly gather to watch Christians being burned at the stake (on the right). The symbolism is clear: The meek and downtrodden (whether Christians in the time of Rome, or Poles in the heyday of Russia and Austria) may be persecuted now but have faith that their noble ideals will ultimately prevail.

• *On the next wall, find...*

Pantaleon Szyndler, *Bathing Girl:* This piece evokes the orientalism popular in 19th-century Europe, when romanticized European notions of the Orient (such as "harem slave girls") were popular artistic themes. Already voyeuristic, the painting was originally downright lewd until Szyndler painted over a man leering at the woman from the left side of the canvas.

• *The huge canvas on this wall is...*

Jan Matejko, *The Prussian Homage:* The last Grand Master of the fearsome Teutonic Knights swears allegiance to the Polish king in 1525. This historic ceremony took place in the Main Market Square in Kraków, the capital at the time. Notice the Cloth Hall balustrade and the spires of St. Mary's Church in the background. Matejko has painted his own face on one of his favorite historical figures, the jester Stańczyk at the foot of the throne.

• *Continue the rest of the way around the room. Keep an eye out for Tadeusz Ajdukiewicz's portrait of Helena Modrzejewska, a popular actress of the time, attending a party in this very building. Finally, backtrack through Room I and continue straight ahead into the...*

Chełmoński Room (Room IV): Featuring works of the late 19th century, this section includes Realism and the first inklings of Symbolism and Impressionism. Just as elsewhere in Europe (including Paris, where many of these painters trained), artists were beginning to throw off the conventions of the Academy and embrace their own muse.

• *As you turn right and proceed counterclockwise through the room, the first stretch of canvases features landscapes and genre paintings. Among these, about halfway down, a particularly fine canvas is...*

Wladyslaw Malecki, *A Gathering of Storks:* The majestic birds stand under big willows in front of the setting sun. Even seemingly innocent wildlife paintings have a political message: Storks are particularly numerous in Poland, making them a subtle patriotic symbol.

• *A few canvases down, find...*

Józef Brandt, *A Meeting on a Bridge:* This dramatic painting shows soldiers and aristocrats pushing a farmer into a ditch—a comment on the state of the Polish people at that time. Just to the right, see Brandt's *Fight for a Turkish Standard.* This artist specialized in battle scenes, frequently involving a foe from the East—as was often the reality here along Europe's buffer zone with Asia.

• *A few more canvases to the left of Brandt's works is...*

Samuel Hirszenberg, *School of Talmudists:* Young Jewish students pore over the Talmud. One of them, deeply lost in thought, may be pondering more than ancient Jewish law. This canvas suggests the inclusion of Jews in Poland's cultural tapestry during this age. While still subject to pervasive bigotry here, many Jewish refugees found Poland to be a relatively welcoming, tolerant place to settle on a typically hostile continent.

• *Dominating the end of the room is...*

Józef Chełmoński, *Four-in-Hand:* In this intersection of worlds, a Ukrainian horseman gives a lift to a pipe-smoking nobleman. Feel the thrilling energy as the horses charge directly at you through splashing puddles.

• *Heading back toward the entrance, on the right wall, watch for...*

Witold Pruszkowski, *Water Nymphs:* Based on Slavic legends (and wearing traditional Ukrainian costumes), these mischievous, siren-like beings have just taken one victim (see his hand in the foreground) and are about to descend on another (seen faintly in the upper-right corner).

Beyond this painting are some travel pictures from Italy and France (including some that are very Impressionistic, suggesting a Parisian influence).

• *Flanking the entrance/exit door are two of this room's best works. First, on the right, is...*

Władysław Podkowiński, *Frenzy:* This gripping painting's title *(Szał),* tellingly, has also been translated as *Ecstasy* and *Insanity.* A pale, sensuous woman—possibly based on a socialite for whom the artist fostered a desperate but unrequited love—clutches an all-fired-up black stallion that's frothing at the mouth. This sexually charged painting caused a frenzy indeed at its 1894 unveiling, leading the unbalanced artist to attack his own creation with a knife (you can still see the slash marks in the canvas).

• *And finally, on the other side of the door is…*

Jacek Malczewski, *Introduction:* A young painter's apprentice on a bench contemplates his future. Surrounded by nature and with his painter's tools beside him, it's easy to imagine this as a self-portrait of the artist as a young man…wondering if he's choosing the correct path. Malczewski was an extremely talented Młoda Polska artist who tends to be overshadowed by his contemporary, Wyspiański. Viewing this canvas—and others by him—makes me feel grateful that he decided to stick with painting.

▲▲Czartoryski Museum (Muzeum Czartoryskich)

This eclectic collection, originally assembled by a precocious aristocrat to celebrate Poland's cultural heritage, is best known to visitors for one painting: Leonardo da Vinci's masterful *Lady with an Ermine*—which alone warrants the ▲▲ rating. The museum also has an excellent (and rare) Rembrandt landscape. The rest of the collection is a historical jumble: decorative arts, tapestries, treasury items, Meissen porcelain figures, old flags and banners, portraits of kings and aristocrats, majolica pottery, ornate suits of armor, a ceremonial Turkish tent from the 1683 siege

of Vienna, and more Czartoryski family portraits than anyone not named Czartoryski would ever care to see. I'd suggest a quick stroll through the rest of the collection, then linger over the Rembrandt and (especially) the stunning Leonardo. Oh, baby!

Cost and Hours: 38 zł, free on Tue; Tue-Sun 10:00-18:00, closed Mon; a short walk from the Florian Gate at Pijarska 15—enter near the brick skybridge, +48 12 370 54 66, http://mnk.pl.

Background: The museum's collection came about, in part, thanks to Poland's 1791 constitution (Europe's first), which inspired Princess Izabela Czartoryska to begin gathering bits and bobs of Polish history and culture. Soon after, when the Partitions dismantled the country, Izabela doubled down on this pursuit—assembling proud Polish bric-a-brac with the motto, "The past for the future," looking ahead to a time when Poland would be reconstituted. That would not happen within her lifetime; she fled with the collection to Paris after the 1830 insurrection. Her son, Adam Czartoryski—who purchased the Leonardo for his mom as a gift—was so influential during this period of exile that he was sometimes called the "uncrowned king of Poland." It took 45 years after the family fled for Izabela's grandson to return the collection to its present Kraków location. During World War II, the Nazis hauled the collection to Germany; although most of it has been returned, some pieces are still missing. The dusty old museum got a serious upgrade starting in 2010 and finally reopened in 2019.

KRAKÓW

⊙ Self-Guided Tour: There are some basic English descriptions, but for the full story, invest in the somewhat long-winded but insightful audioguide (10 zł). Or just follow this selective self-guided commentary for an efficient visit. Spoiler alert: The two all-star paintings are essentially the last things you'll see on this tour. (If you'd like to get to them faster, consider skipping floor 1 and heading right up to floor 2, then speeding through the first few rooms.)

From the ticket desk, head through the lovely courtyard and take the stairs or elevator up to floor 1. You'll begin in two **Rooms of the Czartoryskis,** with portraits and busts of the members of this illustrious family, who were VIPs about two centuries ago. (Their red family crest—with a horseback knight raising his sword—decorates the windows.) You'll see their fancy sabers, ornate jackets and gowns, and a pair of ceremonial keys.

The next few rooms display Princess Czartoryska's collection of Polish artifacts roughly chronologically, by dynasty. In the **Room of the Jagiellonian Dynasty**—tucked among altar paintings, tapestries, tattered flags, and other precious objects—look for the 10 small portraits of the Jagiełło clan in a single frame, done by the workshop of Lucas Cranach the Younger (see his trademark, the small winged lion, in the corner of each one). The **Room of the Vasa Dynasty** is more militaristic, as this was a time of warfare—hence the emphasis on weaponry over simple beauty.

The **Room of the Victory of Vienna** commemorates that fateful battle in 1683, when the Polish King Jan III Sobieski led a pan-European army to success in defending the Austrian capital against an Ottoman siege. The room's centerpiece is a ceremonial tent and a Persian carpet like the ones used by the Ottomans in that battle. On display are actual weapons and equipment (shields, sabers, and saddles) used by the troops that day. Notice the winged hussar suit of armor—those rattling feathers made a fearsome sound when charging full-tilt on horseback. You'll also see Sobieski's ornate divinative shield and a ceremonial saber presented to him by the pope.

The **Room of the Saxons** illustrates how Poland's next dynasty—the Wettins (imported from Dresden, in today's Germany)—squandered their country's resources, ultimately hastening its decline: Notice the expensive Meissen porcelain favored by the Wettins, and the wine glasses, goblets, and plates they used for one of their favorite pastimes...feasting.

The **Room of the Enlightenment**—a bright era for many European lands—coincides with Poland's darkest moment, when the country was chopped up and divided among land-hungry neighbors in a series of three Partitions. The large portrait shows Stanisław August Poniatowski, Izabela Czartoryska's cousin and the final Polish king, who took the throne at age 32 and presided over both Europe's first democratic constitution in 1791...and, just a few years later, the fall of his nation. One case displays his ceremonial swords and medals; the other shows some of his belongings: cane, fan, flute, and powder horn.

Then you'll enter a dimly lit wing with liturgical paraments (amber cross, vestments), then "Pompa Funebris," illustrating the pomp surrounding funeral rituals (see the tattered tombstone banner from 1660, and nearby, the smaller coffin portraits).

The last section on this floor shows off three rooms of **"Oriental Art"**: first from Persia (carpet) and India (bronze statues), then from China (fans, porcelain, a giant bronze dragon), then from Japan (find the display case of *netsuke*—minuscule sculptures carved in ivory or wood).

Now head upstairs to level 2 and cross over the skybridge—looking down over the beautifully restored courtyard at the center of the complex.

While downstairs was mainly about Poland, this floor showcases **European art.** The Antiquity Parlor features paintings, sculptures, and tapestries inspired by ancient Greece and Rome; the Medieval Parlor has gilded altarpieces and other church art; and Northern European Art from the 15th to the 17th century displays...well, exactly that, including some Habsburg portraits.

Finally, we come to the room called Age of the Rembrandt Period. Ignore all the also-rans in this room (for now) and head straight across to the dramatically lit painting: **Rembrandt van Rijn's** *Landscape with the Good Samaritan* (1638). This small, detailed painting depicting the popular parable is one of only a few known landscapes by Rembrandt. In the right foreground, the Samaritan helps the wounded man onto his horse as a little boy watches. To the left, much farther down the road (just beyond the waterfall), find the two tiny figures walking—the priest and the Levite who passed the injured man. The murky colors make it a little tricky to pick out all the details, but Rembrandt's trademark dramatic lighting creates a powerful scene.

There's a small, dimly lit room off of this Rembrandt hall—if you're not looking for it, it's easy to miss. But don't miss it! This is the room where you'll find **Leonardo da Vinci's** *Lady with an*

Ermine. This small (21 x 16 inches) but magnificently executed portrait of a 16-year-old young woman is a rare surviving work by one of history's greatest minds.

Spend some time lingering over the canvas (dating from 1489 or 1490). The subject is likely Cecilia Gallerani, the young mistress of Ludovico Sforza, the duke of Milanand Leonardo's employer. The ermine (white during winter) suggests chastity—thus bolstering Cecilia's questioned virtue—but is also a naughty reference to the duke's nickname, Ermellino—notice that his mistress is sensually, ahem, "stroking the ermine."

Painted before the *Mona Lisa,* the portrait was immediately recognized as revolutionary. Cecilia turns to look at someone, her gaze directed to the side. Leonardo catches this unguarded, informal moment, an unheard-of gesture in the days of the posed, front-facing formal portrait. Her simple body language and faraway gaze speak volumes about her inner thoughts and personality. Leonardo tweaks the generic Renaissance "pyramid" composition, turning it to a three-quarters angle, and softens it with curved lines that trace from Cecilia's eyes and down her cheek and sloping shoulders before doubling back across her folded arms. The background—once gray and blue—was painted black in the 19th century.

Using special lights and cameras, conservators have been able to virtually peel back layers of paint to see earlier "drafts" of the painting (Leonardo was known to tinker with his works over time). They've revealed that the ermine was likely not included in the original version. Perhaps Leonardo added it later as a nod to the duke.

Lady with an Ermine is a rare surviving portrait in oil by Leonardo. She's better preserved than her famous cousin in Paris *(Mona Lisa),* and—many think—simply more beautiful. Can we be sure it's really by the enigmatic Leonardo? Yep—the master's fingerprints were found literally pressed into the paint (he was known to work areas of paint directly with his fingertips).

After this grand finale, you'll pass through the **Polish Hall**—painted a patriotic Polish red—displaying mementos of historical figures and events: gilded shields honoring mighty leaders, small sarcophagi with the remains of great Poles, portraits of monarchs, and flags and banners from the battlefield.

You'll finish by walking through some **temporary exhibits.** The museum also has an exhibit called **The Origins: Ancient Art**

Gallery—with items from Egypt, Greece, and Rome—but it costs extra and isn't worth it for most visitors.

Before you depart, ponder this: The museum technically owns a third masterpiece, **Raphael's** *Portrait of a Young Man*, but its whereabouts are unknown. Arguably one of the most famous and most valuable stolen paintings of all time, it's quite likely a self-portrait (but possibly a portrait of Raphael by another artist), depicting a Renaissance dandy, clad in a fur coat, with a self-satisfied smirk. Painted in 1513 or 1514 and purchased by a Czartoryski prince around the turn of the 19th century, the work was seized by the occupying Nazis during World War II. Along with the paintings by Leonardo and Rembrandt, this Raphael decorated the Wawel Castle residence of Nazi governor Hans Frank. But when Frank and the Nazis fled the invading Red Army at the end of the war, many of their pilfered artworks were lost—including the Raphael.

▲▲Stanisław Wyspiański Museum (Muzeum Stanisława Wyspiańskiego)

One of the great joys of travel is getting to know supremely talented artists you'd never heard of back home. And if you give Stanisław Wyspiański a chance, he may tick that box for you. This concise, beautiful museum assembles many of Wyspiański's best works, offering an ideal introduction to this leader of the Młoda Polska movement (Poland's answer to Art Nouveau; see the sidebar on page 59). If you enjoyed Wyspiański's stained glass and wall paintings in St. Francis Basilica, you'll find even more to like here.

Cost and Hours: 18 zł, free on Tue, audioguide available; Tue and Fri-Sun 10:00-17:00, closed Mon and Wed-Thu; a five-minute walk outside the Planty and west of the Old Town at Plac Sikorskiego 6, +48 12 433 57 60, http://mnk.pl.

Visiting the Museum: With just a few rooms spread over three floors, the museum is easy to see. Most of Wyspiański's works are not paintings or sculptures, but pastels, drawings, and designs for his grand-scale stained-glass windows; as these are fragile, specific items get shuffled in and out of the collection and some things mentioned here may not be on view. (You'll notice some of the more delicate works even have rolled-up curtains hanging above them so they can be covered for protection as needed.)

A dynamic bust of Wyspiański greets you outside the door. Inside, buy your ticket and head into the lone exhibition room on the main floor: **At Home,** featuring an array of landscapes of the countryside around Kraków (plus his iconic pastel of St. Mary's spires viewed from the balcony of the Cloth Hall); Toulouse-Lautrec-like portraits of Wyspiański's contemporaries (including one showing his friend and rival Josef Mehoffer—twice on a single portrait); a variety of self-portraits at various ages (from fresh-faced student, to young and hungry artist, to fatherly family man); and—perhaps most beautiful—intimate portraits of his family members in everyday poses that capture the universality of human experience. These works showcase the personality and endearing behavior of wife Helen, daughter Helenka, and sons Mietek and Staś.

Next head upstairs to level 1. The first room, **Elements,** is devoted to the stunning decorations Wyspiański created for St. Francis Basilica. The theme: a Franciscan love of nature. The centerpiece is a gigantic, life-sized design for his masterpiece—the *God the Father Let It Be* stained-glass window—displayed on a massive roller. Examine the designs for other windows and for the beautiful floral wall decorations. If you've seen these in situ—hanging high on dimly lit walls—this is a wonderful opportunity to examine the details up close.

Next, hook left into the room marked **Apollo Christ.** The focal point here is Wyspiański's design for a window he created for Kraków's House of the Medical Society—titled *Apollo, Copernicus' System.* In addition to Wyspiański's mastery of religious themes, he was captivated by the ancient world, especially the Greeks. Notice how this design juxtaposes the story of Apollo, with a pose resembling Jesus' Crucifixion, all wrapped up in the medieval breakthrough of a scientist who studied here in Kraków.

Also in this room, you'll find some of the plays Wyspiański wrote (and a costume he designed for one of them), designs for his stained-glass windows inside St. Mary's and the Dominican Church (both described elsewhere in this chapter), and some decorative arts handmade by Wyspiański—such as a bench and a tapestry with flowers.

Now cross over—again past the giant *God the Father* roller—to the next section, **Wawel Castle: Drama of Kings.** Yet another of Wyspiański's passions was the evocative architecture of the churches and castles of the Middle Ages. In this room, you'll see some sketches he made of such structures, both in Poland and abroad, and costume sketches (and an actual crown) he designed for a play he wrote about this era. In the center of the room is a model for an imaginative upgrade to Wawel Castle, which would have transformed it into the "Polish Acropolis" he felt it could and should become. (There's even a Circus Maximus-like elongated stadium at the foot of the hill.) If you've been to Wawel, you know that these plans never materialized.

Also in this room are two more large-scale masterpieces. One is Wyspiański's design *(Polonia)* for a stained-glass window in Lviv Cathedral (today in Ukraine, then part of Poland), and another is a hauntingly beautiful wintertime scene of the Planty, with black naked branches of trees lining a boulevard to a mirage-like Wawel Castle, hovering in the distance.

KRAKÓW

Now use the elevator (or stairs) to go down two floors, to level -1. Here are the two final, small exhibits: First is **My Books,** displaying books that Wyspiański wrote, designed illustrations for, or both. Then comes **Metamorphoses,** a deep dive into the plays that Wyspiański wrote (including another costume he designed). In this room, look for the VR headsets; you can sit down, strap one on, and go for a virtual "flight" over Kraków, zooming in for up-close visits to the locations that inspired many of the works we've seen here.

Leaving the museum, it's hard to shake the feeling that there must be many other artists whose fame will never reach the level of their talent. But at least for you and Wyspiański, that's no longer the case.

Bishop Erazm Ciołek Palace (Pałac Biskupa Erazma Ciołka)

This branch of the National Museum features two separate art collections. Upstairs, the extensive "Art of Old Poland" section shows off works from the 12th through the 18th century, with room after room of altarpieces, sculptures, paintings, and more. The "Orthodox Art of the Old Polish Republic" section on the ground floor offers a taste of the remote eastern reaches of Poland, with icons and other ecclesiastical art from the Orthodox faith. You'll see a sizeable section of the iconostasis (wall of icons) from the town of Lipovec. Both collections are covered by the same ticket and are very well presented in a modern facility. Items are labeled in English, but there's not much description beyond the rentable audioguide.

Cost and Hours: 18 zł, free on Tue; open Tue 10:00-18:00, Wed-Sun until 16:00, closed Mon; Kanonicza 17, +48 12 424 9371.

More National Museum Branches

While less interesting than the branches listed earlier, the National Museum's **Main Branch** (Gmach Główny) is worth a visit for museum completists. It features 20th-century Polish art and compelling temporary exhibits (a few blocks west of the Main Market Square at Aleja 3 Maja 1).

The **Szołayski House** (Kamienica Szołayskich), just one short block from the Main Market Square, features high-quality temporary exhibits; art lovers can check what's on (Plac Szczepański 9).

OTHER OLD TOWN ATTRACTIONS

▲▲Rynek Underground Museum (Podziemia Rynku)

In the early 2000s, a renovation of the Main Market Square's pavement unearthed a wealth of remains from previous structures. Now you can do some urban spelunking with a visit to this high-tech medieval-history museum, which is literally underground—beneath all the photo-snapping tourists on the Square above.

Cost and Hours: 32 zł, free on Tue; open Mon and Wed-Thu

10:00-19:00 (but closed the second Mon of each month), Tue until 14:00, Fri-Sun until 20:00, last entry 1.25 hours before closing, Rynek Główny 1, +48 12 426 5060, www.podziemiarynku.com.

Crowd-Beating Tips: This museum can sell out on busy days (especially on Tuesdays—when it's free and closes early—and on summer weekends). Because it's popular with school groups, late afternoons and evenings are quieter. At busy times, it's wise to book ahead online; alternatively, you can buy advance tickets in person at the Museum of Kraków office nearby, at the northwest corner of the Square (see "Tourist Information," earlier).

Visiting the Museum: The **entrance** faces St. Mary's and the pyramid-shaped fountain on the east side of the Cloth Hall (near the fountain), but the **ticket office** is around on the opposite side of the same building. If you already have your tickets, just go to the entrance; if you need to buy tickets, circle around to the ticket office (see locations on page 38).

Once **inside,** climb down a flight of stairs and follow the numbered panels—1 to 70—through the exhibit (all in English). Modern museum technology illuminates life and times in medieval Kraków: Touchscreens let you delve into topics that intrigue you, 3-D virtual holograms resurrect old buildings, and video clips illustrate everyday life on unexpected surfaces (such as a curtain of fog).

All of this is wrapped around large chunks of early structures that still survive beneath the Square; several "witness columns" of rock and dirt are accompanied by diagrams helping you trace the layers of history. Interactive maps emphasize Kraków's Europe-wide importance as an intersection of major trade routes, and several models, maps, and digital reconstructions give you a good look at Kraków during the Middle Ages—when the Old Town looked barely different from today. You'll see a replica of a blacksmith's shop and learn how "vampire prevention burials" were used to ensure that the suspected undead wouldn't return from the grave. In the middle of the complex, look up through the glass of the Square's fountain to see the towers of St. Mary's above. Under the skylight is a model of medieval Kraków. While it looks much the same as today, notice a few key changes: the moat ringing the Old Town, where the Planty is today; and the several smaller market halls out on the Square.

KRAKÓW

Deeper in the exhibit, explore the long corridors of ruined buildings that once ran alongside the length of the Cloth Hall. There are many intriguing cases showing artifacts that shops would have sold (jewelry, tools, amber figurines, and so on). Also in this area, you'll find a corridor with images of the Square all torn up for the renovation, plus a series of five modern brick rooms, each showing a brief, excellent film outlining a different period of Kraków's history. These "Kraków Chronicles" provide a big-picture context to what otherwise seems like a loose collection of cool museum gizmos, and also help you better appreciate what you'll see outside the museum's doors.

Nearby: At the northwest corner of the Square, the **Krzysztofory Palace** (at #35) is the headquarters of Museum of Kraków. At the entrance is a visitors center where you can get information and book tickets and reservations for a variety of these sights (see "Tourist Information," earlier). The building also has a city **history museum,** which offers a sprawling lesson on two floors (28 zł, free on Tue, open daily 10:00-19:00, last entry 1.25 hours before closing, Rynek Główny 35, +48 12 426 5060). While the exhibits try hard, this is best left to serious historians or those looking for a mildly engaging rainy-day activity. In the basement, you'll find paintings, sculptures, suits of armor, busts of royalty, and old street signs; the most interesting section, at the end, is a film showing a virtual reconstruction of medieval Kraków. Upstairs, there are themed rooms (such as "spirituality" and "academia") to complete the story. You'll finish with a walk through a gigantic version of the nativity scenes that are featured in a festival each December.

Jagiellonian University Museum: Collegium Maius

Kraków's historic university building sits in a quiet area a short walk from the Square. While the atmospheric courtyard itself—described earlier in "Kraków's Royal Way Walk"—is worth ▲, the interior is less compelling. They routinely change details for how you enter—sometimes it's with a student guide, other times you're free to roam with an audioguide—but either way, you'll likely see the library, refectory (with a gorgeously carved Baroque staircase), treasury (including Polish filmmaker Andrzej Wajda's honorary Oscar), assembly hall, some old scientific instruments, and other academic artifacts.

Cost and Hours: 15 zł, free on Wed afternoons; guided tours depart 2/hour Mon-Fri 10:00-13:00; unaccompanied visits with audioguide Mon-Fri 13:00-17:00, Sat 10:00-15:00; closed Sun;

two short blocks west of the Square at Jagiellońska 15, +48 12 663 1448, www.maius.uj.edu.pl).

Dominican Church, a.k.a. Holy Trinity Church (Bazylika Trójcy Świętej)

In most towns, this church would be something special. In church-crazy Kraków, it's an also-ran. Still, it's easy to see (just a couple of blocks south of the Square) and worth a peek.

Cost and Hours: Free but donation requested, daily 6:30-13:00 & 16:00-20:00, facing Plac Dominikański at Stolarska 12.

Visiting the Church: Inside, you'll find a Neo-Gothic space that was rebuilt after a devastating 1850 fire. The unique metal chandeliers are one of many modern flourishes added during the late-19th-century restoration of the church. Climb the staircase in the left aisle to reach the chapel of St. Hyacinth. Locally known as St. Jacek, this early Dominican leader—called the "Apostle of the North"—is also the patron saint of pierogi (stuffed dumplings, similar to ravioli). During a famine, St. Jacek supposedly invented pierogi and—in a loaves-and-fishes-type miracle—produced plateful after plateful, feeding the desperate locals. His image adorns Kraków's annual Pierogi Cup contest, and to this day, when old-fashioned Poles are surprised, they might exclaim, *"Święty Jacek z pierogami!"* ("St. Jacek and his pierogi!"). Back down in the main part of the church, stroll slowly past the gorgeously carved wooden seats of the choir area (behind the altar); then, at the main altar, identify the three parts of the Trinity: Jesus (short beard), God (long beard), and Holy Spirit (beardless dove).

Archdiocesan Museum (Muzeum Archidiecezjalne)

This museum, in a building where St. John Paul II lived both as a priest and as a bishop, is a handy place to learn more about Kraków's favorite son (without making the long trip to the St. John Paul II Sanctuary on the outskirts or his family home museum in Wado-wice—both described later). The exhibition includes John Paul II's personal effects, including clothes, handwritten notes, travel gear, bike, kayak, and skis—reminding visitors that he was one sporty pope. Then you'll tour the lavish private apartments where he lived from 1958 until 1967, as archbishop of Kraków. Throughout the collection are many portraits and photographs of the late pontiff—making his cult of personality almost palpable.

Cost and Hours: 10 zł or included in Wawel Cathedral ticket—see earlier, Tue-Sun 10:00-17:00, closed Mon, Kanonicza 19, +48 12 421 8963, www.archimuzeum.pl.

▲Stained-Glass Workshop and Museum (Pracownia i Muzeum Witrażu)

This fascinating, offbeat attraction sits on a busy urban street about a 10-minute walk beyond the Planty west of the Old Town. Its centerpiece is the actual stained-glass workshop, from 1902, where Stanisław Wyspiański and other great artists created windows that decorate many Kraków churches. I like how this place approaches a very old craft with a fresh, youthful enthusiasm. You can take a tour of the production facility, including a demonstration of stained glass being created by hand; you can join a workshop to make your own stained-glass creation; or you can just come and hang out in their chill, easygoing café, decorated with some beautiful samples. Check the schedule and book ahead online, for either the tour or the workshop.

Cost and Hours: 50 zł for a 45-minute tour including a demo, usually Tue-Sat at 12:00 and 15:00; tour plus window-making workshop around 300 zł, longer courses also available; café open Tue-Sat 11:30-13:30 & 14:30-16:30, Sat 10:00-17:00, closed Sun-Mon; kitty-corner from National Museum main branch at Aleja Zygmunta Krasińskiego 23, +48 512 937 979, www.muzeumwitrazu.pl.

Sights in Kazimierz

The neighborhood of Kazimierz (kah-ZHEE-mehzh), 20 minutes by foot or 5 minutes by tram southeast of Kraków's Old Town, is the historic heart of Kraków's once-thriving Jewish community. After years of neglect, the district began a rejuvenation in the early 2000s. Today, while not quite as slick and polished as Prague's Jewish Quarter, Kazimierz's assortment of synagogues, cemeteries, and museums helps visitors appreciate the neighborhood's rich Jewish legacy. At the same time, Kazimierz also happens to be the city's edgy, hipster culture center—jammed with colorful bars, cre-

ative eateries, and designer boutiques. This unlikely combination—where somber synagogues coexist with funky food trucks—makes Kazimierz a big draw among all types of travelers.

Planning Your Visit: Try to visit any day except Saturday, when most Jewish-themed sights are closed (except the Old Synagogue and Galicia Jewish Museum). Monday comes with a few closures of non-Jewish sights: the Ethnographic Museum and Museum of Engineering and Technology. On Monday, the Schindler's Factory Museum is free, but it's open shorter hours and is more crowded than usual. It's always smart to **book ahead for the Schindler's Factory Museum,** which often sells out. For more suggestions on what to do in Kazimierz, see the Shopping, Entertainment, Sleeping, and Eating sections.

Etiquette: To show respect, men cover their heads while visiting a Jewish cemetery or synagogue. Most sights offer loaner yarmulkes, or you can wear your own hat.

Getting to Kazimierz: From Kraków's Old Town, it's about a 20-minute **walk.** From the Main Market Square, head down Ulica Sienna (near St. Mary's Church) and through the Planty park. When you hit the busy ring road, bear right and continue down Starowiślna for 15 more minutes. The **tram** shaves off a few minutes: Find the stop along the ring road, on the left-hand side of Ulica Sienna (across the street from the Poczta Główna, or main post office). Catch tram #3 or #24, and ride two stops to Miodowa. Walking or by tram, at the intersection of Starowiślna and Miodowa, you'll see a tiny park across the street and to the right. To reach the heart of Kazimierz—Ulica Szeroka—cut through this park. The same trams continue to the sights in Podgórze (including the Schindler's Factory Museum), described later.

To return to the Old Town, catch tram #3 or #24 from the intersection of Starowiślna and Miodowa (kitty-corner from where you got off the tram).

Information: An official **TI** is at Ulica Józefa 7.

KAZIMIERZ WALK

This self-guided walk, worth ▲▲, is designed to help you get your bearings in Kazimierz, connecting both its Jewish sights (mostly in "Part 1") and its eclectic other attractions, from trendy bars to underrated museums ("Part 2"). Allow about an hour for the entire walk, not counting museum, cemetery, and synagogue visits along the way. From the end of the walk, you can easily cross the river to this area's biggest sight, the Schindler's Factory Museum.

Part 1: Jewish Heritage on Ulica Szeroka

• *We'll start on Ulica Szeroka ("Broad Street")—the center of the neighborhood, which feels like more of an elongated square than a "street."*

Begin at the bottom (southern) edge of the small, fenced, grassy park, near the strip of restaurants. In the park with the tall trees, look for the low-profile, stone...

Kazimierz Monument

You're standing in the historical heart of Kraków's Jewish community. In the 14th century, King Kazimierz the Great enacted policies that encouraged Jews fleeing other kingdoms to settle in Poland—including in Kraków. He also founded this town, which still bears his name. Originally, Jews lived in the Old Town, but they were scapegoated after a 1495 fire and forced to relocate to Kazimierz. Back then, Kazimierz was still a separate town, divided by a wall into Christian (west) and Jewish (east) neighborhoods. Ulica Szeroka was the main square of the Jewish community. Over time, Jews were more or less accepted into the greater community, and Jewish culture flourished here.

All that would change in the mid-20th century. The **monument** honors the "65 thousand Polish citizens of Jewish nationality from Kraków and its environs"—more than a quarter of the city's pre-WWII population—who were murdered by the Nazis during the Holocaust. When the Nazis arrived, they immediately sent most of Kraków's Jews to the ghetto in the eastern Polish city of Lublin. Soon after, they forced Kraków's remaining 15,000 Jews into a walled ghetto at Podgórze, across the river. The Jews' cemeteries were defiled, and their buildings were ransacked and destroyed. In 1942, the Nazis began transporting Kraków's Jews to death camps (including Płaszów, just on Kraków's outskirts; and Auschwitz-Birkenau).

Only a few thousand Kraków Jews survived the war. During the communist era, this waning population was ignored or mistreated. After 1989, interest in Kazimierz's unique Jewish history was faintly rekindled. But it was only when Steven Spielberg chose to film *Schindler's List* here in 1993 that the world took renewed interest in Kazimierz. (A local once winked to me, "They ought to build a statue to Spielberg on that square.") Although the current Jewish population in Kraków numbers only 200, Kazimierz has become an internationally known destination for those with an interest in Jewish heritage.

• *Facing the park, look to the left. The arch with the Hebrew characters marks the entrance to the...*

Kazimierz Walk

1. Kazimierz Monument
2. Old Jewish Cemetery & Jan Karski Statue
3. Old Shop Fronts
4. Hamsa Rest. & Jarden Bookshop
5. Klezmer-Hois Restaurant
6. New Jewish Cemetery
7. Rubinstein Birthplace
8. Popper Synagogue
9. Old Synagogue
10. Food Trucks
11. Isaac Synagogue
12. Plac Nowy
13. Meiselsa & Bożego Ciała Streets
14. Schindler's List Passage
15. Ulica Józefa
16. Plac Wolnica
17. Ethnographic Museum
18. Old Tram Depot
19. Museum of Engineering & Technology
20. Judah Square
21. Galicia Jewish Museum

▲▲Old Jewish Cemetery (Stary Cmentarz)

This small cemetery was used to bury members of the Jewish community from 1552 to 1800. With more than a hundred of the top Jewish intellectuals of that age buried here, this is considered one of the most important Jewish cemeteries in Europe.

Cost and Hours: 10 zł includes cemetery and attached Remu'h Synagogue; hours vary with demand—especially outside

KRAKÓW

peak season—but generally open Sun-Fri 9:00-16:00, can be open until 18:00 May-Sept, closes earlier off-season and by sundown on Fri, closed Sat year-round, Ulica Szeroka 40.

Visiting the Cemetery: Walk under the arch, pay the admission fee, step into the cemetery, and survey the tidy rows of headstones. This early Jewish resting place (later replaced by the New Cemetery, described later) was desecrated by the Nazis during the Holocaust. In the 1950s, it was discovered, excavated, and put back together as you see here. Shattered gravestones form a mosaic **wall** around the perimeter.

Notice that many graves have a curved top or are engraved with an arch-like pattern—suggesting passage into another realm. As in all Jewish cemeteries and memorials, you'll see many small stones stacked on the graves. The tradition comes from placing stones—representing prayers—over desert graves to cover the body and prevent animals from disturbing it.

Behind the little synagogue to the left, in the elevated, fenced area near the tree, the tallest **tombstone** belonged to Moses Isserles (a.k.a. Remu'h), an important 16th-century rabbi. He is believed to have been a miracle worker, and his grave was one of the only ones that remained standing after World War II. Notice the written prayers crammed into the cracks and crevices of the tombstone.

Near the gate to the cemetery, step into the tiny **Remu'h Synagogue** (c. 1553, covered by cemetery ticket). Tight and cozy, this has been carefully renovated and is fully active. Notice the original 16th-century frescoed walls and ceilings, and the historic donation box at the door. For more on typical synagogue architecture, see the sidebar.

• *Back outside, turn left and continue up to the top of...*

Ulica Szeroka

Just above the cemetery gate, notice a bronze statue of a gentleman seated on a bench. This is a tribute to **Jan Karski** (1914-2000), a Catholic Pole and resistance fighter who published his eyewitness account *The Story of a Secret State* about the Holocaust in 1944. Karski—the ultimate whistleblower—was one of the first people who spoke out about Nazi atrocities, at a time when even many world leaders had only an inkling about what was happening in Hitler's realm. Karski's revelations, so shocking as to be literally unbelievable to many, went ignored by some key leaders—arguably extending the horrors of the Holocaust.

Just above that, at the top corner of the square, notice the side street with a row of rustic old Jewish **shop fronts,** which evoke the bustle of prewar Kazimierz. The Jewish names—Rattner, Weinberg, Nowak, Holcer—stand testament to the lively soul of this neighborhood in its heyday. This lane leads to Miodowa street, which you can follow left to reach two of Kazimierz's lesser-known synagogues (Tempel and Kupa, both described later).

The building at the top of the square houses the recommended **Hamsa** restaurant (with modern Israeli food) and **Jarden Bookshop,** which serves as an unofficial information point for the neighborhood and sells a wide variety of fairly priced books on Kazimierz and Jewish culture in the region (daily, Ulica Szeroka 2).

Kitty-corner from the bookshop, notice **Klezmer-Hois**—one of many restaurants offering live traditional Jewish klezmer music nightly in summer (for more on klezmer music and details on your options, see "Entertainment in Kraków," later).

The **New Jewish Cemetery**—less touristed and a striking contrast to the Old Jewish Cemetery we just saw—is a worthwhile detour, about a five-minute walk away (and described later in this section). To get there, cut through the grassy little lot between Jarden Bookshop and Klezmer-Hois, turn right, cross the busy street, then go through the railway underpass.

When you're ready to move on, do a 180 and head back downhill on Ulica Szeroka. You'll pass the little park again, then come to a row of lively, mostly Jewish-themed **restaurants** with outdoor tables. Some places along here typically feature outdoor klezmer music in good weather—allowing you to get a taste of this unique musical form before committing to a full meal.

Halfway down this side of the square, the green house at #14 is where **Helena Rubinstein** was born in 1870. At age 31, she emigrated to Australia, where she parlayed her grandmother's traditional formula for hand cream into a cosmetics empire. Many cosmetics still used by people worldwide today were invented by Rubinstein, who was just one of many illustrious Jewish residents of Kazimierz.

Two doors past the Rubinstein house, notice the round arch marking the courtyard of the **Popper Synagogue,** which is now home to an extensive bookstore that's worth a peek (daily).

Continue past the restaurants to the very bottom of Ulica Szeroka and pause at the steps before heading down into the sunken area around the Old Synagogue. To the synagogue's left, notice a short, reconstructed stretch of Kazimierz's 14th-century **town wall,** with a roofed rampart on top. This is a reminder that medieval Kazimierz was a separate city from Kraków. It's easy to read some history into a map of Kazimierz (you'll find one on the big panel in front of the Old Synagogue, down the stairs): Today's Starowiślna and Dietla streets—which frame off Kazimierz in a triangle of land hemmed in by the riverbank—were once canals (Kazimierz was built on an island). When King Kazimierz the Great—who reportedly didn't care much for Krakovians—founded this district in 1335, he envisioned it as a separate town to rival Kraków. It wasn't until around 1800 that the two towns merged.

• *The building at the bottom of the square is the...*

Old Synagogue (Stara Synagoga)

The oldest surviving Jewish building in Poland (15th century) sits eight steps below street level. Jewish structures weren't allowed to

be taller than Christian ones— and so, in order to have the proper proportions, the synagogue's "ground floor" had to be underground. Today, the synagogue houses a good three-room museum on local Jewish culture, with informative English descriptions and a well-preserved main prayer hall (18 zł, free on Mon; Mon 10:00-14:00, Tue-Sun until 17:00; shorter hours off-season; Ulica Szeroka 24, +48 12 422 0962).

• *A few more Jewish sights can be found in the surrounding streets; I'll point these out in "Part 2," though the rest of this walk focuses on a more recent chapter of the neighborhood.*

Part 2: Contemporary Kazimierz

• *Stand with your back to the Old Synagogue, at the top of the stairs, and turn left, heading up the little alley next to Szeroka 28—called Lewkowa.*

Hipster Kazimierz

Follow Lewkowa between some old buildings. When you pop out into an open area, angle right, then continue straight along Ulica Ciemna. Soon you'll hit an inviting little **pod of food trucks.** Pause here—perhaps while nursing an açaí smoothie, a Thai-style rolled ice cream, or a taco—and ponder the explosion of youthful culture that's taken place in Kazimierz over the last generation.

At the end of World War II, Kazimierz was badly damaged

The Synagogue

A synagogue is a place of public worship, where Jews gather to pray, sing, and read from the Torah. Most synagogues have similar features, though they vary depending on the congregation.

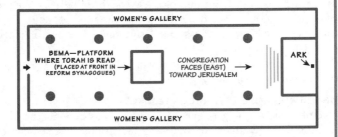

The synagogue generally faces, at least symbolically, toward Jerusalem (in Kraków, worshippers face east). At the east end is an alcove called the **ark,** which holds the Torah. These scriptures (the first five books of the Christian Old Testament) are written in Hebrew on scrolls wrapped in luxuriant cloth. The other main element of the synagogue is the **bema,** an elevated platform from which the Torah is read aloud (the equivalent of a pulpit in a Christian church). In traditional Orthodox synagogues, the bema is near the center of the hall, and the reader stands facing the same direction as the congregation. In other branches of Judaism, the bema is at the front, and the reader faces the worshippers. Orthodox synagogues have separate worship areas for men and women, usually with women in the balcony.

The synagogue walls might be decorated with elaborate patterns of vines or geometric designs, but never statues of people, which could be considered idol worship. A lamp above the ark is always kept lit, as it was in the ancient temple of Jerusalem, and candelabras called menorahs also recall the temple. Other common symbols are the two tablets of the Ten Commandments given to Moses, or a Star of David, representing the Jewish king's shield.

At a typical service, the congregation arrives at the start of Sabbath (Friday evening). As a sign of respect toward God, men don yarmulkes (small round caps). As the cantor leads songs and prayers, worshippers follow along in a book of weekly readings. At the heart of the service, everyone stands as the Torah is ceremoniously paraded, unwrapped, and placed on the bema. Someone—the rabbi, the cantor, or a congregant—reads the words aloud. The rabbi ("teacher") might give a commentary on the Torah passage.

and depopulated. And so it remained for generations, as the communist authorities brushed Jewish heritage under the rug. By the early 2000s, Kazimierz's artistically dilapidated buildings, low rents, and easy proximity to the Old Town became enticing to creative young people. A variety of artsy entrepreneurs took root here, beginning with a cluster of ramshackle, rustic bars (inspired partly by Budapest's "ruin pub" scene). Today, the district has the city's (and probably Poland's) highest concentration of trendy food trucks, cafés, bars, restaurants, and design shops—several of which we'll see as we continue.

• *From the food trucks, continue straight ahead (on Izaaka street). This leads you along the left side of...*

Isaac Synagogue (Synagoga Izaaka)

One of Kraków's biggest synagogues, this was built in the 17th century. Recently under renovation, it may or may not be open to visitors. If you can get inside, notice how the walls in the prayer hall are decorated with giant paintings of prayers for worshippers who couldn't afford to buy books.

• *Just past Isaac Synagogue is the heart of Kazimierz's nightlife zone (also bustling by day). Dive in, passing some characteristic cafés. Then jog right at the glitzy Plac Nowy 1 beer hall to reach...*

Plac Nowy

Kazimierz's endearing "new" market square, Plac Nowy (plats NOH-vee), retains much of the gritty flavor of the district before tourism and gentrification. The circular brick building in the center is a slaughterhouse where Jewish butchers would properly kill livestock, kosher-style. Today, its windows are filled with little stand-up eateries, most of them featuring the traditional, local, pizza-like *zapiekanki*. Circle the market hall and browse for a snack (for more on the Plac Nowy scene, see "Eating in Kraków," later). This square is also ringed by several fun and funky bars—enjoyable by day but hopping at night.

• *Leave Plac Nowy along Meiselsa street (to the left from where you entered, past the yellow Jewish Cultural Center). After one block, pause at the intersection of...*

Meiselsa and Bożego Ciała Streets

The Holocaust was a dark chapter that dominates Kazimierz's history. But this intersection is a reminder that, up until the Nazis arrived, Kazimierz was a place where Jews and Christians lived side by side in relative harmony. Notice the street names, which mix Jewish and Catholic namesakes: Ulica Meiselsa ("Meisels Street"—honoring a deeply respected 19th-century rabbi) and Ulica Bożego Ciała ("Corpus Christi Street"—named for the towering brick church you can see just ahead). As if to celebrate the ecumenism of this intersection, a street artist has painted a graffiti Gene Kelly on the wall...very "happy again" indeed that Kazimierz is blossoming and full of life.

• *Backtrack a few steps up Meiselsa and duck into the courtyard on the right, under the dilapidated arch.*

Schindler's List Passage

This courtyard is a popular tourist spot thanks to its brush with fame as a location for some key scenes in *Schindler's List* (find the black-and-white stills from the movie—and actual historic photos—partway down on the right). Spielberg connection aside, this is a particularly evocative setting to nurse a relaxing drink in the atmospheric beer garden.

• *Carry on all the way through the passage. You'll emerge at...*

Ulica Józefa: Design Street

This street has Kazimierz's highest concentration of funky, one-off boutiques: jewelry, fashion, housewares, and more. It's a great place to browse. There's also a TI just across the street.

• *When you're ready to move along, take Ulica Józefa right a few steps to the intersection with Ulica Bożego Ciała, turn left, and follow it a long block. You'll pass Corpus Christi Church on your left, then arrive at...*

Plac Wolnica

Remember that Kazimierz was originally a separate town from Kraków. This was its main market square, designed to one-up its crosstown rival—right down to the dramatic, red-brick Catholic church on the corner (Corpus Christi).

The former Kazimierz Town Hall at the far end of the square houses an unusually good **Ethnographic Museum** (Muzeum Etnograficzne)—worth ▲. If you're interested in Polish folk culture, it's worth a visit (18 zł, free on Tue, open Tue-Sun 10:00-19:00, closed Mon, Ulica Krakowska 46, +48 12 430 6023, www.etnomuzeum.eu). On the ground floor, you'll find models of traditional rural Polish homes, as well as musty replicas of the interiors (like an open-air folk museum moved inside). The exhibit continues upstairs, where each in a long lineup of traditional Polish folk costumes is identified by specific region. Follow the one-way route through exhibits on village lifestyles, rustic tools, and musical instruments (including a Polish bagpipe). A highlight is the explanation of traditional holiday celebrations—from elaborate crèche scenes at Christmas to a wall of remarkably painted Easter eggs. Some items are labeled in English, but it's mostly in Polish. The top floor features temporary exhibits.

• *There's more to see in Kazimierz. But if you're pooped, several trams run from here back to Wawel Castle, then on to the Plac Wszystkich Świętych stop in the heart of the Old Town (catch tram from along Krakowska street, behind the Ethnographic Museum).*

To continue the walk from Plac Wolnica, head up Ulica Św. Wawrzyńca (at the corner where you entered the square, with the Corpus Christi Church on your left).

Ulica Św. Wawrzyńca: Industrial Kazimierz

By the late 19th century, Kazimierz was not just a Jewish cultural hotspot but also a center of local industry. (It's no coincidence that Oskar Schindler had his factory near here.) After the church, on your left, look for the glass-and-steel arched roof of the Industrial Age **old tram depot,** which now houses a recommended brewpub. In sunny summer weather, the pebbly courtyard is filled with happy drinkers.

Across the street, notice the many tram tracks leading into a courtyard with several more storage sheds for local trams. This gorgeously restored complex now houses the **Museum of Engineering and Technology** (Muzeum Inżynierii i Techniki)—yet another of Kraków's many engaging, well-presented museums (closed Mon, Ulica Św. Wawrzyńca 15, www.mit.krakow.pl).

Continue along Ulica Św. Wawrzyńca a few more steps. At the intersection with Wąska, **Judah Square** (Skwer Judah) is a vacant lot with a gaggle of enticing food carts watched over by a giant mural. Commissioned for Kraków's Jewish Cultural Festival in 2013, the illustration was painted by Israeli street artist Pilpeled. It shows a young boy who feels small and scared but lionhearted nevertheless—a poignant symbol for the Holo-

caust survivors of Kazimierz. If you're ready for a meal or snack, you'll find several good options here.

• *A half-block farther down Ulica Św. Wawrzyńca is another place for refreshment, the recommended Craftownia (Polish microwbrews on tap, on the left at #22). Next you'll reach the intersection with Dajwór street.*

Turn left here and walk a few steps up the street; on the right, you'll find the...

Galicia Jewish Museum (Galicja Muzeum)

This museum, worth ▲ and housed in a restored Jewish furniture factory, focuses on the present rather than the past. The permanent "Traces of Memory" photographic exhibit shows today's remnants of yesterday's Judaism in the area around Kraków (a region known as "Galicia"). From abandoned synagogues to old Jewish gravestones flipped over and used as doorsteps, these giant postcards of Jewish artifacts (with good English descriptions) ensure that an important part of this region's heritage won't be forgotten. Temporary exhibits complement this permanent collection (20 zł, daily 10:00-18:00, one block east of Ulica Szeroka at Ulica Dajwór 18, +48 12 421 6842, www.galiciajewishmuseum.org). The museum also serves as a sort of cultural center, with a good bookstore and café.

• *Our Kazimierz orientation walk is finished. From here, you have several options. To* **return to Ulica Szeroka,** *where we began, walk up Dajwór street past the museum, then angle left through the park at the reconstructed chunk of town wall—you'll wind up at the Old Synagogue.*

For the next two options, you'll first head back down to Ulica Św. Wawrzyńca, turn left, and walk one more block to the intersection with Starowiślna street. Just to the left on Starowiślna, look for the tram stops. The tram stop on the far side of the street takes you **back to the Old Town** *(tram #3 or #24). From the tram stop on the near side of the street, tram #3 or #24 zips you to the* **sights in Podgórze**—*including Ghetto Heroes' Square and the Schindler's Factory Museum (both described later). You can also reach the Podgórze sights on foot by turning right on Starowiślna and crossing the bridge (about a 10-minute walk).*

MORE JEWISH SIGHTS IN KAZIMIERZ

In addition to the sights connected by the walk above, here's another cemetery and a few more synagogues to round out your Jewish Kazimierz experience.

▲New Jewish Cemetery (Nowy Cmentarz)

This burial place—much larger than the Old Jewish Cemetery—has graves of those who died after 1800. It was vandalized by the Nazis, who sold many of its gravestones to stonecutters and used others as pavement in their concentration camps. Many have since been cemented back in their original positions, while others—which could not be replaced—have been used to create the moving mosaic wall and Holocaust monument (on the right as you enter). Most gravestones are in one of four languages: Hebrew (generally the oldest, especially if there's no other language, though some are newer "retro" tombstones), Yiddish (sounds like a mix of German and Hebrew and uses the Hebrew alphabet), Polish (Jews who assimilated into the Polish community), and German (Jews who assimilated into the German community). The earliest graves are simple stones, while later ones imitate graves in Polish Catholic cemeteries—larger, more elaborate, and with a long stone jutting out to cover the body.  Notice that some new-looking graves have old dates. These were most likely put here well after the Holocaust (or even after the communist era) by relatives of the dead.

Cost and Hours: Free, Sun-Fri 8:00-16:00, closed Sat. It's tricky to find: Go under the railway tunnel at the east end of Ulica Miodowa and turn right as you emerge; look for the gate with the small *cmentarz żydowski* sign.

Synagogues

In addition to the three synagogues mentioned on the Kazimierz Walk (Old Synagogue, Isaac, and Remu'h), others welcome visitors. Each of these charges a small admission fee and is closed Saturdays. The **High Synagogue**—so called because its prayer room is upstairs—displays changing exhibits, most of which focus on the people who lived here before the Holocaust (Ulica Józefa 38). **Tempel Synagogue** (Synagoga Templu) has the grandest interior—big and dark, with elaborately decorated, gilded ceilings and balconies (corner of Ulica Miodowa and Ulica Podbrzezie). The **Jewish Community Centre** next door offers activities both for members of the local Jewish community and for tourists (lectures, genealogical research, Friday-night Shabbat meals, Hebrew and Yiddish classes, and so on; https://linktr.ee/jcckrakow). Nearly across the street, the smaller **Kupa Synagogue** (Synagoga Kupa)—clean and brightly decorated—sometimes hosts temporary exhibits (Miodowa 27).

NEAR KAZIMIERZ: PODGÓRZE

The neighborhood called Podgórze (POD-goo-zheh), directly across the Vistula from Kazimierz, has one of Kraków's most famous sights: Schindler's Factory Museum. I've listed the area's sights in the order you'll reach them as you come from Kazimierz or the Old Town.

Background: This is the neighborhood where the Nazis forced Kraków's Jews into a ghetto in early 1941. (*Schindler's List* and the films in the Pharmacy Under the Eagle museum depict the sad spectacle of Jews loading their belongings onto carts and trudging over the bridge into Podgórze.) Non-Jews who had lived here were displaced to make way for the new arrivals. The ghetto was surrounded by a wall with a fringe along the top that resembled Jewish gravestones—a chilling premonition. A short section of this wall still stands along Lwowska street. The tram continued to run through the middle of Podgórze, without stopping—giving Krakovians a harrowing glimpse at the horrifying conditions inside the ghetto.

Getting There: To go directly to Ghetto Heroes' Square, continue through Kazimierz on tram #3 or #24 (described earlier, under "Getting to Kazimierz") to the stop called Plac Bohaterow Getta. Or you can ride the tram or walk 10 minutes across the bridge from the end of my Kazimierz Walk.

KRAKÓW

Ghetto Heroes' Square (Plac Bohaterow Getta)

This unassuming square is the focal point of the visitor's Podgórze. Today, the square is filled with a monument consisting of 68 empty metal chairs—represent-ing the 68,000 people deported from here. This is intended to remind viewers that the Jews of Kazimierz were forced to carry all of their belong-ings—including furni-ture—to the ghetto on this side of the river. It was also  here that many Jews waited to be sent to extermination camps. The small, gray building at the river end of Ghetto Heroes' Square feels like a train car inside, evocative of the wagons that carried people from here to certain death.

▲Pharmacy Under the Eagle (Apteka pod Orłem)

This small but good museum, on Ghetto Heroes' Square, tells the story of Tadeusz Pankiewicz, a Polish Catholic pharmacist who chose to remain in Podgórze when it became a Jewish ghetto. During this time, the pharmacy was an important meeting point for the ghetto residents, and Pankiewicz and his staff heroically aided and hid Jewish victims of the Nazis. (Pankiewicz survived the war and was later acknowledged by Israel as one of the "Righteous Among the Nations"—non-Jews who risked their lives to help the Nazis' victims during World War II. You'll see his medal on display in the white memorial room at the end of the museum.) Today, the pharmacy hosts an exhibit about the Jewish ghetto.

Cost and Hours: 18 zł, free on Wed; open Wed-Sun 10:00-17:00, closed Mon-Tue; Plac Bohaterow Getta 18, +48 12 656 5625.

Visiting the Museum: You'll enter into the re-created pharmacy, where the "windows" are actually screens that show footage from the era. Push buttons, pull out drawers, answer the phone—it's full of interactive opportunities to better understand ghetto life. You'll learn about people who worked in the pharmacy (including riveting interviews with eyewitnesses—some in English, others subtitled) and hear Pankiewicz telling stories about that tense time. You'll also learn a bit about the pharmacy business from that period.

▲▲Schindler's Factory Museum
(Fabryka Emalia Oskara Schindlera)

One of Europe's top museums about the Nazi occupation fills some of the factory buildings where Oskar Schindler and his Jewish employees worked. The museum

tells the wartime story not only of Schindler and his workers but also of all of Kraków. It's loaded with in-depth information (all in English), and touchscreens invite you to learn more and watch eyewitness interviews. Scattered randomly between the exhibits are replicas of everyday places from the age—a photographer's shop, a tram car, a hairdresser's salon—designed to give you a taste of 1940s Kraków. Note that you'll see nothing of the actual factory or equipment, as the threat of the advancing Red Army forced Schindler to move his operation lock, stock, and barrel to Nazi-occupied Czechoslovakia in 1944.

Cost and Hours: 32 zł, free on Mon; open Mon 10:00-14:00, Tue-Sun until 18:00 (except closed the first Tue of each month), last entry 1.5 hours before closing; +48 12 257 1017, www. muzeumkrakowa.pl.

Book Ahead: It's always wise to book ahead for this very busy and popular sight, which frequently sells out. To get your choice of time slots, book at least several days in advance—the sooner, the better—at www.bilety.mhk.pl. (For Mondays, when it's free and extremely busy, you may not be able to prebook online; check the website for the latest policy.) Or, if you arrive in Kraków without a ticket and it's already sold out, stop by the Museum of Kraków Visitors Center on the Main Market Square (see "Tourist Information" on page 37). Ideally, swing by that office the day before you'd like to tour the museum; that's when unsold tickets, previously bought up by local agencies, are returned and become available to procrastinators.

Crowd-Beating Tips: Once inside, the museum can be unpleasantly congested. For a more leisurely experience, the best strategy is to arrive right when it opens, or later in the day—if you have an average appetite for information, planning to arrive 2 hours before closing time should be about right.

Getting There: It's in a gloomy industrial area a five-minute walk from Ghetto Heroes' Square (Plac Bohaterow Getta): Go up Kącik street (to the left of the big, glass skyscraper), go under the railroad underpass, and continue two blocks, past MOCAK (the Museum of Contemporary Art in Kraków, described later) to the second big building on the left (Ulica Lipowa 4). Look for signs to *Emalia*.

Visiting the Museum: Entering on the ground floor, you'll find special exhibits and a "film café" (interesting for fans of the movie) with refreshments. Then head upstairs to the first floor.

First Floor: The 35-minute **film**, called *Lipowa 4* (this building's address), sets the stage with interviews of both Jews and non-Jews describing their wartime experience (find it just off the museum's first, circular room; subtitled in English, it runs continuously).

From here, the one-way route winds through the permanent exhibit, called **"Kraków Under Nazi Occupation 1939-1945."** First, while pleasant music plays, "stereoscopic" (primitive 3-D) photos of prewar Kraków capture an idyllic age when culture flourished and the city's Jews (more than one-quarter of the population) blended more or less smoothly with their Catholic-Pole neighbors. But then, a video explains the Nazi invasion of Poland in early September of 1939: It took them only a few weeks to overrun the country (which desperately awaited the promised help of their British and French allies, who never arrived).

Through the next several rooms, watch the film clip of SS soldiers marching through the Main Market Square—renamed "Adolf-Hitler-Platz"—and read stories about how the Nazis' *Generalgouvernement* attempted to reshape the life of its new capital, "Krakau." (Near the tram car, look for the decapitated head of the Grunwald monument, which had been a powerful symbol of a Polish military victory over German forces.) You'll see the story of a newly German-owned shop selling Nazi propaganda and learn how professors at Kraków's Jagiellonian University were arrested to prevent them from fomenting rebellion among their students. During

Oskar Schindler (1908-1974) and His List

Steven Spielberg's instant-classic, Oscar-winning 1993 film, *Schindler's List,* brought the world's attention to the inspiring story of Oskar Schindler, the compassionate German business-man who did his creative best to save the lives of the Jewish work-ers at his factory in Kraków. Spielberg chose to film the story right here in Kazimierz, where the events actually unfolded.

Oskar Schindler was born in 1908 in the Sudetenland (cur-rently part of the Czech Republic, then predominantly German). Early on, he displayed an idiosyncratic interpretation of ethics that earned him both wealth and enemies. As Nazi aggressions escalated, Schindler (who was very much a Nazi) carried out es-pionage against Poland; when Germany invaded the country in 1939, Schindler smelled a business opportunity. Early in the Nazi occupation of Poland, Schindler came to Kraków and lived in an apartment at Ulica Straszewskiego 7 (a block from Wawel Castle). He took over the formerly Jewish-owned Emalia factory at Ulica Lipowa 4, which produced metal pots and pans that were dipped into protective enamel; later, the factory also began producing ar-maments for the Nazi war effort. The factory was staffed by about 1,000 Jews from the nearby Płaszów Concentration Camp, which was managed by the ruthless SS officer Amon Göth (depicted in *Schindler's List*—based on real events—shooting at camp inmates for sport from his balcony).

At a certain point, Schindler began to sympathize with his Jewish workers, and he increasingly did what he could to protect them and offer them better lives. Schindler fed them far better than most concentration-camp inmates and allowed them to sell some of the pots and pans they made on the black market to make money. After he saw many of his employees and friends murdered during an SS raid in 1943, he ramped up these efforts. He would come up with bogus paperwork to classify those threat-

this time, even Polish secondary schools were closed—effectively prohibiting learning among Poles, whom the Nazis considered in-ferior. But Polish students continued to meet clandestinely with their teachers. You'll also see images of Hans Frank—the hated puppet ruler of Poland—moving into the country's most important symbol of sovereignty, Wawel Castle.

The exhibit also details how early Nazi policies targeted Jews with roundups, torture, and execution. (Down the staircase is an eerie simulation of a cellar prison.) As the Nazis ratcheted up their genocidal activities, troops swept through Kraków on March 3, 1941, forcing all the remaining Jews in town to squeeze into the newly created Podgórze ghetto. At the bottom of the stairs, look for the huge pile of plunder—Jewish wealth stolen by the Nazis.

Second Floor: Climb upstairs using the long **staircase,** which

ened with deportation as "essential" to the workings of the factory—even if they were unskilled. He sought and was granted permission to build a "concentration camp" barracks for his workers on the factory grounds, where they lived in far better conditions than those at Płaszów. These lucky few became known as *Schindlerjuden*—"Schindler's Jews."

As the Soviet army encroached on Kraków in October 1944, word came that the factory would need to be relocated west, farther from the front line. While Schindler could easily have simply turned his workers over to the concentration camp system and certain death—as most other industrialists did—he decided to bring them with him to his new factory at Brünnlitz (Brněnec, in today's Czech Republic). He assembled a list of 700 men and 300 women who worked with him, along with 200 other Jewish inmates, and at great personal expense, moved them to Brünnlitz. At the new factory, Schindler and the 1,200 people he had saved produced grenades and rocket parts—virtually all of them, the workers later claimed, mysteriously defective.

After the war, Schindler—who had spent much of his fortune protecting his Jewish workers—hopped around Germany and Argentina, repeatedly attempting but failing to break back into business (often with funding from Jewish donors). He died in poverty in 1974. In accordance with his final wishes, he was buried in Jerusalem, and today his grave is piled high with small stones left there by appreciative visitors. He has since been named one of the "Righteous Among the Nations" for his efforts to save Jews from the Holocaust. Thomas Keneally's 1982 book *Schindler's Ark* brought the industrialist's tale to a wide audience that included Steven Spielberg, who vaulted Schindler to the ranks of a cultural icon.

was immortalized in a powerful scene in *Schindler's List*. At the top of the stairs on the right is a small room that served as "Schindler's office" for the film (though it's been determined that his actual office was elsewhere; we'll see it soon).

You'll walk through a corridor lined by a replica of the wall that enclosed the **Podgórze ghetto** and see poignant exhibits about the horrific conditions there (including a replica of the cramped living quarters). The Nazis claimed that Jews had to be segregated here, away from the general population, because they "carried diseases."

Continue into the office of Schindler's secretary, with exhibits about Schindler's life and video touchscreens that play testimonial footage of Schindler's grateful employees. Then proceed into the actual **Schindler's office.** The big map (with German names for cities) was uncovered when the factory was being restored. Because Schindler's short tenure here was the only time in the factory's history that these Polish place names would appear in German, it's believed that this map was hung over his desk. Facing the map is a giant monument of enamel pots and pans, like those that were made in this

factory. There are 1,200 pots—one for each Jewish worker that Schindler saved. Inside the monument, the walls are lined with the names on Schindler's famous list. The creaky floorboards are intentional: a reminder that the Nazis knew every step you took.

Proceeding through the exhibit, you'll learn more about everyday life—both for ghetto dwellers and for everyday non-Jewish Krakovians, including the Polish resistance (see the Home Army's underground print shop). More eyewitness accounts relate the terrifying days of March 13 and 14, 1943, when the Podgórze ghetto was liquidated, sending survivors to the nearby Płaszów Concentration Camp. The replica of the Płaszów quarry, where inmates were forced to work in

unimaginably difficult conditions, provides a poignant memorial for those who weren't fortunate enough to wind up on Schindler's list.

Now head all the way back down to the ground floor.

Ground Floor: Exhibits here capture the uncertain days near the end of the war in the summer of 1944, when Nazis arrested between 6,000 and 8,000 suspected saboteurs after the Warsaw Uprising and sent them to Płaszów (see the replica of a basement hideout for 10 Jews who had escaped the ghetto); and later, when many Nazis had fled Kraków, leaving residents to await the Soviet Union's Red Army (see the replica air-raid shelters). The Red Army arrived here on January 18, 1945—at long last, the five years, four months, and twelve days of Nazi rule were over. The Soviets caused their own share of damage to the city before beginning a whole new occupation that would last for generations...but that's a different museum.

Finally, walk along the squishy floor—evoking how life for anyone was unstable and unpredictable during the Nazi occupation—into the **Hall of Choices.** The six rotating pillars tell the stories of people who chose to act—or not to act—when they witnessed atrocities. Think about the ramifications of the choices they made...and what you would have done in their shoes. The final room holds two books: a white book listing those who tried to help, and a black book listing Nazi collaborators. Exiting the museum, notice the portraits of Oskar Schindler's workers who lived long and happy lives after the war.

Nearby: Before heading back to downtown Kraków, consider paying a visit to the superb **Museum of Contemporary Art in Kraków** (Muzeum Sztuki Współczesnej w Krakowie)—or MOCAK for short—that fills the warehouse buildings once occupied by Schindler's workers, behind this main building (closed Mon, www.mocak.pl). Or, for a glass of wine, head just a few doors down from the museum to find the delightful **Krakó Slow Wines** (marked *Lipowa 6F*). This mellow, inviting wine bar and shop is well stocked with wines mostly from Central Europe (daily, +48 669 225 222.

John Paul II Pilgrimage Sights

Catholics coming to Kraków eager to walk in the footsteps of St. John Paul II appreciate the city's dazzling churches and its Archdiocesan Museum. And for most, that's enough. But true pilgrims head for worthwhile sights outside the city center: two sanctuaries related to John Paul II on the outskirts of Kraków and the St. John Paul II Family Home Museum in the town of Wadowice, an hour's drive away.

Sanctuaries in Kraków

The two biggest, most impressive JPII destinations are about four miles south of Kraków's Old Town, in the Łagiewniki neighborhood. While the main attraction here for pilgrims is the John Paul II Sanctuary, historically and geographically you'll come first to the Divine Mercy Sanctuary—so I've covered that first. The sights aren't worth the trek for the merely curious, but they offer a glimpse of the deep faith that characterizes the Polish people.

Getting There: A **taxi** or **Uber** from downtown takes 20-30 minutes and makes things easy. By public transit, you can take **tram #8** from Plac Wszystkich Świętych in the Old Town (next to St. Francis Basilica) or **tram #10** from the Poczta Główna stop, along the Planty at the eastern edge of the Old Town; on either tram, ride about 20 minutes and get off at the Łagiewniki SKA stop. From there, take the pedestrian underpass, turn right, cross the train tracks, and huff a few minutes uphill along the wall to find the entrance to the complex. (You can see the glass steeple of the church from the tram stop—a handy visual landmark.)

After touring the Divine Mercy sights, you'll head to the St. John Paul II Sanctuary—a 15-minute walk or a short, inexpensive taxi or Uber trip. To go directly to the John Paul II Sanctuary from the Old Town, take tram #10 and ride it all the way to the Sanktuarium Bożego Miłosierdzia stop.

Divine Mercy Sanctuary
(Sanktuarium Bożego Miłosierdzia)

This complex, built around a humble red-brick convent, honors the early 20th-century St. Faustina, who saw a miraculous vision of Jesus that became a powerful religious symbol for many Catholics. Today, pilgrims from around the world revere the relics both of Faustina and of John Paul II (who advocated for her sainthood), and learn more about her story from the convent's present-day sisters— many of whom speak English.

Background: One cold and blustery evening in 1931, Sister Faustina Kowalska (1905-1938) answered the convent doorbell to find a beggar asking for some food. Faustina brought some soup to the man, who revealed his true nature: a figure of Jesus Christ clad in a white robe, with one hand raised in blessing and the other touching his chest. Emanating from his chest were twin beams of light: red (representing blood, the life of souls) and white (water, which through baptism washes souls righteously clean). Transformed by her experience, Faustina worked with an artist to create a painted version of the image—called the Divine Mercy—which is one of the most important symbols of Polish Catholicism.

Always frail in health, Faustina died at 33—the same age as Jesus. The story of Faustina deeply moved a young Karol Wojtyła. When he became pope, he dedicated the first Sunday after Easter as the day of Divine Mercy worldwide. In 2000, he made his fellow Krakovian the first Catholic saint of the third millennium. To properly revere the newly important St. Faustina, a futuristic church and visitors center was built alongside her original convent.

Cost and Hours: All parts of the complex are free to enter, but donations are happily accepted. Each part has slightly different hours (listed later; www.faustyna.pl). Note that the daily 15:00 "Hour of Mercy" service—in both the chapel and the modern church—is worth planning around.

Visiting the Complex: Entering the complex through the

side gate, look uphill to find a **walkway** with flags from around the world and plaques translating the Divine Mercy's message—"Jesus, I trust in you"—in dozens of languages.

Just before entering the **original chapel,** look up and to the right—the window with the flowers marks the cell where Faustina died. Inside the chapel (daily 6:00-21:15), the altar to the left of the main altar displays an early copy of Faustina's Divine Mercy painting. Her relics are in the white case just below; in the white kneeler just in front of the chapel, notice the little reliquary holding one of her bones (which worshippers can embrace as they pray).

Leaving the chapel, turn left and go to the far end of the accommodations building. Enter the door on the right to find the **replica of Faustina's cell.** While this is a newer building, here they've created Faustina's convent cell, including many of her personal effects. Drop a coin in the slot for an evocative headphone description of these items, and of the vision of Jesus that put her convent on the map (usually open daily 8:30-18:00).

From here, head downhill and circle around the large brick building—passing (on the right) an area for outdoor Mass.

Dominating the campus is the futuristic, glass-and-steel **main church,** which was consecrated by Pope John Paul II on his final visit to Poland in 2002 (daily 7:00-20:00). The lower level has a variety of small chapels, each one donated by Catholic worshippers in a different country (Germany, Hungary, Slovakia, and so on)—and each with a dramatically different style.

The central chapel on this level has a modern altar and another bone of St. Faustina. Upstairs, the main sanctuary is a sleek cylindrical space with wooden sunbeams sharply radiating from the altar area. That altar—framed by the gnarled limbs of windblown trees, representing the suffering of human existence—contains a replica of the Divine Mercy painting, flanked by the woman who saw the vision (Faustina, on the right) and the Polish pope who made it a worldwide phenomenon (John Paul II, on the left).

Head back out to the terrace surrounding the church. The bold **tower**—as tall as St. Mary's on Main Market Square—has an elevator to a glassed-in viewpoint offering panoramas over the Divine Mercy campus, the adjacent John Paul II Sanctuary complex, and—on the distant horizon—the spires of Wawel Cathedral and Kraków's Old Town (daily 8:00-19:00). Near the base of the tower is a **canopy** where Mass is said on Divine Mercy Sunday each year, before a crowd of 100,000 who fill the fields below.

Connecting to the St. John Paul II Sanctuary: You can see the rectangular, brick tower of the JPII Sanctuary from the Divine Mercy Sanctuary; it's about a 15-minute walk through the park (downhill, then uphill). Alternatively, you can make a short, inexpensive trip in a taxi (see if any are waiting at the parking lot in front of the sanctuary's hotel—the boxy, white building; otherwise, ask the receptionist to call one, or order an Uber).

KRAKÓW

St. John Paul II the Great Sanctuary (Sanktuarium Św. Jana Pawła II Wielkiego)

This complex, funded entirely by private donors, celebrates the life and sainthood of Kraków's favorite son. A visit has two parts: the giant sanctuary (church) and the nearby museum.

Cost and Hours: Sanctuary—free, daily 7:30-19:00, until 18:00 in winter, www.sanktuariumjp2.pl; museum—15 zł, daily 9:00-17:00.

Sanctuary of St. John Paul II the Great: This hypermodern church is big and splendid. In the **downstairs** area, the cen-
tral chapel features paintings of JPII's papal visits to various pilgrimage sites, both in Poland (Częstochowa) and abroad (Fátima, Lourdes). Ringing that central area is a variety of interesting smaller chapels.

On the outer wall, look for three in particular: The Kaplica Kapłańska is a replica of the St. Leonard's Crypt under Wawel Cathedral—where a young priest named Karol Wojtyła celebrated his first Mass. In this chapel, you'll see JPII's empty papal tomb from the crypt beneath St. Peter's Basilica at the Vatican. (When he became a saint, his remains—which, controversially, are kept in Rome rather than his homeland—were moved up into the main part of the church in Rome, and a simple grave marker was donated to the church here.) You'll also see a reliquary in the shape of a book with fluttering pages, holding a small amount of John Paul II's blood (for the story of the book, see page 72). This blood was kept in secret by JPII's personal secretary, only revealed after his death, when it was divvied up among a select few churches. Nearby, another chapel holds the tombs of a few recent cardinals; as they're running out of space below Wawel Cathedral, this chapel is poised to handle the overflow. And the Kaplica Św. Kingi features finely executed reliefs in rock salt, in the style of Wieliczka Salt Mine.

Head upstairs to the sleek, modern **main sanctuary.** The concrete structure supports large walls, providing a canvas for dynamic mosaics of Bible stories. Above the main altar, in the middle, you'll see the Three Kings delivering their gifts to the Baby Jesus and the Virgin Mary—with St. John Paul II serenely overlooking the scene. Other scenes include Adam and Eve, Jesus calming the storm, the wedding feast at Cana, and the Last Supper. In the back-left corner, a smaller chapel displays the blood-spattered vestments that St. John Paul II was wearing on May 13, 1981, when he was shot by a would-be assassin.

The sanctuary anchors a sprawling complex of conference facilities and other attractions for pilgrims. Poke around. The museum, described next (and on the right as you exit the sanctuary's main door), is the sight most worth visiting.

St. John Paul II Museum: This collects many of the gifts bestowed on the beloved pope (African carved masks and ivory tusks; Latin American tapestries; the key to the city of Long Branch, New Jersey; a pair of glass doves of peace given to him—perhaps with a touch of irony—by US vice president Dick Cheney), ornate worship aids (chalices, crosses, and so on), and modern art that celebrates the modern pope and his life's work. There are also personal items, from his papal ski and hiking gear to the place settings from his Vatican dinner table to his stylish red leather shoes. You'll also see the throne from his last visit to Poland in 2002, and a replica of the humble room across the street from St. Francis Basilica where he stayed on visits back to his homeland.

Returning to Kraków: Taxis may be waiting at the sanctuary; otherwise, you can ask the museum desk to call one for you (or order an Uber). Or, you can walk downhill through the park to find the Sanktuarium Bożego Miłosierdzia stop; tram #10 goes back to the Old Town.

Wadowice—St. John Paul II's Hometown

Karol Wojtyła was born and lived until age 18 in Wadowice (VAH-doh-veet-seh, pop. 20,000), about 30 miles southwest of Kraków. This working-class town, known for its woodworkers and factories, seems an unassuming place to have produced such a globally influential figure. And today, it's a place of pilgrimage for admirers of the man young "Lolek" would become.

Getting There: Wadowice is about an hour's drive from Kraków. As it's roughly in the same direction as Auschwitz, a local guide or driver can help you connect both places for one very busy day of contrasts—though you'll want to time things carefully. (If using public transit, doing both is not realistic.) Buses run frequently from Kraków to Wadowice's train station (about 1.25

hours one-way, departs every 20 minutes); from there, you can walk about 10 minutes to the main square and museum.

Visiting Wadowice: The town of Wadowice has a beautifully restored **main market square** (Plac Jana Pawła II). Information

panels around the square tell the story of the local boy done very, very good, and plaques in the cobbles list the cities and countries John Paul II visited. At the top of the square (opposite the church), the green *cukiernia* (pastry shop) sells the local cream cake, *kremówki,* which the pope raved about—having a slice is practically obligatory on a visit to Wadowice.

The square is dominated by the pretty Baroque steeple of the home **church** of young Karol Wojtyła (officially the Basilica of the Presentation of the Blessed Virgin Mary). Today, a larger-than-life statue of John Paul II stands outside that church, whose outer walls are plastered with plaques, photos, and information boards about the saint. Inside the church, in the chapel left of the main altar, you can see the font where he was baptized (a photo of him visiting the font as pope hangs on the wall nearby). He also took his First Communion and served as an altar boy here.

Immediately to the right of the church, across a narrow lane, stands the house where Karol Wojtyła was born and grew up—now an impressive museum.

▲▲St. John Paul II Family Home Museum

This thoughtfully presented multimedia museum tells the story of Karol Wojtyła, his journey to the papacy, and his legacy. It fills four

floors of the tenement building where his family lived through his adolescence. Worth ▲▲▲ for the faithful, it's engaging and informative to anyone—though detractors will note the complete omission of any criticism. The museum is essentially an exercise in lionizing a giant historical figure, and that it does very well; it's a well-executed combination of important artifacts and stirring storytelling.

Cost and Hours: 39 zł includes audioguide, free on Tue; April-Oct Wed-Mon 9:00-18:00, Tue from 12:00, Nov-March until 16:00, May-Sept open until 19:00 Fri-Sun, closed last Tue of month year-round; last entry 1.25 hours before closing; on the main square next to the town church at Ulica Kościelna 7, +48 33 823 2662, https://domjp2.pl. Be sure to book ahead online to visit on Tuesdays, when the museum is free and very busy.

Tours: You can see the museum on your own (with an audioguide) or join a guided tour. If you already know the story of John Paul II, you may prefer to see it on your own to linger over the riveting exhibits—which offer lots to unpack—at your own pace. A tour is handy for those looking for an efficient introduction (or a refresher) on his life story. English tours run irregularly—check and book ahead on the website.

Visiting the Museum: You'll begin with a wall of photographs featuring Karol Wojtyła's parents and his youth—back when he was known as Lolek. The apartment in this tenement building was above a Jewish-run general store; that storefront has been recreated in the entryway. Inside is an homage to the approximately 20 percent of young Karol's neighbors who were Jewish, many of whom died in the Holocaust. You'll also see a hologram reconstruction of the town synagogue (destroyed by the Nazis) and footage of John Paul II's historic visits to the Rome synagogue and the Wailing Wall in Jerusalem. (As pope, he was noted for his ecumenism—which the museum credits partly to his many Jewish friends and neighbors here in Wadowice.)

Next, you'll learn of Karol's deep spiritual ties to the nearby village of Kalwaria Zebrzydowska, which he visited more than 100 times. And you'll see the skis and hiking gear he used to explore the nearby hills.

Upstairs is the three-room **apartment** where Karol's family lived. Most of the furniture is from the period, but not actually the family's; a few exceptions are in glass cases. You'll see the parlor; the bedroom, where Karol was born and which he later shared with his father (see the two single beds); and the kitchen. The kitchen table looks out at a sundial on the side of the adjacent church. The motto Karol saw there every day—"Time flies; eternity dwells"—became one of his mantras. Perhaps this soulfulness at such a young age was inspired by the many losses in his life: He lost his mother at age 9, his brother at age 12, and his father at age 20.

Then you'll step into the **museum** proper. The large red room covers the 40 years Karol Wojtyła spent in Kraków—from his time as a student, and then as a priest, archbishop, and cardinal, until he was called to the papacy. These stages are represented by the various robes, actually worn by him, displayed here.

Next, the replica of St. Peter's boat marks his transition to the papacy. You'll see a room about the attempt on his life in 1981 (the actual handgun used is in a glass case in the floor); a hall commemorating his eight pilgrimages home to Poland (the first three while it was still controlled by the communists); a rotunda with a replica of the Jubilee Doors at St. Peter's Basilica in Rome, under a dome supported by giant illustrated versions of his encyclicals; and a room documenting the staggering 129 countries Pope John Paul II visited during his 104 pilgrimages. In the floor, transparent boxes hold soil from many of these countries (commemorating the pope's tradition of kissing the ground in each place), and a nearby display case shows off some unusual mementos from those travels: an embroidery with the Lord's Prayer in Inuit, a Congolese statue of Jesus with strongly African features, a Marvel comic book about the life of John Paul II, and a Burger King-branded cardboard periscope for catching a glimpse of the Popemobile over the crowds.

Use the elevator to descend to the basement and continue the visit. You'll see the kayak he took on camping trips with his students in the 1970s, and a room dedicated to the World Youth Days he was instrumental in creating. (Conspicuously absent is any mention of John Paul II's inaction when it came to protecting children who were molested by priests on his watch.)

The exhibit ends with the final days of John Paul II's earthly life; you'll see his bedside clock, stopped at the hour of his death, and a Bible displaying the final words he heard (as a nun was reading to him when he died). The red hall features a backup copy of the book of his funeral Mass, which famously flipped closed in the wind; and actual red robes worn by attendees. Then, the white room commemorates his sainthood—with an illustration of St. John Paul II surrounded by some of the many people he himself had sainted as pope; and walls of letters left behind by visitors to Rome around the time of his funeral, asking for his intercession.

Rounding out the museum are some temporary exhibits. You'll return onto the square where young Karol Wojtyła spent his childhood. Now...time for some cream cake. Lolek would have wanted it that way.

Sights Outside Kraków

The following sights—an impressive salt mine, a purpose-built communist town, and an unusual earthwork—require a bus, tram, or train ride to reach. Also near Kraków are the St. John Paul II Family Home Museum in Wadowice (described above) and the poignant memorial at Auschwitz-Birkenau Concentration Camp (covered in the next chapter).

▲▲Wieliczka Salt Mine (Kopalnia Soli Wieliczka)

Wieliczka (veel-EECH-kah), a salt mine southeast of Kraków, is beloved by Poles. Hundreds of feet beneath the ground, the mine is filled with sculptures that miners have lovingly carved out of the

salt. You'll explore this unique gallery—learning both about the art and about medieval mining techniques—on a required tour. Though the sight is a bit overrated, it's unique and practically obligatory if you're in Kraków for a few days. In my experience, about half of those who visit love Wieliczka, while half feel it's a waste of time—but it can be hard to predict which half you're in. Read this description before you decide. And expect a lot of walking.

Cost and Hours: The standard "Tourist Route" costs 126 zł and is by guided tour only. English-language tours leave at the top of each hour, daily 8:00-18:00 (these are first and last tour times), with shorter hours off-season. More in-depth routes (such as the interactive "Miners' Route," where visitors wear coveralls and helmets and operate some of the old equipment) are explained on the website.

Information: The mine is in the town of Wieliczka at Ulica Daniłowicza 10 (+48 12 278 7302, www.kopalnia.pl).

Crowd-Beating Tips: This popular sight can be packed, and there's a strict limit on how many people can be in the mine at once. It's busiest between 10:00 and 16:00—try to arrive before or after those times (the ticket office opens at 7:30; since the last English tour leaves at 18:00 in summer, arriving in the afternoon can be a good way to stretch your sightseeing day). It's most crowded on weekends and in the summer and overrun on long holiday weekends. Given the possibility of selling out, it's smart to **book an entry time** on the website in advance (no extra charge).

Getting There: The salt mine is 10 miles from Kraków. By far the easiest option is to hop on **train SKA1** at Kraków's main train station (2/hour, 7 zł, 25 minutes, get off at Wieliczka Rynek-Kopalnia; from there, walk up through the parking lot and follow signs to the Daniłowicza shaft and entrance, about 5 minutes). In a pinch, you can take **bus #304** (at the Dworzec Główny Zachód stop, on Ogrodowa street, at the opposite side of Galeria Krakowska mall from the train station); while these depart frequently, they take longer (about 40 minutes) and are subject to traffic delays. **Private drivers** also make this trip (see page 47).

Visitor Information: While taking pictures is allowed, flash photos often don't turn out, thanks to the irregular reflection of the salt crystals. Dress warmly—the mine is a constant 57 degrees Fahrenheit. Before entering, you'll have to check large bags.

Eating: There's a good little **$ cafeteria** deep down in the mine, at the end of the tour route. Up at the surface is a wide range of eateries, from snack stands to sit-down restaurants.

Background: Going all the way back to Neolithic times, prehistoric tribes gathered salt from springs in this area. In the 1280s, Wieliczka Salt Mine began producing salt in earnest. Under Kazimierz the Great, one-third of Poland's income came from these precious deposits—back in an age when salt was called "white gold" and was extremely valuable for its ability to preserve foods. (The Romans even paid workers in salt—*salarium,* the origin of our word "salary.") The mines were so important that Kazimierz the Great enacted laws protecting the miners—the first known instance of worker-protection laws in Europe. Wieliczka was controlled by the Polish crown and, after the Partitions, by the Austro-Hungarian Empire (which outfitted miners with military-style uniforms). During this time, around the Industrial Revolution (and under efficient Austrian management), the mine hit peak productivity.

Wieliczka miners spent much of their lives underground, leaving for work before daybreak and returning after sundown, rarely emerging into daylight. To pass the time, beginning in the 17th century, miners carved figures, chandeliers, and even entire underground chapels out of the salt. For many modern visitors, these carvings are the most memorable part of Wieliczka.

Until just a few years ago, the mine still produced salt. Today's miners—about 400 of them—primarily work on maintaining the 200 miles of chambers. This entire network is supported by pine beams—over time, the salt strengthens the wood (some you'll see are more than 200 years old), whereas metal would rust. Per tradition, the wood beams are painted white to reflect the dim light of the miners' oil lamps. Today, visitors see only about 1.5 percent of the sprawling mines. (You would not want to visit the original medieval mines, which have tunnels only about three feet tall.)

Visiting the Mine: For the main tour ("Tourist Route"), head for the Daniłowicz shaft, and buy your ticket if you haven't already. At the appointed time, find the English tour area to wait for your guide, who leads you 380 steps down a winding staircase. If you've always wanted to experience true vertigo, peer between the banisters on your way down. Once at level 1, you begin a 1.5-mile stroll, generally downhill (more than 800 steps down altogether), past 20 of the mine's 2,000 chambers (with signs ex-

plaining when they were dug), finishing 443 feet below the surface (at level 3). When you're done, an elevator beams you back up.

As you spelunk, your guide offers a canned commentary about the history of the mines. You'll learn how the miners lived and worked, using horses who spent their entire adult lives without ever seeing the light of day. You'll see the gigantic horse-pulled wheels used to operate lifts within the mines and find out why igniting pockets of methane gas near the ceiling was the most dangerous part of the job (the mortality rate for miners was about 1 in 10). All along the way, you'll walk through tunnels caved out of the rock salt; although it can be dark in color (mixed with other minerals such as sandstone and gypsum), it's about 90 percent pure salt. To transport the salt out of the mine, the miners would either carve it into big blocks or crush it and pour it into barrels.

The tour takes you through vast underground caverns, past subterranean lakes (32 percent salt—like the Black Sea, the maximum allowed by nature), and introduces you to some of the mine's many sculptures. You'll see Copernicus (who actually visited here in the 15th century), an army of salt elves, the Polish military hero Józef Piłsudski, and this region's favorite son, St. John Paul II.

Expect to be wowed by the enormous **Chapel of St. Kinga**, carved over three decades in the early 20th century. Look for the salt-relief carving of the Last Supper (its 3-D details are astonishing, considering it's just six inches deep). The chapel is still used for services every Sunday morning at 7:30.

From there, you'll see a few more chambers, including one with a big lake and a brief sound-and-light show. Your tour finishes in a deep-down shopping zone about 1.5 hours after you started. From here you can decide whether to return to the surface or add on the Mine Museum.

Returning to the Surface: You'll loop around through a handy cafeteria, then take an old-school elevator through the Daniłowicz shaft, back up to where you began. (If it's extremely busy, they may send you up the modern Regis shaft, which pops you out closer to the town center of Wieliczka—about a 10-minute walk through a pretty park back to the entrance building.)

Optional Add-On—Mine Museum: If you're not pooped, you can tack on a visit to the museum (included in your ticket)—which adds about an hour and a mile more walking. While overkill for most, the museum provides a bit more historical context. A guide will take you through the exhibits, showing you the fancy Habsburg-era miner uniforms; historic maps and etchings of the networks of mines, and cutaway scenes of life below the surface; tools and mining equipment (including a variety of Aladdin-style oil lamps, and huge slings used to lower horses into the mines); a photo gallery of famous visitors, including kings, queens, popes,

KRAKÓW

presidents, and Lech Wałęsa; and a remarkably detailed model of the town of Wieliczka circa 1645.

Nearby: Near the parking lot, you'll see the **"Graduation Tower,"** a modern fort-like structure with a wooden walkway up top. The tower is designed to evaporate and then condense the supposedly very healthy brine from deep underground. The resulting moist, salty air is used to treat patients with lung problems. While locals are prescribed visits here, for most tourists it's not worth the extra money.

▲Nowa Huta

Nowa Huta (NOH-vah HOO-tah, "New Steel Works"), an enormous planned workers' town five miles east of central Kraków, offers a glimpse into the stark, grand-scale aesthetics of the communists. Although challenging to appreciate on your own, it's particularly well suited to a guided tour (options noted below). While Nowa Huta is lost on many visitors, it's a must for those curious for a look at large-scale artifacts of the communist period.

Getting There: Tram #4 goes from near Kraków's Old Town (catch the tram on the ring road near Kraków's main train station, at the Dworzec Główny stop) along John Paul II Avenue (Aleja Jana Pawła II) to Nowa Huta's main square, Plac Centralny (about 30 minutes total), then continues a few minutes farther to the main gate of the Tadeusz Sendzimir Steelworks—the end of the line. From there, it returns to Plac Centralny and back to Kraków.

Tours: For a thoughtful look at Nowa Huta, book with **Kraków Urban Tours** (see page 47). Or, for something looser and more off-the-wall, consider Mike Ostrowski's **Crazy Guides,** which offers private tours to Nowa Huta in genuine communist-era vehicles (mostly Trabants and Polski Fiats) with a laid-back hipster guide (€110/2 people for a 1.5-hour tour by car; €155/2 people for 2.5-hour version that adds a walking tour; see www.crazyguides. com for other options and to book, +48 500 091 200). If you're already hiring a **local guide** or **private driver** in Kraków, consider paying a little extra to add a quick spin through Nowa Huta.

Background: Nowa Huta was the communists' idea of paradise. It's one of only three towns outside the Soviet Union that were custom-built to showcase socialist ideals. (The others are Dunaújváros—once called Sztálinváros—south of Budapest, Hungary; and Eisenhüttenstadt—once called Stalinstadt—near Brandenburg, Germany.) Completed in just 10 years (1949-1959), Nowa Huta was built here primarily because the Soviets felt that smart and sassy Kraków needed a taste of heavy industry. Farmers and villagers were imported to live and work in Nowa Huta. Many new residents, who weren't accustomed to city living, brought along their livestock (which grazed in the fields around unfinished buildings).

For commies, Nowa Huta was idyllic: Dad would cheerily ride the tram into the steel factory, mom would dutifully keep house, and the kids could splash around at the artificial beach and learn how to cut perfect red stars out of construction paper. But Krakovians had the last laugh: Nowa Huta, along with Lech Wałęsa's shipyard in Gdańsk, was one of the home bases of the Solidarity strikes that eventually brought down the regime. Now, with the communists long gone, Nowa Huta remains a major suburb of Poland's cultural capital, with a whopping 200,000 residents.

Touring Nowa Huta: Nowa Huta's focal point used to be known simply as **Central Square** (Plac Centralny), but in a fit of poetic justice, it was later renamed for the anticommunist crusader, Ronald Reagan.

A map of Nowa Huta looks like a clamshell: a semicircular design radiating from Central/Reagan Square. Numbered streets fan out like spokes on a wheel, and trams zip workers directly to the immense factory.

Nowa Huta's designers found inspiration in a surprising source: the Italian Renaissance (which, thanks to the textbook Renaissance design of the Cloth Hall and other landmarks, Soviet architects considered typically Polish). Notice the elegantly predictable arches and galleries that would make Michelangelo proud. The settlement was loosely planned on the gardens of Versailles (both with axes radiating from a central hub).

Nowa Huta was delightfully orderly, primly painted, impeccably maintained, and downright beautiful...if a little boring. It was practical, too: Each of the huge apartment blocks is a self-contained unit, with its own grassy inner courtyard, school, and shops. Each is labeled with *Os.* (meaning "section"), plus a name and a number. Driveways, which appear to dead-end at underground garage doors, lead to vast fallout shelters.

Wander around. Poke into the courtyards, which often are filled with green parks, cheerful playgrounds, and ventilation for the fallout shelters beneath. The enclosed architecture makes you feel safe...but also *monitored.*

Reflect on what it would be like to live here. It may have been more pleasant than you imagine; the looming buildings are packed with happy little apartments filled with color, light, and warmth. These days, Nowa Huta is a very desirable place to live, partly because everything is smartly designed to be close at hand and easily connected to the city center by public transit—precisely what today's urban planners aspire to.

For those interested to learn more, Museum of Kraków operates a **Nowa Huta Museum** (Muzeum Nowej Huty) along the main road south of Central/Reagan Square (closed Mon-Tue, Os. Centrum E 1, www.muzeumkrakowa.pl).

The wide boulevard running northeast of Central/Reagan Square, now called Solidarity Avenue (Aleja Solidarności, lined with tracks for tram #4), leads to the **Tadeusz Sendzimir Steelworks.** Originally named for Lenin, this factory was supposedly built using plans stolen from a Pittsburgh plant. It was designed to be a cog in the communist machine—reliant on iron ore from Ukraine and therefore worthless unless Poland remained in the Soviet Bloc. Down from as many as 40,000 workers at its peak, the steelworks now employs about 10,000. Today, there's little to see other than the big sign, stern administration buildings, and smokestacks in the distance. Examine the twin offices flanking the sign—topped with turrets and a decorative frieze inspired by Italian palazzos, these continue the Renaissance theme of the housing districts.

Another worthwhile sight in Nowa Huta is the **Lord's Ark Church** (Arka Pana, several blocks northwest of Central/Reagan Square on Ulica Obrońców Krzyża). Back when he was archbishop of Kraków, Karol Wojtyła fought for years to build a church in this most communist of communist towns. When the regime refused, he insisted on conducting open-air Masses before crowds in fields, until the communists finally capitulated. No "official" building supplies  were allowed to be used; all materials had to be sourced through back channels. Consecrated in 1977, the Lord's Ark Church has a Le Corbusier–esque design that looks like a fat, exhausted Noah's Ark resting on Mount Ararat—encouraging Poles to persevere through the deluge of communism. Inside, the giant crucifix depicts Christ in agony...while also, seemingly, about to take flight. The Carrara marble altar was donated by Italian Catholics.

Kościuszko Mound (Kopiec Kościuszki)

On a sunny day, the parklands west of the Old Town are a fine place to get out of the city and commune with Krakovians at play. On the outskirts of town is the Kościuszko Mound, a nearly perfectly conical hill erected in 1823 to honor Polish and American military hero Tadeusz Kościuszko. The mound incorporates soil that was brought here from battlefields where the famous general fought, both in Poland and in the American Revolution. Later, under Habsburg rule, a citadel with a chapel was built around the mound, which provided a fine lookout over this otherwise flat terrain. And more recently, the hill was reinforced with steel and cement to prevent it from eroding away. You'll pay to enter the walls and walk to the top—up a curlicue path that makes the mound resemble a giant soft-serve cone—and inside you'll find a modest Kościuszko museum. While not too exciting, this is a pleasant place for an excursion on a nice day.

Cost and Hours: 24 zł, includes museum, mound open daily 9:00-dusk, museum open daily 9:30-19:00—shorter hours off-season, café, +48 12 425 1116, www.kopieckosciuszki.pl.

Getting There: Ride tram #1 (from in front of the Wyspiański Pavilion or the main post office) to the end of the line, called Salwator. From here, you can either follow the well-marked path uphill for 20 minutes or hop on bus #100 to the top.

Shopping in Kraków

Two of the most popular Polish souvenirs—amber and pottery—come from areas far from Kraków. You won't find any great bargains on those items here, but several shops specializing in them are listed below. Somewhat more local are the many wood carvings you'll see.

The **Cloth Hall,** smack-dab in the center of the Main Market Square, is the most convenient place to pick up Polish souvenirs. It has a good selection at respectable prices (summer Mon-Fri 9:00-18:00, Sat-Sun until 15:00—but many stalls remain open later; winter Mon-Fri 9:00-16:00, Sat-Sun until 15:00).

Jewelry

The popular **amber** *(bursztyn)* you'll see sold around town is found on northern Baltic shores; if you're also heading to Gdańsk, wait until you get there (for more on amber, see page 267). One unique alternative that's a bit more local is "**striped flint**" *(krzemień pasiasty),* a stratified stone that's polished to a high shine. It's mined in a very specific subregion near Kraków. Each piece has its own unique wavy, sandy patterns.

Jewelry shops abound in the Old Town. For a good selection of striped flint, amber, and other jewelry, try the no-name shop on **Plac Mariacki,** the little square facing the side entrance of St. Mary's Church; they also have a selection of Polish folk costumes in the basement (at #9—look for *Amber Souvenir* in window). A few

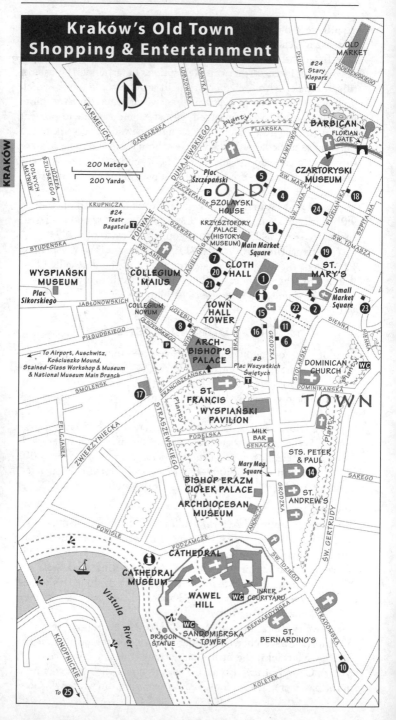

Kraków's Old Town Shopping & Entertainment

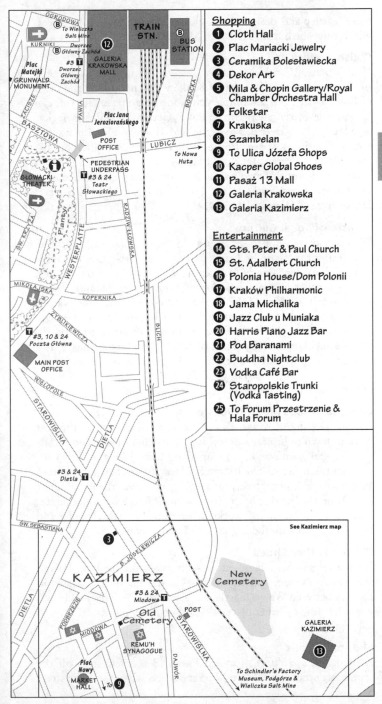

KRAKÓW

Shopping
1. Cloth Hall
2. Plac Mariacki Jewelry
3. Ceramika Bolesławiecka
4. Dekor Art
5. Mila & Chopin Gallery/Royal Chamber Orchestra Hall
6. Folkstar
7. Krakuska
8. Szambelan
9. To Ulica Józefa Shops
10. Kacper Global Shoes
11. Pasaż 13 Mall
12. Galeria Krakowska
13. Galeria Kazimierz

Entertainment
14. Sts. Peter & Paul Church
15. St. Adalbert Church
16. Polonia House/Dom Polonii
17. Kraków Philharmonic
18. Jama Michalika
19. Jazz Club u Muniaka
20. Harris Piano Jazz Bar
21. Pod Baranami
22. Buddha Nightclub
23. Vodka Café Bar
24. Staropolskie Trunki (Vodka Tasting)
25. To Forum Przestrzenie & Hala Forum

more jewelry and design shops cluster along Sławkowska street, which runs north from the Main Market Square.

Polish Pottery

"Polish pottery," with distinctive blue-and-white designs, is made in the region of Silesia, west of Kraków (in and around the town of Bolesławiec). But assuming you won't be going there, you can browse one of the shops in Kraków. **Ceramika Bolesławiecka,** on a busy urban street between the Old Town and Kazimierz, has a tasteful, affordable selection of pottery that's oriented more toward locals than tourists (closed Sun, Starowiślna 43). In the Old Town—and with inflated prices to match—two places face each other across Sławkowska street, just a block north of the Square: **Dekor Art** at #11 and **Mila** at #14.

A Taste of Local Culture

While tacky souvenir shops abound in the streets near the Square, two locally run places sell mementos more closely tied to Polish culture. **Folkstar,** along Grodzka street just south of the Square, has all manner of products adorned with the exuberantly colorful floral folk patterns of the local countryside (daily, Grodzka 14). **Krakuska,** named for (and run by) female Krakovians, is a lovingly cluttered hole-in-the-wall with more folk items (daily, Szewska 9).

Szambelan, a block south of the Main Market Square, is a fun concept for vodka lovers: Peruse the giant casks of three dozen different flavored vodkas, buy an empty bottle, and they'll fill and seal it to take home (daily, Gołębia 2 at the corner with Bracka).

Designer Shops along Ulica Józefa, in Kazimierz

As the epicenter of Kraków's hipster scene, Kazimierz is the best place in town to browse one-off boutiques (both design and fashion). Several good options line up along Ulica Józefa, mostly concentrated along a two-block stretch. Head just one block south from Plac Nowy on Estery street, turn right, and survey the possibilities (mostly on the left side of the street). You'll find jewelry boutiques, vintage ware, fascinating works by untrained artists, clothing and housewares from local designers, and much more.

Polish Leather Shoes

Kacper Global has a large outlet selling colorful, made-in-Poland shoes in styles from athletic to casual to stylish. They're located in the area between Wawel Castle and Kazimierz—a handy add-on if you're heading to either place (closed Sun, Stradomska 21, https://kacperglobal.pl).

Shopping Malls

A small but swanky mall called **Pasaż 13** is a few steps off the southeast corner of the Main Market Square, where Grodzka street enters the square. Enter the mall under the balcony marked *Pasaż 13*. You'll find a cool brick-industrial interior, with upscale international chains...and not much that's Polish (daily).

Two enormous shopping malls lie just beyond the tourist zone. The gigantic **Galeria Krakowska,** with nearly 300 shops, shares a square with the train station (daily, kids' play area upstairs from the main entry). Only slightly smaller is **Galeria Kazimierz** (daily, just a few blocks east of the Kazimierz sights, along the river at Podgórska 24).

Entertainment in Kraków

As a town full of both students and tourists, Kraków has plenty of fun options, especially at night.

IN THE OLD TOWN

For locations of the following places, see the "Kraków's Old Town Shopping and Entertainment" map, earlier).

Main Market Square

Intoxicating as the Square is by day, it's even better at night...pure enchantment. Have a meal or sip a drink at an outdoor café, or just grab a bench and enjoy the scene. There's often live al fresco music coming from somewhere (either at restaurants, at a temporary stage set up near the Town Hall Tower, or from talented buskers). You could spend hours doing slow laps around the Square after dark and never run out of diversions. For a great view over the Square at twilight, nurse a drink at **Café Szał**—on the Cloth Hall's upper terrace (long hours, enter through Gallery of 19th-Century Polish Art).

Concerts

You'll find a wide range of musical events, from tourist-oriented Chopin concerts and classical "greatest hits" selections in quaint old ballrooms and churches, to folk-dancing shows, to serious philharmonic performances. The best all-around site for concert information is KrakowCulture.pl; also look for the hefty, free quarterly magazine *Kraków Culture* (at the TI). Other good listings can be found at CracowConcerts.com and Facebook.com/orkiestrasm. Hotel lobbies are stocked with fliers, but to get all of your options, visit the TI north of the Square on Ulica Św. Jana, which specializes in cultural events.

Popular Classical Concerts: The three main choices are organ concerts in churches (usually at 17:00), orchestral or chamber music, or Chopin (either can happen anytime between 18:00 and 20:00). The going rate for most concerts is around 60-70 zł. Many are held in churches (such as **Sts. Peter and Paul** on Ulica Grodzka and **St. Adalbert** on the Square). You'll also find concerts in fancy mansions on or near the Main Market Square (including the **Polonia House/Dom Polonii** upstairs from Wierzynek restaurant at #14, near Ulica Grodzka; and the **Chopin Gallery**—also billed as the **Royal Chamber Orchestra Hall**—just up Sławkowska street from the Square at #14). Occasionally in summer, they're held in various gardens around town.

Serious Concerts: The **Kraków Philharmonic** (Filharmonia im Krakowie) puts on concerts aimed at local music lovers rather than tourists—more serious than crowd-pleasing—in a 700-seat hall just west of the Planty (Zwierzyniecka 1, + 48 506 625 430, www.filharmonia.krakow.pl).

Folk Music: Various venues present a small, hardworking ensemble of colorfully costumed Krakovian singers, dancers, and musicians who put on a fun little folk show as you dine. While this is obviously a very touristy scene, it's fun if you approach it with the right spirit—and the performers try hard to involve members of the audience in the polkas and circle dances. The Old Town lineup changes from year to year; start by checking at the historic **Jama Michalika,** with its dusty old Art Nouveau interior right along Floriańska street (150 zł includes dinner; Wed and Sat at 19:00; Floriańska 45, +48 12 422 1561, www.cracowconcerts.com). If you have a car, you can reach a more rustic venue 30 minutes outside the city: **Skansen Smaków,** filling a log cabin-like building, has shows each Thursday night (170 zł, book ahead, +48 12 357 1006, www.skansensmakow.pl).

Jazz

Kraków has a surprisingly thriving jazz scene. Several popular clubs hide on the streets surrounding the Main Market Square (open nightly, most shows start around 21:30, sometimes free or a cover of 20-30 zł for better shows). **Jazz Club u Muniaka** is the most famous and best for all-around jazz in a sophisticated cellar environment (Ulica Floriańska 3, +48 12 423 1205, www.jazzumuniaka.club). **Harris Piano Jazz Bar,** right on the Square (at #28), is more casual and offers a mix of traditional and updated "fusion" jazz, plus blues (+48 12 421 5741, www.harris.krakow.pl).

Nightlife in the Old Town

The entire Old Town is crammed with nightclubs and discos pumping loud music on weekends. On a Saturday, the pedestrian streets can be more crowded at midnight than at noon. Most of these nightspots are garden-variety dance clubs, lacking any personality or creativity. Worse, to save money, young locals stand out in front of nightclubs to drink their own booze (BYOB) rather than pay high prices for the drinks inside—making the streets that much more crowded and noisy. For low-key hanging out, people choose a café on the Square; otherwise, they head for Kazimierz, with a more interesting variety of nightspots.

That said, there are a few places right around the Square—in addition to the jazz options listed earlier—that are worth checking out.

First, at the southwest corner of the Square, go down the corridor with the Starbucks at #27, then find the staircase that descends to **Pod Baranami** ("Under the Rams"). This historic spot—once home to a subversive, counterculture cabaret show (and still hosting occasional performances)—feels like a mysterious speakeasy where well-dressed grown-ups meet to sip cocktails and relive their younger days. Cozy tables sprawl through several rooms (daily, +48 12 421 25 00, www.piwnicapodbaranami.pl).

Across the Square, on the east side (where it meets Grodzka street), are two more places worth checking out. At #6, head into the passage to find the **Buddha** nightclub, with comfy lounge sofas under awnings in an immaculately restored old courtyard. For something funkier and even more local, go down the passage at #19, which runs a surprisingly long distance through the block—passing a shot bar called Szototo. Soon you'll start to see tables for the **Herring Embassy;** you'll eventually emerge at **Stolarska street,** a still enjoyable but far less touristy scene (for more on the Herring Embassy and Stolarska, see pages 144-145).

If you have (or would like to cultivate) an appreciation for vodka, stop by the **Vodka Café Bar,** serving more than 100 types of vodkas, liquors, and hard drinks. You can buy a tasting flight board with six small shots; they'll help you narrow down your options. It's a mellow, uncluttered space that lets you focus on the vodka and the company (daily from 15:00, weekends from 13:00, Mikołajska 5).

IN KAZIMIERZ

Aside from the Old Town's gorgeous Square, Kraków's best area to hang out after dark is Kazimierz. Although this is also the former Jewish quarter, the Jewish Sabbath has nothing to do with the bar scene here. You can, however, still hear traditional Jewish music called klezmer. For tips on enjoying a concert of klezmer music, see the sidebar.

Bars and Clubs

Squeezed between centuries-old synagogues and cemeteries are enticing hangouts running the full gamut from sober and tasteful to wild and clubby. The classic recipe for a Kazimierz bar: Find a dilapidated old storefront, fill it with ramshackle furniture, turn the lights down low, pipe in old-timey jazz music from the 1920s, and sprinkle with alcohol. Serves one to two dozen hipsters. After

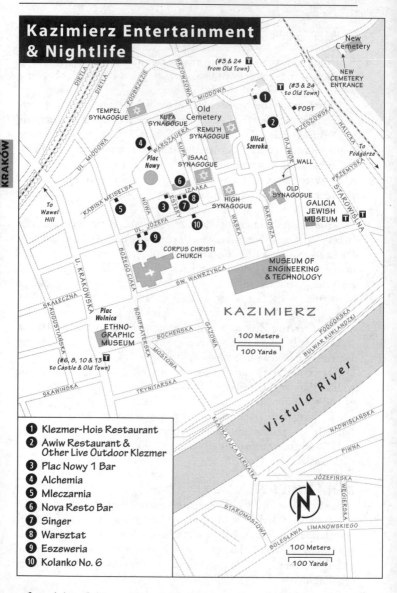

Kazimierz Entertainment & Nightlife

❶ Klezmer-Hois Restaurant
❷ Awiw Restaurant &
   Other Live Outdoor Klezmer
❸ Plac Nowy 1 Bar
❹ Alchemia
❺ Mleczarnia
❻ Nova Resto Bar
❼ Singer
❽ Warsztat
❾ Eszeweria
❿ Kolanko No. 6

a few clubs of this type caught on, a more diverse cross-section of nightspots began to move in, including some loud dance clubs. The whole area is bursting with life. For locations, see the map on this page.

On and near Plac Nowy: The highest concentration of bars rings the Plac Nowy market square. Do a loop to browse your options. **Plac Nowy 1** specializes in Polish microbrews and upmarket

KRAKÓW

Klezmer Music in Kazimierz

On a balmy summer night, Kazimierz's main square, Ulica Szeroka, is filled with the haunting strains of klezmer—traditional Jewish music from 19th-century Poland, generally with violin, string bass, clarinet, and accordion. Skilled klezmer musicians can make their instruments weep or laugh like human voices. There are two main ways to enjoy some klezmer music: at a restaurant or at a concert.

Restaurants: Several eateries on Ulica Szeroka offer klezmer music, typically starting between 19:00 and 20:00. The musicians move from room to room, and the menus tend to be a mix of traditional Jewish and Polish cuisine (which are quite similar). But don't come here just for the food—it's an afterthought to the music. While most places claim to do concerts "nightly year-round," they can be canceled anytime it's slow (especially off-season)—confirm ahead.

Some old-school restaurants offer reasonably priced food but charge 40 zł per person for the music. Probably your best choice is the well-established **$$$ Klezmer-Hois,** filling a venerable former Jewish ritual bathhouse and making you feel like you're dining in a rich grandparent's home (daily 8:00-22:00, at #6, +48 12 411 1245, www.klezmer.pl).

Some restaurants with outdoor seating on Ulica Szeroka offer "free" al fresco klezmer music for customers (though the food tends to be that much more expensive). Because the music is free, anybody (at neighboring restaurants, or simply strolling past) can enjoy a taste of klezmer. Just show up, comparison-shop music and menus, and—if you like what you hear—pick a place for dinner or a drink. **$$$ Awiw** (at #13, overpriced food) is one such option.

Within the **Old Town,** there are also sometimes klezmer concerts at Sławkowska 14 (a.k.a. the Royal Chamber Orchestra Hall, www.cracowconcerts.com). However, for most visitors it's worth the easy trek to Kazimierz to enjoy a concert.

Don't worry too much about seeking out a particular musician—they are equally good, and each brings a unique style to the music. Many venues share musicians, so on any given night it's hard to predict who's performing where. Bottom line: If you're interested in klezmer music, you can't go wrong in Kazimierz.

pub grub in a bright, sleek (and arguably "un-Kazimierz") setting. Across the square, **Alchemia,** one of the first—and still one of the best—bars in Kazimierz, is candlelit, cluttered, and claustrophobic, with cavelike rooms crowded with rickety old furniture, plus a cellar used for live performances (Estery 5, www.alchemia.com.pl). Late at night, the little windows in the Plac Nowy **market hall** do a big business selling *zapiekanki* (baguette with toppings) to hungry bar-hoppers.

On Rabina Meiselsa street, just a half-block off Plac Nowy, under the arch to a characteristic courtyard is **Mleczarnia,** a beer garden with rickety tables squeezed under the trees and its cozy old-fashioned pub across the street (at #20).

Near Isaac Synagogue: A block east of Plac Nowy, a few more places cluster on the wide street in front of Isaac Synagogue. The huge **Nova Resto Bar** dominates the scene with a long covered terrace, a vast interior, and seating in their courtyard. This feels upscale and a bit pretentious compared to many of the others, but it's the place to be seen (Estery 18, www.novarestobar.pl). Facing Nowa are some smaller, more accessible options: **Singer** is classy and mellow, with most of its tables made of old sewing machines (Estery 20), while **Warsztat** has an exploding-instruments-factory ambience (Izaaka 3, www.restauracjawarsztat.pl).

On Józefa Street: Yet more good bars are just a short block south. Along Józefa, you'll find a pair of classic Kazimierz joints: **Eszeweria,** which wins the "best atmosphere" award, feels like a Polish speakeasy that's been in mothballs for the last 90 years—a low-key, unpretentious, and inviting hangout (Józefa 9). A block up, **Kolanko No. 6** has a cozy bar up front, a pleasant beer garden in the inner courtyard, and a fun events hall in back (Józefa 17, www.kolanko.net).

Beach Bar on the Riverbank

South of the river, roughly between Kazimierz and Wawel Castle, **Forum Przestrzenie** fills a dilapidated concrete hotel—a mostly abandoned dinosaur from com-munist times. But now the ground floor has been taken over by a lively hipster bar—especially appealing in the balmy summer months, when comfy low-slung chairs sprawl across a tidy lawn and a pebbly "beach" with views across the Vistula to Wawel Castle. They serve coffee, wine, beer, summery cocktails, and a wide variety of bar food. A few artists and designers also have boutiques here, and in the summer, they have live music and DJs (open daily in good weather until late, skip the trip if it's not nice out, Ulica Marii Konopnickiej 28, +48 515 424 724, www.forumprzestrzenie.com). The enticing **Hala Forum** food hall is next door, and you may also see a Ferris wheel and/or a hot-air balloon ride nearby—making this lively scene easy to spot from afar.

Sleeping in Kraków

Kraków has ample accommodation choices, and healthy competition keeps prices reasonable and makes choosing a hotel fun rather than frustrating. I've focused my accommodations in two areas: in and near the Old Town; and in Kazimierz, a hipper, more affordable neighborhood that's home to both the old Jewish quarter and a thriving dining and nightlife zone.

Both neighborhoods can suffer from discos that thump loud music on weekend nights to attract roving gangs of rowdy drinkers. I've tried to avoid the areas most plagued by noise, but to help your odds, ask for a quiet room when you reserve...and bring earplugs.

IN AND NEAR THE OLD TOWN

Most of my listings are inside (or within a block or two of) the Planty park that rings the Old Town. Sleeping inside the Old Town comes with pros (maximum atmosphere; handy location for sightseeing and dining) and cons (high prices; the potential for noise—especially on weekends—as noted earlier). Places just outside the Old Town are still handy, but quieter and cheaper. If you need a room in a pinch, several slick, international chains (Ibis, Mercure, Puro) have branches near the train station.

$$$$ Hotel Copernicus is the top splurge inside Kraków's Old Town, with 29 rooms in a historic shell on one of the finest, most serene streets in the historical center. The service is polished—verging on snobby—and the rooms are decorated with heavy beams, hand-painted frescoes, and antique furniture (air-con, elevator, Kanonicza 16, +48 12 424 3400, www.hotel.com.pl, copernicus@hotel.com.pl).

$$$ Donimirski Boutique Hotels are a reliably comfortable option that set the bar for quality and value (www.donimirski.com). All have friendly staff, discounts for my readers, and classy little extras that add up to a memorable hotel experience. **Hotel Polski Pod Białym Orłem** ("White Eagle") has 60 classic rooms conveniently located near the Florian Gate just inside the Old Town walls (RS%, apartments available, air-con, elevator, Ulica Pijarska 17, +48 12 422 1144, hotel.polski@donimirski.com). **Hotel Gródek** offers 23 rooms a three-minute walk behind St. Mary's Church, on a quiet dead-end street overlooking the Planty park (RS%, air-con, elevator, pay parking, Na Gródku 4, +48 12 431 9030, grodek@donimirski.com). They also have a six-room annex, **Hotel Pugetów,** that can be rented by a small group (Ulica Starowiślna 15A, pugetow@donimirski.com).

$$ Hotel Senacki is a business-class place renting 20 comfortable rooms between Wawel Castle and the Main Market Square. The staff is warm, professional, and conscientious, and the loca-

KRAKÓW

> ## Sleep Code
>
> Hotels in this book are categorized according to the average price of a standard double room with breakfast in high season. 4 zł = about $1.
>
> **$$$$**   **Splurge:** Most rooms over 900 zł (€200)
> **$$$**   **Pricier:** 700-900 zł (€150-200)
> **$$**   **Moderate:** 500-700 zł (€100-150)
> **$**   **Budget:** 250-500 zł (€50-100)
> **¢**   **Backpacker:** Under 250 zł (€50)
> **RS%**   **Rick Steves discount**
>
> Unless otherwise noted, credit cards are accepted and hotel staff speak basic English. Comparison-shop by checking prices at several hotels (on each hotel's own website, on a booking site, or by email). For the best deal, *book directly with the hotel.* Ask for a discount if paying in cash; if the listing includes **RS%,** request a Rick Steves discount.

tion is perfect, making this an ideal spot to stay. Top-floor "attic" rooms have low beams, skylight windows, and a flight of stairs after the elevator (air-con, elevator to all but the attic rooms, ask about nearby pay parking, Ulica Grodzka 51, +48 12 422 7686, www.hotelsenacki.pl, senacki@hotelsenacki.pl).

$$ Grand Ascot Hotel sits just beyond the end of the lively, pedestrianized Krupnicza dining drag—a pleasant walk away from the Old Town. With 63 business-class rooms over a plush lobby, it feels a bit posh yet reasonably priced (family rooms, air-con, elevator, sauna and fitness area, Józefa Szujskiego 4, +48 12 446 7600, www.grandascot.pl, rezerwacja@grandascot.pl).

$$ Hotel Wawel has 39 rooms on a well-located street that's quieter than the Old Town norm. It's colorful and serene; above the swanky marble lobby are hallways creatively painted with the history of the building and images from around Kraków. Out back, a fountain gurgles in a cute little courtyard (air-con, elevator—but doesn't go to top floor, Ulica Poselska 22, +48 12 424 1300, www.hotelwawel.pl, hotel@hotelwawel.pl).

$$ Bracka 6, conveniently located one short block off the Main Market Square, is a sort of a hybrid between a hotel and an apartment house. The 16 stylish rooms—with sleek lines, lots of glass, and exposed brick—each have a kitchen, so breakfast is optional and extra (at a nearby café). The lack of full hotel amenities keeps the prices affordable for this level of modern elegance. In this central location, request a quieter room in back (air-con, elevator, laundry service, limited reception hours—let them know when you're arriving, Bracka 6, +48 608 000 609, www.bracka6.pl, info@bracka6.pl).

$ Hotel Wielopole sits a block outside the Planty, on the way to the lively Kazimierz district. Its 35 tight rooms are tucked down a side street just past the main post office, facing a big Holiday Inn. The staff are proud of their attentive service, and they post an informative little newsletter daily (air-con, elevator, Italian restaurant in cellar, Wielopole 3, +48 12 422 1475, www.wielopole.pl, office@wielopole.pl).

$ Hotel Amber sits on a dreary urban street just outside the Planty park but still less than a 10-minute walk from the Square. Run by the same company as Hotel Wielopole (described above), it has an equally pleasant emphasis on welcoming service. The hotel has two parts: 18 perfectly fine, if smallish, rooms in the original building; and 20 slightly more upscale rooms in the newer "design" section. Both parts share a small gym, sauna, and garden in back (air-con, elevator, Garbarska 8-10, +48 12 421 0606, www.hotel-amber.pl, office@hotel-amber.pl).

$ Cracowdays is the farthest of my listings from the center of town, about a 15-minute walk away (a tram can cut a few minutes off the trek). But it's also a notch more refined than the places listed previously. It sits in a pleasant residential neighborhood west of the Main Market Square, with eight beautifully decorated and thoughtfully tended rooms, all sharing a central kitchen (plus two stand-alone studio apartments in another building). Owner Magdalena, a great traveler, prides herself on creating an atmosphere where fellow wanderers can feel welcome far from home (air-con, Grabowskiego 7, +48 604 460 860, www.cracowdays.com, reservation@cracowdays.com).

$ Kraków for You Apartments offers 16 studios and one- and two-bedroom units with kitchenettes around a courtyard along one of Kraków's most happening streets, just a few steps off the Main Market Square. A few of their rooms are elsewhere in the Old Town (reception open daily 10:00-20:00, request quieter courtyard room, lots of stairs with no elevator, go down the passage at Grodzka 4, +48 660 541 085, www.krakowforyou.com, info@krakowforyou.com, Mikołaj).

¢ Globtroter Guest House offers 17 basic, somewhat stuffy, rustic-feeling rooms with high ceilings and big beams around a serene garden courtyard. Marek (Mark) conscientiously focuses on value—keeping prices reasonable by not offering needless extras (RS%, 2 people can cram into a single to save money, family rooms, breakfast at nearby café extra, pay laundry service, fun 700-year-old brick cellar lounge, go down passageway at #7 at the square called Plac Szczepański, +48 12 422 4123, www.globtroter-krakow.com, globtroter@globtroter-krakow.com).

KRAKÓW

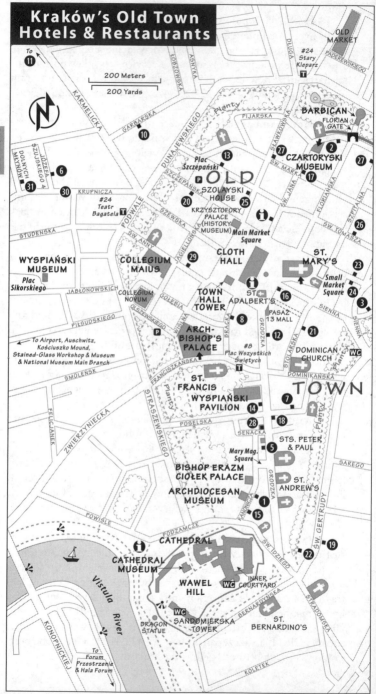

Kraków's Old Town Hotels & Restaurants

To 11

200 Meters
200 Yards

OLD MARKET

#24 Stary Kleparz T

BARBICAN

FLORIAN GATE

27 CZARTORYSKI MUSEUM
2
17

10

31
6
30
#24 Teatr Bagatela T

Plac Szczepański
13
SZOLAYSKI HOUSE
20
25
KRZYSZTOFORY PALACE (HISTORY MUSEUM)
Main Market Square

OLD

27

26

WYSPIAŃSKI MUSEUM
Plac Sikorskiego

COLLEGIUM MAIUS
29
CLOTH HALL
ST. MARY'S
23

Small Market Square
24
3

COLLEGIUM NOVUM

TOWN HALL TOWER
ST. ADALBERT'S
16
8
PASAŻ 13 MALL
12
21
DOMINICAN CHURCH
WC

ARCH-BISHOP'S PALACE
#8 Plac Wszystkich Świętych

To Airport, Auschwitz, Kościuszko Mound, Stained-Glass Workshop & Museum & National Museum Main Branch

ST. FRANCIS
WYSPIAŃSKI PAVILION
14
7

TOWN

28
18

Mary Mag. Square
5
STS. PETER & PAUL

BISHOP ERAZM CIOŁEK PALACE
ARCHDIOCESAN MUSEUM
1
15
ST. ANDREW'S

CATHEDRAL
CATHEDRAL MUSEUM
WAWEL HILL
INNER COURTYARD
WC

22
19

ST. BERNARDINO'S

DRAGON STATUE
WC
SANDOMIERSKA TOWER

Vistula River

To Forum Przestrzenie & Hala Forum

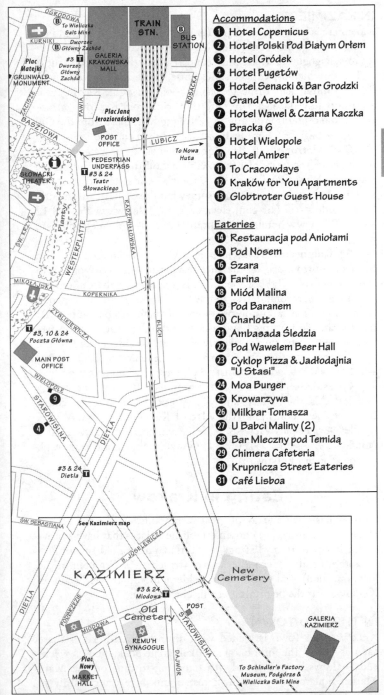

KRAKÓW

Accommodations

1. Hotel Copernicus
2. Hotel Polski Pod Białym Orłem
3. Hotel Gródek
4. Hotel Pugetów
5. Hotel Senacki & Bar Grodzki
6. Grand Ascot Hotel
7. Hotel Wawel & Czarna Kaczka
8. Bracka 6
9. Hotel Wielopole
10. Hotel Amber
11. To Cracowdays
12. Kraków for You Apartments
13. Globtroter Guest House

Eateries

14. Restauracja pod Aniołami
15. Pod Nosem
16. Szara
17. Farina
18. Miód Malina
19. Pod Baranem
20. Charlotte
21. Ambasada Śledzia
22. Pod Wawelem Beer Hall
23. Cyklop Pizza & Jadłodajnia "U Stasi"
24. Moa Burger
25. Krowarzywa
26. Milkbar Tomasza
27. U Babci Maliny (2)
28. Bar Mleczny pod Temidą
29. Chimera Cafeteria
30. Krupnicza Street Eateries
31. Café Lisboa

IN KAZIMIERZ

Kazimierz is both Kraków's Jewish heart and soul, and its trendiest eating and nightlife zone. Sleeping here puts you in close proximity to synagogues and klezmer concerts, as well as to food trucks and hip nightclubs (expect some noise, especially on weekends). Keep in mind that, while pleasant in its own right, Kazimierz is a 20-minute walk or a 5-minute tram ride from Kraków's atmospheric old center (for details on getting to Kazimierz from the Old Town, see page 95). For locations, see the map on page 148.

$$$ Metropolitan Boutique Hotel is an upscale refuge a block before the heart of Kazimierz (just off the busy road on the way to Kraków's Old Town). Its 59 rooms—with exposed brick and slick modern style—sit along a somewhat dreary but conveniently located side street (air-con, elevator, gym, Joselewicza 19, +48 12 442 7500, www.hotelmetropolitan.pl, hotel@hotelmetropolitan.pl).

$$ Rubinstein Residence sits right in the middle of Ulica Szeroka—surrounded by klezmer restaurants and synagogues, in the heart of the neighborhood. It fills a painstakingly restored old townhouse (parts of it dating to the 15th century) with heavy wood beams and 30 swanky rooms—some of them palatial suites that incorporate old features like frescoes and pillars. The rooftop terrace—open to the public, with views over Kazimierz and to the Old Town—sets this place above (air-con, elevator, Szeroka 12, +48 12 384 0000, www.rubinstein.pl, recepcja@rubinstein.pl).

¢ Residence Tournet, well run by friendly Piotr and Sylwia Działowy, is your cheap-and-cheery option, offering 18 colorful, perfumed rooms near the edge of Kazimierz toward Wawel Castle (elevator plus a few stairs, reception open 7:00-22:00, Ulica Miodowa 7, +48 12 292 0088, www.accommodation.krakow.pl, tournet@nocleg.krakow.pl).

Eating in Kraków

Kraków has a wide array of great restaurants. As the food scene changes constantly, I've chosen established places that have a proven track record. In my listings, you'll find a mix of old-school Polish eateries and modern alternatives (which are still rooted in the local tradition). You could also consider a food tour (see "Tours in Krakow" near the beginning of this chapter).

IN THE OLD TOWN

Kraków's Old Town is loaded with dining options. All of these eateries (except the milk bars) are likely to be booked up on weekends—always reserve ahead. It's tempting to dine on the Main Market Square; however, most restaurants here cater mainly to

KRAKÓW

Restaurant Code

Eateries in this book are categorized according to the average cost of a typical main course. Drinks, desserts, and splurge items (steak and seafood) can raise the price considerably. 4 zł = about $1.

$$$$	**Splurge:** Most main courses over 90 zł (€20)
$$$	**Pricier:** 70-90 zł (€15-20)
$$	**Moderate:** 50-70 zł (€10-15)
$	**Budget:** Under Under 50 zł (€10)

In Poland, a milk bar or takeout spot is **$**; a basic sit-down eatery is **$$**; a casual but more upscale restaurant is **$$$**; and a swanky splurge is **$$$$**.

---

tourists and—other than Szara, recommended below—don't provide the best value for the money. To enjoy the same experience more affordably, have just a drink on the Square and dine elsewhere.

$$$ Restauracja pod Aniołami ("Under Angels") offers a dressy, candlelit atmosphere on a wonderful covered patio or in a deep, steep, romantic cellar with rough wood and medieval vaults. Peruse the elaborately described menu of medieval nobles' dishes. The cuisine is traditional Polish, with an emphasis on grilled meats and trout (on a wood-fired grill). Every meal begins with *smalec* (spread made with lard, fried onion, bacon, and apple). Don't go here if you're in a hurry—only if you want to really slow down and enjoy your dinner. Reservations are smart (daily from 13:00, Ulica Grodzka 35, +48 12 421 3999, www.podaniolami.pl).

$$$$ Pod Nosem ("Under the Nose") is a worthwhile splurge for refined, updated Polish cuisine in a sophisticated, untouristy atmosphere. It's tucked at the far end of sleepy Kanonicza lane, just beyond the tourists and before Wawel Castle. In a tight dining room that skips the kitsch, they offer an extensive wine list and a short menu of artfully executed Polish dishes (daily, Kanonicza 22, +48 12 376 0014, www.kanonicza22.com).

$$$$ Szara owns a prime location right on the Main Market Square, in the 14th-century Kamienica Szara ("Grey House"). The restaurant is a well-regarded option for a higher-end meal of elevated Polish cuisine, with a short menu of meat and fish dishes. The interior feels rich and dressy, with gilded vaults and Józef Mehoffer-painted ceilings soaring overhead, and the outdoor tables own a prime location facing the Square. If you're looking to splurge memorably for a special occasion, this is a fine choice (daily, Rynek Główny 6, +48 12 421 6669, www.szara.pl).

$$ Czarna Kaczka ("Black Duck") features Polish fare with an emphasis on duck (of course) and dumplings. The cozy, steamy, arched interior is a central choice for traditional food done well, but not too rustic. As it fills up, book ahead (daily from 13:00, next to Hotel Wawel at Poselska 22, +48 500 195 149, https://czarnakaczka.pl).

$$$ Farina, specializing in international/Mediterranean fish and seafood dishes from chef Monika Turasiewicz, is a dressy, upscale-feeling, well-established choice for a memorable meal. It's smart to reserve ahead (closed Mon, Św. Marka 16, +48 519 399 474, https://farina.com.pl).

$$ Miód Malina ("Honey Raspberry") is an acceptably kitschy Polish-Italian fusion restaurant filled with the comforting aroma of its wood-fired oven. The menu is mostly Polish, with a few Italian dishes thrown in. Sit in the cozy, warmly painted interior or out in the courtyard (reservations smart, daily, Ulica Grodzka 40, +48 12 430 0411, www.miodmalina.pl).

$$$ Pod Baranem ("Under the Ram") is a solid midrange bet for well-executed, traditional Polish food. Respected by locals, it sits just outside the tourist chaos, quietly facing the Planty near Wawel Castle. Several cozy rooms—tasteful but not stuffy—sprawl through a homey old building (daily from 13:00, Św. Gertrudy 21, +48 12 429 4022, www.podbaranem.com).

Youthful Style at Plac Szczepański: While seemingly every corner of the Old Town is jammed with tourists, the pleasant square called Plac Szczepański—tucked at the northwest corner of the Old Town—feels more like the terrain of university students. While just two short blocks from the Square, this small array of cafés and galleries has a vibe that's more Warsaw-urbane than ye olde Kraków. Among these, **$ Charlotte** is a winner—it's a classy, French-feeling bakery/café/wine bar. They make their own breads and pastries in the basement (with lots of seating—you can watch the bakers work if you come early enough in the morning), cultivate a stay-awhile coffeehouse ambience upstairs, and throw in a few square-facing sidewalk tables to boot. The food is light café fare—sandwiches, pastries, and salads—rather than a filling dinner (daily, Plac Szczepański 2, +48 12 431 5610).

On Stolarska Street: Stolarska street, a neatly pedestrianized, oddly untrammeled "embassy row" just a block away from the Main Market Square, is worth exploring for a meal or a drink. Stolarska has a fun variety of more locals-oriented bars and cafés. Begin at the Small Market Square (Maly Rynek) behind St. Mary's Church and head south. On the left, look for the ridiculously long sign that perfectly identifies the business: *Pierwszy Lokal Na Stolarskiej Po Lewej Stronie Idąc Od Małego Rynku* ("The first pub on the left side of Stolarska coming from the Small Market Square"). Notice that this once-sleepy street is lined with embassies and consulates—it's easy to spot the flags of Germany, the US, and France. On the left, in the stretch of cafés under canopies, you'll see the **$$ Ambasada Śledzia** ("Herring Embassy"), with a divey, youthful atmosphere and a "Polish tapas" approach: A dozen different types of herring and other light meals, plus a variety of vodka to wash it down, are posted on the menu. You'll order at the bar, then find a table or take it to go (daily, Stolarska 8). Across the street and 50 paces back up, the Pasaż Bielaka (look for the low-profile stone doorway at #5) runs through the middle of the block all the way out to the Main Market Square (emerging at Rynek Główny #19); in here is another sprawling branch of the Herring Embassy.

Beer Hall: The rollicking Czech-style **$ Pod Wawelem** ("Under Wawel") is right on the Planty park near Wawel Castle. It's packed with locals seeking big, sloppy, greasy portions of meaty fare, with giant mugs of various beers on tap (including Polish and Bavarian). Choose between the bustling interior and the outdoor terrace right on the Planty. Locals come here not for a romantic dinner but for a rowdy evening out with friends (different specials every day—such as giant schnitzel, pork ribs, or roasted chicken; daily, Ulica Św. Gertrudy 26-29, +48 12 421 2336).

Pizza: Cozy and charming **$ Cyklop** has good wood-fired pizzas, with 10 tables wrapped around the cook and his busy oven (daily, near St. Mary's Church at Mikołajska 16, +48 12 421 6603).

Burgers (and Vegan Burgers): Gourmet hamburgers are all the rage in Poland. One of the best options in the center is **$ Moa Burger,** with a dozen different types of big, sloppy, "New Zealand-style" hamburgers. Order at the counter, then find a seat at a shared table. This isn't "fast food"—everything is made to order (daily, Mikołajska 3, +48 12 421 2144). For vegan burgers, a handy place in the center is **$ Krowarzywa** (a pun roughly meaning both "Cow Alive" and "Cow Vegetable")—with a hip atmosphere and an enticing menu of meatless options (daily, Sławkowska 8, +48 531 777 136).

Milk Bars and Other Quick, Cheap, Traditional Eats

Kraków is a good place to try the cheap cafeterias called "milk bars." For pointers on eating at a milk bar, review the sidebar on page 26.

$ Milkbar Tomasza is an upgraded milk bar popular with local students. Modern and relatively untouristy, it serves big, splittable portions of high-quality food—a mix of Polish and international—plus breakfast dishes all day (great big salads, daily specials, open Tue-Sun until 18:00, closed Mon, Ulica Tomasza 24, +48 12 422 1706).

$ U Babci Maliny ("Granny Raspberry"), with a grinning Granny on the sign, is well established and much appreciated for its big portions of flavorful traditional food. One location, frequented almost entirely by Krakovians and designed for university students and staff, is tucked into an inner courtyard of the Science Academy. Find the door at Sławkowska 17, then make your way into the inner courtyard, with an entrance to a rustic cellar where it looks like a kitschy cottage bomb went off. Another location is across the street from the National Theater building at Szpitalna 38. The main floor, also done up in gaudy cottage style, is self-service and budget priced, while the cellar—with a drawing-room vibe—has table service and slightly higher prices (both are open daily). Both locations have walls of photos of the owner posing with bodybuilders and ultimate fighters...not quite in keeping with the country theme.

$ Jadłodajnia "U Stasi" is a throwback that makes you feel like you're in on Kraków's best-kept secret. Its hidden location—tucked at the far end of the passage with the recommended Cyklop pizzeria—attracts a wide range of loyal local clientele, from hardscrabble seniors to politicians, artists, and actors. They're all here for well-executed, unpretentious, home-style Polish lunch grub. There can be a bit of a language barrier, so go with the flow: Pick up the English menu as you enter, find a table, wait for them to take your order, enjoy your meal, then pay as you leave. This is an excellent value and a real, untouristy Polish experience. The short menu changes every day—and when they're out, they're out (Mon-Fri until 17:00, closed Sat-Sun, Mikołajskiej 16).

Throwback Milk Bars on Grodzka Street: Just a couple of blocks south of the Main Market Square, on busy Ulica Grodzka, two classic milk bars some-how survive the onslaught of the modern world. First, at the corner with Senacka, is the remarkably basic and traditional milk bar, **$ Bar Mleczny pod Temidą.** The next best thing to a time machine to the communist era, this place has grumpy monolingual service, a mostly local clientele, and cheap but good food (daily). A few more

steps down, also on the right (just before the two churches), **$ Bar Grodzki** is a single tight little room with shared tables. They specialize in tasty potato pancake dishes *(placki ziemniaczane).* Order high on the menu and try the rich and hearty "Hunter's Delight"—potato pancake with sausage, beef, melted cheese, and spicy sauce. The English menu posted by the counter makes ordering easy. Order, sit, and wait to be called to fetch your food (daily).

$ Chimera Cafeteria, just off the Main Market Square, is a handy spot for a quick lunch in the center. It serves fast traditional meals to a steady stream of students. You'll order at the counter—choose a big plate (6 items) or medium plate (4 items) and select from an array of salads and main dishes by pointing to what you'd like. Then eat on their quiet, covered garden courtyard (good for vegetarians, daily, near the university at Ulica Św. Anny 3). I'd skip their expensive full-service restaurant (in the basement), which shares an entryway.

Lively Student Zone Just West of the Old Town

A few minutes' walk west of the Old Town is a trendy, energetic neighborhood with more students than tourists. If ye olde Kraków is getting a little olde, this area is a closer, easier escape than Kazimierz. The spine of this zone is **Krupnicza street,** a pedestrianized strip that begins just across the ring road from the Planty. To get here, head out Szewska street from the middle of the Square (to the west), cross the busy ring road, and fork left at the Teatr Bagatela. Several eateries along here are worth considering: **$ Meat & Go,** a cellar restaurant with hearty meat dishes (at #3 on the right); a pod of **$ food trucks** (just beyond #6 on the left, under the mural); **$$ Dynia,** with a hip brick interior and an inviting garden courtyard (at #20 on the left); and **$ Meho Café,** a casual place with drinks, light food, and delightful seating in the garden behind the Józef Mehoffer House Museum (at #26 on the left). At the end of the street, hook right to find the best place in the area for a sweet treat: **$ Café Lisboa,** which serves great coffee and excellent *pastéis de nata*, the national dessert of Portugal—made by a Pole who went to Belém to learn how to make it just right (Dolnych Młynów 3).

IN KAZIMIERZ

The entire district is bursting with lively cafés and bars—it's a happening night scene. For locations, see the map on the next page.

Fast and Cheap

Kazimierz has some great takeout and street food—handy for a lunch break from daytime sightseeing here, or for an affordable dinner break from bar-hopping.

$ Food Trucks: Kazimierz has two pods of fun-to-browse food trucks—most open daily for lunch and dinner. **Judah Square,** named for its big graffiti mural by an Israeli street artist, is tucked at the southern fringe of the tourists' Kazimierz, near the old tram depot (corner of Św. Wawrzyńca and Wąska). Mainstays here include Andrus (super-decadent and gooey roasted pork sandwiches), Boogie Truck burgers, Yatai sushi, Belgian-style fries, Pan Kumpir baked potatoes, and the beloved Chimney Cake Bakery, which

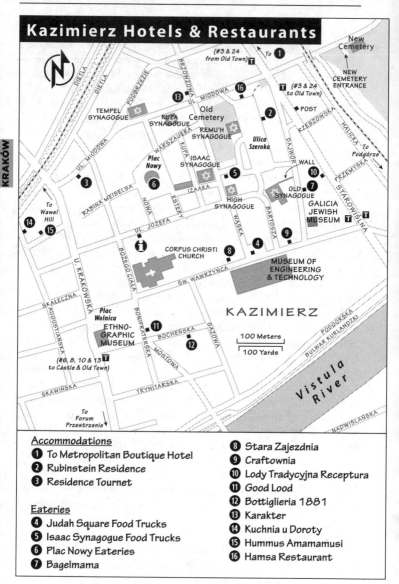

Kazimierz Hotels & Restaurants

Accommodations
1 To Metropolitan Boutique Hotel
2 Rubinstein Residence
3 Residence Tournet

Eateries
4 Judah Square Food Trucks
5 Isaac Synagogue Food Trucks
6 Plac Nowy Eateries
7 Bagelmama
8 Stara Zajezdnia
9 Craftownia
10 Lody Tradycyjna Receptura
11 Good Lood
12 Bottiglieria 1881
13 Karakter
14 Kuchnia u Doroty
15 Hummus Amamamusi
16 Hamsa Restaurant

rotisserie-roasts dough and sugar into a sweet and crunchy cake, then fills it with ice cream and other toppings—a Hungarian treat. Right in the heart of the tourist zone, another food truck pod fills a vacant lot **behind Isaac Synagogue,** just steps from Ulica Szeroka. Here you'll find painted-wooden-pallet furniture, hammocks, twinkle lights, and a mellow vibe. Likely options include hot dogs, Mexican tacos, açaí smoothies, burgers, veggie wraps, Thai ice cream, and—of course—more chimney cakes. Note that any and all of these could reshuffle their carts—or be gone entirely, replaced by a ritzy new building—at any moment. But it's clear that, in general, Kazimierz's food-truck scene is here to stay.

Polish Fast Food on Plac Nowy: The centerpiece of the Plac Nowy market is a circular brick slaughterhouse, which has recently been taken over by Kazimierz foodies. Each of the shop windows—which once housed butchers and basic Polish grub—is now operated by a different pop-up eatery, most of them serving the Poles' beloved *zapiekanki:* toasted baguettes with cheese, ketchup, and a bewildering array of other toppings. You can take a spin around the building to survey your options—noting where the lines are longest (locals know which *zapiekanek* is best).

Bagels: A casual shop popular with expats and locals, **$ Bagelmama** is run by an American named Nava (who once worked as a private chef for tennis star John McEnroe). The bagels come dressed with a wide variety of spreads, and they also sell sandwiches, soups, salads, desserts, and fresh juices. You can eat in or get it to go (Mon-Fri until 16:00, Sat-Sun until 17:00, Ulica Dajwór 10, +48 12 346 1646).

Beer: Beer lovers find two different experiences along Św. Wawrzyńca. **$$ Stara Zajezdnia** ("Old Tram Depot") fills exactly that—a cavernous old industrial hall—with tables and happy drinkers, draining huge mugs of the five different types of beer brewed on the premises (You can also order a sampler.) In good weather, the vast courtyard out front becomes an idyllic, self-service beer garden filled with relaxing lounge chairs (Św. Wawrzyńca 12, +48 664 323 988). For craft beer aficionados, **Craftownia** has 18 Polish microbrews on tap (and many more by the bottle) in a nondescript setting (daily from 14:00, Św. Wawrzyńca 22, +48 515 010 565).

Hip Bars with Food: Several of the bars listed under "Entertainment in Kraków," earlier, serve decent food. If you're looking for classic ramshackle Kazimierz ambience first and something to munch on second, consider these **$$** options: **Alchemia** (daily, Estery 5), **Kolanko No. 6** (daily, Józefa 17), and **Warsztat** (daily, Izaaka 3). For locations, see the "Kazimierz Entertainment and Nightlife" map, earlier.

Ice Cream: True to its name, **Lody Tradycyjna Receptura** has some of the best "ice cream from a traditional recipe" in Kraków—if not in Poland. The straightforward, seasonal flavors—just a few varieties—are made fresh each morning and sold until they run out. Locals line up here—and if you have a sweet tooth, you should, too (daily, Starowiślna 83). **Good Lood** (a pun on *lody*—ice cream) is newer and hipper but based on the same concept: creative flavors made fresh daily. Once they're out...they're out (daily, Plac Wolnica 11).

Dining in Kazimierz

In addition to its hip, fast, and cheap eateries, Kazimierz is emerging as a foodie hotspot for sit-down, take-your-time meals. In fact, this neighborhood owns Kraków's only Michelin star (at the first listing, below).

$$$$ Bottiglieria 1881—a chic, sophisticated restaurant tucked unassumingly just off Plac Wolnica—recently earned a Michelin star. Chef Przemysław Klima delicately constructs fixed-price menus of modern Polish and international fare. The cellar is stocked with wines from all over the world (with an emphasis on Italian). As this is one of Kraków's top "destination" restaurants, be sure to book ahead (closed Sun-Mon, Bochenska 5, +48 660 661 756, www.1881.com.pl).

$$$ Karakter, a short walk from the core of Kazimierz, feels lively, trendy, fresh, and upmarket. They take a meat-focused, international approach, but with ample Polish influences. You'll peruse a tempting menu of everything from pastas, mussels, and steaks to more innovative dishes like horse tenderloin tartare or beef tongue in wasabi sauce (Mon dinner only, Tue-Sun lunch and dinner, Brzozowa 17, +48 795 818 123).

$ Kuchnia u Doroty is a hidden gem for affordable, authentic, Grandma-style Polish food with zero pretense. Tucked along a forgotten side street at the edge of Kazimierz, its no-frills, welcoming interior is a haven for those seeking hearty local cuisine at a great value (cheap daily specials, open daily, Augustiańska 4, +48 517 945 338).

Middle Eastern: Hole-in-the-wall **$ Hummus Amamamusi** is a bar selling creamy, top-quality homemade hummus with various toppings, bread, and veggies. They also make their own soft drinks and have great coffee. The delicious food here is worth the short walk from the core of Kazimierz (daily until 17:00, Meiselsa 4, +48 533 306 288). **$$$ Hamsa,** with a prime location at the top of Ulica Szeroka and lots of tempting tables out front, offers "hummus and happiness," with an updated take on Israeli food (that's Middle Eastern, not traditional Jewish fare). Don't come here for matzo balls and klezmer music, but for an enticing menu of *mezes* (small plates, like hummus and various dips) and grilled meat dishes in a modern, hip atmosphere (daily, Ulica Szeorka 2, +48 515 150 145).

Kraków Connections

For getting between Kraków and **Auschwitz,** see the next chapter. To confirm rail journeys, check specific times at the main train station or online (www.intercity.pl). You can also buy tickets on this website; you'll be sent an eticket, which you can show to the conductor on board.

From Kraków by Train to: Warsaw (about hourly, 2.5 hours, slick EIC express train, requires seat reservation), **Gdańsk** (6/day direct, 5.5 hours on EIC express, plus night train, 9 hours), **Toruń** (7/day, 5.5 hours, most transfer at Warsaw's Zachodnia station), **Prague** (2/day direct, 7.5 hours, plus 1 night train, 10 hours; additional connections may be possible with change in Katowice and other points; some connections are operated by private Czech rail company Leo Express, www.leoexpress.com), **Berlin** (2-3/day, 9-10 hours with change at Warsaw's Zachodnia station, more options with multiple changes), **Budapest** (2/day direct—one during the day in 9 hours, the other overnight in 10 hours; additional connections possible with changes; also consider long-distance bus, www.flixbus.com), **Vienna** (2/day direct—1 during the day in 6 hours, the other overnight in 8.5 hours; additional connections possible with changes).

By Bus: For certain journeys between major cities—both domestic and international—you can save time and money by taking a bus instead of a train. Check your options with Flixbus (www.flixbus.com).

AUSCHWITZ-BIRKENAU

The unassuming regional capital of Oświęcim (ohsh-VEENCH-im) was the site of one of humanity's greatest crimes: the systematic murder of at least 1.1 million innocent people. From 1940 until 1945, Oświęcim was the home of Auschwitz, the biggest, most notorious concentration camp in the Nazi system. Today, Auschwitz is the most poignant memorial anywhere to the victims of the Holocaust.

"Auschwitz" (OWSH-vits) actually refers to a series of several camps in German-occupied Poland—most importantly Auschwitz I, in the town of Oświęcim (50 miles west of Kraków), and Auschwitz II—Birkenau (about 1.5 miles west of Oświęcim). Visitors generally start with Auschwitz I, then ride a shuttle bus to Birkenau. **Auschwitz I,** where public transportation from Kraków arrives, has the main museum building, the *Arbeit Macht Frei* gate, and indoor museum exhibits in former prison buildings. **Birkenau** (BEER-keh-now), on a much bigger scale and mostly outdoors, has the infamous guard tower, a vast field with ruins of barracks, a few tourable barracks, the notorious "dividing platform," a giant monument flanked by remains of destroyed crematoria, and a prisoner processing facility called "the Sauna."

A visit here is obligatory for Polish 14-year-olds; students usually come again during their last year of school. And it's an important pilgrimage for school groups from other countries. Many visitors leave flowers and messages; one message—from a German visitor—reads, "Nations who forget their own history are sentenced to live it again."

GETTING THERE

To reach Auschwitz from Kraków, it's easiest to join a package tour or hire a private guide or driver (1.5-hour drive each way). But the trip is also doable by train or bus (allow about 2 hours each way). For details, see "Auschwitz Connections," at the end of this chapter.

Orientation to Auschwitz

Cost: Most of the time, you're required to join a guided tour of Auschwitz I for 90 zł. (Alternatively, you could join a "study tour," or hire your own guide—see the "Guided Tours at Auschwitz" sidebar.) At off-peak times (April-Sept after 16:00, March and Oct after 15:00, Feb after 14:00, Jan and Nov after 13:00, Dec after 12:00), the tour is not required—you are allowed to visit on your own for free, though donations are appreciated. For any visit, **reservations are required** to enter Auschwitz I (see later). Any time of year, Birkenau grounds can be toured without a guide.

Hours: The museum opens daily at 7:30. Closing times change with the season: June-Aug at 19:00, April-May and Sept at 18:00, March and Oct at 17:00, Feb at 16:00, Jan and Nov at 15:00, and Dec at 14:00. These are "last entry" times; the grounds at Auschwitz I stay open 1.5 hours later (though many buildings—including the national memorials—close promptly at these times). The grounds at Birkenau, where most groups end their visits, may stay open even later.

Information: +48 33 844 8100, www.auschwitz.org.

AUSCHWITZ-BIRKENAU

Why Visit Auschwitz?

Why visit a notorious concentration camp on your vacation? Auschwitz-Birkenau is one of the most moving sights in Europe, and certainly the most important of all the Holocaust memorials. Seeing the camp can be difficult: Many visitors are overwhelmed by sadness and anger, as well as inspiration at the remarkable stories of survival. Auschwitz survivors and victims' families want tourists to come here and experience the scale and the monstrosity of the place. In their minds, a steady flow of  visitors will ensure that the Holocaust is always remembered—so nothing like it will ever happen again.

Auschwitz isn't for everyone. But I've never met anyone who toured Auschwitz and regretted it. For many, it's a profoundly life-altering experience—at the very least, it will forever affect the way you think about the Holocaust.

Mandatory Reservations: With well over one million visitors each year, Auschwitz struggles with crowds. Reservations are required—even if you're visiting late in the day, on your own. Book as soon as your dates are set—ideally weeks in advance—at https://visit.auschwitz.org. Entrance slots for individuals typically become available 90 days before the date of visit (and can fill quickly, especially for May and June, when school groups crowd the site). These details can change—confirm on the website.

If an English tour isn't available for your preferred date, consider booking one in a foreign language; once inside, you can use this chapter's self-guided tour.

After you've booked your reservation, you'll be sent a barcode; to get in, you'll need both the barcode (on your phone) and an ID for each person in your group. (This system, while cumbersome, prevents scalpers from buying up tickets and reselling them at inflated prices.)

Last-Minute Options: I don't recommend arriving in Kraków without an advance ticket. But if you do, there are a couple of last-minute options: You can book a **day tour** through a private company in Kraków, which includes both transportation and a tour of the camp (see the "Guided Tours at Auschwitz" sidebar). Or take your chances and **just show up**—a few tickets are reserved for same-day visitors. The visitors center opens at 7:30; typically, the later you arrive, the longer the wait. You can pass any wait time by first going to Birkenau, which has less strict timing requirements.

Getting from Auschwitz I to Birkenau: Buses shuttle visitors two miles between the camps (free, typically every 10-20 minutes, schedule posted at bus stops at each site, timed to correspond with tours). Taxis are also standing by (about 20-25 zł). Or you can walk the 30-40 minutes between the camps, which gives you a chance for reflection. Along the way, you'll pass the Judenrampe, an old train car like the ones used to transport prisoners.

Services: The visitors center at Auschwitz I has an information desk, bookshops, baggage storage (large bags must be checked), and WCs. The guard tower at Birkenau has another bookshop and more WCs.

Eating: You'll find eating options at the visitors center; additional choices are nearby.

Expect Changes: The Auschwitz museum is continually maintained and updated. Some things may be different than described here, but everything is well signposted.

Etiquette: The camp encourages visitors to remember that Auschwitz is the place where more than a million people lost their lives. Behave and dress here as you would at a cemetery. Photos are allowed inside some buildings, as posted.

Auschwitz Tour

Although most visitors will (and should) take a guided tour, the self-guided commentary below is worth reading before your visit to get your head around the history and the scope of what you're about to experience. If you visit on your own without a tour, read the text ahead of time, then use it to guide you through the camp.

Regardless of how you arrive, you'll begin at the new visitors center for Auschwitz I. This area can be crowded and chaotic; show your ticket, go through the security checkpoint, and get oriented. When ready, you'll go through an underground tunnel and arrive at the main entrance building. This is where the tour begins. You'll start with an eight-minute **movie,** which offers a concise history of the camp and sets the stage for what you'll see.

• *To begin your visit, stand by the main building and look over the grassy field to get oriented.*

AUSCHWITZ I
Before World War II, this camp was a base for the Polish army. When Hitler occupied Poland, he took over these barracks and

turned the site into a concentration camp for his Polish political
enemies. The location was ideal:
The industrial city of Oświęcim
was already an established rail
junction, with good connections to Germany and the rest
of Europe. (In fact, in the decades leading up to the war, tens
of thousands of Polish families
emigrating to North America

came through Oświęcim.) Nearby rivers also provided natural protective boundaries.

An average of 14,000 prisoners were kept at this camp at one
time. (Birkenau could hold up to 100,000.) In 1942, Auschwitz
became a death camp for the extermination of European Jews
and others whom Hitler considered "undesirable." By the time the
camp was liberated in 1945, at least 1.1 million people had been
murdered here—approximately 960,000 of them Jewish.

• *Go closer to the camp entrance, approaching the notorious...*

"Arbeit Macht Frei" Gate

Although this gate imparts the message "Work Sets You Free," it's
cruelly ironic. The only way out of the camp for the prisoners was
through the crematorium chimneys. Note that the "B" was welded
on upside down by belligerent inmates, who were forced to make
this sign (and much of the camp). The sign is a replica; the original
was stolen one night in December 2009, then recovered two days
later, cut up into several pieces. The original is now safely in the
museum's possession but no longer displayed.

Just inside the gate and to the right, the camp orchestra (made
up of prisoners) used to play marches; having the prisoners march
made them easier to count.

• *From the gate, proceed straight up the "main street" of the camp.*

You'll pass two rows of barracks. The first one holds a variety
of national memorials. We'll circle back here later, if you'd like to
enter some of them. The second row of barracks holds the main
museum exhibitions. Blocks 4 and 5 focus on how Auschwitz
prisoners were killed. Blocks 6, 7, and 11 explore the conditions
for prisoners who survived here a little longer than most. In each
block, arrows guide you on a one-way route through the numbered
rooms; in many cases, exhibits are both downstairs and upstairs—
don't miss these.

• *Start with the third block you come to, on your right.*

Guided Tours at Auschwitz

While you can see it on your own (using this chapter's self-guided tour), most visitors take a guided tour—in fact, these are required at peak times. Even during these busy times, you can enter Birkenau without a guide.

Organized Museum Tours: The Auschwitz Museum's excellent guides are serious and frank historians who feel a strong sense of responsibility about sharing the story of the camp. The regularly scheduled 3.5-hour English tour covers Auschwitz and Birkenau (90 zł; 130 zł for 6-hour "study tour"). These tours must be prebooked at https://visit.auschwitz.org. Arrive for your scheduled tour 30 minutes early.

Private Official Museum Guides: If you have a special interest or a small group, it's affordable and worthwhile to hire one of the museum's guides for a private tour. Choose between the basic 3.5-hour tour (620 zł) or a longer "study tour" (800 zł/6 hours, 890 zł/spread over 2 days); rates are higher for more than 10 people. Because English-speaking guides are limited, reserve as far in advance as possible—ideally, when time slots open up 90 days ahead—at https://visit.auschwitz.org.

Day Tours from Kraków: Various Kraków-based companies sell round-trip tours from Kraków to Auschwitz, which include a guided tour of the camp (typically around 140-170 zł). I can't vouch for their quality, but the main outfits are **See Kraków** (www.seekrakow.com), **Discover Cracow** (www.discovercracow.com), **Kraków Booking** (www.krakowbooking.com), and **Cracow City Tours** (www.cracowcitytours.com)—for details, see page 50.

Local Guides and Drivers from Kraków: For easy transportation to Auschwitz-Birkenau, hire a Kraków-based guide or driver (about 600-700 zł per carload). They will clearly explain how to reserve a time slot for entry, then provide an easy, no-stress connection between your hotel and the museum, with commentary about what you're seeing in the countryside en route. I've listed my favorite guides and drivers on page 47.

Block 4: Extermination

In Room 1, a map identifies the countries from which Auschwitz prisoners were brought—as far away as Norwegian fjords and Greek isles. In an alcove along the side of the room is an urn filled with ashes, a symbolic memorial to all the camp's victims. At the end of the hall is a giant photo of arriving prisoners from Hungary.

Room 2 shows photographs of Jewish ghettos from all over Europe being "liquidated"—that is, the residents assembled and deported to various concentration camps. Thanks to its massive occupancy, Auschwitz was a destination for many.

Room 3 displays rare photos of scenes inside the camp. To pre-

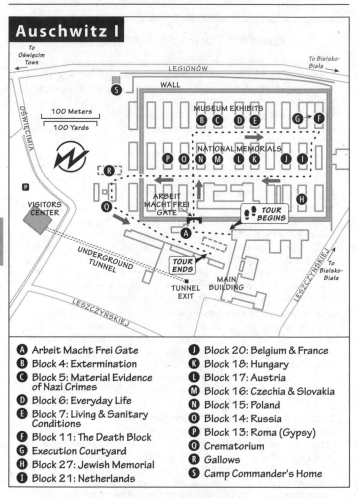

Auschwitz I

To Oświęcim Town

To Bielsko-Biała

LEGIONÓW

WALL

MUSEUM EXHIBITS

B **C** **D** **E** **G** **F**

100 Meters

100 Yards

NATIONAL MEMORIALS

P **O** **N** **M** **L** **K** **J** **I**

S

R

H

Q

ARBEIT MACHT FREI GATE

A

TOUR BEGINS

P

VISITORS CENTER

OŚWIĘCIMIA

UNDERGROUND TUNNEL

TOUR ENDS

TUNNEL EXIT

MAIN BUILDING

LESZCZYŃSKIEJ

To Bielsko-Biała

LESZCZYŃSKIEJ

AUSCHWITZ-BIRKENAU

A Arbeit Macht Frei Gate
B Block 4: Extermination
C Block 5: Material Evidence of Nazi Crimes
D Block 6: Everyday Life
E Block 7: Living & Sanitary Conditions
F Block 11: The Death Block
G Execution Courtyard
H Block 27: Jewish Memorial
I Block 21: Netherlands

J Block 20: Belgium & France
K Block 18: Hungary
L Block 17: Austria
M Block 16: Czechia & Slovakia
N Block 15: Poland
O Block 14: Russia
P Block 13: Roma (Gypsy)
Q Crematorium
R Gallows
S Camp Commander's Home

vent a riot, the Nazis claimed at first that this was only a transition camp for resettlement in Eastern Europe.

Upstairs in Room 4 is a model of a Birkenau crematorium. People entered on the left, then undressed in the underground rooms (hanging their belongings on numbered hooks and encouraged to remember their numbers to retrieve their clothes later). They then moved into the "showers" and were

killed by Zyklon-B gas (hydrogen cyanide), a German-produced

Chilling Statistics: The Holocaust in Poland

The majority of people murdered by the Nazis during the Holocaust were killed right here in Poland. For centuries, Poland was known for its relative tolerance of Jews, and right up until the beginning of World War II, Poland had Europe's largest concentration of Jews: 3,500,000. Throughout the Holocaust, the Nazis murdered 4,500,000 Jews in Poland (many of them brought in from other countries) at camps, including Auschwitz, and in ghettos such as Warsaw's.

By the end of the war, only 300,000 Polish Jews had survived—less than 10 percent of the original population. Many of these survivors were granted "one-way passports" (read: deported) to Israel, Western Europe, and the US by the communist government in 1968 (following a big student demonstration with a strong Jewish presence). Today, only about 10,000 Jews live in all of Poland.

cleaning agent that is lethal in high doses. This efficient factory of murder took about 20 minutes to kill 8,000 people in four gas chambers. Elevators brought the bodies up to the crematorium. Members of the *Sonderkommand*—Jewish inmates who were kept isolated and forced by the Nazis to work here—removed the corpses' gold teeth and shaved off their hair (to be sold) before putting the bodies in the ovens. It wasn't unusual for a *Sonderkommand* worker to discover a wife, child, or parent among the dead. A few of these workers committed suicide by throwing themselves at electric fences; those who didn't were systematically executed by the Nazis after a two-month shift. Across from the model of the crematorium are empty canisters of Zyklon-B.

Across the hall in the dimly lit Room 5 is one of the camp's most powerful exhibits: a wall of actual victims' hair—4,400 pounds of it. Also displayed is cloth made of the hair, used to make Nazi uniforms. The Nazis were nothing if not efficient...not even human body parts could be wasted.

Back downstairs in Room 6, you may see an exhibit on the plunder of victims' personal belongings. People being transported here were encouraged to bring luggage—and some victims had even paid in advance for houses in their new homeland. After they were killed, everything of value was sorted and stored in warehouses that prisoners named "Canada" (after a country they associated with great wealth). Although the Canada warehouses were destroyed, you can see a few of these items in the next building.

• *Head next door, to the left.*

Block 5: Material Evidence of Nazi Crimes

The exhibits in this block consist mostly of piles of the victims' goods, a tiny fraction of everything the Nazis stole. As you wander through the rooms, you'll see eyeglasses, fine Jewish prayer shawls, crutches and prosthetic limbs (the first people the Nazis exterminated were mentally and physically ill German citizens), and a pile of pots and pans.

Then, upstairs, you'll witness a seemingly endless mountain of shoes, children's clothing, and suitcases with names of victims—many marked *Kind*, or "child." Visitors often wonder if the suitcase with the name "Frank" belonged to Anne, one of the Holocaust's most famous victims. After being discovered in Amsterdam by the Nazis, the Frank family was transported here to Auschwitz, where they were split up. Still, it's unlikely this suitcase was theirs. Anne Frank and her sister Margot were sent to the Bergen-Belsen camp in northern Germany, where they died of typhus shortly before the war ended. Their father, Otto Frank, survived Auschwitz and was found barely alive by the Russians, who liberated the camp in January 1945.

• *Cross over to the next block.*

Block 6: Everyday Life

Although the purpose of Auschwitz was to murder its inmates, not all were killed immediately. After an initial evaluation, about 20 percent of prisoners were registered and forced to work. (This did not mean they were chosen to live—just to die later.) This block shows various aspects of daily existence at the camp.

19472
DĄBROWSKI JAN
ur.8.2.1920 r., robotnik
przybył: 30.7.1941, zginął wrzesień 1942.

The halls are lined with photographs of victims, each identified with a name, birthdate, occupation, date of arrival at Auschwitz, date of death, and camp registration number. The dates reveal that these people survived here an average of two to three months. Similar photographs hang in several other museum buildings; as with the plundered items in the last block, keep in mind that these represent only a tiny fraction of the masses of people murdered at Auschwitz. In fact, most of the faces you see in these halls are non-Jewish Poles, who were among the early inmates at the camp. Later—when new arrivals were predominantly Jewish—photographing each prisoner became too expensive, so they were tattooed instead.

The room on the right displays drawings of the arrival process. One end of the room displays actual camp uniforms. After the ini-

St. Maksymilian Kolbe (1894-1941)

Among the many inspirational stories of Auschwitz is that of a Polish priest named Maksymilian Kolbe. Before the war, Kolbe traveled as a missionary to Japan, then worked in Poland for a Catholic newspaper. While he was highly regarded for his devotion to the Church, some of his writings had an unsettling anti-Semitic sentiment. But during the Nazi occupation, Kolbe briefly ran an institution that cared for refugees—including Jews.

In 1941, Kolbe was arrested and interned at Auschwitz. When a prisoner from Kolbe's block escaped in July of that year, the Nazis punished the remaining inmates by selecting 10 of them to be put in the Starvation Cell until they died—based on the Nazi "doctrine of collective responsibility." After the selection had been made, Kolbe offered to replace a man who expressed concern about who would care for his family. The Nazis agreed. (The man Kolbe saved is said to have survived the Holocaust.)

All 10 of the men—including Kolbe—were put into Starvation Cell 18. Two weeks later, when the door was opened, only Kolbe had survived. The story spread throughout the camp and Kolbe became an inspiration to the inmates. To squelch the hope he had given the others, Kolbe was executed by lethal injection.

In 1982, Kolbe was canonized by the Catholic Church. Some critics—mindful of his earlier anti-Semitic rhetoric—still consider Kolbe's sainthood controversial. But most Poles feel he redeemed himself through this noble act at the end of his life.

tial selection, those chosen to work were showered, shaved, and photographed. Pictures show the tattoos used to register prisoners: on the chest, on the arm, or—for children—on the leg. A display shows the symbols that prisoners had to wear to show their reason for internment—Jew, Roma (Gypsy), homosexual, political prisoner, and so on.

Across the hall, Room 4 shows the starvation that took place here. The 7,500 survivors that the Red Army found when the camp was liberated were essentially living skeletons (the "healthier" inmates had been forced to march to Germany). Of those liberated, one-fifth died soon after of disease and starvation.

In Room 5, you can see scenes from the prisoner's workday (sketched by survivors after liberation). Prisoners worked as long as the sun shone—8 hours in winter, up to 12 hours in summer—mostly on farms or in factories.

Another room is about Auschwitz's child inmates, 20 percent of the camp's victims. Blond, blue-eyed children were either "Germanized" in special schools or, if younger, adopted by German families. Dr. Josef Mengele conducted gruesome experiments here on children, especially twins and triplets, ostensibly to find ways to increase fertility for German mothers.

• *Next up is…*

Block 7: Living and Sanitary Conditions

Tours sometimes skip this block because it's a bottleneck, and most of what you'll see inside is similar to exhibits elsewhere in the camp. The focus is on the living conditions of prisoners held in these barracks—at first about 700 per building, and eventually up to 1,000. As you progress down the hall, you'll see how conditions grew more and more unpleasant: At first, the floor was strewn with hay, or with straw-filled mattresses. Later, three-tiered bunk beds (with two or eventually three prisoners per bed) were crammed into each room. You'll also see the washrooms (with trough-like sinks) and the latrines (with individual toilets—rather than the long, communal benches we'll see later at Birkenau). The Block Elder's Room showed how supervisors—selected from among the prisoners—had special privileges.

• *Blocks 8-10 are vacant (medical experiments were carried out in Block 10). Block 11 was the most notorious of all.*

Block 11: The Death Block

Head into the **"Death Block"** (#11), from which nobody ever left alive. Death here required a "trial"—but it was never a fair trial.

Room 2 (on the left as you enter) is where these sham trials were held, lasting about two minutes each. In Rooms 4 and 5, you can see how prisoners lived in these barracks—more three-level bunks, with three prisoners sleeping in each bed (they had to sleep on their sides so they could fit). In Room 6, people undressed before they were executed.

In the **basement,** you'll see several types of cells. In the Standing Cells (#22), four people would be forced to stand together for hours at a time (amid bricks that went all the way to the ceiling then). In the Dark Cell (#20), which held up to 30, there was only a small window for ventilation—and if it became covered with snow, the prisoners suffocated. The Starvation Cell (#18) held prisoners selected to starve to death when a fellow prisoner escaped; Maksymilian Kolbe spent two weeks here to save another man's life (see sidebar on Kolbe). The basement is also where Nazi scientists carried out the first tests of Zyklon-B.

If the **upstairs** is open, you'll find gallows and a bench used for administering lashes. Filling this floor are exhibits on various forms of punishment, mostly focusing on resistance within the camp, escapees, and local Poles who were executed—either for trying to assist the prisoners or for fighting with Nazi officers.

Finally, step into the walled-in **courtyard** between Blocks 10 and 11. The wall at the far end is where the Nazis shot several thousand political prisoners, leaders of camp resistance, and religious leaders. Notice that the windows are covered so that nobody could witness the executions. Also take a close look at the memorial—the back of it was made of a material designed by Nazis to catch the bullets without a ricochet. Inmates were shot at short range—about three feet. There are usually fresh flowers and other memorials placed at this poignant location.

• *Leaving Block 11, proceed straight ahead, between the buildings, to the other row of barracks. Several of these blocks house...*

National Memorials

These exhibits were created not by museum authorities but by representatives of the home countries of the camps' victims. As these memorials overlap with the general exhibits and are designed for Europeans to learn more about the victims from their own homelands, most visitors skip this part of the site. On the other hand, while the main museum exhibits await renovation and modernization, the displays in these national memorials tend to be slicker and better-presented than the ones we just saw. As you walk along this street toward our next stop (the crematorium), consider stepping into the ones that interest you.

The first one you see is the memorial to **Jewish** victims (Block 27), and this powerful memorial may be the one most worth entering. The entryway displays the words *SHOAH—Holocaust.* A large room with black-and-white footage captures the joyful flowering of Jewish culture in the interwar period—when Europe and the Mediterranean basin had some 10.8 million Jews. Upstairs, clips of Hitler speeches spout the hateful propaganda that led to the Holocaust. The "Geography of Murder" room shows the locations of death camps and killing sites where Jews were murdered. You'll watch eyewitness testimony from survivors and see art penciled on blank walls that was inspired by actual children's art from concentration camps. The final room contains the gigantic Book of Names—individually listing each and every one of the nearly 6 million Jews murdered in the Holocaust. The book practically fills an entire room.

Most of the other national memorials are on the right side

of the street. Across from the Jewish memorial, Block 21 honors **Dutch Jews,** including perhaps the most famous Dutch victim of the concentration camp, Anne Frank.

Block 20, a former hospital block, is shared by **Belgium** and **France.** A room near the entrance explains how some prisoners were killed by lethal injection, with portraits and biographical sketches of victims. Upstairs is the powerful Belgium exhibit, with a room featuring victims' portraits. Block 18 holds a very modern, conceptual exhibit about **Hungary**'s victims, with an eerie heart-beat sound pervading the space; Block 17 memorializes victims from **Austria.** Across from this block, notice the long **gallows** used for mass hangings and the **wooden guard booth** where the SS took roll call. If someone was missing, the entire group had to stand at attention—perhaps for hours—until that person was located. Block 16 contains a well-presented exhibit about **Czech** and **Slovak** victims.

Block 15 honors victims from **Poland,** focusing on the 1939 Nazi invasion of the country, which resulted in the immediate internment of Polish political prisoners. Exhibits explain the process of "Germanization"—such as renaming Polish streets with German names—and (upstairs) the underground resistance that fought to get back some control over Poland.

Block 14 is the **Russian** national memorial. However, this one's a bit controversial: While Russia claims to have lost "Russian" Jews to the Holocaust, virtually all of them were technically Polish Jews who had been living within Russia. (They spoke Polish, not Russian.) To sidestep the hot topic of how to identify these victims, this memorial focuses not on victims, but on the Russian liberation of the camp.

Block 13 houses the **Roma (Gypsy)** exhibit. You'll learn that the Roma, along with the Jews, were considered no better than "rats, bedbugs, and fleas," and explore elements of the so-called *Zigeunerfrage*—the "Gypsy question" about what to do with this "troublesome" population.

• *At the end of this row of barracks, you reach a guard tower and a barbed-wire fence. Jog a few steps to the right, through the hole in the fence, then angle left toward the earthen mound with the giant, ominous brick chimney. Enter on the right side.*

Crematorium

You'll enter into the big **"shower room."** Up to 700 people at a time could be gassed here. People undressed outside, or just inside the door. Look for the vents in the ceiling—this is where the SS men dropped the Zyklon-B.

In the adjacent room is a replica of the **furnace.** This facility could burn 340 bodies a day—so it took two days to burn all of the bodies from one round of executions. (The Nazis didn't like this "inefficiency," so they built four more huge crematoria at Birkenau.)

• *Exiting the crematorium, you're facing the main building where we began the tour. But first, circle around to the opposite side of the crematorium—near where you entered—for the closest thing this story has to a happy ending.*

Shortly after the war, camp commander Rudolf Höss was tried, convicted, and sentenced to death. Survivors requested that he be executed at Auschwitz, and in 1947, he was hanged here. The **gallows** are preserved behind the crematorium, about a hundred yards from his home where his wife—who is said to have loved her years here—raised their children in a villa maintained by enslaved people and furnished with possessions of the dead.

• *Take your time with Auschwitz I. When you're ready, continue to the second stage of the camp—Birkenau.*

AUSCHWITZ II—BIRKENAU

In 1941, realizing that the original Auschwitz camp was too small to meet their needs, the Nazis began a second camp in some nearby farm fields. The original plan was for a camp that could hold 200,000 people, but at its peak, Birkenau (Brzezinka) held about 100,000. They were still adding onto it when the camp was liberated in 1945.

AUSCHWITZ-BIRKENAU

• *Train tracks lead past the main building and into the camp. The first sight that greeted prisoners was the...*

Guard Tower

If you've seen *Schindler's List,* the sight of this icon of the Holocaust—shown in stirring scenes from the movie—may make you queasy.

Go through the gate to survey the camp: a vast field of chimneys and a few intact wooden and brick barracks. Some of the barracks were destroyed by Germans. Most were dismantled to be used for fuel and building materials shortly after the war. But the first row has been reconstructed (using components from the original structures). The train tracks lead straight back to the dividing platform, and then dead-end at the ruins of the crematorium and camp monument at the far side.

• *Turn right (passing the WCs) and walk through the barbed-wire fence to reach the...*

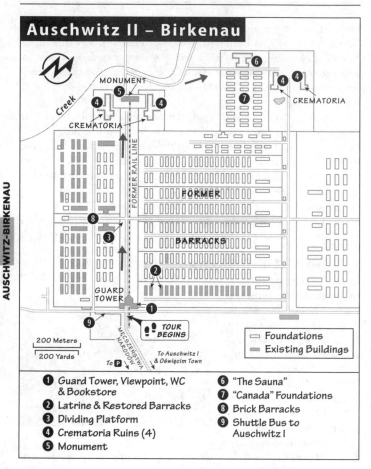

Auschwitz II – Birkenau

MONUMENT

Creek

CREMATORIA

FORMER RAIL LINE

FORMER

BARRACKS

CREMATORIA

GUARD TOWER

TOUR BEGINS

MIECSZEWSTWA NARODÓW

To Auschwitz I & Oświęcim Town

To P

200 Meters
200 Yards

☐ Foundations
▬ Existing Buildings

1 Guard Tower, Viewpoint, WC & Bookstore
2 Latrine & Restored Barracks
3 Dividing Platform
4 Crematoria Ruins (4)
5 Monument
6 "The Sauna"
7 "Canada" Foundations
8 Brick Barracks
9 Shuttle Bus to Auschwitz I

AUSCHWITZ-BIRKENAU

Wooden Barracks

The first of these barrack buildings was the **latrine:** The front half of the building contained washrooms, and the back was a row of toilets. There was no running water, and prisoners were in charge of keeping the latrine clean. Because of the resulting unsanitary conditions and risk of disease, the Nazis were afraid to come in here—so the latrine became the heart of the black market and the inmates' resistance movement.

The third barrack was a **bunkhouse.** Each inmate had a personal number, a barrack number, and a bed number.

Inside, you can see the bunks (angled so that more could fit). An average of 400 prisoners—but up to 1,000—would be housed in each of these buildings. These wooden structures, designed as stables by a German company to fit 51 horses (look for the horse-tying rings

on the wall), came in prefab pieces that made them cheap and convenient. Two chimneys connected by a brick duct provided a little heat. The bricks were smoothed by inmates who sat here to catch a bit of warmth.

• *Return to the train tracks and follow them toward the monument about a half-mile away, at the back end of Birkenau. At the intersection of these tracks and the perpendicular gravel road (halfway to the monument)—now marked by a lonely train car—was the gravel pitch known as the...*

Dividing Platform

A Nazi doctor would stand facing the guard tower and evaluate each prisoner. If he pointed to the right, the prisoner was sentenced to death, and trudged—unknowingly—to the gas chamber. If he pointed to the left, the person would be registered and live a little longer. It was here that families from all over Europe were torn apart forever. (Photographs near the wooden building show the sad scene.)

Now carry on along the train tracks. As you walk on the camp's only road, imagine the horror of this place—all the barracks packed with people, smoke billowing from the busy crematoria.

• *At the end of the tracks, go 50 yards to the left and climb the three concrete steps to view the ruins of the...*

Crematorium

This is one of four crematoria here at Birkenau, each with a capacity to cremate more than 4,400 people per day. At the far-right end of the ruins, see the stairs where people entered the rooms to undress. They were given numbered lockers, conning them into thinking they were coming back. (The Nazis didn't want a panic.) Then they piled into the "shower room"—the underground passage branching away from the memorial—and were killed. Their bodies were burned in the crematorium (on the left), giving off a scent of sweet almonds (from the Zyklon-B). Beyond the remains of the crematorium is a hole—once a gray lake where tons of ashes were dumped.

AUSCHWITZ-BIRKENAU

This efficient factory of death was destroyed by the Nazis as the Red Army approached, leaving the haunting ruins you see today.

When the Soviets arrived on January 27, 1945, the nightmare of Auschwitz-Birkenau was over. The Polish parliament voted to turn these grounds into a museum so that the world would understand, and never forget, the horror of what happened here.

• *At the back of the camp stands the...*

Monument

Built in 1967 by the communist government in its heavy "Socialist Realist" style, this monument represents gravestones and the chimney of a crematorium. The plaques, written in each of the languages spoken by camp victims (including English, far right), explain that the memorial is "a cry of despair and a warning to humanity."

• *With more time, you could continue deeper into the...*

Rest of the Camp

There's much more to see for those who are interested—Birkenau sprawls for a frightening distance. One worthwhile extension is the reception and disinfection building that prisoners called **"the Sauna"** (the long building with four tall chimneys). It was here that prisoners would be forced to strip and be deloused; their belongings were seized and taken to the "Canada" warehouses (described earlier) to be sorted. Walking through here

(on glass floors designed to protect the original structure below), you'll see artifacts of the grim efficiency with which prisoners were "processed"—their heads were shaved, they were tattooed with a serial number, and they were assigned uniforms and wooden clogs to wear. Portraits at the end of the building humanize those who passed through here. Look for the cart, which was used to dispose of ashes.

In front of the Sauna is a field of foundations of the **"Canada" warehouses.** Nearby are the other two destroyed **crematoria.**

• *On your way back out of the camp, consider detouring to the right to look inside one of the...*

Brick Barracks

Enter one of these buildings. The supervisors lived in the two smaller rooms near the door. Farther in, most barracks still have the wooden bunks that held about 700 people per building. Four

On the Way to Auschwitz: The Polish Countryside

You'll spend an hour or two gazing out the window as you drive or ride to Auschwitz—offering a good look at the Polish countryside. Ponder these thoughts about what you're passing...

The small houses you see are traditionally inhabited by three generations at the same time. Nineteenth-century houses (the few that survive) often sport blue stripes, which in those days announced that a daughter was eligible for marriage. Once they saw these blue lines, local boys were welcome to come a-courtin'.

Some of the houses are bigger, very boxy, and have almost flat roofs rather than angled ones. These prefab homes generally date from the communist period and are sturdily built (of concrete) so they can handle the heavy snow loads in winter. While some have been nicely colorized, most are a drab gray or beige.

Big churches mark small villages. In fact, Polish Catholics like to show off their civic and spiritual pride by building wildly imaginative churches. Like in the US, tiny roadside memorials and crosses indicate places where fatal accidents have occurred.

Polish farmers traditionally had small lots that were notorious for not being very productive. These farmers somewhat miraculously survived the communist era without having to merge their farms. For years, they were Poland's sacred cows: producing little, paying almost no tax, and draining government resources. But after Poland joined the European Union in 2004, many had to collectivize their farms after all.

Since most people don't own cars, bikes are common and public transit is excellent. There are lots of bus stops, as well as minibuses that you can flag down. The bad roads are a legacy of communist construction, exacerbated by heavy truck use and brutal winters.

Poland has more than 2,000 counties, or districts, each with its own coat of arms; you'll pass several along the way. The forests are state owned, and locals enjoy the right to pick berries in the summer and mushrooms in the autumn (you may see people—often young kids—selling their day's harvest by the side of the road). The mushrooms are dried and then boiled to make tasty soups in the winter.

or five people slept on each bunk; the floor was reserved for new arrivals. There were chamber pots at either end of the building. After a Nazi doctor died of typhus, sanitation improved, and these barracks got running water.

Auschwitz Connections

The Auschwitz Museum is in the town of Oświęcim, about 50 miles west of Kraków. The drive takes around 1.5 hours, depending on traffic. By public transit, it's about 2 to 2.5 hours each way, including travel time to and from the bus or train station.

FROM KRAKÓW TO AUSCHWITZ

The easiest way to reach Auschwitz is with a **package tour** or **private guide or driver;** both of these options are described on page 46.

If you're using public transportation, here are your choices (each option costs around 20 zł):

The most comfortable public transit option is to take a **public bus** (hourly, 1.5 hours, get current schedule at any Kraków TI, buses depart from Kraków's main bus station behind the train station, run by Lajkonik). Look for buses to "Oświęcim" (not necessarily "Auschwitz"). Note that these buses can be full, and there's no way to reserve a seat—line up early (generally about 15 minutes ahead). Be sure the driver knows you're heading to the *Muzeum*. Once in Oświęcim, buses stop first at the train station, then continue on to the museum's visitors center.

Your other option is to ride the **train** to Oświęcim (about 4/day direct, 2 hours), but be aware that it takes about 20-25 minutes to walk from the train station to the camp/visitors center. Instead, you can take a taxi (likely around 20 zł).

RETURNING FROM AUSCHWITZ TO KRAKÓW

Upon arrival at Auschwitz I, plan your departure by visiting the information desk. They can give you a schedule of departures and explain where the bus leaves from. If you intend to stay late into the afternoon, make a point of figuring out the last bus or train back to Kraków. Plan accordingly, and remember to allow enough time to make it from Birkenau back to Auschwitz I to catch your ride.

WARSAW

Warszawa

Warsaw (Warszawa, vah-SHAH-vah in Polish) is Poland's capital and biggest city. It's huge, famous, and important...but not particularly romantic. If you're looking for Old World quaintness, head for Kraków. If you're tickled by spires and domes, get to Prague. But if you want to experience a truly 21st-century city, Warsaw's your place.

A decade ago, Warsaw was dreary and uninviting. But things have changed here dramatically. The Varsovians (as locals are called) are chic and sophisticated, and here by choice; according to some studies, as many as 8 out of every 10 Varsovians weren't born in Warsaw. Young professionals dress and dine as well as the Parisians and Milanese, and they've mastered the art of navigating an urban jungle in heels or a man bun. Today's Warsaw has gleaming new office towers, glitzy shopping malls, swarms of international

businesspeople, inviting parks and pedestrian zones, hipster culture to rival Brooklyn or Portland, and a gourmet coffee shop or designer pastry store on every corner.

Stroll down revitalized boulevards that evoke the city's glory days, pausing at an outdoor café to sip coffee and nibble at a *pączek* (the classic Polish jelly doughnut). Drop by a leafy park for an al fresco Chopin concert, packed with patriotic Poles. Commune with the soul of Poland at the city's many state-of-the-art museums—take your pick: Poland's artists (National Museum), its favorite composer (Chopin Museum), its dramatic histo-

WARSAW

Warsaw History: Ebbs and Flows

Warsaw has good reason to be a city of the future: The past hasn't been very kind. Historically, Warsaw has seen wave after wave of foreign rulers and invasions—especially during the last hundred years. But in this horrific crucible, the enduring spirit of the Polish people was forged. Years ago, one proud Varsovian told me, "Warsaw is ugly because its history is so beautiful."

Founded around 1300, Warsaw gradually gained importance through the late Middle Ages. In the mid-16th century, it became the seat of the Sejm (parliament of nobles), and it took over as seat of the royal court (and therefore Poland's capital) in 1596.

The city's golden age was between the World Wars, when Poland—newly reconstituted after a century and a half of foreign rule under the Partitions—was proudly independent. Interwar Warsaw saw a flourishing of commerce, construction, and the arts almost unmatched in Europe at that time, when it was also the largest and most culturally rich Jewish city in Europe.

This age of optimism was cut brutally short by the city's darkest days, as the Nazis occupied the city (and all of Poland) at the outbreak of World War II. First, its Jewish residents were forced into a tiny ghetto. They rose up...and were slaughtered (the Ghetto Uprising—see page 215). Then, in the war's waning days, its surviving residents rose up...and were slaughtered (the Warsaw Uprising—see page 222). Fed up with the troublesome Varsovians, Hitler sent word to systematically demolish the entire city, block by block. At the war's end, Warsaw was virtually gone. An estimated 800,000 residents were dead—nearly two out of every three souls.

The Poles almost gave up on what was then a pile of rubble, planning to build a brand-new capital city elsewhere. But ultimately, they decided to rebuild, creating a city of contrasts: painstakingly restored medieval lanes and retrofitted communist apartment blocks (*bloki* in Polish). And its evolution continues. Since the end of communism, Warsaw has become a hub of international trade and diplomacy—adding sleek skyscrapers to its skyline. Finally emerging from the gloom of the 20th century, Warsaw is no longer ugly. The city—and its history—are more beautiful than ever.

ry (Museum of Warsaw and Warsaw Uprising Museum), its dedication to the sciences (Copernicus Science Center), and its Jewish story (Museum of the History of Polish Jews). You can also dig into one of Europe's most interesting foodie scenes, where a world of wildly creative chefs open new restaurants all the time—at budget prices. If you picture a dreary metropolis, think again. Warsaw is full of surprises.

PLANNING YOUR TIME

One day is the absolute minimum to get a quick taste of Warsaw—but you'll have to sightsee very selectively. The city can easily fill two or three days, and even then you'll need to pick and choose. Review your museum-going options to decide how much time you need.

No matter how long you stay, get your bearings by taking a stroll through Polish history, following my Royal Way Walk from Palm Tree Circle to the Old Town. With more time, extend your stroll on my Old Town Walk for a sampling of Warsaw's historic core. Then visit other sights according to your interests and time: Jewish history, the Warsaw Uprising, Polish artists, royalty, hands-on science gizmos, hipster hangouts, or Chopin. To slow down and take a break from the city, relax in Łazienki Park.

For dinner, buck the tourist trend by leaving the overpriced Old Town and riding a tram or the Metro, or taking a taxi or an Uber to the hip Śródmieście district, which has the highest concentration of quality eateries.

Orientation to Warsaw

Warsaw sprawls with 1.8 million residents. Everything is on a big scale—it seems to take forever to walk just a few "short" blocks.

Get comfortable with public transportation (or taxis or Uber) and plan your sightseeing to avoid backtracking.

The tourist's Warsaw blankets a mild hill on the west bank of the Vistula River (in Polish: Wisła, VEES-wah). To break things into manageable chunks, I think of the city as three major zones (from north to south):

The **Old Town and Royal Way,** at Warsaw's northern edge, is the most touristy area. Here you'll find the Old Town (Stare Miasto, STAH-reh mee-AH-stoh), the adjacent and nearly-as-old New Town (Nowe Miasto, NOH-vay mee-AH-stoh), the Royal Castle on Castle Square (Plac Zamkowy, plahts zahm-KOH-veh), and the historical artery called the Royal Way (Trakt Królewski, shwock kroh-LEHV-skee). This bustling strip has strollable boulevards, genteel cafés, expansive squares and parks, and stately landmarks both historic and faux-historic (much of this area was rebuilt after World War II).

WARSAW

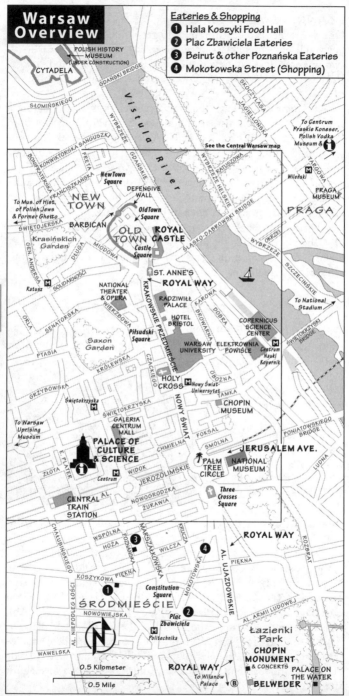

Warsaw Overview

Eateries & Shopping

1. Hala Koszyki Food Hall
2. Plac Zbawiciela Eateries
3. Beirut & other Poznańska Eateries
4. Mokotowska Street (Shopping)

CYTADELA

POLISH HISTORY MUSEUM (UNDER CONSTRUCTION)

SŁOMIŃSKIEGO

GDAŃSKI BRIDGE

WYBRZEŻE GDAŃSKIE

Vistula River

SKOCZYLASA

JAGIELLOŃSKA

To Centrum Fraskie Koneser, Polish Vodka Museum &

TARGOWA

Wileński

PRAGA MUSEUM

PRAGA

See the Central Warsaw map

WYBRZEŻE HELSKIE

KATUSZOWA

NewTown Square

NEW TOWN

DEFENSIVE WALL

NOWE TOWN Square

To Mus. of Hist. of Polish Jews & Former Ghetto

BARBICAN

Old Town Square

OLD TOWN

ROYAL CASTLE

ŚLĄSKO-DĄBROWSKI BRIDGE

OKRZEI

WYBRZEŻE

SZCZECIŃSKIE

ŚWIĘTOJERSKA

Krasińskich Garden

DŁUGA

MIODOWA

Castle Square

ST. ANNE'S

ROYAL WAY

To National Stadium

GEN. ANDERSA

SOLIDARNOŚCI

Ratusz

KRAKOWSKIE PRZEDMIEŚCIE

NATIONAL THEATER & OPERA

WIERZBOWA

RADZIWIŁŁ PALACE

KAROWA

DOBRA

COPERNICUS SCIENCE CENTER

Centrum Nauki Kopernik

ŚWIETOKRZYSKI BRIDGE

OKLA

SENATORSKA

Saxon Garden

Piłsudski Square

CZACKIEGO

BROWARNA

HOTEL BRISTOL

WARSAW UNIVERSITY

ELEKTROWNIA POWIŚLE

PTASIA

KRÓLEWSKA

GRZYBOWSKA

Świętokrzyska

ŚWIETOKRZYSKA

NOWY ŚWIAT

HOLY CROSS

Nowy Świat-Uniwersytet

OBOŻNA

TAMKA

CHOPIN MUSEUM

PONIATOWSKIEGO BRIDGE

To Warsaw Uprising Museum

GALERIA CENTRUM MALL

FOKSAL

SMOLNA

JEROZOLIMSKIE

E. PLATER

ZŁOTA

PALACE OF CULTURE & SCIENCE

Centrum

CHMIELNA

WIDOK

JEROZOLIMSKIE

PALM TREE CIRCLE

JERUSALEM AVE.

NATIONAL MUSEUM

LUDNA

CENTRAL TRAIN STATION

NOWOGRODZKA

ŻURAWIA

Three Crosses Square

CHAŁUBIŃSKIEGO

WSPÓLNA

HOŻA

MARSZAŁKOWSKA

POZNAŃSKA

WILCZA

3

KRUCZA

4

ROYAL WAY

ROZBRAT

AL. UJAZDOWSKIE

PIĘKNA

AL. NIEPODLEGŁOŚCI

KOSZYKOWA

PIĘKNA

1

Constitution Square

MOKOTOWSKA

ŚRÓDMIEŚCIE

NOWOWIEJSKA

2

Plac Zbawiciela

Łazienki Park

CHOPIN MONUMENT & CONCERTS

Politechnika

WAWELSKA

0.5 Kilometer

0.5 Mile

ROYAL WAY

To Wilanów Palace

AL. ARMII LUDOWEJ

PALACE ON THE WATER

BELWEDER

WARSAW

"**Palm Tree Circle**" is my nickname for the center of the city, near the traffic circle with a fake palm tree—where busy Jerusalem Avenue (Aleja Jerozolimskie, ah-LAY-uh yeh-ro-zoh-LIM-skyeh) crosses the shopping street called Nowy Świat (NOH-veh SHVEE-aht). Nearby are some good accommodations, trendy upscale eateries, pedestrianized shopping streets and glitzy malls, the National Museum (Polish art), the Palace of Culture and Science (communist-era landmark skyscraper), and the central train station (Warszawa Centralna).

The **Śródmieście** (SHROD-myesh-cheh, "Downtown") district, to the south, is a mostly residential zone with the city's best restaurant and nightlife scene and some good accommodations. The only real sight here is lush Łazienki Park, with its summertime al fresco Chopin concerts.

In sprawling Warsaw, many more sights—including some major ones—lie outside these three areas, but all are within a long walk or a short ride on public transit or in a taxi/Uber. These include the Museum of the History of Polish Jews and the Warsaw Uprising Museum (to the west) and the Copernicus Science Center (to the east, along the river). Across the river is the hardscrabble but gentrifying Praga district.

TOURIST INFORMATION

Warsaw's TI is helpful, but the locations are less than handy: one at the **Palace of Culture and Science** (enter on the side facing the train station, on Emilii Plater; daily 9:00-19:00, Oct-April until 18:00) and the other across the river in Praga, at the trendy **Koneser Center** (same hours, Plac Konesera 2). There's also a privately run TI partner on Castle Square, but it's a souvenir shop first and far less helpful—drop by here only if you want to grab some brochures (Plac Zamkowy 1/13). The general information number for all TIs is +48 503 033 720. All information is also available online (www.warsawtour.pl).

Sightseeing Pass: Busy sightseers might consider the **Warsaw Pass,** which covers admission to most major sights, the best hop-on, hop-off bus tour, and a Chopin concert, but no city transit (149 zł/24 hours, 199 zł/48 hours, 239 zł/72 hours, sold at the TI). If your museum-going plans are ambitious, do the math.

ARRIVAL IN WARSAW
By Train

Most trains arrive at the **central train station** (Warszawa Centralna, vah-SHAH-vah tsehn-TRAHL-nah), a communist-era monstrosity that has been renovated with surprising grace. (Don't get off at Warszawa Zachodnia or Warszawa Wschodnia—the

Western and Eastern stations, respectively—which are far from the tourist area.)

Warszawa Centralna can be tricky to navigate: Three parallel concourses run across the tracks, accessed by three different sets of escalators from each platform, creating a subterranean maze (with well-signed lockers, ticket windows, and lots of shops and eateries). Be patient: To get your bearings, ride up on your platform's middle escalator, then look for signs to the wide-open **main hall** (follow signs for *hala główna/main hall*). Here you'll  find a row of ticket windows, eateries, waiting areas (upstairs), and (from outside, near the taxi stand) views of the adjacent Palace of Culture and Science and Złota 44 skyscrapers. If you have a little time to kill, walk across the street to the super-modern Złote Tarasy shopping mall.

Getting into Town: To reach the tourist zone and most of my recommended hotels, a taxi/Uber is the easiest choice, while the bus is more economical (but more challenging to find).

Taxis wait outside the main hall. To get a fair fare, look for one with a company logo and telephone number, and ask for an estimate up front (the ride should cost no more than about 20-30 zł for most of my recommended hotels). You can also order an **Uber,** but it can be tricky to identify a pick-up location near the station—consider walking out to a busy road with pullouts and ordering it from there.

From the station, **bus #175** or **#128** takes you to the Royal Way and Old Town in about 10 minutes. (Credit-card-operated ticket machines are at major bus stops and often on board; for details on getting tickets, see "Getting Around Warsaw," later.) You can catch either bus in front of the skyscraper with the Hotel Marriott, across busy Jerusalem Avenue from the station. Because it's hard to find this stop from the station's mazelike corridors, it's probably simplest to ascend to street level (on the Aleja Jerozolimskie side) and cross surface streets to reach the well-marked Marriott tower. Both buses terminate just off Piłsudski Square, a five-minute walk from the Old Town. **Bus #160** also goes to the Old Town (though not via the Royal Way), but it departs from the opposite side of the station: To find its stop from the main hall, go out the side door toward *Ulica Emilii Plater*.

Buying Train Tickets: Lining one wall of the main arrival hall *(hala główna)* are 16 ticket windows; window #1 is for information. There are also ticket machines throughout the station, and you can book online at Intercity.pl. If buying tickets in person, allow plenty of time to wait in line. At one corner of the main hall, the InfoDworzec office can help you get oriented to the station but doesn't sell tickets (daily 7:00-21:00). Remember: Even if you have a rail pass, a reservation is still required on many express trains (including EIC trains to Kraków or Gdańsk). If you're not sure, ask. To get to your train, first find your way to the right platform (*peron,* as noted on schedules), then keep an eye on both tracks *(tor)* for your train.

By Plane
Fryderyk Chopin International Airport
Warsaw's Fryderyk Chopin International Airport (Lotnisko Chopina Waszawa, code: WAW, www.lotnisko-chopina.pl) is about six miles southwest of the center.

To get into town, you can take the train or bus (similar prices, around 5 zł). The train is faster, but the bus makes more stops in the city center and may get you closer to your hotel. From the arrivals area, just follow signs to either option.

The **train** departs about twice hourly and takes 20-30 minutes. The line into town is operated by two different companies (SKM and KM)—take whichever one departs first. Be ready for your stop: Half the trains make fewer stops and take you to Centralna station; others make a few more stops and use the Warszawa Śródmieście station—which feeds into the same underground passages as Centralna (these trains also continue one more stop to the Warszawa Powiśle station, which is closer to Nowy Świat and nearby hotels). Whether arriving at Centralna station or Warszawa Śródmieście, see the "By Train" arrival instructions, earlier.

Bus #175 departs from the curb in front of arrivals every 15-20 minutes and runs into the city center (Centralna station, the Royal Way, and Piłsudski Square near the Old Town, 30-45 minutes depending on traffic; buy ticket from machine before you board).

For a **taxi,** head to the official taxi stand. Taxis have a fixed rate of about 50 zł to most downtown hotels (trip takes 30 minutes depending on traffic). It's generally cheaper to order an **Uber** (except at very busy times).

Modlin Airport
Modlin Airport (code: WMI, www.modlinairport.pl), about 21 miles northwest of the city center, primarily serves budget airlines (especially Ryanair). A **taxi** into downtown Warsaw should be about 150 zł (the maximum legitimate fare is 200 zł, or 250 zł at night). There may be a direct **bus** operated by Flixbus (www.flixbus.com), or you can take the well-coordinated **bus-plus-train connection:** Take a shuttle bus to Modlin's main train station, then hop on a

train to Warszawa Centralna station (about 20 zł total, runs about hourly, 1-1.5 hours total, www.mazowieckie.com.pl).

GETTING AROUND WARSAW

Sprawling Warsaw can be exhausting to get around. Get comfortable with public transportation and taxis/Uber.

By Public Transit: Warsaw's efficient, affordable public transportation network includes buses, trams, and the two-line Metro (transit info: www.wtp.waw.pl). Everything is covered by the same tickets. Most rides within the tourist zone take less than 20 minutes, so the default is the 3.40-zł 20-minute ticket *(bilet 20-minutowy)*. For longer journeys, a single ticket *(bilet jednorazowy)* covers any trip up to 75 minutes for 4.40 zł. A 24-hour travelcard *(bilet dobowy)*—which pays for itself if you take at least five trips—costs 15 zł. Ticket machines, which are at most major stops and on board many buses and trams, are easy to use; they have English instructions and take credit cards. Be sure to validate your ticket as you board by inserting it into the little yellow box. You can also buy tickets on the Jakdojade app, which has a route finder.

Most of the city's major attractions line up on a single axis, the Royal Way, which is served by several different buses (but no trams). **Bus #175**—particularly useful on arrival—links Chopin Airport, the central train station, the Royal Way, and the Old Town (it terminates at Piłsudski Square, about a five-minute walk from Castle Square). Once you're in town, the designed-for-tourists **bus #180** conveniently connects virtually all the significant sights and neighborhoods: the former Jewish Ghetto and Museum of the History of Polish Jews, Castle Square/the Old Town, the Royal Way, Łazienki Park, and Wilanów Palace (south of the center). This user-friendly bus lists sights in English on the posted schedule inside (other buses don't). **Bus #111** is another handy option for those going to the Jewish Museum; from there, it runs parallel to the bus #180 route, cutting over to the Royal Way just south of Piłsudski Square, then down to Nowy Świat, before turning off to the east with a stop in front of the National Museum and then over the river.

Bus routes beginning with "E" (marked in red on schedules) are express, so they go long distances without stopping (these don't run July-Aug). Note that on Saturdays and Sundays in summer (May-Sept), the Nowy Świat-Krakowskie Przedmieście section of the Royal Way is closed to traffic, so the above routes detour along a parallel street.

Trams are useful for reaching the trendy Śródmieście district in the south. Several trams run along the north-south Marszałkowska corridor, with stops at Plac Konstytucji (Constitution Square, the heart of the Śródmieście) and at Plac Zbawiciela (with a cluster of great eateries).

Warsaw's two-line **Metro** system, designed for commuters, can be useful for hops between certain sights—especially line 2, which runs east to west; its most convenient stops are Rondo Daszyńskiego (near the Warsaw Uprising Museum), Świętokrzyska (where you can transfer to line 1), Nowy Świat-Uniwersytet (in the middle of the Royal Way, near the Copernicus Monument), Centrum Nauki Kopernik (on the riverbank, near the Copernicus Science Center), Stadion Narodowy (National Stadium, across the river), and Wileński (near the heart of the Praga district). The north-south line 1, which stops at the train station (Centrum), is less useful for visitors.

By Taxi: Use only cabs that are clearly marked with a company logo and telephone number; official cabs have a mermaid decal on the front door (or call your own: Locals like City Taxi, +48 19459; MPT Radio Taxi, +48 19191; or Ele taxi, +48 22 811 1111). All official taxis have similar rates: 8 zł to start, then 3 zł per kilometer (4.50 zł after 22:00, on weekends, or in the suburbs). **Uber** also works well in Warsaw and is typically cheaper than a taxi.

Tours in Warsaw

Walking Tours
Each year, new companies crop up offering walking tours in Warsaw. These tend to have one of two approaches: a "free" tour of the main sights (with generous tipping expected); or communism-themed tours, often with a ride to a gloomy apartment-block area for a taste of the Red old days. The TI and most hotels have brochures. Survey the latest offerings, do some homework (check online reviews), and pick a tour that suits your interests.

Private Guides
Having a talented local historian as your guide in this city, with such a complex and powerful story to tell, greatly enhances your experience. I've worked with two great guides, who charge around 750 zł for a four-hour walking tour: **Jola Postrzygacz** (+48 602 252 707, jolanta@postrzygacz.pl) and **Hubert Pawlik** (various tours, includes options by car, see descriptions on his website, +48 502 298 105, www.warsaw-citytours.com, guide@warsaw-citytours.com).

Food Tours
Eat Polska does excellent food and vodka tours around this fast-changing foodie mecca. A top-quality guide will take your small group to a variety of restaurants and bars around the city, with tasting samples at each one. The guides provide insightful context

WARSAW

WARSAW

Central Warsaw

Accommodations

1. Hotel Indigo
2. Between Us B&B & Między Nami
3. Chopin Boutique
4. Apple Inn
5. Oki Doki City Hostel
6. Hotel Bristol
7. Hotel Le Régina
8. Duval Apartments
9. Castle Inn
10. To Hotel Nobu

Eateries

11. Bibenda
12. Soul Kitchen
13. Le Cabaret
14. Drugie Dno
15. Żywioły
16. Kamanda Lwowska
17. A. Blikle
18. E. Wedel Pijalnia Czekolady
19. Elektrownia Powiśle Eateries
20. Warszawa Powiśle
21. Browary Warszawskie Eateries
22. Fabryka Norblina Eateries
23. To Centrum Praskie Koneser Eateries
24. Żyto & Freta 33
25. Pyzy, Flaki Gorące!
26. Zapiecek (5)

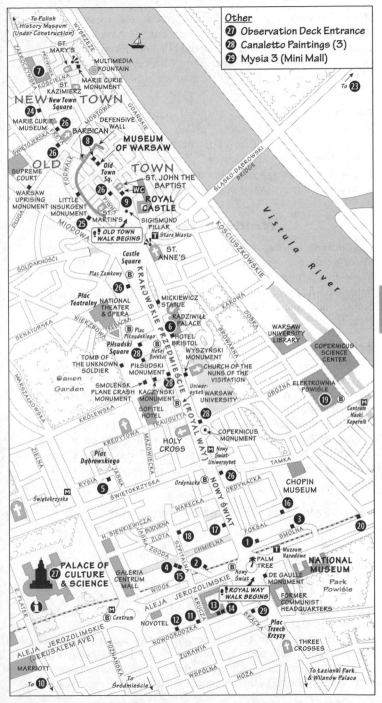

Other
- 27 Observation Deck Entrance
- 28 Canaletto Paintings (3)
- 29 Mysia 3 (Mini Mall)

To Polish History Museum (Under Construction)

ST. MARY'S
ST. KAZIMIERZ
MULTIMEDIA FOUNTAIN
MARIE CURIE MONUMENT

NEW TOWN New Town Square

MARIE CURIE MUSEUM
BARBICAN
DEFENSIVE WALL

MUSEUM OF WARSAW

OLD TOWN

Old Town Sq.
ST. JOHN THE BAPTIST

SUPREME COURT

WARSAW UPRISING MONUMENT
LITTLE INSURGENT MONUMENT
ST. MARTIN'S

WC
ROYAL CASTLE

SIGISMUND PILLAR

Stare Miasto

OLD TOWN WALK BEGINS

Castle Square

ST. ANNE'S

Plac Zamkowy

Plac Teatralny
NATIONAL THEATER & OPERA

MICKIEWICZ STATUE
RADZIWIŁŁ PALACE

Plac Piłsudskiego
Piłsudski Square
HOTEL BRISTOL
WYSZYŃSKI MONUMENT

TOMB OF THE UNKNOWN SOLDIER
PIŁSUDSKI MONUMENT

CHURCH OF THE NUNS OF THE VISITATION

SMOLEŃSK PLANE CRASH MONUMENT
KACZYŃSKI MONUMENT
SOFITEL HOTEL

Uniwersytet
WARSAW UNIVERSITY

COPERNICUS MONUMENT

HOLY CROSS

Nowy Świat-Uniwersytet

COPERNICUS SCIENCE CENTER

ELEKTROWNIA POWIŚLE

Centrum Nauki Kopernik

Plac Dąbrowskiego

Świętokrzyska

Ordynacka

CHOPIN MUSEUM

PALACE OF CULTURE & SCIENCE

GALERIA CENTRUM MALL

ROYAL WAY WALK BEGINS

Muzeum Narodowe
NATIONAL MUSEUM

DE GAULLE MONUMENT
FORMER COMMUNIST HEADQUARTERS

Park Powiśle

Plac Trzech Krzyży

NOVOTEL

ALEJA JEROZOLIMSKIE (JERUSALEM AVE.)

MARRIOTT

To Śródmieście

THREE CROSSES

To Łazienki Park & Wilanów Palace

WARSAW

Vistula River

WARSAW UNIVERSITY LIBRARY

ŚLĄSKO-DĄBROWSKI BRIDGE

To 23

PALM TREE

Nowy Świat

about what you're tasting, making this educational about both Polish cuisine and Polish culture in general. If you have a serious interest in food, this is the most worthwhile tour in town (food tours typically daily at 13:00, vodka tours with food pairings daily at 17:00, either tour is about 400 zł/person, get details and book at www.eatpolska.com).

Bus Tours

Warsaw's spread-out landscape makes it a natural for a hop-on, hop-off bus—although heavy traffic may make you wish you'd taken a tram or the Metro instead. The best choice is CitySightseeing, with red buses (85 zł/24 hours, 90 zł/48 hours, two routes). Skip City-Tour (yellow buses), which is less reliable.

Walks in Warsaw

I've outlined two self-guided walks in Warsaw. The Royal Way Walk covers the most interesting one-mile section of the Royal Way—in the heart of the city, from Palm Tree Circle to Castle Square. It's followed by the Old Town Walk, which starts in Castle Square and explores Warsaw's Old Town, ending in the adjacent New Town. Allow about two hours to do both walks back-to-back.

ROYAL WAY WALK

The Royal Way (Trakt Królewski) is the six-mile route that the kings of Poland used to travel from their main residence (at Castle Square in the Old Town) to their summer home (Wilanów Palace, south of the center and not worth visiting). This busy boulevard changes names from Nowy Świat to Krakowskie Przedmieście as it stretches from south to north. Not counting sightseeing stops, figure about 30 minutes to walk along Nowy Świat ("Part 1"), then another 45 minutes along Krakowskie Przedmieście to the Old Town ("Part 2").

Part 1: Palm Tree Circle and Nowy Świat
• Start this walk at the traffic circle officially named for Charles de Gaulle but colloquially known as...

Palm Tree Circle

This is one of the city's main intersections, marked by the iconic palm tree. Stand near the communist-era monument under the spruce trees (on the curb, kitty-corner from the biggest building) and get oriented.

You're standing at the intersection of two major boulevards: **Nowy Świat** (where we're heading next) and **Jerusalem Avenue** (Aleja Jerozolimskie, which heads from Warszawa Centralna station across the river). This street once led to a Jewish settlement

Warsaw at a Glance

▲▲▲**Museum of the History of Polish Jews** Exceptional, expansive exhibit on the full Jewish experience through Polish history. **Hours:** Wed-Mon 10:00-18:00, Sat until 20:00, closed Tue. See page 214.

▲▲**Castle Square** Colorful spot with whiffs of old Warsaw—Royal Castle, monuments, and a chunk of the city wall—and cafés just off the square. See page 193.

▲▲**Royal Castle** Warsaw's best palace, rebuilt after World War II, but retaining its former opulence and many original furnishings. **Hours:** Tue-Sun 10:00-18:00, Oct-April until 17:00, closed Mon year-round. See page 199.

▲▲**Old Town Market Square** Re-creation of Warsaw's glory days, with lots of colorful architecture. See page 196.

▲▲**National Museum** Collection of mostly Polish art, with unknown but worth-discovering works by Jan Matejko and the Młoda Polska (Art Nouveau) crew. **Hours:** Tue-Sun 10:00-18:00, Fri until 20:00, closed Mon. See page 205.

▲▲**Warsaw Uprising Museum** State-of-the-art space tracing the history of the Uprising and celebrating its heroes. **Hours:** Wed-Mon 8:00-18:00, Sat-Sun from 10:00, closed Tue. See page 221.

▲**Copernicus Science Center** Spiffy science museum with well-explained, hands-on exhibits in English; Warsaw's best family activity. **Hours:** Mon-Thu 8:00-18:00, Fri until 20:00, Sat-Sun 9:00-19:00. See page 210.

▲**Łazienki Park** Lovely, sprawling green space with Chopin statue, peacocks, and Neoclassical buildings. **Hours:** Always open; wonderful outdoor Chopin concerts mid-May-late Sept generally Sun at 12:00 and 16:00. See page 224.

▲**Museum of Warsaw** In-depth treatment of the history of Warsaw, with excellent movie in English. **Hours:** Tue- Fri 9:00-17:00, Thu until 19:00, Sat-Sun 11:00-18:00, closed Mon. See page 203.

▲**Marie Skłodowska-Curie Museum** Honors the great Polish scientist who studied radiation, in her birth home. **Hours:** Tue-Sat 12:00-18:00, closed Sun-Mon. See page 204.

WARSAW

called New Jerusalem. Like so much else in Warsaw, it's changed names many times. Between the World Wars, it became "May 3rd Avenue," celebrating Poland's 1791 constitution (Europe's first). But this was too nationalistic for the occupying Nazis, who called it simply Bahnhofstrasse ("Train Station Street"). Then the communists switched it back to "Jerusalem," strangely disregarding the religious connotations of that name. (Come on, guys—what about a good, old-fashioned "Stalin Avenue"?) The strikingly wide boulevards were part of the city's post-WWII Soviet rebuilding. Communist urban planners felt that eight-to-twelve-lane roads were ideal for worker pageantry like big May Day parades...and, when the workers weren't happy, for Soviet tanks to thunder around, maintaining order.

You can't miss the giant **palm tree** in the middle of Jerusalem Avenue. When a local artist went to the real Jerusalem, she was struck by the many palm trees—and wanted to erect one along Warsaw's own little stretch of "Jerusalem." This artificial palm tree went up in 2002 as a temporary installation. It was highly controversial, dividing the neighborhood. One snowy winter day, the pro-palm tree faction—who appreciated the way the tree spiced up this otherwise dreary metropolis—camped out here in bikinis and beachwear to show their support. They prevailed, and the tree is now a permanent fixture.

The big, blocky building across the street (on the left side of the intersection) was the **headquarters of the Communist Party,** built in 1948. *Nowy Świat* translates as "New World," inspiring a popular communist-era joke: What do you see when you turn your back on the Communist Party? A "New World." Ironically, when the economy was privatized in 1991, this building became home to Poland's stock exchange. And then the country's only dealership for Ferraris—certainly not an automobile for the proletariat—moved in downstairs.

On the corner in front of the former Communist Party HQ, a statue of **Charles de Gaulle** strides confidently up the street. A gift from the government of France, this celebrates the military tactician who came to Warsaw's rescue when the Red Army invaded from the USSR after World War I.

To the left of the Communist Party building is the vast **National Museum**—a good place for a fascinating lesson in Polish art (see the self-guided tour later, under "Sights in Warsaw").

Before walking down Nowy Świat, notice the small but powerful **monument** near you. In 1956, this was dedicated to the "Poles who fought for People's Poland"—with a strong communist connotation. In a classic example of Socialist Realism, the communists

appropriated a religious theme that Poles were inclined to embrace (this pietà composition)...and politicized it. But in 2014, the statue was rededicated to the "*partyzantom* who fought for free Poland in World War II." "Partisan" was a bad word in the 1950s, when it was used to describe the soldiers of the Polish Home Army—which fought against both the Nazis and the Soviets.

• *From here, turn your back to the Communist Party building and head into a new world— down Nowy Świat—to the first intersection. As you stroll, notice how massive, intense Warsaw suddenly becomes more intimate and accessible.*

Nowy Świat

This charming shopping boulevard, lined with boutiques, cafés, and restaurants, feels upscale and elegant. Before World War II,

Nowy Świat was Warsaw's most popular neighborhood. And today, once again, rents are higher here than anywhere else in town. While most tourists flock into the Old Town, Varsovians and visiting businesspeople prefer this zone and farther south.

The city has worked hard to revitalize this strip with broad sidewalks, flower boxes, old-time lampposts, and strict restrictions on traffic (only buses and taxis—and on summer weekends, it's entirely traffic-free).

Look down the street and notice the harmonious architecture. In the 1920s, this street was anything but cohesive: an eclectic and decadent strip of Art Deco facades, full of individualism. Rather than rebuild in that "trouble-causing" style, the communists used an idealized, more conservative, Neoclassical style, which feels more like the 1820s than the 1920s.

Ulica Chmielna, the first street to the left, is an appealing pedestrian street leading to Emil Wedel's chocolate heaven (a five-minute walk away—down Chmielna and then right on Szpitalna street; described later, under "Eating in Warsaw"). Between here and the Palace of Culture and Science stretches one of Warsaw's top shopping neighborhoods (culminating at the Galleria Centrum mall).

Across the street from Chmielna (on the right) is the restaurant street called **Foksal.** On a balmy summer evening, this street is filled with chatty al fresco diners. For more ideas on eating along either of these streets—Foksal or Chmielna—see page 232.

A few steps farther down Nowy Świat, on the left, look for the recommended **A. Blikle** pastry shop and café—a venerable spot for Polish sweets, especially *aczki* (rose-flavored jelly doughnuts). Don't miss the chance to sample this distinctly Polish treat. Step inside for a dose of the 1920s: good-life Art Deco decor and historical photos. Or, if you're homesick for Starbucks, drop in to one of the second-wave coffee shops that line this stretch of Nowy Świat—many with American-style lattes "to go."

A half-block down the street (on the left, at #39) is a rare surviving bit of preglitz Nowy Świat: Bar Mleczny Familijny, a classic **milk bar**—a government-subsidized cafeteria filled with locals seeking a cheap meal (an interesting cultural artifact, but not recommended for a meal; for more about milk bars, see the sidebar on page 26). But don't be surprised if it's gone by the time you visit; in this high-rent district, it's unlikely that these few remaining holdovers from the old days will survive for much longer.

Eat and shop your way along Nowy Świat. About one more block down, **Ordynacka street** (on the right) leads downhill to the Chopin Museum, worth considering for musical pilgrims.

Keep going. At the intersection with busy Świętokrzyska is a handy **Metro stop** for the M2 line; you can use this to reach the Warsaw Uprising Museum to the west, or the Copernicus Science Center or Praga district to the east.

• *Continuing straight along Nowy Świat through a duller stretch, you'll walk alongside a hulking, gloomy building on your left before popping out in a pleasant square with a big statue of Copernicus.*

Part 2: Krakowskie Przedmieście

• *The street name changes to Krakowskie Przedmieście (meaning, roughly, "suburb in the direction of Kraków") at the big...*

Copernicus Statue

This statue, by the great Danish sculptor Bertel Thorvaldsen, stands in front of the Polish Academy of Science. **Mikołaj Kopernik** (1473-1543) was born in Toruń and went to college in Kraków. The Nazis stole his statue and took it to Germany (which, like Poland, claims Copernicus as its own). Now it's back where it belongs. The concentric circles radiating from the front of the

statue represent the course of the planets' orbits, from Mercury to Saturn.

Just to Copernicus' left is a low-profile, black-marble **Chopin bench**—one of many scattered around the center. These benches mark points related to his life (in this case, his sister lived across the street). Each of these benches plays Chopin's music with the push of a button (though because of passing traffic, this one is tough to hear).

Directly in front of the statue, in the glass case, find a replica of a **Canaletto painting** of this same street scene in 1778 and compare it to today's reality. As the national archives were destroyed, city builders referred to historic paintings like these for guidance after World War II. You'll see other Canaletto replicas like this one scattered around the city.

• *Across from Copernicus, the Church of the Holy Cross is worth a look.*

Church of the Holy Cross (Kościół Św. Krzyża)

We'll pass many churches along this route, but the Church of the Holy Cross is unique (and free to enter). Composer **Fryderyk Cho-pin's heart** is inside one of the pillars of the nave (first big pillar on the left, look for the marker). After two decades of exile in France, Chopin's final wish was to have his heart brought back to his native Poland after his death. During World War II, the heart was hidden away in the countryside for safety.

Check out the bright gold chapel, located on the left as you face the altar, near the front of the church. It's dedicated to a saint whom Polish Catholics believe helps them with **"desperate and hopeless causes."** People praying here are likely dealing with some tough issues. The beads draped from the altarpieces help power their prayers, and the many little brass plaques are messages of thanks for prayers answered.

In the back-left corner (as you face the altar) is a chapel dedicated to Poland's favorite son, **St. John Paul II.** His ghostly image appears out of the wall; beneath him is a rock inscribed with the words *Tu es Petrus* (Latin for "You are Peter"—what Jesus said when he made St. Peter the first-ever pope), embedded with a capsule containing JPII's actual blood.

Just opposite, in the back-right corner, behind the giant barbed wire, is a memorial to the 22,000 Polish POWs—mostly officers and prominent civilians—massacred by Soviet soldiers in 1940 near **Katyń,** a village in today's Russia. Stalin was determined to decapitate Poland's military intelligentsia in a ruthless mass killing, which Poles have never forgotten.

Leaving the church, notice the 19th-century, bronze-and-granite **statue of Christ bearing the cross** along the balustrade. In front, a placard reads, "Lift up your hearts." Even as Warsaw bore the burden of Russian occupation, this statue inspired them to remain strong and not lose hope.

• *Cross the street (appreciating how pedestrian-friendly it is—crossing here used to be a real-life game of Frogger), and continue left.*

Warsaw University

A long block up the street on the right, you'll see the gates (marked *Uniwersytet*) to the main campus of **Warsaw University,** founded in 1816. This lively student district has plenty of bookstores *(księgarnia)* and cafeterias.

Keep strolling, appreciating the fine facades. The 18th century was a time of great political decline for Poland, as a series of incompetent foreign kings mishandled crises and squandered funds. But ironically, it was also Warsaw's biggest economic boom time. Along this boulevard, aristocratic families of the period built **mansions**—most of them destroyed in World War II and rebuilt since. Some have curious flourishes (just past the university on the right, look for the doorway supported by four bearded brutes admiring their overly defined abs...it's supposed to be a six-pack, but I count ten). Over time, many of these families donated their mansions to the university.

• *The bright-yellow church a block up from the university, on the right, is the...*

Church of the Nuns of the Visitation (Kościół Sióstr Wizytek)

This Rococo confection from 1761 is the only church on this walk that survived World War II, and is notable because Chopin was briefly the organist here.

The monument in front of the church commemorates **Cardinal Stefan Wyszyński,** who was the head of the Polish Catholic Church from 1948 to 1981. The communist authorities opposed the Church but also realized it would be risky for them to shut down the churches in such an ardently religious country. The Communist Party and the Catholic Church coexisted tensely in Poland, and when Wyszyński protested a Stalinist crackdown in 1953, he was arrested and imprisoned. Three years later, in a major victory for the Church, Wyszyński was released. He continued to fight the communists, becoming a great hero of the Polish people in their struggle against the regime—so much so, he's been called the "uncrowned king of Poland."

Across the street is another then-and-now Canaletto illustration.

• *Farther up (on the right, past the park) is the elegant, venerable...*

Hotel Bristol

A striking building with a round turret on its corner, the Hotel Bristol was used by the Nazis as a VIP hotel and bordello, and survived World War II. If you wander through any fancy Warsaw lobby... make it this one. Step in like you're staying here and explore its fine public spaces, with fresh Art Deco and Art Nouveau flourishes. The café in front retains its Viennese atmosphere, but the *pièce*

de résistance is the stunning Column Bar deeper in, past the dramatically chandeliered lounge.

• *Leave the Royal Way briefly here for a worthwhile detour. With the corner turret of Hotel Bristol at your back, cross the street and bear left between the buildings—passing the fancy Raffles Europejski Hotel. You'll pop out at a vast expanse. Continue straight ahead across the street and stand at the edge of...*

Piłsudski Square (Plac Marszałka Józefa Piłsudskiego)

The oversized, empty-feeling Piłsudski Square (pew-SOOD-skee) has been important Warsaw real estate for centuries, constantly changing with the times. In the 1890s, the Russians who controlled this part of Poland began construction of a huge and magnificent Orthodox cathedral on this spot. But soon after it was completed, Poland regained its independence, and anti-Russian sentiments ran hot. So in the 1920s, just over a decade after the cathedral went up, it was torn down. During the Nazi occupation, this square took the name "Adolf-Hitler-Platz." Under the communists, it was Zwycięstwa, meaning "Victory" (of the Soviets over Hitler's fascism).

When the regime imposed martial law in 1981, the people of Warsaw silently protested by filling the square with a giant cross made of flowers. The huge **plaque** in the ground near the road commemorates two monumental communist-era Catholic events on this square: John Paul II's first visit as pope to his homeland on June 2, 1979; and the May 31, 1981, funeral of Cardinal Stefan Wyszyński, whom we met across the street. The **cross** nearby also honors the 1979 papal visit, with one of his most famous and inspiring quotes to his countrymen: "Let thy spirit descend, let thy spirit descend, and renew the face of the earth—of *this* earth" (meaning Poland, in a just-barely-subtle-enough dig against the communist regime that was tolerating his visit).

Now walk deeper into the square and stand in the center, near the giant **flagpole,** with the Royal Way at your back, for this quick spin tour orientation: Ahead are the Tomb of the Unknown Soldier and Saxon Garden; 90 degrees to the right is the old National The-ater, eclipsed by a modern business center/parking garage; another 90 degrees to the right is a statue of Piłsudski (which you passed to get here); and 90 more degrees to the right is the Sofitel—formerly the Victoria Hotel, the ultimate plush, top-of-the-top hotel where all communist-era VIPs stayed.

In front of the hotel, the monument that resembles a **giant black staircase** commemorates the 2010 crash in Smoleńsk, Rus-sia, of a plane carrying 96 top government officials, including President Lech Kaczyński. There were no survivors. (A week later, the funeral for Kaczyński on this square drew more than 100,000 mourners.) Now look to the left to see a giant statue of Kaczyński at the edge of the square—striding in this direction, with his hand over his heart. You'll see lots of relatively new Kaczyński memorials throughout Warsaw (and Poland). On the one hand, it's a shocking trauma for a nation to lose a president unexpectedly midterm—think of all the things named for JFK in the US. On the other hand, the party Kaczyński co-founded (Law and Justice) still holds power in Poland—in fact, his twin brother is its chairman—so it's also politically expedient for them to lionize him as a martyr.

To the right of the hotel, on the horizon, you can see Warsaw's quickly expanding skyline. The imposing Palace of Culture and Science, which once stood alone over the city, is now joined by a cluster of glittering postcommunist skyscrapers, giving Warsaw a Berlin-esque vibe befitting its important role as a business center of Central Europe.

Deeper into the square, you may see fences on either side, or you may see a sprawling **construction zone.** The city is finally get-ting around to rebuilding some of the buildings that were leveled by the Nazis: the Saski Palace, the Brühl Palace, and three tene-ment houses that once fronted Królewska street. (The colonnade straight ahead—described below—was once part of the Saski Pal-ace.) If the fences are still up, peer through the holes to see the brick foundations they've already excavated.

If it's accessible, walk to the fragment of colonnade by the park that marks the **Tomb of the Unknown Soldier** (Grób Nieznanego Żołnierza). The Saski Palace (this is all that's left) was built by the Saxon prince electors (Dresden's Augustus the Strong and his son), who became kings of Poland in the 18th century. After the palace was destroyed in World War II, this fragment was kept to memorialize Polish soldiers. The names of key battles over 1,000 years are etched into the columns, the urns contain dirt from major Polish battlefields, and two soldiers stand stiffly at attention. Every hour on the hour, they do a crisp Changing of the Guard—which, poignantly, honors those who have perished in this country, so shaped by wars against foreign invaders.

Just behind the tomb is the stately **Saxon Garden** (Ogród Saski), inhabited by genteel statues, gorgeous flowers, and a spurt-

ing fountain. This park was also built by the Saxon kings of Poland. Like most foreign kings, Augustus the Strong and his son cared little for their Polish territory, building gardens like these for themselves instead of investing in more pressing needs. Poles say that foreign kings such as Augustus did nothing but "eat, drink, and loosen their belts" (it rhymes in Polish). According to Poles, these selfish absentee kings were the culprits in Poland's eventual decline. But they do appreciate having such a fine venue for a Sunday stroll.

Walk back out toward the Royal Way, stopping at the statue you passed earlier. In 1995, the square was again renamed—this

time for **Józef Piłsudski** (1867-1935), the guy with the big walrus mustache. With the help of a French captain named Charles de Gaulle (whom we met earlier), Piłsudski forced the Russian Bolsheviks out of Poland in 1920 in the so-called "Miracle on the Vistula." Piłsudski is credited with creating a once-again-independent Poland after more than a century of foreign oppression, and he essentially ran Poland as a virtual dictator after World War I. Of course, under the communists, Piłsudski was swept under the rug. But since 1989, he has enjoyed a renaissance as many Poles' favorite prototype anticommunist hero. His name adorns streets, squares, and bushy-mustachioed monuments all over the country.

• *Return to Hotel Bristol, turn left, and continue your Royal Way walk.*

Radziwiłł Palace

Next door to the hotel, you'll see the huge Radziwiłł Palace. The Warsaw Pact was signed here in 1955, officially uniting the Soviet satellite states in a military alliance against NATO. This building has also, from time to time, served as the Polish "White House." Along the street in front of the palace is another monument to the 2010 Smoleńsk plane crash, which effectively decapitated Poland's leadership.

• *Beyond Radziwiłł Palace, on the right, you'll reach a park with a...*

Statue of Adam Mickiewicz

Poland's national poet, Adam Mickiewicz spearheaded Poland's cultural survival during more than a century when the country disappeared from maps—absorbed by Austria, Prussia, and Russia. This was an age when underdog nations (and peoples without nations) all over Europe had their own national revival movements. The statue was erected in 1898 with permission from the Russian czar, as long as the people paid for it themselves. It's still an important part of community life: Polish high school students have a big formal ball (like a prom) 100 days before graduation. After the ball, if students come here and hop around the statue on one leg, it's supposed to bring them good luck on their finals. Mickiewicz, for his part, looks like he's suffering from a heart attack—perhaps in response to the impressively ugly National Theater and Opera a block in front of him.

• *Continue to the end of the Royal Way, marked by the big pink palace. Just before the castle, on your right, is...*

St. Anne's Church

This Rococo church has playful Corinthian capitals inside and out and a fine pulpit shaped like the prow of a ship—complete with

a big anchor. The richly ornamented apse, behind the altar, survived World War II. This church offers organ concerts nearly daily in summer (see "Entertainment in Warsaw," later).

For a scenic finale to your Royal Way stroll, climb the 150 steps of the **view tower** by the church (10 zł, generally open daily 10:00-18:00, later in summer, closed in bad winter weather).

You'll be rewarded with excellent views—particularly of Castle Square and the Old Town. From up top, visually retrace your steps along the Royal Way, and notice the emerging skyline surrounding the Palace of Culture and Science. The tower also affords a good look at the Praga district across the river, where the Red Army waited for the Nazis to level Warsaw during the uprising. Help was so close at hand...but stayed right where it was.

• *Just across from the view tower entrance, look for another Chopin bench (in front of #79). From St. Anne's Church, it's just a few more steps to Castle Square and the start of my Old Town Walk.*

OLD TOWN WALK

In 1945, not a building remained standing in Warsaw's "Old" Town (Stare Miasto). Everything you see here is rebuilt, mostly finished by 1956. Some think the Old Town seems artificial, in a Disney World kind of way. For others, the painstaking postwar reconstruction feels just right, with Old World squares and lanes charming enough to give Kraków a run for its money.

This concise walk, which can be done in about 45 minutes (and is a natural continuation of the Royal Way Walk outlined earlier), offers a quick overview of Warsaw's rebuilt historic core. We'll begin at Castle Square; wind through the streets and squares of the Old Town; pop out at the far side, at the Barbican; and have the opportunity to venture a few minutes farther, into the pretty and mellow New Town. For those looping back, there's also an optional, lightly guided return to this point via sleepy back streets.

• *Begin by standing on the gateway square to the Old Town, at the base of the tall pillar.*

Castle Square (Plac Zamkowy)

This beautiful square (rated ▲▲) is packed with Polish history. Get comfy for a quick overview:

Historically, the Polish kings called Kraków home. But things began to change in 1572, with the expiration of the second great Polish dynasty—the Jagiellonians. Rather than elevate another Polish aristocratic family to the throne, the Polish nobility decided to keep power in their own hands. From that point on, Poland was ruled by the Sejm, or Republic of Nobles—consisting of the kingdom's wealthiest 10 percent. The Sejm elected various foreign kings for limited stints on their throne. While this system kept Poland under its own control (to a degree), it wound up being unworkable: Poor choices of sovereigns, coupled with in-fighting among the nobles, paralyzed Poland and ultimately led to it being wiped from the map of Europe for a century and a half.

The guy on the 72-foot-tall **pillar** is Sigismund III, the first Polish king from the Swedish Vasa dynasty (or Waza in Polish). In 1596, it was Sigismund who relocated his royal seat from Kraków to Warsaw: Warsaw was the meeting point of the Sejm, and it was closer to the center of 16th-century Poland (which had expanded to the east).

Turn your attention to the big, pink **Royal Castle.** A castle has stood here since Warsaw was founded around 1300, but it grew much more important after Warsaw became the capital: It was both the meeting place of the Sejm and the residence of the king...sort of like Buckingham Palace and the Houses of Parliament rolled into one. The palace reached its peak under Stanisław August Poniatowski—the final Polish king—who imported artists and architects to spiff up the interior.

During World War II, Luftwaffe bombs all but obliterated the palace—only one wall remained standing. Reconstruction stalled because Stalin considered it a palace for the high-class elites. It was finally rebuilt in the more moderate 1970s, funded by local donations. The castle's opulent interior is well worth touring—see listing later, under "Sights in Warsaw." (I'll wait while you tour the castle...then let's meet out here to resume the walk.)

Along the right side of the castle, notice the **two previous pillars** lying on their sides. The first one, from 1644, was falling apart and had to be replaced in 1887 by a new one made of granite. In 1944, a Nazi tank broke this second pillar—a symbolic piece of Polish heritage—into the four pieces (still pockmarked with bullet holes) that you see here today. As Poland rebuilt, its citizens put Sigismund III back on his pillar. Past the pillars are views of Warsaw's red-and-white National Stadium across the river—built for the Euro Cup soccer tournament in 2012.

Across the square from the castle, you'll see the partially re-constructed **defensive wall.** This rampart once enclosed the entire Old Town. Like all of Poland, Warsaw has seen invasion from all sides.

Explore the café-lined lanes that branch off Castle Square. Street signs indicate the year that each lane was originally built.

The first street is **Ulica Piwna** ("Beer Street"). If you take a little detour up this street, you'll find **St. Martin's Church** (Kościół Św. Martina, on the left). Run by Franciscan nuns, this church has a simple, modern interior. Walk up the aisle and find the second pillar on the right. Notice the partly destroyed crucifix—it's the only church artifact that survived World War II. Across the street and closer to Castle Square, admire the carefully carved doorway of the house called *pod Gołębiami* ("Under Doves")—dedicated to the memory of an old woman who fed birds amidst the Old Town rubble after World War II.

Back on Castle Square, find the white **plaque** on the wall (at Plac Zamkowy 15/19). It explains that 50 Poles were executed by Nazis on this spot on September 2, 1944. You'll see plaques like this all over the Old Town, each one commemorating victims or opponents of the Nazis. The brick planter under the plaque is often filled with fresh flowers to honor the victims.

• *Leave the square at the far end, on* **St. John's street** *(Świętojańska). On the plaque under the street name sign, you can guess what the dates mean, even if you don't know Polish: This building was constructed from 1433 to 1478, destroyed in 1944, and rebuilt from 1950 to 1953.*

Partway down the street on the right, you'll come to the big brick...

Cathedral of St. John the Baptist (Katedra Św. Jana Chrzciciela)

This cathedral-basilica is the oldest (1370) and most important church in Warsaw. Superficially unimpressive, the church's own

archbishop admitted that it was "modest and poor"—but "the historical events that took place here make it magnificent" (much like Warsaw itself). Poland's constitution was consecrated here on May 3, 1791. Much later, this church became the final battleground of the 1944 Warsaw Uprising—when a Nazi "tracked mine" (a huge bomb on tank tracks—this one appropriately named *Goliath*) drove into the church and exploded, massacring the rebels. You can still see part of that tank's tread hanging on the outside wall of the church (through the passage on the right side, between the buttresses).

Cost and Hours: Cathedral—free, crypt—5 zł, both open to tourists Mon-Sat 10:00-17:00, Sun from 15:00, closed during services and summertime organ concerts (see "Entertainment in Warsaw," later).

Visiting the Cathedral: Head inside. Typical of brick churches, it has a "hall church" design, with three naves of equal height. In the back-left corner, find the chapel with the tomb of Cardinal Stefan Wyszyński—the great Polish leader who, as Warsaw's archbishop, morally steered the country through much of the Cold War. (Notice the request to pray for his beatification, as Poles would love to see him become a saint.) Nearby, the crypt holds graves of several important Poles, including Stanisław August Poniatowski (the last Polish king) and Nobel Prize-winning author Henryk Sienkiewicz. Then head up the nave to the main altar, which holds a copy of the Black Madonna—proclaimed "everlasting queen of Poland" after a victory over the Swedes in the 17th century. The original Black Madonna is in Częstochowa (125 miles south of Warsaw)—a mecca for Slavic Catholics, who visit in droves in hopes of a miracle. In the chapel left of the high altar, look for the crucifix ornamented with real human hair.

Nearby: Those interested in Cold War espionage may want to seek out a nearby exhibit about **Ryszard Kukliński** (1930-2004), a Polish military officer who worked closely with USSR authorities...all the while collecting priceless intelligence for the CIA. Kukliński's story, with many twists and turns, is riveting. The excellent exhibit about this superspy was recently slated to be folded into a brand-new **Cold War Museum,** which you'll likely find in the streets immediately behind the cathedral (for the latest, see www.muzeumzimnejwojny.com).

• *Continue up the street and enter Warsaw's grand...*

WARSAW

Old Town Market Square (Rynek Starego Miasta)

For two centuries, this was a gritty market square. Sixty-five years ago, it was a pile of bombed-out rubble. And today, like a phoe-

nix from the ashes, it's risen to remind residents and tourists alike of the prewar glory of the Polish capital (which is why it's rated ▲▲).

Head to the **mermaid fountain** in the middle of the square. The mermaid is an important symbol in Warsaw—you'll see her everywhere. Legend has it that a mermaid *(syrenka)* lived in the Vistula River and protected the townspeople. While this siren supposedly serenaded the town, she's most appreciated for her strength (hence the sword). This square seems to declare that life goes on in Warsaw, as it

always has. Children frolic here, oblivious to the turmoil their forebears withstood. When the fountain gurgles, the kids giggle.

Each of the square's four sides is named for a prominent 18th-century Varsovian: Kołłątaj, Dekert, Barss, and Zakrzewski. These men served as "Presidents" of Warsaw (mayors, more or less), and Kołłątaj was also a framer of Poland's 1791 constitution. Take some time to explore the square. Enjoy the colorful architecture. Notice that many of the buildings were intentionally built to lean out into the square—to approximate the higgledy-piggledy wear and tear of the original buildings.

If you'd like to learn more about Warsaw's history, visit the Museum of Warsaw on the Dekert (north) side of the square (described later, under "Sights in Warsaw").

• *Exit the square on Nowomiejska (at the mermaid's 2 o'clock, next to the Museum of Warsaw, under the second-story niche sculpture of St. Anne). After a block, you'll reach the* **Barbican** *(Barbakan). This defensive gate of the Old Town, similar to Kraków's, protected the medieval city from invaders. Once you've crossed through the Barbican, you're officially in Warsaw's...*

New Town (Nowe Miasto)

This 15th-century neighborhood is "new" in name only: It was the first part of Warsaw to spring up outside the city walls (and is therefore slightly newer than the Old Town). The New Town is a fun place to wander: only a little less charming than the Old Town, but with a more real-life feel—people live and work here. While busy sightseers may choose to skip the New Town, if you stick with me for a few minutes longer, it's worth the extra time. Continue straight ahead from the Barbican on Nowomiejska, which becomes Freta. As you proceed deeper into the New Town, you can feel the tourism slowly melt away. You'll pass an outpost of the E. Wedel chocolate empire, and some funky galleries and boutiques. On the right is the informative **museum about Marie Skłodowska-Curie,** who grew up in this neighborhood (at #16; see listing later, under "Sights in Warsaw").

Just beyond, for some modern "design"-oriented souvenirs, watch on the left for the endearing **Love Poland Design shop** (at #29/31)...pierogi pillow, anyone?

That shop also marks the entrance to the mellow, easy-to-like **New Town Square** (Rynek Nowego Miasta). A few recommended restaurants line its top edge, and its bottom is dominated by the distinctive green dome of St. Kazimierz Church. While just a short walk from the Old Town, this feels a world apart—a fine spot to relax in the heart of this giant city, enjoy an al fresco meal, sit on a bench, do some people-watching...and just enjoy.

• *To finish our walk with a scenic overview, cross through to the bottom end of the square and turn left, then right (with the green dome on your right). Keep going with the red-brick St. Mary's Church (Kościół*

Mariacki) on your left-hand side. Soon you'll emerge at a park with a monument and an overlook.

The **Marie Skłodowska-Curie monument** honors the woman whose museum we passed earlier. Maria Skłodowska (1867-1934) grew up in this neighborhood at a time when Warsaw was under Russian control, so women were not allowed to pursue a university education. Instead, she left in 1891 for Paris, where—while studying at the Sorbonne—she met and fell in love with a fellow scientist named Pierre Curie. The two wed and became partners in life and in research (and the Polish "Maria" became French "Marie").

They were the first to identify and explain the phenomenon of radioactivity, and they discovered two new elements: polonium (which Marie named after her native land—in the monument she's holding an object that represents that discovery) and radium. They were awarded the Nobel Prize in Physics; later, Marie also won a Nobel Prize in Chemistry, for how her discoveries revolutionized the world's understanding of how the elements function.

After Pierre died in a horse-cart accident, Marie took over his professorship at the Sorbonne and continued her research; among other accomplishments, she founded the Radium Institute, which still carries out important cancer research. (Marie and Pierre were the first to treat certain tumors with radiation.) Few scientists of her generation had so great an impact on our understanding of the world than this brilliant woman from Warsaw.

Madame Curie is looking out over a **panorama** of the Vistula River and Warsaw's more rugged and wild eastern embankment. Down below is an inviting park with a "multimedia fountain" that performs a sound-and-light show on weekends in the summer (ask the TI for the schedule)—which can be viewed from either up here or down along the river. Speaking of which, notice the inviting promenade that runs along the Vistula—in good weather, it's packed with locals enjoying their city. Why not join them?

• *Our walk is finished. You can head back the way you came to reach the Old Town Square. Or, to see a side of the Old Town that many tourists miss, consider this scenic detour back to Castle Square.*

Optional Return Detour: From the Barbican to Castle Square

Go back through the Barbican and over the little bridge, turn right, and walk along the houses that line the inside of the wall. You'll pass a leafy garden courtyard on the left—a reminder that people actually live in the tourist zone within the Old Town walls. Just beyond the garden on the right, look for the carpet-beating rack, used to clean rugs (these are common fixtures in people's backyards). Go left into the square called Szeroki Dunaj ("Wide Danube"), walk to its end, then turn right at Wąski Dunaj ("Narrow Danube").

After about 100 yards, you'll pass the city wall. Just to the right (outside the wall), you'll see the monument to the **Little Insurgent** of 1944, a child wearing a grown-up's helmet and too-big boots, and carrying a machine gun. Children—especially Scouts (Harcerze)—played a key role in the resistance against the Nazis. Their job was mainly carrying messages and propaganda.

Continue around the wall, admiring more public art. Circling all the way back around, soon before you hit the giant pillar, look for the statue honoring **Jan Zachwatowicz** (1900-1983)—the architect who oversaw the rebuilding of Old Warsaw after World War II. If you've enjoyed your visit, offer him a thank-you to end this tour.

Sights in Warsaw

THE OLD TOWN
These sights are linked by my Old Town Walk, earlier.

▲▲Royal Castle (Zamek Królewski)
Warsaw's Royal Castle, dominating Castle Square at the entrance to the Old Town, has the most opulent interior in Poland. Many

of its furnishings are original (hidden away when it became clear the city would be demolished in World War II). A visit to the castle is like perusing a great Polish history textbook. In fact, you'll likely see grade-school classes sitting cross-legged on the floors. Watching the teachers quizzing eager young history buffs, try to imagine what it's like to be a young Pole growing up in a country with such a tumultuous history. The "Royal Route" (the lavish apartments) is worth paying for, but unless you're an art lover, I'd skip the extra cost of the Gallery of Masterpieces. Wednesday is a good day to visit—it's free, and although some royal rooms are closed, enough are open to make a visit worthwhile.

Cost and Hours: Royal Route—50 zł, Gallery of Masterpieces—40 zł, more for special exhibits, free on Wed (when some royal rooms are closed); open Tue-Sun 10:00-18:00, Oct-April until 17:00, closed Mon year-round, last entry one hour before closing; Plac Zamkowy 4, +48 22 355 5170, www.zamek-krolewski.pl.

Tours: The castle's well-produced audioguide is included in the ticket price (10 zł on Wed, when entry is free). Good English information is posted throughout. For an efficient visit, use my commentary to follow the one-way route through the castle.

Services: A public WC is on the courtyard just around the corner of the castle, with more inside and downstairs.

Visiting the Castle: Because the castle visitor route often changes, it's possible you won't see the rooms in this exact order; match the labels in each room to the corresponding text below.

Entering the courtyard, find the ticket office, then cross to the opposite side to enter. (Downstairs are the mandatory coat check and the audioguide desk.) In the lobby, turn left, pass the gift shop and café, then follow *Castle Route* signs upstairs.

The first big room is the **Council Chamber,** where a "Permanent Council" consisting of the king, 18 senators, and 18 representatives met to chart Poland's course. Next is the **Great Assembly Hall,** heavy with marble and chandeliers. The statues of Apollo and Minerva flanking the main door are modeled after King Stanisław August Poniatowski and Catherine the Great of Russia, respectively. (The king enjoyed a youthful romantic dalliance with Catherine on a trip to Russia, and never quite seemed to get over her...much to his wife's consternation, I'm sure.)

Step into the **Knights' Hall,** with yet more busts and portraits of VIPs—Very Important Poles. The statue of Chronos—god of time, with the globe on his shoulders—is actually a functioning clock, though now it's stopped at 11:15 to commemorate the exact time in 1944 when the Nazis bombed this palace to bits. Attached to this hall is the **Marble Room,** with more portraits of Polish greats ringing the top of the room. Above the fireplace is a portrait of Stanisław August Poniatowski (the last Polish king).

Next, step into the **Throne Room.** Notice the crowned white eagles, the symbol of Poland, decorating the banner behind the throne. The Soviets didn't allow anything royal or aristocratic, so postwar restorations came with crownless eagles. Only after 1989 were these eagles crowned again. Peek into the **Conference Room,** with portraits of Russia's Catherine the Great, England's George III, and

France's Louis XVI—in whose esteemed royal league Poniatowski liked to consider himself.

Pass through four more grand rooms: the King's Study, Dressing Room, and Bedchamber (with a gorgeous green silk canopy over the bed), then the Old Audience Chamber. Finally, you'll enter the **Canaletto Room,** filled with canvases of late 18th-century Warsaw painted in exquisite detail by this talented artist. (This Canaletto, also known for his panoramas of Dresden, was the nephew of another more famous artist with the same nickname, known for painting Venice's canals.) Paintings like these helped post-WWII restorers resurrect the city from its rubble. Straight ahead as you enter, on the lower wall, the biggest canvas features the view of Warsaw from the Praga district across the river; pick out the few landmarks that are still standing (or, more precisely, have been resurrected). The castle you're in dominates the center of the painting, overlooking the river. Notice the artist's self-portrait in the lower left. On the facing wall is Canaletto's depiction of the election of Stanisław August Poniatowski as king, in a field outside Warsaw (notice the empty throne in the middle of the group). Among the assembled crowd, each flag represents a different Polish province.

From here, look left of the big "view of Warsaw" painting into the **side chapel,** reserved for the king. In a box to the left of the altar is the heart of Tadeusz Kościuszko, a hero of both the American Revolution and the Polish struggle against the Partitions (for more about the Partitions, see page 18).

As you cross over to the other part of the castle, you'll pass through the **Four Seasons Gallery** (with some fine but faded Gobelin tapestries) before entering a few rooms occupied by the houses of parliament—a reminder that this "castle" wasn't just the king's house but also the meeting place of the legislature. In the giant red room called the **New Deputies' Chambers,** notice the maps over the doors showing Poland's constantly in-flux borders—a handy visual aid for the many school groups that visit here.

After several rooms, you'll reach the grand **Senators' Chamber,** with the king's throne, surrounded by different coats of arms.

Each one represents a region that was part of Poland during its golden age, back when it was united with Lithuania and its territory stretched from the Baltic to the Black Sea (see the map on the wall between the doors). In this room, Poland adopted its 1791 constitution (notice the replica in the display case to the left of the throne). It was the first in Europe, written soon after America's and just months before France's. And, like the Constitution of the United States, it was very progressive, based on the ideals of the Enlightenment. But when the final Partitions followed in 1793 and 1795, Poland was divided between neighboring powers and ceased to exist as a country until 1918—so the constitution was never fully put into action.

At the end of this impressive chamber, you'll turn right into a room with two giant canvases by the great historical painter **Jan Matejko,** showing a very high point and a very low point in Polish history (for more on Matejko, see page 206). First, on the right wall, the *Constitution of 3 May 1791* shows the giddy procession (with the Marshall of the Sejm crowd-surfing through the Old Town, and this castle in the background) heading up the street to the Cathedral of St. John the Baptist to consecrate the first constitution in Europe. But from there, Poland's fortunes tumbled dramatically. Straight ahead from where you entered, *Rejtan—The Fall of Poland* shows the nobleman Tadeusz Rejtan (on the right) lying in front of a door and pulling his shirt open in violent protest against his colleagues in the Sejm debating the First Partition in 1773, which ceded some Polish territory to neighboring Russia, Prussia, and Austria. Two Partitions later, Poland was erased from the map of Europe for a century and a half.

In the next room is another Matejko painting (on the right): *Stefan Batory at Pskov,* in which the Polish king negotiates with Ivan the Terrible's envoys to break their siege of a Russian town. Notice the hussars—fearsome Polish soldiers wearing winged armor.

From here, you'll work your way back down to the lobby where you began. There you'll also find the entrance to another sight...

Gallery of Masterpieces: This gallery of paintings, sculpture, and decorative arts may please art lovers, but it's not essential viewing for most. Inside is a fine cabinet of silver and crystal, and the 36 paintings of the Lanckroński Collection. In the final room, take your time appreciating two canvases by Rembrandt (both from 1641). *Girl in a Picture Frame* is exactly that—except that she's "breaking the frame" by resting her hands on a faux frame that Rembrandt has painted inside the real one...shattering the fourth wall in a way that was unusual for the time. The other, *A Scholar at His Writing Table,* shows the hirsute academic glancing up from his notes. Circle around behind the canvases to see X-rays of the paintings, which have helped experts better understand the master's techniques.

Other Castle Sights: Consider a detour to the **Kubicki Arcades** (Arkady Kubiciego), the impressively excavated arcades deep beneath the castle. From the entrance lobby, head downstairs to the

area with the cloakroom, bathrooms, and bookshop, then find
the long escalator that takes you
down to the arcades. It's free to
wander the long, cavernous, and
newly clean and gleaming space,
made elegant by grand drapes.

The **"Tin-Roofed Palace"**
(Pałac pod Blachą) features an
extensive oriental carpet collec-
tion and seven unimpressive apartments of Prince Józef Poniatowski, the king's brother; it's not worth the 30 zł extra.

▲Museum of Warsaw (Muzeum Warszawy)

Four adjoining townhouses on the north side of the Old Town
Square have been connected and turned into this in-depth museum
that tells the story of Warsaw. While there's too much detail for a
casual visitor's attention span, it's well presented and offers some
interesting insight into this great city.

Cost and Hours: 25 zł, includes audioguide, free on Tue;
open Tue-Fri 9:00-17:00, Thu until 19:00, Sat-Sun 11:00-18:00,
closed Mon; Rynek Starego Miasta 28–42, +48 22 277 4300, www.
muzeumwarszawy.pl.

Visiting the Museum: The permanent collection, called
"Warsaw in 23 Rooms," offers exactly that. Pick up the detailed
map and the dense-but-informative audioguide, and head down
into the cellars for an orientation to the city's history—with a timeline, lots of graphs, maps, and helpful models of key landmarks.
Then head upstairs and weave your way through the labyrinthine
collection; your geo-tagged audioguide knows (roughly) where you
are and offers commentary.

Back up on the ground floor, in the courtyard, you'll find architectural decorations from city buildings, as well as the original
mermaid statue from the square. Then work your way up through
four floors: Floor 1 has a photography gallery, paintings of Warsaw, and a model of the Old Town in the late 18th century. Floor
2 features bronzes, silverwork, portraits of important Varsovians,
and clothing. Floor 3 has a moving collection of "relics" from the
difficult WWII days and a more lighthearted exhibit on "Warsaw
packaging"—with nostalgic vintage advertising. Floor 4 features
antique clocks and the "Schiele Room"—named not for the artist,
but for the local merchant family whose furnishings and personal
objects you can see here. You can continue all the way up into the
attic ("viewing platform") to look down over the square, and to see
panoramas of the Old Town's rooftops.

The museum sporadically presents a poignant 20-minute film

(in English) tracing the tragic WWII experience of this city—from a thriving interwar metropolis, to a bombed-out wasteland, to the focus of a massive rebuilding effort. This only runs a couple of times each week; consider calling or dropping by to find out when, so you can time your visit accordingly (10 zł).

▲Marie Skłodowska-Curie Museum

Maria Skłodowska (1867-1934)—who, as Marie Curie, would go on to accomplish many firsts, including pioneering the study of radioactivity and becoming the only person to win Nobel Prizes in two different disciplines—was born in this building and grew up in the neighborhood before she moved to Paris to study. This concise, endearing museum is happy to introduce visitors to Madame Curie's world and work. Just a few rooms on one floor, it's made meaningful by the good included audioguide.

Cost and Hours: 11 zł, free on Tue; open Tue-Sat 12:00-18:00, closed Sun-Mon; Ulica Freta 16, +48 22 831 8092, www.mmsc.waw.pl.

Visiting the Museum: Buy your ticket, pick up your audioguide, and head upstairs to tour the exhibit. First you'll learn about Maria Skłodowska's childhood (with lots of black-and-white photos). Then you'll step into a re-creation of the glass-roofed Parisian shed where she and her husband, Pierre, conducted early experiments. You'll see old instruments and equipment, and learn more about the couple and their revolutionary discoveries. On the wall are copies of the two Nobel Prizes she won—one jointly with Pierre, the other solo (later, other members of her family would also go on to win Nobels). Then you'll walk through a room of biographical panels describing different stages of her life—for example, during World War I, where she contributed to the war effort by operating a mobile X-ray unit to treat injured soldiers. Finally, you'll see a re-creation of a drawing room like the one she grew up in, including items from her family. A short film provides a recap of all you've learned about this remarkable, often unheralded scientist. Downstairs are temporary exhibits and a well-stocked shop of Skłodowska swag (say that three times fast).

Polish History Museum

This ambitious new museum is being built north of the New Town, at Warsaw's Citadella. The project has been ongoing for years; it could open as early as 2024. Once open, this promises to become a big and important draw for all visitors—especially Poles. To check on the progress, see muzhp.pl. They're also planning a Polish Army Museum nearby.

NEAR PALM TREE CIRCLE

These sights are in the city center, near Palm Tree Circle—where Jerusalem Avenue crosses Nowy Świat.

East of the Royal Way (Toward the River)
▲▲National Museum (Muzeum Narodowe)

A celebration of underrated Polish artists, this museum offers a surprisingly engaging and—if you follow my tour—concise overview of this country's impressive painters (many of whom are unknown outside their home country). A modern, state-of-the-art exhibition space allows these unsung canvases to really belt it out.

Cost and Hours: 25 zł, more for temporary exhibits, permanent collection free on Tue; Tue-Sun 10:00-18:00, Fri until 20:00, closed Mon, last entry 45 minutes before closing; one long block east of Nowy Świat at Aleja Jerozolimskie 3, bus #111 stops right out front, +48 22 629 3093, www.mnw.art.pl.

➔ **Self-Guided Tour:** The collection fills several separate galleries. The museum's strongest point—and the bulk of this tour—is its 19th-century Polish art. But before diving in, consider some of the other collections.

Overview: To get your bearings, pick up a floor plan as you enter. On the ground floor are Ancient Art (from Greek pieces to artifacts left by early Polish tribes), the Faras Gallery (highlighting the museum's fine collection of archaeological findings from that ancient Egyptian city), and a good collection of Medieval Art, which gathers altarpieces from churches around Poland—organized both chronologically and geographically—and displays some of the most graphic crucifixes and pietàs I've seen.

Upstairs (floor 1) is the excellent Gallery of 19th-Century Art, which is described by the tour below. Nearby, through the gift shop, is the worthwhile 20th- and 21st-Century Art collection, with an impressive array of Modern and Postmodern Polish artists, including photographers and filmmakers. The underwhelming Gallery of Old Masters fills floor 2.

To cut to the chase, focus on the **Gallery of 19th-Century Art.** We'll start with the granddaddy of Polish art, Jan Matejko.

• *From the entrance lobby, head up the left staircase, then turn left across the mezzanine and ascend a few more stairs to enter the collection. Matejko is hiding at the far end of this wing: Entering the collection, angle right, then left, heading all the way to the room at the far end, which is dominated by a gigantic battlefield canvas. (If you get lost, ask the attendants, "mah-TAY-koh?")*

Jan Matejko: While not the most talented of artists—he's a fairly conventional painter, lacking a distinctive, recognizable style—Matejko more than made up for it with vision and productivity. His typically super-sized paintings are steeped in proud

Jan Matejko (1838-1893)

Jan Matejko (yawn mah-TAY-koh) is Poland's most important painter, period. In the mid-to-late 19th century, the nation of Poland had been dissolved by foreign powers, and Polish artists struggled to make sense of their people's place in the world. Rabble-rousing Romanticism seemed to have failed (inspiring many brutally suppressed uprisings), so Polish artists and writers turned their attention to educating the people about their history, with the goal of keeping their traditions alive.

Matejko was at the forefront of this so-called "positivist" movement. He saw what the tides of history had done to Poland and was determined to make sure his countrymen learned from it. He painted two types of works: huge, grand-scale epics depicting monumental events in Polish history; and small, intimate portraits of prominent Poles. Polish schoolchildren study history from books with paintings of virtually every single Polish king—all painted by the incredibly prolific Matejko.

Matejko is not admired for his technical mastery or for the literal truth of his works—he was notorious for fudging historical details to give his canvases a bit more propagandistic punch. But he is revered for the emotion behind—and inspired by—his works. His paintings are utilitarian, straightforward, and dramatic enough to stir the patriot in any Pole. The intense focus on history by Matejko and other positivists is one big reason why today's Poles are still so in touch with their heritage.

You'll see Matejko's works in Warsaw's National Museum and Royal Castle, as well as in Kraków's Gallery of 19th-Century Polish Art (above the Cloth Hall). You can also visit his former residence in Kraków.

Polish history. Matejko's biggest work here—in fact, the biggest canvas in the whole building—is the enormous *Battle of Grunwald*. This epic painting commemorates one of Poland's high-water marks: the dramatic victory of a Polish-Lithuanian army over the Teutonic Knights, who had been terrorizing northern Poland for decades (for more on the Teutonic Knights, see page 317). On July 15, 1410, some 40,000 Poles and Lithuanians (led by the sword-waving Lithuanian in red, Grand Duke Vytautas) faced off against 27,000 Teutonic Knights (under their Grand Master, in white) in one of the medieval world's bloodiest battles. Matejko plops us right in the thick of the battle's climax, painting life-size figures and framing off a 32-foot-long slice of the two-mile battle line.

In the center of the painting, the Teutonic Grand Master is about to become a shish kebab. Duke Vytautas leads the final charge. And waaaay up on a hill (in the upper-right corner, on horseback, wearing a silver knight's suit) is Władysław Jagiełło, the first king of the Jagiellonian dynasty...ensuring his bloodline will survive another 150 years.

Matejko spent three years covering this 450-square-foot canvas in paint. The canvas was specially made in a single seamless piece. This was such a popular work that almost as many fans turned out for its unveiling as there are figures in the painting.

From Poland's high point in the *Battle of Grunwald,* look over your right shoulder for another, much smaller Matejko canvas, **Stańczyk,** to see how Poland's fortunes shifted drastically a century later. This more intimate portrait depicts a popular Polish figure: the court jester Stańczyk, who's smarter than the king, but not allowed to say so. This complex character, representing the national conscience, is a favorite symbol of Matejko's. Stańczyk slumps in gloom. He's just read the news (on the table beside him) that the city of Smoleńsk has fallen to the Russians after a three-year siege (1512-1514). The jester had tried to warn the king to send more troops, but the king was too busy partying (behind the curtain). The painter Matejko—who may have used his own features for Stańczyk's face—also blamed the nobles of his own day for fiddling while Poland was partitioned.

More Matejkos fill this room. On the left wall as you face *Grunwald* is a self-portrait of the gray-bearded artist (compare his features to Stańczyk's), flanked by Matejko's portraits of his children and his wife.

On the final wall is a smaller but very dramatic scene, *The Sermon of Piotr Skarga.* In the upper-right corner, this charismatic, early 17th-century Jesuit priest waves his arms to punctuate his message: Poland's political system is broken. Skarga is addressing fat-cat nobles and the portly King Sigismund III Vasa (seated and wearing a ruffled collar), who were acting in their own self-interests instead of prioritizing what was best for Poland. Notice that Skarga's audience isn't hearing his ravings—they seem bored, bugged, or both. The king is even taking a nap. They should have listened: Poland's eventual decline is often considered the fault of its unworkable political system. After the Partitions, the ahead-of-his-time Skarga was rehabilitated as a visionary who should have been heeded. Notice that, like Stańczyk, Skarga is a self-portrait of Matejko.

• *Leaving Matejko, we'll pass through several more rooms of lesser-known Polish painters to the opposite wing, where we'll meet several of Matejko's students—each of whom developed his own style and left his mark on the Polish art world. On the way, I'll point out a few canvases worth a pause.*

Other Polish Painters: First, head back down the long corridor the way you came (passing some Matejko copycats), cutting through a corner of the Portrait Gallery. When you reach the door you came in, bear right to stay inside the gallery. At the end of that first, large room, you'll find some battle scenes by **Józef Brandt** (1845-1915)—the only painter who rivaled Matejko in capturing epic warfare on canvas. Many of Brandt's scenes focus on confronting an enemy from the east, which was Poland's lot for much of its history. His biggest work here, *Rescue of Tatar Captives*, is typical of his scenes.

Continue straight into the next room, with some fine landscape scenes. This room (the partition in the middle) also has works by the talented **Józef Chełmoński** (1849-1914): *Indian Summer* and (around back) *Storks*—a young boy and his grandfather look to the sky as a formation of storks flies overhead. Storks, which are rare in many places but abundant in Poland, are a proud national symbol.

Turn right and go through one more long room, watching for **Aleksander Gierymski**'s (1850-1901) small, evocative, personality-filled *Jewish Woman Selling Oranges* (on the left wall).

• *You'll emerge into a big, violet-walled room that kicks off the collection of...*

Młoda Polska: Matejko's pupils took what he taught them and incorporated the Art Nouveau styles that were emerging around Europe to create a new movement called "Young Poland" (see page 59). This room features works by two of the movement's big names.

On the left wall are paintings by **Jacek Malczewski** (1854-1929), some of them depicting the goateed, close-cropped artist in a semisurrealistic, Polish countryside context. Malczewski painted more or less realistically, but enjoyed incorporating one or two subtle, symbolic elements evocative of Polish folkloric tradition—magical realism on canvas. *The Death of Ellenai* (1907) shows the pivotal scene in Juliusz Słowacki's epic 1838 poem, *Anhelli*, in which a young nobleman exiled from Poland during the Partitions is forced to make his way through the wastelands of Siberia. When his young and idealistic travel companion, Ellenai, perishes, Anhelli kisses her feet and abandons all hope.

Most of the works on the opposite wall are by **Józef Mehoffer** (1869-1946), who paints with brighter colors in a more stylized form, with more abstraction. Mehoffer's hypnotic *Strange Garden* (from 1902-1903) is a bucolic vision of blue-clad Mary Poppinses, nude cherubs, lots of flowers...and a gigantic, hovering, golden dragonfly that places the otherwise plausible scene in the realm of pure fantasy. In the middle of the room, the small version of Auguste Rodin's *The Kiss* reminds us how this emotion-conveying style, called Symbolism, was also finding expression elsewhere in Europe.

WARSAW

The next room, at the end of the hall, features some lesser-known painters from the age. Among these, **Olga Boznańska** (1865-1940) is worth lingering over: Her gauzy, almost Impressionistic portraits skillfully capture the humanity of each subject.

Head back into the Malczewski/Mehoffer room and find the small, darkened adjoining rooms. The first one features additional Malczewski paintings; the second is a treasure trove of works by the founder and biggest talent of Młoda Polska, **Stanisław Wyspiański** (1869-1907). The specific items in this room are subject to change—as Kraków, which owns the best collection of hometown boy Wyspiański, shuffles his works in and out of special exhibitions—but you'll likely see both paintings and pastel works by this Art Nouveau juggernaut. Wyspiański also designed stage sets and redecorated some important churches; some of the large pastel-on-paper works you may see here were used as studies for those projects. And you'll likely see some self-portraits and portraits of his wife and children.

Pondering the works here—and throughout the museum—think about how such a talented artist from a small country can be left out of textbooks across the ocean. The rest of the museum is yours to explore. If you're craving lesser works by more recognizable names, they're upstairs.

Chopin Museum (Muzeum Fryderyka Chopina)

The reconstructed Ostrogski Castle houses this museum honoring Poland's most famous composer, with manuscripts, letters, and original handwritten compositions. You'll learn about Chopin's early life in Żelazowa Wola and Warsaw; see a replica of his drawing room in Paris, and his last piano, which he used for composing during the final two years of his life (1848-1849); and

learn about the women who loomed large in his life (including his older sister Ludwika, his mother Justyna, and George Sand—the French author who took a male pseudonym in order to be published, and who was romantically linked with Chopin). Listening stations give you the chance to deepen your appreciation for Chopin's talent. While this is all riveting to Chopin devotees, casual fans may find the museum falls a bit short in igniting enthusiasm for the composer—for that, it's worth attending a concert, either here or elsewhere in Warsaw (see "Entertainment in Warsaw," later).

Cost and Hours: 25 zł, free (and crowded) on Wed; open Tue-

Sun 10:00-18:00, closed Mon, last entry 45 minutes before closing; 3 blocks east of Nowy Świat at Ulica Okólnik 1, +48 22 441 6251, https://muzeum.nifc.pl.

Concerts: Under the palace is a **concert hall,** which hosts a variety of performances from May through September—ranging from frequent weekend piano recitals to "young talents" afternoon concerts by local music students. Some are included in museum entry, while others require a separate ticket. Check the schedule and book at Bilety.nifc.pl.

Nearby: The park next to the museum surrounds the Chopin University of Music; hanging out here, you'll often hear students rehearsing inside.

Other Chopin Sight: The composer's tourable **birth house** is in a park in Żelazowa Wola, 34 miles from Warsaw. While interesting to Chopin devotees, it's not worth the trek for most (closed Mon, details at museum website, +48 46 863 3300).

▲Copernicus Science Center (Centrum Nauki Kopernik)

This facility, a wonderland of completely hands-on scientific doodads that thrill kids and kids-at-heart, is a futuristic romper room. (For kids, it's worth at least ▲▲.)

Filling two floors of an industrial-mod, purpose-built space, this is Warsaw's best family activity. Exhibits are described in both Polish and English, and there are frequent demonstrations and special events—ask when you buy your ticket, or check their website.

Cost and Hours: 40 zł, 28 zł for kids, slightly more on weekends; Mon-Thu 8:00-18:00, Fri until 20:00, Sat-Sun 9:00-19:00, last entry one hour before closing; Wybrzeże Kościuszkowskie 20, +48 22 596 4100, www.kopernik.org.pl.

Crowd-Beating Tips: This popular attraction can be busy on weekends and school holidays. If you anticipate crowds, book ahead on their website to secure your preferred entry time.

Getting There: It's an easy downhill walk from Warsaw's Royal Way, but the hike back up is fairly steep. Near the modern bridge—about a five-minute walk from the museum—are a Metro stop and a bus stop (both called Centrum Nauki Kopernik). Metro line 2 connects the science center to the National Stadium, the Royal Way (near the Copernicus statue), and the Warsaw Uprising Museum.

Visiting the Center: The science center is a sprawling, two-floor playhouse of hands-on, interactive exhibits. The specifics are always in flux, so pick up a map as you enter and just enjoy exploring. Kids love trying out the various tools and machines, playing with the air cannons, and running a slinky down an inclined treadmill. On the main floor is a special area for kids under five (called "Buzzz!"). Every visitor finds their own highlights, but favorites include the talking Copernicus robot and the "High Voltage Theater." The attached planetarium has a constantly changing schedule of performances (these cost extra and run about hourly at :30 past the hour, in Polish with English headset, ask for schedule and book at main ticket desk).

Nearby: The **riverside embankment** near the center has a few areas that are fun to stroll; it was created when the busy riverfront highway was rerouted into an underground tunnel. A giant Warsaw mermaid raises her sword at passing joggers, cyclists, and rollerbladers. From here, you have good views of the modern Holy Cross Bridge (Most Świętokrzyski) and the National Stadium, proudly wrapped in the patriotic red and white of the Polish flag. These riverbanks are a popular hangout by day and after dark; in the summer, a stroll along here reveals a world of picnics, family outings, and impromptu parties.

Also don't miss the postindustrial, futuristic **Elektrownia Powiśle** dining and shopping complex, just across the street from the museum (described later, under "Eating in Warsaw").

West of the Royal Way (near Centralna Station)
Palace of Culture and Science
(Pałac Kultury i Nauki, or PKiN)

This massive skyscraper, dating from the early 1950s, is still one of the tallest buildings in Europe (760 feet with the spire). While you can ride the lift to its top for a commanding view, the highlight is simply viewing it up close from ground level.

Viewing the Skyscraper: This building was a "gift" from Stalin

that the people of Warsaw couldn't refuse. Varsovians call it "Stalin's Penis"... using cruder terminology than that. (There are seven such "Stalin Gothic" erections in Moscow.) If it feels like an Art Deco Chicago skyscraper, that's because the architect was inspired by the years he spent studying and working in Chicago in the 1930s. Because it was to be "Soviet in substance, Polish in style," Soviet architects toured Poland to absorb local culture before starting the project. Notice the frilly decorative friezes that top each level—evocative of Poland's many Renaissance buildings (such as Kraków's Cloth Hall). The clock was added in 1999 as part of the millennium celebrations. Since the end of communism, the younger generation doesn't mind the structure so much—and some even admit to liking it for the way it enlivens the predictable glass-and-steel skyline springing up around it.

Everything about the Pałac is big. Approach it from the east side (facing the busy Marszałkowska street and the slick Galeria Centrum shopping mall). Stand in front of the granite tribune where communist VIPs surveyed massive May Day parades and pageantry on the once-imposing square, which today holds a sloppy parking lot. From there, size up the skyscraper—its grand entry flanked by massive statues of Copernicus on the right (science) and the great poet Mickiewicz on the left (culture). It's designed to show off the strong, grand-scale Soviet aesthetic and architectural skill. The Pałac contains various theaters (the culture), museums of evolution and technology (the science), a congress hall, a multiplex, an observation deck, and lots of office space. With all this Culture and Science under one Roof, it's a shame that only the ground-floor lobby (which feels like stepping into 1950s Moscow and is free to enter) and the 30th-floor observatory deck are open to the public (25 zł to zip up on retrofitted Soviet elevators, daily 10:00-20:00, may be open later in summer, www.pkin.pl).

Nearby: Behind the Pałac sprawls Warsaw's new skyline of glittering skyscrapers. **Varso Tower,** which opened in 2022, finally eclipsed the Pałac's height record, at 1,020 feet tall (the tallest building in the EU). But the most interesting skyscraper is **Złota 44,** with its dramatic swooping lines rising high into the air. This was designed by Poland-born architect Daniel Libeskind, perhaps best known for Berlin's Jewish Museum and for his role as master architect in redeveloping the World Trade Center site in New York City. The tower's shape evokes an eagle (a symbol for Poland) just beginning to take flight. At its base—and immediately behind Centralna station, easy to check out while waiting for your train—is **Złote Tarasy shopping mall,** featuring a funky, undulating glass-and-steel roof (https://zlotetarasy.pl).

JEWISH WARSAW

In the early 1600s, an estimated 80 percent of all Jews lived in Poland—then the largest country in Europe. And particularly between the two World Wars, Jewish culture flourished here. But after centuries of dwelling in relative peace in tolerant and pragmatic Poland, Warsaw's Jews suffered terribly at the hands of the Nazis. Several sights in Warsaw commemorate those who were murdered, and those who fought back. Because the Nazis leveled the ghetto, there is nothing left except the street plan, a few scattered monuments, and the heroic spirit of its former residents. However, the top-notch Museum of the History of Polish Jews is a magnet for those interested in this chapter of Polish history.

Getting There: To reach Ghetto Heroes Square and the museum from the Old Town, you can hop in a **taxi** or an **Uber,** or take a **bus** (to the Nalewki-Muzeum stop; bus #180 is particularly useful; bus #111 reaches this stop from farther south—Piłsudski Square, Nowy Świat, Palm Tree Circle, and the National Museum). You can also **walk** there in about 15 minutes: Go through the Barbican gate two blocks into the New Town, turn left on Świętojerska, and walk straight 10 minutes—passing the green-glass Supreme Court building. En route, at the corner of Świętojerska and Nowiniarska, watch for the pattern of bricks in the sidewalk, marking *Ghetto Wall 1940-1943.*

▲Ghetto Heroes Square (Plac Bohaterow Getta)

The square is in the heart of what was the Jewish ghetto—now surrounded by bland Soviet-style apartment blocks. After the uprising, the entire ghetto was reduced to dust by the Nazis, leaving the communists to rebuild to their own specifications. Today, the district is called Muranów ("Rebuilt").

The **monument** in the middle of the square commemorates those who fought and died "for the dignity and freedom of the Jew-

ish Nation, for a free Poland, and for the liberation of humankind." The statue features heroic Jewish men who knew that an inglorious death at the hands of the Nazis awaited them. Flames in the background show Nazis burning the ghetto. The opposite side features a sad procession of Jews trudging to concentration camps, with subtle Nazi bayonets and helmets moving things along.

As you face the monument, look through the trees to the right to see a seated statue. **Jan Karski** (1914-2000) was a Catholic Pole and resistance fighter who traveled extensively through Poland during the Nazi occupation, collected evidence, and then reported on the Warsaw Ghetto and the Holocaust to the leaders of the Western Allies (including a personal meeting with FDR). In 1944, while the Holocaust was still going on, Karski published his eye-witness account, *The Story of a Secret State* (which you can see on this statue's armrest). After the war he became a US citizen, and in 2012 President Barack Obama awarded him a posthumous Presidential Medal of Freedom.

The huge, glassy building facing the monument from across the square is the Museum of the History of Polish Jews (described next).

▲▲▲Museum of the History of Polish Jews (Muzeum Historii Żydów Polskich, a.k.a. POLIN)

This world-class attraction thoughtfully traces the epic, millennium-long story of Jews in Poland. This is not a "Holocaust museum"; rather, it provides stirring, comprehensive documentation of the very rich Polish Jewish experience across the centuries. In-depth, engaging, vividly illustrated, and eloquently presented, the exhibits present a powerful context for the many Jewish cultural sites around Poland—offering insights both for

people familiar with the story and for those who aren't. The museum is at once expansive and intimate, with ample descriptions, videos, and touchscreens; you could spend all day here, but two hours is the minimum. Its name, POLIN, means "rest here" in Hebrew and also evokes birdsong. It wins my vote for the best museum in Poland, and it's easily Europe's best Jewish museum—and a strong contender for the best European historical museum, period. The building also hosts cultural events and temporary exhibits.

Cost and Hours: Core exhibition—45 zł, includes essential audioguide, more for temporary exhibits; Wed-Mon 10:00-18:00, Sat until 20:00, closed Tue, last entry two hours before closing; Anielewicza 6, +48 22 471 0300, www.polin.pl.

Visiting the Museum: Before entering, view the building's striking **exterior** (designed by Finnish architect Rainer Mahlamäki). You'll enter (and go through a security checkpoint) at the large, asymmetrical hole in the side of the building. Once you're inside, the symbolism becomes clear: This represents Moses parting the Red Sea. (While the main exhibit covers the thousand years of Jews in Poland, this goes back even further—to the Jewish origin story.)

Buy your tickets for the core exhibition and pick up the invaluable 60-stop audioguide, which helps provide a concise structure for your exploration of the sprawling exhibitions. The main floor has a children's area and the good **$ Warsze** café, with a tempting cafeteria line of Polish and Jewish classics.

Warsaw's Jews and the Ghetto Uprising

From the Middle Ages until World War II, Poland was a relatively safe haven for Europe's Jews. While other kings were imprisoning and deporting Jews in the 14th century, the progressive king Kazimierz the Great welcomed Jews into Poland, even granting them special privileges (see page 57).

By the 1930s, there were more than 380,000 Jews in Warsaw—nearly a third of the population (and the largest concentration of Jews in any European city). The Nazis arrived in 1939. Within a year, they had pushed all of Warsaw's Jews into one neighborhood and surrounded it with a wall, creating a miserably overcrowded ghetto (crammed with an estimated 460,000 people, including many from nearby towns). There were nearly 600 such ghettos in cities and towns all over Poland.

By the summer of 1942, more than a quarter of the Jews in the ghetto had either died of disease, committed suicide, or been murdered. The Nazis started moving Warsaw's Jews (at the rate of 5,000 a day) into what they claimed were "resettlement camps." Most of these people—300,000 in all—were actually murdered at Treblinka or Auschwitz. Finally, the waning population—now about 60,000—began to get word from concentration camp escapees about what was actually going on there. Spurred by this knowledge, Warsaw's surviving Jews staged a dramatic uprising.

On April 19, 1943, the Jews attacked Nazi strongholds. The overwhelming Nazi war machine—which had rolled over much of Europe—imagined they'd be able to put down the rebellion easily. Instead, they struggled for a month to finally crush the Ghetto Uprising. The ghetto's residents and structures were "liquidated." About 300 of Warsaw's Jews survived, thanks in part to a sort of "underground railroad" of courageous Varsovians.

Warsaw's Jewish sights are emotionally moving, but even more so if you know some of their stories. You may have heard of **Władysław Szpilman,** a Jewish concert pianist who survived the war with the help of Jews, Poles, and even a Nazi officer. Szpilman's life story was turned into the Oscar-winning film *The Pianist,* which powerfully depicts events in Warsaw during World War II.

Less familiar to non-Poles—but equally affecting—is the story of Henryk Goldszmit, better known by his pen name, **Janusz Korczak.** Korczak wrote imaginative children's books that are still enormously popular among Poles. He worked at an orphanage in the Warsaw ghetto. When his orphans were sent off to concentration camps, the Nazis offered the famous author a chance at freedom. Korczak turned them down, choosing to die at Treblinka with his children.

Then head downstairs and follow the one-way route. In this high-tech, interactive space, exhibits in eight galleries mingle with actual artifacts to bring history to life.

You'll begin by passing through a simulated forest—evocative of legends about the Jews' arrival in Poland—to reach the **First Encounters** exhibit. Here you'll learn how Jewish merchants made their way to Poland in the 10th century (with maps of their trade routes and samples of what they sold). The story is told partly from the perspective of Ibrahim ibn Yakub, a Sephardic Jew who penned early travelogues about Europe. Look for the display case that holds a coin from the ninth century, with Hebrew characters, that was minted in Poland. In 1264, Duke Bolesław the Pious—the first of many tolerant Polish rulers—extended rights and protections to his Jewish subjects, allowing them to thrive. In the next room, on the left wall are illustrations of the leading Polish cities of the time, and on the right wall are Polish medieval monarchs, with in-depth explanations of each one's policies toward their Jewish subjects.

Next, the **Paradisus Iudaeorum** explains how, as Jews became more established in Polish society in the 15th and 16th centuries,

they enjoyed better and better living conditions. (Meanwhile, anti-Semites bitterly complained that Poland was becoming a "Jewish Paradise"—the name of this exhibit.) The centerpiece here is a gigantic, interactive model of Kraków and its Jewish quarter, Kazimierz. In the library section, you can flip through virtual pages of books from the era—representing the flourishing of education during this time. Poland was a rare place where books would actually be printed in Hebrew.

Continuing into the next area, you'll enter a dark hallway that explains the Khmelnytsky Uprising—a mid-17th-century Cossack rebellion against the Polish lords and the Jews who served them. This brought a new wave of pogroms and 10,000 Jewish deaths, mainly in present-day Ukraine.

After the uprising, Polish lords invited Jews to privately owned market towns—called *shtetls*—to help reestablish the economy. **The Jewish Town** offers a fascinating look at different walks of life in a typical Jewish community: the market, where Jews and Christians could mingle at the tavern; the home, where a family would live, work, eat, and sleep in a single room; the cemetery (touchscreens invite you to learn about the symbolism of Jewish tombstones); and the synagogue, with a gloriously colorful replica of a ceiling and bema (prayer platform) from a wooden synagogue from the village of Gwoździec—dripping with symbolism that's explained on nearby touchscreens. The depictions of "exotic" animals were influenced by Ottoman art and painted by local artists, who had never actually seen these beasts—leading to several errors, including an elephant with claws and an "ostrich" that looks more like an eagle. An exhibit also traces the mid-18th-century rise of Hasidism—a mystical branch of Judaism—in the eastern Polish lands (today's Ukraine).

With the Partitions of the late 18th century (when Polish territory was divided among neighboring powers), the Jewish population—who had spent centuries carving out a vital niche in a united Poland—now found themselves split among three different empires (symbolized by giant portraits of the rulers of Prussia, Russia, and Austria, all facing the Polish throne).

Encounters with Modernity examines how Jews in different parts of the Polish lands had very different experiences. Some were required by the new authorities to adopt surnames for the first time. Flippable panels illustrate how Russian authorities required both men and women to change their traditional clothing. You'll see a replica salon of a wealthy Jewish family who mingled with elites, and learn about the debate at that time of what the role of Jews in society should be (illustrated by a fine collection of items from Jewish ceremonies commemorating rites of passage). You'll also learn about the competing movements within Judaism that emerged during this era: Hasidism, led by charismatic Tzadiks who promised a closer spiritual connection to God, and the more reform-minded Haskalah, an intellectual approach inspired by the Enlightenment.

A mesmerizing, painterly film follows a day in the life of a young student at a *yeshiva* (school). A railway station represents the Industrial Revolution, when the world got smaller. You'll learn how some Jews worked hard to integrate with their dominant cultures (such as the painter Maurycy Gottlieb). This period also saw the emergence of modern anti-Semitism, including a brutal pogrom in Warsaw in 1881. As Jews sought to define a modern Jewish identity in the late 19th century, many emigrated—some to North or South America, and still others to the Holy Land (the beginnings of Zionism).

All of this sets the stage for World War I, when Jews were drafted into various armies—and often forced to fight one another. But at war's end, Poland was reconstituted as an independent nation. You'll step out onto **The Jewish Street,** which re-creates an interwar shopping street from a Jewish community. ("The Jewish Street" was also slang for the Jewish world in general.) It was between the world wars—when a newly independent Poland extended full citizenship and voting rights to its Jewish citizens—that Jewish cultural life flourished as never before. Three million Jews lived in Poland—including one-third of Warsaw's population. You'll see re-created Warsaw sites relating to newspapers, cinema, writers, and artists; and you'll learn about Jewish tourism of the era (when middle-class Jews would travel around Poland and Europe to visit Jewish cultural sites). Don't miss the mezzanine area, with exhibits about education and reform—including bilingual schooling (Yiddish and Polish), the beloved educator and author Janusz Korczak, and the debate over "ghetto benches" (segregated seating areas in schools).

This was also a time of rising anti-Semitism, segregation, boycotts, and anti-Jewish quotas. After one more nostalgic stroll down "The Jewish Street," you come to September 1, 1939, when the Nazis invaded Poland. They stripped Jews of their rights and possessions; humiliated, labeled, tortured, and executed them; and eventually implemented the **Holocaust.**

The exhibit traces, step by step, the escalation of the Nazis' "Final Solution," with a focus on events here in Warsaw: forcing Jews into a ghetto (you'll walk across a platform representing the bridge that connected the two parts of the ghetto, offering Jewish people fleeting glimpses of "normal" life going on outside their walls), the liquidation of the ghetto and the movement of Warsaw's Jews to the death camp at Treblinka, and the Ghetto Uprising, a desperate last stand in which the dwindling number or Warsaw's Jews put up a valiant, but ultimately doomed, fight. Making these stories personal are contemporaneous diaries, documents, and photographs.

The exhibit poses difficult questions about how non-Jewish Poles helped—or did not help—the Jews who were gradually disappearing from their cities. And it explains how a sort of "underground railroad" worked at great peril to save as many Jews as possible—as depicted in the movie *The Pianist*. (Look for the chess set carved by a Jew in hiding.) All told, 9 out of every 10 Polish Jews were murdered in the Holocaust. Only about 300,000 survived.

Finally, **The Postwar Years** follows Holocaust survivors in the years just after the war, when, astonishingly, they were scapegoated for war crimes. About 150,000 more (half the total survivors) fled to the newly created state of Israel, and those who remained had to navigate an unfriendly, anti-Semitic communist regime. In 1968, the communists launched an "anti-Zionist" campaign; eventually around 15,000 Polish Jews lost their citizenship and left for Israel,

Western Europe, and the US. Not until the fall of communism could the rest finally enter a world of new possibilities. The final room poses a powerful question: Given this rich yet traumatic history, what is the future for Jews in Poland?

The creation of this museum—the first time that the full story of the Jews of Poland has ever been told in such a mainstream way, and in all its epic scope—represents a critical milestone in celebrating a culture that has survived a harrowing history.

Ghetto Walking Tour

For a poignant stroll through what was the ghetto, with faint echoes of a tragic history, take this brief, lightly guided walk for a few blocks. The neighborhood itself is drab and boxy, though increasingly gentrified. It was rebuilt in characterless communist style after it was leveled during the Holocaust. You'll have to work hard to resurrect the memory of what went on here.

Stand along the street facing the back side of the monument, with the museum behind it. Turn right and walk along Zamenhofa—which, like many streets in this neighborhood, is named for a hero of the Ghetto Uprising. From here, you'll follow a series of three-foot-tall, black stone memorials to uprising heroes—the **Path of Remembrance.** Like stations of the cross, each recounts an event of the uprising. Every April 19th (the day the uprising began), huge crowds follow this path.

In a block and a half, just beyond the corner of Miła (on the left, partly obscured by some bushes), you'll find a **bunker** where about 100 organizers of the uprising hid (and where they committed suicide when the Nazis discovered them on May 8, 1943).

Continue following the black stone monuments up Zamenhofa (which becomes Dubois), then turn left at the corner, onto broad and busy Stawki. The ugly gray building on your left (a half-block down at #5, near the tram stop) was the **headquarters of the SS** within the ghetto. This is where the transportation of Warsaw's Jews to concentration camps was organized.

Using the crosswalk at the tram stop, cross Stawki and proceed straight ahead into the gap between the two buildings. At the back of this parking lot is a surviving part of the red-brick **ghetto wall,** with a few remaining scraps of 1940s barbed wire.

Farther up Stawki street, on the right, is the finale of this walk: the **Umschlagplatz** monument. That's German for "transfer place," and it marks the spot where the Nazis brought Jewish families to prepare them to be loaded onto trains bound for Treblinka or Auschwitz. This was the actual site of the touching scene in the film *The Pianist* where the grandfather shares bits of chocolate with his family before being forever separated. In the walls of the monument are inscribed the first names of some of the victims.

Other Warsaw Ghetto Sights

There are several other powerful sights relating to the ghetto, but they're spread far and wide around the city. Ideally, join a tour or hire a guide to weave them together. Here are some of the key locations; the first two are closer to the Palace of Culture and Science, while the final one is west of the Museum of the History of Polish Jews.

A rare, small surviving section of the **ghetto wall** that surrounded Warsaw's Jews during the Nazi occupation is behind a stretch of humdrum buildings just west of the Palace of Culture and Science. Enter through the passage at Ulica Złota 62 and bear right; you'll find it tucked back in a courtyard.

The **Nożyk Synagogue,** just north of the Palace of Culture and Science, is the only synagogue that survived World War II; it's relatively new, dating from 1902 (Twarda 6). After the liquidation of the ghetto, the building was kept intact to use as stables by occupying Nazi forces. Rebuilt in 1983, it's still used today as a place of worship and gathering, and is not typically open to the public.

Several blocks northeast, a monument called the **Footbridge of Remembrance** (Kładka Pamięci) spans Chłodna street near the intersection with Żelazna street. This recalls the wartime period when the walled Jewish ghetto included a corridor where local trams could pass through. In order to cross between the "Large Ghetto" (to the north of here) and the "Small Ghetto" (to the south), Jews had to walk over a footbridge—giving them a cruelly enticing glimpse of the "outside world." (This scene was vividly staged in *The Pianist,* and there's a conceptual re-creation of the bridge in the Museum of the History of Polish Jews.) A few steps up Chłodna street is a different monument from a different era, honoring Jerzy Popiełuszko, the outspoken, pro-Solidarity priest who was murdered by the communist secret police during martial law in 1984; he lived in the house at #15.

WARSAW UPRISING SIGHTS

For those interested in the 1944 Warsaw Uprising, it's worth visiting two sights: one a monument, the other a museum. Neither is right along the main tourist trail; the monument is closer to the core sightseeing zone, while the museum is a subway, tram, or taxi/Uber ride away.

Warsaw Uprising Monument

The most central sight related to the Warsaw Uprising is the monument at Plac Krasińskich (intersection of Ulica Długa and

Miodowa, one long block and about a five-minute walk southwest of the New Town Square). Larger-than-life soldiers and civilians race for the sewers in a desperate attempt to flee the Nazis. Just behind the monument is the oxidized-copper facade of Poland's Supreme Court.

▲▲Warsaw Uprising Museum
(Muzeum Powstania Warszawskiego)

Thorough, modern, and packed with Polish field-trip groups, this museum celebrates the heroes of the uprising (or, as this museum calls it, the Warsaw Rising). It's a bit cramped, and finding your way through the exhibits can be confusing, but it works hard to illuminate this complicated chapter of Warsaw's history. The location is inconvenient (a taxi/Uber or public transit ride west of Centralna station) and, because it takes some time to visit, may not be worth the trek for those with a casual interest. But history buffs find it worthwhile.

Cost and Hours: 30 zł, free on Mon; open Wed-Mon 8:00-18:00, Sat-Sun from 10:00, closed Tue; +48 22 539 7947, www.1944.pl.

Audioguide: The informative, two-hour audioguide is ideal if you want to delve into the whole story (10 zł, rent it in the gift shop). But the museum is so well described, you can just wander aimlessly and be immersed in the hellish events.

Eating: The museum's **$ café** is oddly pleasant, serving drinks and light snacks amidst genteel ambience from interwar Warsaw. In summer you can dine on a peaceful terrace. You'll also find a few business lunch-type places in the surrounding office zone.

Getting There: The museum is on the western edge of downtown—a long, dull walk—at Ulica Przyokopowa 28. While it's easiest to reach by taxi or Uber (figure about 10 minutes and 20 zł from the Royal Way), you can get close on public transit: Ride the Metro or a bus to Rondo Daszyńskiego, or a tram to the Muzeum Powstania Warszawskiego stop. From any of these, it's a short walk to the museum (can be tricky to find, as it's tucked around on the back side of the block).

Visiting the Museum: Buy your ticket at the little house at the far end of the entrance courtyard (marked *kasa*), then head into the main hall. The high-tech main exhibit sprawls across three floors. It tells the story of the uprising chronologically, with a keen focus on military history. The exhibit covers several topics but doesn't provide a big-picture narrative; to fully understand the context of what you're seeing, read the sidebar before your visit.

As you enter, the **Room of the Little Insurgent** on the right is a children's area, reminding visitors young and old that Varsovian kids played a role in the Warsaw Uprising, too.

The Warsaw Uprising

By the summer of 1944, it was becoming clear that the Nazis' days in Warsaw were numbered. The Red Army drew near, and by late July, Soviet tanks were within 25 miles of downtown Warsaw.

The Varsovians could simply have waited for the Soviets to cross the river and force the Nazis out. But they knew that Soviet "liberation" would also mean an end to Polish independence. The Polish Home Army numbered 400,000—30,000 of them in Warsaw alone—and was the biggest underground army in military history. The uprisers wanted Poland to control its own fate, and they took matters into their own hands. The symbol of the resistance was an anchor made up of a *P* atop a *W* (which stands for *Polska Walcząca,* or "Poland Fighting"—you'll see this icon all around town). Over time, the Home Army had established an extensive network of underground tunnels and sewers, which allowed them to deliver messages and move around the city without drawing the Nazis' attention. These tunnels gave the Home Army the element of surprise.

On August 1, 30,000 Polish resistance fighters launched an attack on their Nazi oppressors. They poured out of the sewers and caught the Nazis off guard. The ferocity of the Polish fighters stunned the Nazis. But the Nazis regrouped, and within a few days, they had retaken several areas of the city—murdering tens of thousands of innocent civilians as they went. In one notorious incident, some 5,500 Polish soldiers and 6,000 civilians who were surrounded by Nazis in the Old Town were forced to flee through the sewers; many drowned or were shot. (This scene is depicted in the Warsaw Uprising Monument on Plac Krasińskich.)

Two months after it had started, the Warsaw Uprising was over. The Home Army called a cease-fire. About 18,000 Polish uprisers had been killed, along with nearly 200,000 innocent civilians. An infuriated Hitler ordered that the city be destroyed—which it was, systematically, block by block, until virtually nothing remained.

Through all of this, the Soviets stood still, watched, and waited. When the smoke cleared and the Nazis left, the Red Army marched in and claimed the wasteland that was once called Warsaw. After the war, General Dwight D. Eisenhower said that the scale of destruction here was the worst he'd ever seen. The communists later tracked down the surviving Home Army leaders, killing or imprisoning them.

Depending on whom you talk to, the desperate uprising of Warsaw was incredibly brave, stupid, or a little of both. As for the Poles, they remain fiercely proud of their struggle for freedom. In 2004, 60 years after the uprising, the Warsaw Uprising Museum opened to document and commemorate this tragedy.

The **ground floor** sets the stage with Germany's invasion and occupation of Poland. The Generalgouvernement (Nazi puppet government of occupied Poland, ruled by Hans Frank in Kraków) wasted no time in asserting its control over the Poles; you'll learn how they imprisoned and executed priests, professors, and students. You'll also hear the story of the earlier, smaller uprisings that preceded the Warsaw Uprising, including the Poland-wide Operation Tempest (Burza) in 1943. During those earliest rebellions, Warsaw was intentionally left out of the fray...but only for the time being. The print shop shows how propaganda was spread during the occupation despite the watchful eye of the Nazis.

To keep with the chronological flow, skip the middle floor for now and ride the elevator to the **top floor** (#2), which covers the main part of the uprising. You'll meet some of the uprising's heroes and learn about their uniforms, weapons, and methods. The room in the middle, with felt drapes, tells the story of the Wola Massacre, in which some 40,000 residents of that Warsaw neighborhood were executed in just three days. Beyond that, the "Kino Palladium" movie screen shows fascinating Home Army newsreel footage from the period (with English subtitles). To the right of the screen, you'll walk through a simulated sewer, reminiscent of the one that many Home Army soldiers and civilians used to evade the Germans. Imagine terrified troops quietly traversing a sewer line like this one more than a mile long (but with lower ceilings)—and doing it while knee-deep in liquid sewage. At the end of the "sewer," stairs lead down to the middle floor.

The **middle floor** focuses on the grueling aftermath of the uprising. The later days of the uprising are outlined, battle by battle. A chilling section describes how Warsaw became a "city of graves," with burial mounds and makeshift crosses scattered everywhere. One room honors the Field Postal Service, which, at great personal risk, continued mail delivery of both military communiqués and civilian correspondences. Many of these brave "mailmen" were actually Scouts who were too young to fight. Nearby, another room recreates a clandestine radio broadcast station set up in a living room. If you need a break, look for the red corridor leading through the USSR section to the **café** and WC.

End your visit by walking down the stairs into the **main hall,** which is dominated by two large-scale exhibits: a replica of an RAF Liberator B-24 J, used for airborne surveillance of wartime Warsaw; and a giant movie screen showing more newsreels assembled by the Home Army's own propaganda unit during the uprising. Under the screen, behind the black curtains, an exhibit tells the story of Germans in Warsaw, along with another, more claustrophobic walk-through sewer.

Also in the main hall, look for the entrance to the seven-minute 3-D film *City of Ruins (Miasto Ruin)*, with virtual aerial footage of the postwar devastation. This gives you a look at the reality of the thousand people (nicknamed "Robinson Crusoes") who lived in bombed-out Warsaw immediately after the war. It's worth waiting in line to see this powerful film.

The **park** surrounding the building features several thought-provoking sights. A Chevy truck armored by the Home Army is both a people's tank and an example of how outgunned they were. Along the back is the Wall of Memory, a Vietnam War Memorial-type monument to soldiers of the Polish Home Army who were killed in action. You'll see their rank and name, followed by their code name, in quotes. The Home Army observed a strict policy of anonymity, forbidding members from calling each other by anything but their code names. The bell in the middle is dedicated to the commander of the uprising, Antoni Chruściel (code name "Monter").

SOUTH OF THE CENTER
▲Łazienki Park (Park Łazienkowski)

The huge, idyllic Łazienki Park (wah-ZHYEN-kee) is where Varsovians go to play. The park is sprinkled with fun Neoclassical buildings, strutting peacocks, and young Poles in love. It was built by Poland's very last king (before the final Partition), Stanisław August Poniatowski, to serve as his summer residence and provide a place for his citizens to relax.

On the edge of the park (along Belwederska) is a **monument to Fryderyk Chopin.** The monument, in a rose garden, is flanked by platforms, where free summer piano **concerts** of Chopin's music are given weekly (mid-May-late Sept only, generally Sun at 12:00 and 16:00—confirm at TI). The statue shows Chopin sitting under a wind-blown willow tree. Although he spent his last 20 years and wrote most of his best-known music in France, his inspiration came  from wind blowing through the willow trees of his native land, Poland. The Nazis were quick to destroy this statue, which symbolizes Polish culture. They melted the original (from 1926) down for its metal. Today's copy was recast after World War II. Savor this spot; it's great in summer, with roses wildly in bloom, and in autumn, when the trees provide a golden backdrop for the romantic statue.

Venture down into the ravine and to the center of the park, where (after a 10-minute hike) you'll find King Poniatowski's striking **Palace on the Water** (Pałac na Wodzie)—liter-ally built in the middle of a river. Nearby, you'll spot a clever amphitheater with seating on the riverbank and the stage on an island. The king was a real man of the Enlightenment, host-

ing weekly Thursday dinners here for artists and intellectuals. But Poland's kings are long gone, and proud peacocks now rule this roost.

Getting There: The park is just south of the city center on the Royal Way. Buses #116 and #180 run from Castle Square in the Old Town along the Royal Way directly to the park (get off at the stop called Łazienki Królewskie, by Belweder Palace—you'll see Chopin squinting through the trees on your left). Maps at park entrances locate the Chopin monument, the Palace on the Water, and other park attractions.

WARSAW

EAST OF THE CENTER: THE PRAGA DISTRICT

If you're in Warsaw for a longer stay, or are curious to see an emerg-ing hipster zone, cross the river to the Praga district. Praga was spared the worst of the WWII bombs; in fact, this is where the Red Army watched and waited as Hitler's forces leveled the historic city center. And today, Praga's relatively low rents and easy access to downtown make it a popular place for creative young Poles to live, eat, and party.

From Castle Square, the Śląsko-Dąbrowski Bridge rumbles over the Vistula (with ample tram and bus connections) right to the heart of this "other side of the river" neighborhood. (The Wileński stop, on the M2 Metro line, is also handy.) You can stroll along the traditional-feeling main drag, **Targowa**—a wide street with easy tram access, local shops and cafés, and Praga's own history museum (closed Mon, www.muzeumpragi.pl). Or, for a look at contempo-rary Praga, walk 10 minutes east to the postindustrial **Centrum Praskie Koneser**—a former distillery that has been transformed into a hip dining and entertainment complex (for an events calen-dar, see www.koneser.eu). Wander through the red-brick buildings to find a tempting place for a meal. Or, if you need an excuse to cross the river, sign up for a tour and tasting at the **Polish Vodka Mu-**

seum—filling one part of the former Koneser distillery. After a tour and a look at both old and new methods for making vodka, you'll enjoy an educational tasting designed to train your palate (closed Mon, smart to book ahead at www.muzeumpolskiejwodki.pl).

Shopping in Warsaw

You'll notice that many Varsovians are chic, sophisticated, and very well dressed. To see where they outfit themselves, go window-shopping. **Mysia 3** is a super-hip mini mall with three concise floors dedicated to mostly Polish fashion designers, but also has cutting-edge housewares and decor (daily, across Jerusalem Avenue from Nowy Świat, inside the former communist propaganda office at Mysia 3, www.mysia3.pl). Warsaw's main "fashion row" is a bit farther south, in the Śródmieście district. **Mokotowska street,** which angles northeast from trendy Plac Zbawiciela, is lined with dozens of chichi boutiques, jewelry shops, shoe stores, designer pastry shops, hair salons, and hipster barbers. The highest concentration is a few short blocks north of Plac Zbawiciela, north of Piękna. If you enjoy this zone, the area immediately to the west—along Wilcza and Poznańska streets—has more of the same.

Entertainment in Warsaw

Warsaw fills the summer with live music. In addition to more serious options (opera, symphony, etc.), consider these crowd-pleasing choices.

CHOPIN

My favorite Warsaw music option is to enjoy a Chopin performance. There's nothing like hearing Chopin's compositions passionately played by a teary-eyed Pole who really feels the music. The best option is the outdoor concert in front of the big Chopin statue in **Łazienki Park,** but it is held only one day a week in summer (free, mid-May–late-Sept generally Sun at 12:00 and 16:00, www.lazienki-krolewskie.pl; for more on this option, see the Łazienki Park listing on page 224).

If you're not in town on a Sunday, the next best thing is the **Chopin Salon.** Jarek Chołodecki, who runs the recommended Chopin Boutique lodging, hosts an intimate piano concert in his delightful salon nightly at 19:00. The performance can cover a range of musical styles and composers—but generally there are piano pieces featuring Chopin. The concert lasts around 45 minutes and is followed by wine, homemade cakes, and social time. A small group of locals and travelers gathers around Jarek's big, shiny Steinway grand to hear great music by talented young artists in a great city (70 zł, half-price for hotel guests, Ulica Smolna 14, reservations required, +48 22 829 4801, www.bbwarsaw.com).

The **Chopin Museum** features a variety of quality piano recitals—including several presented by local music students. These typically take place from May through September, and many are included in the museum's admission price (for details, see the museum listing on page 209).

Additionally, various **touristy Chopin concerts** are popping up all over the city; figure 85 zł for a piano performance set in a drawing room or small theater. Ask at the TI for the latest fliers.

OTHER MUSIC
Two big, historic churches in and near the Old Town put on 30-minute **organ concerts** most days. Choose between the Cathedral of St. John the Baptist, with an austere brick interior, right in the heart of the Old Town (25 zł, Mon-Sat at 12:00, no concerts Sun); and the frilly, Rococo St. Anne's Church, with a more sumptuous interior, just outside the Old Town (25 zł, May-early Oct Mon-Sat at 12:00, no concerts Sun). Both are run by the same company (+48 501 158 477, www.kapitula.org).

Free outdoor **jazz concerts** take place each Saturday in summer right on the Old Town Square (July-Aug at 19:00). In the summer, in good weather, the recommended Chopin Boutique hotel hosts **rooftop concerts** with sweeping views over Warsaw; the music varies, but it's often smooth jazz (free, usually May-Sept daily at 16:00, confirm schedule at https://bbwarsaw.com).

LIVELY HANGOUT ZONES
The Old Town and New Town are totally for tourists. To find some more interesting areas to explore and hang out after dark, your first stop should be **Plac Zbawiciela** in Śródmieście and the surrounding streets (see page 234). Locals also enjoy spending a balmy afternoon or evening on the **Vistula riverbanks.** Long ignored by Varsovians, the left (west) bank has undergone a dramatic renovation, with beautiful parklike embankments ideal for strolling. Meanwhile, the right (east) bank is still rugged and undeveloped, with forests and natural beaches; the biggest beach is around the eastern base of the Poniatowski Bridge (where Jerusalem Avenue crosses the river).

Sleeping in Warsaw

Warsaw is affordable for a European capital—for what you'd spend on a decent midrange room in Rome or Amsterdam, you can get a palatial room in a top-end hotel here. That said, two of my Warsaw favorites—Chopin Boutique and Duval Apartments—are both affordable and characteristic, making them great all-around choices.

I've arranged my listings by neighborhood. For locations, see the "Central Warsaw" map, earlier. Keep in mind that in the Old Town, you'll rarely see a local, while in Śródmieście, you'll rarely see a tourist. Choose your Warsaw experience.

NEAR PALM TREE CIRCLE
(NOWY ŚWIAT AND JERUSALEM AVENUE)

Considering how spread out Warsaw is, this is a convenient location for reaching various sights around the city. While comfortable inside, these hotels are in big buildings on uninspiring urban streets.

$$ Hotel Indigo, part of a high-end chain, surrounds a sleek and glassy atrium with 60 posh rooms at reasonable prices. A row of nearby nightclubs can generate lots of noise on the weekends—ask for a quieter room, and pack earplugs (air-con, elevator, Smolna 40, +48 22 418 8900, www.indigowarsaw.com, reservation@indigowarsaw.com).

$$ Between Us B&B is an inviting home-away-from-home for hipsters in Warsaw. Beata rents three trendy rooms above a recommended café centrally located in downtown Warsaw. As this place books up early, reserve far ahead (on second floor, no elevator, check in at Między Nami café downstairs, Bracka 20, +48 22 828 5417 or +48 603 096 701, www.between-us.eu, info@between-us.eu).

$ Chopin Boutique offers comfort, class, personality, hospitality, and value in an ideal location. Jarek Chołodecki, who lived near Chicago for many years, returned to Warsaw and converted this beautifully renovated apartment building into a bed-and-breakfast with 38 endearingly creaky, creatively decorated, antique-furnished rooms. Quirky, charming Jarek is a good host (you'll feel like you're staying with your Warsaw sophisticate cousin), and his staff provide

a warm professionalism. You'll enjoy breakfast at big communal tables in the cellar restaurant, escape from the city in the garden courtyard, and have the opportunity to take in a nightly Chopin concert in the ground-floor salon—see "Entertainment in Warsaw," earlier. Jarek prides himself on his hotel's eco-friendliness and sustainability—with solar panels on the roof and much of the produce grown on the premises (RS%, elevator, free loaner bikes, rooftop deck with sweeping views over Warsaw, some rooms have street noise—ask for a quieter one in back, Ulica Smolna 14, +48 22 829 4801, https://bbwarsaw.com, info@bbwarsaw.com).

$ Apple Inn, with 10 tight, modern rooms that have small windows high above the streets of Warsaw, is your cheap-and-cheery option in the center. It's in the attic of the former Jabłkowski Brothers department store—and, since *jabłko* means "apple," the name is a clever pun (air-con, shared kitchen and library, sometimes unstaffed—clearly communicate your arrival time, Chmielna 21, unit 22B—ride elevator to fourth floor, +48 601 746 006, www. appleinn.pl, Marta).

¢ Oki Doki City Hostel, on a pleasant square a few blocks in front of the Palace of Culture and Science, is colorful, creative, and easygoing. Each of its 37 rooms was designed by a different artist with a special theme—such as Van Gogh, Celtic spirals, heads of state, or Lenin. It's run by Ernest—a Pole whose parents loved Hemingway—and his wife Łucja, with help from their sometimes-jaded staff (private rooms available, up lots of stairs with no elevator, Plac Dąbrowskiego 3, +48 22 828 0122, www.okidoki.pl, okidoki@okidoki.pl).

In Śródmieście ("Downtown"): Foodies, people who hate tourists, and travelers who really want to disappear into Warsaw choose to sleep in Śródmieście, a 10-to-15-minute walk (or quick tram ride) south of Jerusalem Avenue. **$$$$ Hotel Nobu,** part of a high-end international chain, is a sophisticated home base in urbane Śródmieście. Its 117 rooms come in two types: The majority are sleek Asian minimalism, with bare-concrete hallways and well-decorated rooms. The rest are in a historic hotel building next door, with classic Art Deco style (air-con, elevator, Wilcza 73, nearest tram/bus stop at Koszykowa, +48 22 551 8888, https://warsaw.nobuhotels.com).

IN OR NEAR THE OLD TOWN

The Old Town area has some fine splurges and easy access to the romantic, rebuilt historic core. But it's less handy to Warsaw's trendier side.

$$$$ Hotel Bristol is Warsaw's top splurge—as much a landmark as a hotel (see description on page 189), this classic address on the Royal Way is where you're likely to spot visiting dignitaries and celebrities. (Just inside the round entrance on the corner, find the wall of brass knobs identifying past VIP guests—from Pablo Picasso to Ed Sheeran.) The public spaces are palatial, with sumptuous Art Deco lounges, bars, and coffee shops that make you want to dress up just to hang out. And the 206 rooms are fresh, elegant, and well equipped. If you like a posh home base, check the rates here first—you may be surprised at how affordable opulence can be (air-con, classy old vintage elevator, gym, swimming pool, sauna, Krakowskie Przedmieście 42, +48 22 551 1000, www. hotelbristolwarsaw.pl, bristol@luxurycollection.com).

$$$ Hotel Le Régina, part of the Mamaison group, is another tempting splurge, buried in the quiet and charming New Town (just north of the Old Town, a short walk away). From elegant public spaces to its 61 rooms, everything here is done with class (air-con, elevator, exercise room, pool, Kościelna 12, +48 22 531 6000, www.mamaisonleregina.com, reservations.leregina@ mamaison.com).

$ Duval Apartments, named for a French woman who supposedly had an affair with the Polish king in this building, offers four nicely appointed rooms above a café and teahouse (called Same Fusy) a few steps off the square in the Old Town. Each spacious room has a different theme: traditional Polish, Japanese, glass, or retro. Offering B&B comfort with hotel anonymity, this is a solid value in a dreamy location. Especially on busy weekends, there may be some noise from revelers in the street out front—light sleepers can request a quieter back room (lots of stairs with no elevator, no breakfast—but ample options nearby, between the Barbican and Old Town Square at Nowomiejska 10, +48 608 679 346, www. duval.net.pl, duval@duval.net.pl). Arrange a meeting time with Agnieszka or Marcin when you reserve.

$ Castle Inn, sitting on Castle Square at the entrance to the Old Town, is run by the owners of Oki Doki Hostel (described earlier). Each of its 22 creative and colorful rooms has different decor. While not plush, it's central and well priced (portable air-con in "deluxe" rooms in summer—otherwise no air-con, lots of stairs and no elevator, can be noisy—request quiet room, Świętojańska 2, +48 22 425 0100, www.castleinn.pl, castleinn@castleinn.pl).

Eating in Warsaw

Warsaw is, quite unexpectedly, one of Central Europe's best food cities...not that the tourists who stick to the kitschy Old Town restaurants would know. While there are some fine places in the historic center to sample traditional Polish food, that's better done in Old World Kraków; in Warsaw, don't be shy about exploring some local neighborhoods to find a more eclectic, modern, cosmopolitan food scene. Prices are low, so even a "splurge" restaurant lets you experience high-end

cuisine for a fraction of the cost of a similar place in a Western European capital.

But be warned: The food scene here changes at a bewildering pace. What's hot and new one year is shuttered the next. Don't be surprised if some places I list here are closed when you visit. On the upside, that means there's always something new to check out. Ask around, and do some research to find out what's trending right now.

Unless otherwise noted, see the "Central Warsaw" map, earlier, for locations.

NEAR PALM TREE CIRCLE (NOWY ŚWIAT AND JERUSALEM AVENUE)

These practical options are right in the middle of your sightseeing plans. The clientele is a mix of local yuppies, savvy business travelers, and tourists smart enough to steer clear of Old Town restaurants.

Nowogrodzka Street

This otherwise unassuming street, one block south of busy Jerusalem Avenue, is a burgeoning foodie strip for local urbanites. The best choice here is **$$ Bibenda,** a rustic-trendy bar with cocktails and an enticing seasonal menu of Polish fusion dishes. The creative chefs use Polish classics as a starting point, then jazz them up with elements borrowed from corresponding dishes in other cultures. For example, you might see fried chicken (a Polish staple) marinated in buttermilk (from the American south) with a raspberry/chipotle glaze (from Mexico). Or perhaps a *gołąbki* (Polish cabbage roll) done in the style of a Turkish *dolma* (stuffed grape leaves). Or perhaps a beet salad with Sicilian citrus and radicchio. You may not see these exact dishes, as the menu changes constantly, but what you eat will invariably be creative, delicious, and surprisingly affordable. They have outstanding craft cocktails, too. They don't take reservations, so arrive early or line up (Mon dinner only, Tue-Sun lunch from 13:00 and dinner, Nowogrodzka 10, +48 502 770 303, www.bibenda.pl).

Also along Nowogrodzka, you'll find **$$$ Soul Kitchen,** a more upscale-feeling place with international cuisine in a sophisticated cellar (daily, downstairs at #18A, +48 519 020 888, www.soulkitchen.pl); **$$ Le Cabaret,** a dressy, grown-up-feeling "jazz café bistro" with a throwback-upscale interior, a short menu of hot and cold small plates, and live jazz music (daily, at #4A, +48 536 976 403); and **$ Drugie Dno,** an industrial microbrew taproom with bare brick, eight beers on tap, and affordable burgers (daily from 16:00, at #4, +48 22 625 3709, www.drugiedno.pl).

Near the Heart of Nowy Świat

The first cross street you reach on Nowy Świat (coming from Jerusalem Avenue) has a concentration of dining options in both directions. To the right (east, toward the river) runs **Foksal street,** lined with an ever-changing lineup of lively, contemporary eateries where diners cram the al fresco tables. This enticing strip feels generic and a bit touristy. (The recommended Kamanda Lwowska, described below, is a bit farther down Foksal.) To the left (west, toward the Palace of Culture and Science) runs **Chmielna street.** This grubby urban corridor has an entirely different vibe: Rather than upscale sit-down places, it's an intriguing lineup of hole-in-the-wall and takeaway joints: Vietnamese, kebabs, pizza slices, Belgian fries, bubble tea, fancy ice cream, and so on.

After a couple of blocks, Chmielna opens up into a lovely traffic-free square (with modern benches) at **Szpitalna street.** Here the vibe changes again, with some appealing, upmarket, hangout hipster cafés where you can grab a good drink or a bite: The sleek and modern **$$ Żywioły** ("Elements") bakery, filling the ground floor of the modernized Jabłkowski Brothers department store building, is a good and obvious choice (daily, straight ahead at Chmielna 19, +48 501 984 040, www.zywioly.pl); just to the left, find the hipper **$ Między Nami,** with ramshackle secondhand furniture, a short but tempting menu, and an ambience that encourages hanging out (closed Sun, Bracka 20, downstairs from recommended Between Us B&B, +48 22 828 5417, www.miedzynamicafe.com). Emil Wedel's chocolate heaven, described later under "Classic Polish Treats," is a block north.

Very Traditional Polish Food: $$ Kamanda Lwowska is the best spot in central Warsaw for big portions of homestyle Polish cooking. It's named for the former Polish city that's now in Ukraine (Lwow, a.k.a. Lviv). It has a few outdoor seats in a parklike setting and a charming, cluttered old cellar with just a touch of kitsch. The friendly and fun staff serves up well-executed Polish classics (daily from 13:00, Foksal 10, +48 22 828 1031, www.kamandalwowska.pl).

Classic Polish Treats: *Pączki* and Chocolate

These places are on or close to the busy Nowy Świat boulevard.

A. Blikle, Poland's most famous pastry shop, serves a wide variety of delicious treats. This is where locals shop for cakes when they're having someone special over for coffee. The specialty is *pączki* (PONCH-kee), the quintessential Polish doughnut, filled with rose-flavored jam. You can get your goodies "to go" in the shop, or pay double to enjoy them with coffee in the swanky, classic café with indoor or outdoor seating (daily, Nowy Świat 35, +48 22 828 6601). They also have a sit-down restaurant, but I come here only for the *pączki*. You'll see many other A. Blikle branches around town, but this is the original.

E. Wedel Pijalnia Czekolady thrills chocoholics. Emil Wedel made Poland's favorite chocolate, and today, his former residence houses this chocolate shop and genteel café. This is the spot for delicious pastries and a *real* hot chocolate—*czekolada do picia* ("drinking chocolate"), a cup of melted chocolate, not just hot chocolate milk. Or, if you fancy chocolate mousse, try *pokusa*. Wedel's was *the* Christmas treat for locals under communism. Cadbury bought the company when Poland privatized, but they kept the E. Wedel name, which is close to all Poles' hearts...and taste buds (daily, Szpitalna 8, +48 22 827 2916, www.wedelpijalnie.pl).

IN POWIŚLE, NEAR THE RIVERBANK

The low-lying Powiśle neighborhood—squeezed in the little canyon between the Royal Way and the river—is trendy, thanks partly to its proximity to the inviting riverbank parks and Copernicus Science Center. These places aren't worth a big detour, but a trip here lets you escape the congested urban center, explore a quieter side of town, and combine a meal with a stroll along the river.

Elektrownia Powiśle is a sprawling, futuristic complex that fills a former electric plant across the street from the Copernicus Science Center. It preserves an original red-brick hall, newly adorned with lots of steel, glass, and steampunk accents. The core of the complex is dedicated to dining, surrounded by a sprawling designer mall (if you're in the market for modern Polish fashion or upmarket tennis shoes, this is the place). The **$ food hall** is a handy place to browse for a meal—the eclectic lineup includes everything from microbrews, smash burgers, and gourmet hot dogs to sushi, ramen, dim sum, and tacos. There are also a few attached **$$-$$$$ sit-down restaurants.** Even if you're not looking for a meal, the dramatic old-meets-new architecture makes this worth a stroll-through (closed Sun, Dobra 42, www.elektrowniapowisle.com).

$ Warszawa Powiśle is a café/bar occupying the old, communist-style ticket office for the suburban train station of the same name. Tucked along a picturesque bike lane beneath the towering legs of a bridge, its sidewalk is jammed with cool Varsovians and in-the-know visitors. I'd skip the basic food (light sandwiches, dumplings) and instead

just enjoy the vibe with a drink (daily, Kruczkowskiego 3B, +48 22 474 4084).

IN ŚRÓDMIEŚCIE ("DOWNTOWN")

Warsaw's Śródmieście district is the epicenter of Polish hipster/foodie culture—where you'll find young Varsovian foodies digging into affordable dishes at the trendiest new places. This area is a 15-minute walk south of Jerusalem Avenue and also well served by public transportation (several trams run frequently along the main north-south Marszałkowska corridor to Plac Zbawiciela); the Politechnika Metro stop is also nearby. Listed next are a few different restaurant-hunting zones, with a handful of specific recommendations. For locations of the places listed in this section, see the "Warsaw Overview" map, on page 174.

Hala Koszyki

This trendy food hall (pronounced koh-SHEE-kee), which opened in 2016 in a renovated brick market hall from 1906, is your handiest one-stop shop for sampling Warsaw's current dining scene. Outside—sandwiched between the two brick entrances—is a sprawling zone of al fresco tables amidst lush trees strewn with twinkle lights. Inside, you'll find more than a dozen entirely different eateries, covering all of the culinary bases: Spanish  tapas, sushi, Indian, Latin American, Italian, Thai, hummus bar, dim sum, beer hall, tea salon, gourmet chocolates, *gelateria,* Portuguese, the grotesquely over-the-top "Jeff's American Food," and more (most are **$-$$**). It's anchored by the big bar in the middle, surrounded by communal seating.

The upper level, ringed by design studios, has quieter seating and views over the action. The complex also has some serious sit-down eateries, including **$$$ Ćma** ("Moth"), with updated Polish fare and occasional DJs (daily, Koszykowa 63, www.koszyki.com). They also have live performances (ranging from concerts for kids to Polish stand-up comedy)—check the website for details.

On Plac Zbawiciela

Named "Holiest Savior Square" for the looming church, this is a dizzying six-way intersection with a big traffic circle ringed by hulking old colonnades. To get a quick taste of the Śródmieście scene, come here first and just do a slow loop around the circle, surveying your options. Starting to the right of the steeple and

moving clockwise, here are a few
options you'll see (all open daily):
$$ Izumi Sushi, **$ Karma** coffee
shop (drinks, sandwiches, and sal-
ads), and **$$ Tuk Tuk** Thai street
food are all popular, with great
seating out on the square. Continuing two crosswalks around the circle, you'll cross Mokotowska; looking left here, you may spot a line
of people at **Sucré**—an unpretentious hole-in-the-wall serving all-
natural, homemade ice cream. The
next section (after Mokotowska)

has **Pałaszowanie,** serving cheap but creative *zapiekanki* (French
bread pizza), followed by the trendy **$$ Charlotte** designer bak-
ery and wine bar, with homemade treats and sandwiches at tables
spilling out all over the square. Up above, **Plan B** is a hipster dive
bar with drinks, snacks, and views down over the square; this is
where revelers head at 2 in the morning, after the restaurants are
closed (find the graffiti-slathered staircase up just past Charlotte).

On and near Poznańska Street

A few short blocks west of Plac Zbawiciela, this street is also
lined with trendy and youthful eateries (especially around the in-
tersection with Wilcza street; the nearest tram/bus stop is Hoża,
and it's also not far from Plac Konstytucji). Strolling this strip,
you'll find several enticing options. **$$ Beirut,** a rustic and casual
bar serving up good Middle Eastern food, is the culinary anchor
of this neighborhood—always packed and lively. The hummus
bar, on the left, has a wide variety of *mezes* (small plates) and
grilled meats, while the "Kraken Rum Bar" on the right has fish
dishes (portions are modest—plan to share a few, order at the
counter then find a table, daily, Poznańska 12). **$$ Tel Aviv,** with
gluten-free and vegan Middle Eastern food across the street, is
the upscale and more user-friendly answer to Beirut...and enjoys
handling its overflow (daily, Poznańska 11). A few steps away, at
the intersection with Wilcza, is **$$$$ Nolita,** one of Warsaw's
top-end, white-tablecloth, fine-dining splurges (closed Sun-Mon,
Sat dinner only, Wilcza 46, www.nolita.pl).

OTHER HIP, POSTINDUSTRIAL HANGOUTS

In addition to **Hala Koszyki** (in Śródmieście) and **Elektrownia
Powiśle** (near the river and Copernicus Science Center)—both
recommended above—Warsaw has several other trendy food-
and-drink zones that fill rejuvenated former industrial com-

plexes. Scattered around the city, these capitalize on a Poland-wide obsession with postindustrial hipness; if you're near any of them, or if you're simply interested in exploring a different chunk of this sprawling city, these are worth a browse. At each, you'll find a range of options, from food-hall counters slinging tempting global cuisine, to sit-down splurges, to convivial pubs. All have eateries that are open daily; for the current lineup, see the websites.

Browary Warszawskie, near the Warsaw Uprising Museum in the Wola district west of downtown, fills the former home of Haberbusch and Schiele—Poland's largest brewery in the 19th century. Leveled in World War II, now it's been rebuilt in modern style under the name "Warsaw Breweries" (Grzybowska 60, www.browarywarszawskie.com.pl).

Fabryka Norblina, also in Wola, is the former factory of Norblin, a huge facility that produced metal items in the 19th and early 20th centuries. Now it's a thriving entertainment zone, with ample bars, restaurants, and "Food Town," with two dozen global food counters. If you'd like to learn more about the complex's industrial history, they also have a museum and guided tours (Żelazna 51/53, www.fabrykanorblina.pl).

Centrum Praskie Koneser—or Koneser Center for short—offers a good excuse to visit the Praga district, across the river (described on page 225). In addition to housing the Polish Vodka Museum, this former distillery complex has a wide array of dining, drinking, and entertainment venues (Plac Konesera 8, https://koneser.eu).

IN OR NEAR THE OLD TOWN

The restaurants within the Old Town and surrounding streets are 100 percent for tourists. Dining right on the Old Town Market Square is exorbitantly expensive, but could be worth it for those who treasure a romantic memory. Still, I'd rather walk a block or two to one of these options. The first two are on the New Town Square—an enjoyable five-minute stroll beyond the Barbican; with each step, you feel the tourist-to-local ratio dropping.

$$ Żyto is a cozy, stylish spot facing the New Town Square, where you can sample Ukrainian cuisine. Perusing the menu is actually educational: You'll see Ukrainian spins on what you might think are "Polish" dishes, like pierogi; and you'll notice influences from other parts of that huge country—Hungarian-style *borgacz,* Georgian-style salad with walnut paste, and so on (daily, Freta 29/31, +48 575 806 296). For more on Ukrainian food, see page 30.

$$ Freta 33, next door, has decent international fare (such as pastas), fine outdoor seating, and a contemporary subway-tile interior. It feels modern and hip for this ye olde neighborhood (daily, Freta 33, +48 22 635 0931).

$ Pyzy, Flaki Gorące! is close to Castle Square, but just across the street from the Old Town wall, which helps it feel less touristy. The name—meaning "Hot Dumplings and Tripe!"—is also the menu. Cozy and casual, with a dash of trendy and kitschy, it's a fine spot for updated-traditional Polish flavors. Most of the dishes—dumplings with various toppings, soups (including the namesake tripe soup, *flaki po warszawsku*), and herring—all come in jars, a homage to Poland's historic propensity for preserving foods through the long, hard winters. They also have flatbreads with very Polish toppings (daily, Podwale 5, +48 722 255 245, www.pyzyflakigorace.pl).

$ Zapiecek, with a half-dozen locations in and near the Old Town, is a kitschy chain serving up cheap and cheery traditional Polish dishes. Yes, it's definitely touristy. But the prices are reasonable, and the food is better and more authentic than it has any right to be. They proudly make their prizewinning pierogi by hand every morning. If you need a quick, traditional meal anywhere near the Old Town, you could do much worse (handiest location faces the Cathedral of St. John the Baptist at Świętojańska 13, others are on the main drag through the New Town at Freta 1 and Freta 18, two more on the Royal Way at Nowy Świat 64 and Krakowskie Przedmieście 55, all open long hours daily).

Warsaw Connections

Almost all trains into and out of Warsaw go through hulking Warszawa Centralna station (described earlier, under "Arrival in Warsaw," including ticket-buying tips).

If you're heading to Gdańsk, note that the red-brick Gothic city of Toruń and the impressive Malbork Castle are both on the way but are on separate train lines—making it difficult to do both en route (see the Gdańsk and Pomerania chapters). Also be aware that EIC and IC express trains to many destinations—including Kraków and Gdańsk—require seat reservations, even if you have a rail pass.

You can buy most tickets online (www.intercity.pl). To confirm rail journeys, check specific times online or at the station.

From Warszawa Centralna Station by Train to: Kraków (about hourly, 2.5 hours), **Gdańsk** (hourly, 3 hours), **Malbork** (hourly, 2.5 hours), **Toruń** (every 2 hours direct, 3 hours on express IC train, more with changes), **Prague** (2/day direct, more with change in Ostrava, 8.5 hours), **Berlin** (4/day direct, 6.5 hours, no direct night train), **Budapest** (1/day direct, 11.5 hours;

1/day overnight, 13 hours; more with change in Břeclav, Czech Republic), **Vienna** (2/day direct, 7.5 hours; plus 1 night train, 11.5 hours).

By Bus: Flixbus—described on page 339—runs bus routes throughout Poland and to international destinations (www.flixbus.pl).

GDAŃSK & THE TRI-CITY

Gdańsk (guh-DAYNSK), on the Baltic Coast of Poland, may be *the* great undiscovered Central European destination—rich with history and culture, slathered with gorgeous architecture old and new, loaded with world-class museums and great restaurants...and just plain fun.

Exploring Gdańsk is a delight. It feels like Poland's answer to Amsterdam or Scandinavia. The historical center is a gem, with block after block of red-brick churches and narrow, colorful, ornately decorated Hanseatic burghers' mansions. The riverfront embankment, with its trademark medieval crane, oozes salty maritime charm. Gdańsk's history is also fascinating—from its 17th-century golden age to the headlines of the late 20th century, big things happen here. You might even see ol' Lech Wałęsa still wandering the streets. And yet Gdańsk is also unmistakably a city of the future, with state-of-the-art construction projects popping up all over.

Gdańsk and two nearby towns (Sopot and Gdynia) together form an area known as the "Tri-City," offering several day-trip opportunities north along the coast (see page 299). The belle époque seaside resort of Sopot beckons to holidaymakers, while the modern burg of Gdynia sets the pace for today's Poland. Beyond the Tri-City, the sandy Hel Peninsula is a popular spot for summer sunbathing, and Malbork Castle (covered in the next chapter) is an easy half-hour train ride away.

PLANNING YOUR TIME
Gdańsk, with more than its share of great sights (and tempting side trips), demands two full days—which also makes the long trip up

here more worthwhile. (Add a night in Toruń, while you're at it.) If you're in a rush and have a limited appetite for sightseeing, you could squeeze it into one day. If you have more time, Gdańsk will fill it.

Gdańsk sightseeing has three major components: the Royal Way (historic main drag with good museums); the river embankment, leading to the WWII history museum; and the modern shipyard where Solidarity was born (with a fascinating museum). If you have just one (very busy) day, follow my self-guided walk through the Main Town and then out to the Solidarity sights, followed by a spin through the WWII museum (closed Mon) and a stroll along the riverfront back into town.

With two days, I'd devote one day to the Main Town, riverbank, and WWII museum; and a second day to the Solidarity sights, rounding out your time with other attractions: Art lovers enjoy the National Museum (with a stunning altar painting by Hans Memling), history buffs make the pilgrimage to Westerplatte (where World War II began), castle fans side-trip to Malbork, and church and pipe-organ fans might visit Oliwa Cathedral in Gdańsk's northern suburbs (on the way to Sopot).

If you have more time, consider the wide variety of side trips. The most popular option is the half-day round-trip to Malbork Castle (30-45 minutes each way by train, plus two or three hours to tour the castle—see next chapter). It only takes a quick visit to enjoy the resort town of Sopot (25 minutes each way by train), but on a sunny day, that town's beaches may tempt you to laze around longer. Gdynia is skippable, but it does have one great sight (the Emigration Museum) and rounds out your take on the Tri-City. If you have a full day and great weather, and you don't mind fighting the crowds for a patch of sandy beach, go to Hel.

Gdańsk gets very busy in late June, when school holidays begin, and it's crowded with (mostly German, Norwegian, and Swedish) tourists from July to mid-September—especially during St. Dominic's Fair (Jarmark Św. Dominika, three weeks from late July to mid-Aug), with market stalls, concerts, and other celebrations.

Closed (and Free) Days: Most sights in Gdańsk close one day each week, typically either Tuesday (Museum of Gdańsk branches) or Monday (other museums). And some sights are free one day each week—for example, the Museum of Gdańsk branches are free on Monday. Check these details when planning your sightseeing (as these days tend to change from year to year). If you're in town when major museums are closed, good alternatives include visiting churches (including St. Mary's) or the European Solidarity Center. If side-tripping anywhere, check ahead for closed days: For example, Malbork Castle's interiors and Gdynia's Emigration Museum are closed on Mondays.

Orientation to Gdańsk

With 460,000 residents, Gdańsk is part of the larger urban area known as the Tri-City (Trójmiasto, total population of one million).

But the tourist's Gdańsk is compact, welcoming, and walkable—virtually anything you'll want to see is within a 20-minute stroll of everything else.

Focus on the Main Town (Główne Miasto), home to most of the sights described, including the spectacular Royal Way main drag, Ulica Długa. The Old Town (Stare Miasto) has a handful of old brick buildings and faded, tall, skinny houses—but the area is mostly drab and residential, and not worth much time. Just beyond the northern end of the Old Town (about a 20-minute walk from the heart of the Main Town) is the entrance to the Gdańsk Shipyard, with the excellent European Solidarity Center and its top-notch museum. From here, shipyards sprawl for miles.

Crossing the River: In addition to the big, permanent bridge in front of the Green Gate, Gdańsk has two pedestrian bridges in the tourist zone: a **swing bridge** near the Crane (connecting to the sleek modern strip on Granary Island) and a **drawbridge** farther north (just beyond the carousel on Fishmarket Square). Both bridges are available to pedestrians from :30 past each hour until the top of the hour; when the clock approaches :00, you'll hear a siren and a recorded warning to clear the bridges so they can open for boat traffic. Then, after 30 minutes, they click back into place for pedestrians again. If exploring across the river, keep an eye on the time...unless you don't mind taking a longer route back. You may also see a small **ferry** (named the *Motława*, like the river) that occasionally shuttles visitors back and forth on the extremely quick crossing between the Crane and the old granaries across the way (small fee, operated by the Maritime Museum).

Language Barrier: The second language in this part of Poland is German, not English. As this was a predominantly German city until the end of World War II, German tourists flock here in droves. But you'll win no Polish friends if you call the city by its more familiar German name, Danzig.

Cruise Crowds: Gdańsk is an increasingly popular cruise destination, with about 100 ships calling here each year (most dock at the nearby city of Gdynia, and passengers take a bus or train in). During summer daytime hours, the town is filled with little excursion groups.

TOURIST INFORMATION

Gdańsk has two different TI organizations. Most helpful is the **regional TI,** which occupies the Upland Gate, at the start of my self-guided walk (daily 9:00-18:00, off-season until 17:00, +48 58 732 7041, www.pomorskie.travel). The **city TI** is conveniently located at the bottom end of the main drag, at Długi Targ 28 (just to the left as you face the river gate; daily 9:00-17:00, +48 58 301 4355, www.visitgdansk.com). There's also a TI desk at the airport, and there may be one in the future at the Solidarity Center.

Sightseeing Pass: Busy sightseers should consider the **Tourist Card,** which includes entry to several sights in Gdańsk, Gdynia, and Sopot, and discounts at others (such as 20 percent off the European Solidarity Center). Check the list of what's covered, and do the arithmetic (65 zł/24 hours, 85 zł/48 hours, 105 zł/72 hours, pay more to add local transit, sold only at TIs).

ARRIVAL IN GDAŃSK

By Train at Gdańsk's Main Train Station (Gdańsk Główny): If you're on a PKP train, get off at the Gdańsk Główny stop. This station is a pretty brick palace on the western edge of the old center. (To save money, architects in Colmar, France, copied this exact design to build their city's station.) As this station has been under construction, details may be in flux. But generally, trains to other parts of Poland (marked *PKP*) typically use platforms 1 or 2; regional trains with connections to the Tri-City (marked *SKM*) use platform 3. The bus station (Dworzec PKS) is behind the train station, accessible via the pedestrian tunnel that connects the platforms.

To **walk** into town, use the pedestrian underpass to go beneath the busy road; from where you emerge, it's a 10-to-15-minute walk to the heart of town and most hotels (bear right from the underpass and head for all the red-brick church towers). Considering the stairs and the distance, it's easier—and affordable—to hop in a **taxi** or request an **Uber** (about 20-25 zł); from the tunnel under the tracks, exit toward *ul. Podwale Grodzkie* to pop out at the busy road, where you can meet your Uber or find a taxi.

By Train at Gdańsk Śródmieście: If you're arriving in

Gdańsk on a commuter SKM train, consider getting off at the Gdańsk Śródmieście station, which is a slightly shorter walk to the start of my Gdańsk Walk. From Gdańsk Śródmieście, use the underpass to reach the gigantic Forum shopping mall. Walk straight through the mall to the far end; after exiting, if you look to the right, you'll see a pedestrian underpass leading to the Upland Gate and the start of my walk.

By Plane: Gdańsk's architecturally impressive, user-friendly airport, named for Lech Wałęsa, is about five miles west of the city center (code: GDN, www.airport.gdansk.pl). From the arrivals area, follow signs to the handy train, which zips to the main train station in about 30 minutes (5 zł, 1-2/hour). Public **bus** #210 also heads to the main train station; you can get off one stop earlier, at Hucisko, for a slightly shorter walk to the main part of town (5 zł, buy ticket at machine before boarding, 2/hour Mon-Fri, hourly Sat-Sun, 40 minutes). The 25-minute **taxi** ride into town should cost around 60-80 zł; an **Uber** typically costs less (except during peak times).

GETTING AROUND GDAŃSK

Nearly everything is within easy walking distance of my recommended hotels, but public transportation can be useful for reaching outlying sights such as Oliwa Cathedral, Westerplatte, Sopot, Gdynia, and Hel (specific transportation options for these places are described in each listing).

By Public Transportation: Gdańsk's trams and buses work on the same tickets: single-ride ticket—4.80 zł, 24-hour ticket—18 zł. Major stops have user-friendly ticket machines, which take credit cards; otherwise, buy tickets *(bilety)* at kiosks marked *RUCH*. In the city center, the stops worth knowing about are Plac Solidarnośći (near the European Solidarity Center), Gdańsk Główny (in front of the main train station), and Brama Wyżynna (near the Upland Gate and the Gdańsk Śródmieście commuter train station).

By Taxi or Uber: Taxis cost about 8 zł to start, then 2-3 zł per kilometer (a bit more at night). However, taxis waiting at stands often have inflated rates; it's safer to call a cab (try Neptun, +48 19686 or +48 585 111 555; EcoCar, +48 123 456 789; or Dajan, +48 58 19628). Uber works well in Gdańsk and is typically cheaper than a taxi.

Tours in Gdańsk

Private Guides

Hiring a local guide is an exceptional value. **Agnieszka Syroka**—personable and knowledgeable—is a wonderful guide (750 zł/half-day tour, more for all day, +48 502 554 584, www.tourguidegdansk.

Gdańsk at a Gdlance

▲▲▲**Gdańsk Walk** Stroll down the city's colorful showpiece main drag, ending at the famous shipyards and the European Solidarity Center. See page 245.

▲▲▲**Solidarity Sights and Gdańsk Shipyard** Home to the beginning of the end of Eastern European communism, with a towering monument and excellent museum. **Hours:** Memorial and shipyard gate—always open. European Solidarity Center exhibit—Mon-Fri 10:00-19:00, Sat-Sun until 20:00; Oct-April Wed-Mon 10:00-17:00, Sat-Sun until 18:00, closed Tue. See page 270.

▲▲**Main Town Hall** Ornate meeting rooms, town artifacts, and tower with sweeping views. **Hours:** June-Sept Tue-Sun 10:00-18:00, Mon from 12:00; Oct-May Wed-Mon 10:00-16:00, Thu until 18:00, closed Tue. See page 264.

▲▲**Artus Court** Grand meeting hall for guilds of golden-age Gdańsk, boasting an over-the-top tiled stove. **Hours:** Same as Main Town Hall. See page 266.

▲▲**St. Mary's Church** Giant red-brick church crammed full of Gdańsk history. **Hours:** Mon-Sat 8:00-17:30, Sun from 13:00, until 18:30 in July-Aug, tower typically open later in summer but generally closed in winter. See page 256.

▲▲**Museum of the Second World War** Poland's definitive museum on the most devastating conflict in human history. **Hours:** Tue 10:00-16:00, Wed-Sun 10:00-18:00 (until 20:00 in July-Aug), closed Mon year-round. See page 281.

▲**Amber Museum** High-tech exhibit of valuable golden globs of petrified tree sap. **Hours:** July-Aug Mon 12:00-20:00, Tue-Sun 10:00-20:00; Sept-June Wed-Mon 10:00-18:00, closed Tue. See page 266.

▲**Uphagen House** Tourable 18th-century interior, typical of the pretty houses that line Ulica Długa. **Hours:** Same as Main Town Hall. See page 264.

▲**St. Bridget's Church** Home church of Solidarity, with poignant memorials and a massive amber altar. **Hours:** Mon-Sat 10:00-18:30, Sun from 13:30. See page 261.

com, syroka.agnieszka@gmail.com). Other guides include **Izabel-la Daszkiewicz** (similar rates, +48 506 511 752, gedanka@op.pl, www.gedanka.pl) and **Jacek "Jake" Podhorski,** who teaches economics at the local university (500 zł/4 hours, more for all day and/or with his car, +48 603 170 761, jacek.podhorski@ug.edu.pl).

Gdańsk Walk

In the 16th and 17th centuries, Gdańsk was the wealthiest city in the Polish lands, with gorgeous architecture (much of it in the

Flemish Mannerist style) rivaling that in the two historic capitals, Kraków and Warsaw. During this golden age, Polish kings would visit this city of well-to-do Hanseatic League merchants and gawk along the same route trod by tourists today.

The following self-guided walk—rated ▲▲▲—introduces you to the best of Gdańsk. It bridges the two historic centers (the Main Town and the Old Town), dips into St. Mary's Church (the city's most important church), and ends at the famous shipyards and Solidarity Square (where Poland began what ultimately brought down the USSR). I've divided the walk into two parts (making it easier to split up, if you like): The first half focuses on a loop through the Main Town, with most of the high-profile sights; while the second part carries on northward, through the less touristy (but still interesting) Old Town to the shipyards.

PART 1: THE MAIN TOWN
• *Begin at the west end of the Main Town, just beyond the last gate at the edge of the busy road—across from the mega-shopping mall.*

❶ Upland Gate (Brama Wyżynna)
The Main Town's fortifications were expanded with a Renaissance wall bound by the Upland Gate (built in 1588). "Upland" refers to the low hills you see beyond—considered high country in this flat region. Standing with your back to the busy arterial (which traces the old moat), study the gate. Find its three coats of arms (the black eagle for Royal Prussia, the crowned white eagle for Poland, and the two crosses for Gdańsk). Recall that this city has, for almost the entirety of its history before the mid-20th century, been bicultural: Germanic and Polish, coexisting more or less peacefully. Also notice the little wheels that once hoisted a drawbridge.

GDAŃSK & THE TRI-CITY

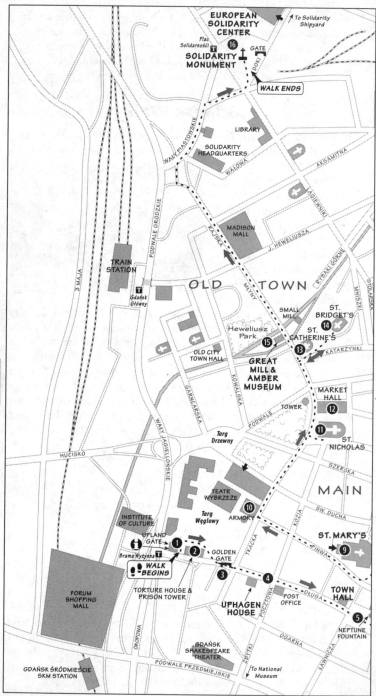

To Solidarity Shipyard

EUROPEAN
SOLIDARITY
CENTER

Plac
Solidarności

SOLIDARITY
MONUMENT 16

GATE

WALK ENDS

WAŁY PIASTOWSKIE

LIBRARY

SOLIDARITY
HEADQUARTERS

WAŁOWA

AKSAMITNA

ŁAGIEWNIKI

PODWALE GRODZKIE

3 MAJA

TRAIN
STATION

Gdańsk
Główny

KAŁSKA

MADISON
MALL

J. HEWELIUSZA

RYBAKI GÓRNE

MNISZKI

STOLARSKA

OLD   TOWN

MŁYNY

Heweliusz
Park

SMALL
MILL

ST.
BRIDGET'S 14

ST.
CATHERINE'S
13

OLD CITY
TOWN HALL

GREAT
MILL &
AMBER
MUSEUM 15

KOWALSKA

KATARZYNKI

GARNCARSKA

WAŁY JAGIELLOŃSKIE

PODWALE

TOWER

MARKET
HALL
12

ST.
NICHOLAS 11

HUCISKO

Targ
Drzewny

SZEROKA

MAIN

ŚW. DUCHA

TEATR
WYBRZEŻE

Targ
Węglowy

ARMORY 10

KOZIA

ST. MARY'S 9

INSTITUTE
OF CULTURE

UPLAND
GATE 1

TKACKA

PIWNA

Brama Wyżynna

WALK
BEGINS

2

GOLDEN
GATE

3

4

DŁUGA

TOWN
HALL

POCZTOWA

POST
OFFICE

5

NEPTUNE
FOUNTAIN

FORUM
SHOPPING
MALL

TORTURE HOUSE &
PRISON TOWER

UPHAGEN
HOUSE

OKOPOWA

ŻBIKA

OGARNA

ŁAWNICZA

GDAŃSK
SHAKESPEARE
THEATER

To National
Museum

GDAŃSK ŚRÓDMIEŚCIE
SKM STATION

PODWALE PRZEDMIEJSKIE

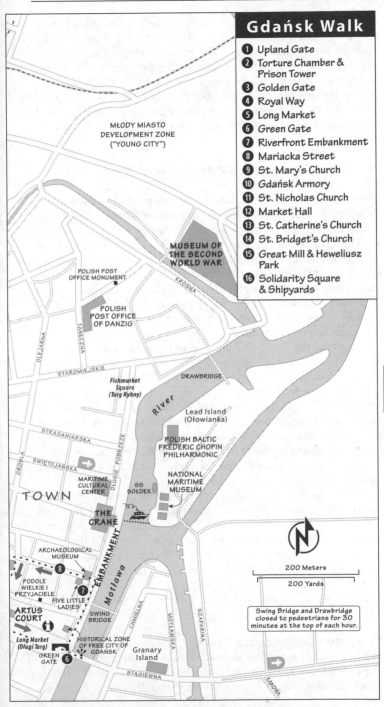

Gdańsk Walk

1. Upland Gate
2. Torture Chamber & Prison Tower
3. Golden Gate
4. Royal Way
5. Long Market
6. Green Gate
7. Riverfront Embankment
8. Mariacka Street
9. St. Mary's Church
10. Gdańsk Armory
11. St. Nicholas Church
12. Market Hall
13. St. Catherine's Church
14. St. Bridget's Church
15. Great Mill & Heweliusz Park
16. Solidarity Square & Shipyards

MŁODY MIASTO DEVELOPMENT ZONE ("YOUNG CITY")

MUSEUM OF THE SECOND WORLD WAR

POLISH POST OFFICE MONUMENT

KROSNA

POLISH POST OFFICE OF DANZIG

OLEJARNA

TANECZNA

STAROMIEJSKIE

DRAWBRIDGE

Fishmarket Square (Targ Rybny)

River

Lead Island (Ołowianka)

STRAGANIARSKA

POLISH BALTIC FREDERIC CHOPIN PHILHARMONIC

GROBLA

ŚWIĘTOJAŃSKA

MARITIME CULTURAL CENTER

DŁUGIE POBRZEŻE

NATIONAL MARITIME MUSEUM

SS SOŁDEK

TOWN

THE CRANE

ARCHAEOLOGICAL MUSEUM

8

EMBANKMENT

Motława

PODOLE WIELKIE I PRZYJACIELE

7

FIVE LITTLE LADIES

ARTUS COURT

SWING BRIDGE

CHMIELNA

MOTŁAWSKA

SZAFARNIA

Long Market (Długi Targ)

HISTORICAL ZONE OF FREE CITY OF GDAŃSK

GREEN GATE

6

Granary Island

STAGIEWNA

ŁĄKOWA

N

200 Meters

200 Yards

Swing Bridge and Drawbridge closed to pedestrians for 30 minutes at the top of each hour.

GDAŃSK & THE TRI-CITY

Now look across the busy street, to the supermodern **Forum shopping center.** Controversial for its over-the-top design (and for covering over a historic canal), this replaced a ragtag old flea market area. A lion—symbol of Gdańsk—perches high on the corner of the rust-colored main building. I'm not in the habit of telling travelers to visit shopping malls...but this one really is worth a peek.

• *It's a straight line from here to the river. Walk around the arch (which houses a good TI—find the entrance on the back side) to the next arch, just a few steps ahead.*

❷ Torture Chamber (Katownia) and Prison Tower (Wieża Więzienna)

The tall, Gothic brick gate before you was part of an earlier protective wall made useless after the Renaissance walls were built in 1588. The evocative passage is generally open (and free) to walk through. Inside, find gargoyles (on the left, a town specialty) and the shackles from which prisoners were hung (on the right). Look waaaay up at the inside of the high gable to find the headless man, identifying this as the torture chamber. (If you stand in just the right spot, you can "reattach" his head to his body.) This old jail—with its 15-foot-thick walls—was used as a prison even in modern times, under Nazi occupation.

Leaving the Torture Chamber and Prison Tower through the far end, look to your left (100 yards away) to see a long, brick building with four fancy, uniform gables. This is the **armory** *(zbrojownia),* one of the finest examples of Dutch Renaissance architecture anywhere. Though this part of the building appears to have the facades of four separate houses, it's an urban camouflage to hide its real purpose from potential attackers. But there's at least one clue to what the building is really for: Notice the exploding cannonballs at the tops of the turrets. (We'll get a better look at the armory from the other side, later in this walk.)

The round, pointy-topped tower next to the armory is the **Straw Tower** (Baszta Słomiana). Gunpowder was stored here, and the roof was straw—so if it exploded, it could easily blow its top without destroying the walls. And to the left you'll see the sleek, modern **Teatr Wybrzeże** performing arts complex—one of many new venues that have opened around this cultural hub in recent years.

• *Straight ahead, the final and fanciest gate between you and the Main Town is the...*

❸ Golden Gate (Złota Brama)

While the other gates were defensive, this one's purely ornamental. The four women up top represent virtues that the people of Gdańsk should exhibit toward outsiders (left to right): Peace, Freedom,

Prosperity, and Fame. The gold-lettered inscription, a psalm in medieval German, compares Gdańsk to Jerusalem: famous and important. Directly above the arch is the Gdańsk coat of arms: two white crosses under a crown on a red shield. We'll see this symbol all over town. Photographers love the view of the Main Town framed in this arch. Inside the arch, you may see old photos showing the 1945 bomb damage. Heartbreaking aerial views of the city in 1945 illustrate how 80 percent of its buildings were in ruins.

• *Passing through the Golden Gate, you reach the Main Town's main drag.*

❹ The Royal Way

Before you stretches Ulica Długa (cleverly called the "Long Street")—the main promenade of what, 600 years ago, was a tremendously wealthy city, thanks to its profitable ties to the Hanseatic League of merchant cities. This promenade is nicknamed the "Royal Way" because (just as in Warsaw and Kraków) the king would follow this route when visiting town.

Walk half a block and then look back at the Golden Gate. The women on top of this side represent virtues the people of Gdańsk should cultivate in themselves (left to right): Wisdom, Piety, Justice, and Concord (if an arrow's broken, let's take it out of the quiver and fix it). The inscription—sharing a bit of wisdom as apropos today as it was in 1612—reads, "Concord makes small countries develop, and discord makes big countries fall." Gdańsk was cosmopolitan and exceptionally tolerant in the Middle Ages, attracting a wide range of people, including many who were persecuted elsewhere: Jews, Scots, Dutch, Flemish, Italians, Germans, and more. Members of each group brought with them strands of their culture, which they wove into the tapestry of this city—demonstrated by the eclectic homes along this street. Each facade and each gable was different, as nobles and aristocrats wanted to display their wealth. On one visit, a traveler seeing this street for the first time gasped to me, "It's like stepping into a Fabergé egg."

During Gdańsk's golden age, these houses were taxed based on frontage (like the homes lining Amsterdam's canals)—so they were built skinny and deep. The widest houses belonged to the super-elite. Different as they are from the outside, every house had the same general plan inside. Each had three parts, starting with the front and moving back: First was a fancy drawing room, to show off for visitors. Then came a narrow corridor to the back rooms—often

Gdańsk History

Visitors to Gdańsk are surprised at how "un-Polish" the city's history is. In this cultural melting pot of German, Dutch, and Flemish merchants (with a smattering of Italians and Scots), Poles were only a small part of the picture until the city became exclusively Polish after World War II. However, in Gdańsk, cultural backgrounds traditionally took a back seat to the bottom line. Wealthy Gdańsk was always known for its economic pragmatism—no matter who was in charge, merchants here made money.

Gdańsk is Poland's gateway to the waters of Europe, where its main river (the Vistula) meets the Baltic Sea. The town was first mentioned in the 10th century and was seized in 1308 by the Teutonic Knights (who called it "Danzig"; for more on the Teutonic Knights, see page 317). The Knights encouraged other Germans to settle on the Baltic coast, and gradually turned Gdańsk into a wealthy city. In 1361, Gdańsk joined the Hanseatic League, a trade federation of mostly Germanic merchant towns that provided mutual security. By the 15th century, Gdańsk was a leading member of this mighty network, which virtually dominated trade in northern Europe (and also included Toruń, Kraków, Lübeck, Hamburg, Bremen, Bruges, Bergen, Tallinn, Novgorod, and nearly a hundred other cities).

In 1454, the people of Gdańsk rose up against the Teutonic Knights, burning down their castle and forcing them out of the city. Three years later, the Polish king borrowed money from wealthy Gdańsk families to hire Czech mercenaries to take the Teutonic Knights' main castle, Malbork (described in the next chapter). In exchange, the Gdańsk merchants were granted special privileges, including exclusive export rights. Gdańsk now acted as a middleman for much of the trade passing through Polish lands, and paid only a modest annual tribute to the Polish king.

The 16th and 17th centuries were Gdańsk's golden age. Now a part of the Polish kingdom, the city had access to an enormous hinterland of natural resources to export—yet it maintained a privileged, semi-independent status. Like Amsterdam, Gdańsk became a progressive and booming merchant city. Its mostly Germanic and Dutch burghers imported Dutch, Flemish, and Italian architects to give their homes an appropriately Hanseatic flourish. At a time of religious upheaval in the rest of Europe, Gdańsk became known for its tolerance—a place that opened its doors to all visitors (many Mennonites and Scottish religious refugees emigrated here). It was also a haven for great thinkers, including philosopher Arthur Schopenhauer, women's rights activist Käthe Schirmacher, and scientist Daniel Fahrenheit (who invented the mercury thermometer).

Along with the rest of Poland, Gdańsk declined in the late 18th century and became part of Prussia (today's northern Germany) during the Partitions. But the people of Gdańsk—even those of German heritage—had taken pride in their independence and weren't enthusiastic about being ruled from Berlin. After World War I, in a unique compromise to appease its complex ethnic makeup, Gdańsk once again became an independent city-state: the Free City of Danzig (about 750 square miles, populated by 400,000 ethnic Germans and 15,000 Poles). Like a holdover from medieval fiefdoms in modern times, it even issued its own currency (the Gulden) and stamps. Danzig, along with the so-called Polish Corridor connecting it to Polish lands, effectively cut off Germany from its northeastern territory. On September 1, 1939, Adolf Hitler started World War II when he invaded Gdańsk in order to bring it back into the German fold. Later, nearly 80 percent of the city was destroyed when the Soviets "liberated" it from Nazi control.

After World War II, Gdańsk officially became part of Poland and was painstakingly reconstructed. In 1970, and again in 1980, the shipyard of Gdańsk witnessed strikes and demonstrations that would lead to the fall of European communism. Poland's great anticommunist hero and first postcommunist president, Lech Wałęsa, still lives here. When he flies around the world to give talks, he leaves from Gdańsk's "Lech Wałęsa Airport."

A city with a recent past that's both tragic and uplifting, Gdańsk celebrated its 1,000th birthday in 1997. Very roughly, the

city has spent about 700 years as an independent entity, and about 300 years under Germanic overlords (the Teutonic Knights, Prussia, and the Nazis). But today, Gdańsk is decidedly its own city. And, as if eager to prove it, Gdańsk has made big improvements at a stunning pace: museums (the European Solidarity Center and WWII museum), cultural facilities (the Shakespeare Theater), sports venues (a stadium that resembles a blob of amber, built for the 2012 Euro Cup tournament), and an ongoing surge of renovation and refurbishment that has the gables of the atmospheric Hanseatic quarter gleaming once again.

along the side of an inner courtyard. Because the houses had only a few windows facing the outer street, this courtyard provided much-needed sunlight to the rest of the house. The residential quarters were in the back, where the family actually lived: bedroom, kitchen, office. To see the interior of one of these homes, pay a visit to the interesting **Uphagen House** (at #12, on the right, a block and a half in front of the Golden Gate; described later).

Pause in front of Uphagen House, look around, and ponder this beautiful street's very ugly history. At the end of World War II, the Royal Way was in ruins. That epic war actually began here, in what was then the "Free City of Danzig." Following World War I, nobody could decide what to do with this influential and multi-ethnic city. So, rather than assign it to Germany or Poland, it was set apart as its own little autonomous statelet. In 1939, Danzig was 80 percent German-speaking—enough for Hitler to consider it his. And so, on September 1 of that year, the Nazis seized it in one day with relatively minor damage (though the attack on the Polish military garrison on the city's Westerplatte peninsula lasted a week).

But six years later, when the Soviets arrived (March 30, 1945), they devastated the city. This was the first traditionally German city that the Red Army took on their march toward Berlin. And, while it was easy for the Soviets to seize the almost empty city, the commander then insisted that it be leveled, building by building—in retaliation for all the pain the Nazis had caused in Russia. (Soviets didn't destroy nearby Gdynia, which they considered Polish rather than German.) Soviet officers turned a blind eye as their soldiers raped and brutalized residents. An entire order of horrified nuns committed suicide by throwing themselves into the river.

It was only thanks to detailed drawings and photographs that these buildings could be so carefully reconstructed. Notice the cheap plaster facades done in the 1950s—rough times under communism, in the decade after World War II. (Most of the town's medieval brick was shipped to Warsaw for a communist-sponsored "rebuild the capital first" campaign.) While the fine facades were restored, the buildings behind the facades were completely rebuilt to modern standards.

Just beyond Uphagen House, on the left at #73, **Grycan** has been a favorite for ice cream here for generations. Just a few doors down, also on the left, are some of the most striking **facades** along the Royal Way. The blue-and-white house with the three giant heads is from the 19th century, when the

hot style was eclecticism—borrowing bits and pieces from various architectural eras. This was one of the few houses on the street that survived World War II.

At the next corner on the right is the huge, blocky, red **post office,** which doesn't quite fit with the skinny facades lining the rest of the street. Step inside. With doves fluttering under an airy glass atrium, the interior's a class act.

A few doors farther down on the left, just past #62/63, notice the **colorful scenes** over the windows. These are slices of life from 17th-century Gdańsk: drinking, talking, shopping, playing music. The ship is a *koga,* a typical symbol of Hanseatic ports like Gdańsk.

Across the street and a few steps down are the fancy facades of three houses belonging to the very influential medieval **Ferber family,** which produced many burghers, mayors, and even a bishop. On the house with the little dog over the door (#29), look for the heads in the circular medallions. These are Caesars of Rome. At the top of the building is Mr. Ferber's answer to the constant question, "Why build such an elaborate house?"—*PRO INVIDIA,* "For the sake of envy."

A few doors down on the right (at #33/34), is Gdańsk's most scenically situated milk bar, **Bar Mleczny Neptun.** Back in communist times, these humble cafeterias were subsidized to give workers an affordable place to eat out. To this day, they offer simple and very cheap grub.

Before you stands the **Main Town Hall** (Ratusz Głównego Miasta) with its mighty brick clock tower. Consider climbing its observation tower and visiting its superb interior, which features ornately decorated meeting rooms for the city council (described later, under "Sights in Gdańsk").

As you stroll along this street—and throughout your time in Gdańsk—you'll periodically hear cheerful **carillon music** playing from the top of the Main Town Hall tower. This 14-bell instrument, which dates from 1561, chimes throughout the day, providing a lovely soundtrack to a Gdańsk visit. On Saturdays at noon, there's a longer concert (www.carillongdansk.pl).

• *Just beyond the Main Town Hall, Ulica Długa widens and becomes...*

❺ Long Market (Długi Targ)

Step from the Long Street into the Long Market and do a slow, 360-degree spin to appreciate the amazing array of proud architecture. The centerpiece of this square is one of Gdańsk's most important landmarks, the statue of **Neptune**—god of the sea. He's a fitting symbol for a city that dominates the maritime life of Poland. Behind him is another worthwhile museum, the **Artus Court.** Step up to the magnificent door on the right side and study the golden relief just above, celebrating the Vistula River (in so many ways the lifeblood of the Polish nation): Lady Vistula is exhausted after her heroic journey and is finally carried by Neptune to her ultimate destination, the Baltic Sea. (This is just a preview of the ornate art that fills the interior of this fine building—described later.)

Midway down the Long Market (on the right, across from the Hard Rock Café) is a glass case with the **thermometer and barometer of Daniel Fahrenheit.** Although that scientist was born here—his birth house is just a few blocks away—he did his groundbreaking work in Amsterdam.

• *At the end of the Long Market is the...*

❻ Green Gate (Zielona Brama)

This huge gate (named for the Green Bridge just beyond) was built as a residence for visiting kings...who usually preferred to stay back by Neptune instead (maybe because the river, just on the other side of this gate, stank).

A few steps down the skinny lane to the left is the endearing little **Historical Zone of the Free City of Gdańsk** museum, which explains the interwar period when "Danzig" was an independent and bicultural city-state (described later). During this period, four out of five people living in the free city identified themselves not as Germans or Poles but as "Danzigers."

• *Now go through the gate, walk out onto the Green Bridge, anchor yourself in a niche on the left, and look downstream.*

❼ Riverfront Embankment

The Motława River—a side channel of the mighty Vistula—flows into the nearby Baltic Sea. This port was the source of Gdańsk's phenomenal golden-age wealth. This embankment was jam-packed in its heyday, the 14th and 15th centuries. It was so crowded with boats that you would hardly have been able to see the water, and boats had to pay a time-based moorage fee for tying up to a post.

Look back at the **Green Gate** and notice that these bricks are much smaller than the locally made ones we saw earlier on this walk. These bricks are Dutch: Boats from Holland would come here empty of cargo but with a load of bricks for ballast. Traders filled their ships with goods for the return trip, leaving the bricks behind.

See any pirate ships? The old-fashioned **galleons** and other tour boats depart hourly for a fun cruise to Westerplatte (where on

September 1, 1939, Germans fired the first shots of World War II) and back. Though kitschy, the galleons are a fun way to get out on the water (see details on page 289).

Across the river is **Granary Island** (Wyspa Spichrzów), where grain was stored until it could be taken away by ships. Before World War II, there were some 400 granaries here; almost all were destroyed...and this island remained rubble until the mid-2010s, when developers began erecting a passel of modern new buildings (evoking the old Gdańsk gables) and wrapped the island in a scenic boardwalk—a wonderful place for a stroll. While there's not much sightseeing value along here, it's a delightful place to promenade, enjoy views back on the historic skyline across the river, and perhaps browse for a meal or drink. The three older-looking granaries downstream, in the distance on the next island, house exhibits for the National Maritime Museum (described later).

From your perch on the bridge, look down the embankment (about 500 yards, on the left) and find the huge wooden **Crane** (Żuraw) bulging over the water. This monstrous 15th-century crane—a rare example of medieval port technology—was once used for loading and repairing ships...beginning a shipbuilding tradition that continued to the days of Lech Wałęsa. The crane mechanism was operated by several workers scrambling around in giant hamster wheels. Treading away to engage the gears and pulleys, they could lift 4 tons up 30 feet, or 2 tons up 90 feet.

Near the Crane, notice the white, modern **swing bridge** that makes it easier for pedestrians to do a loop along both embankments. At the top of each hour, it swings parallel to the river to allow boats to pass, making it inaccessible for 30 minutes. (The similar white drawbridge, farther downstream, works on the same schedule.) You'll hear a big commotion every time it's about to swing; watch the tourists scurry.

• *Walk along the embankment about halfway to the Crane. Along the way, you may pass the moorings for **excursion boats** heading to the Westerplatte monument. (Or these may be farther down along the embankment, beyond the Crane.)*

*Pause when you reach the big brick building with green window frames and a tower. This red-brick fort houses the **Archaeological Museum** (described later). Its collection includes the five ancient stones in a small garden just outside its door (on the left). These are the **Prussian***

Hags—mysterious sculptures from the second century AD (a.k.a. "Five Little Ladies," each described in posted plaques).

Turn left through the gate in the middle of the brick building. You'll find yourself on the most charming lane in town...

❽ Mariacka Street

The calm, atmospheric "Mary's Street" leads from the embankment to St. Mary's Church. Stroll the length of it, enjoying the most romantic lane in Gdańsk. (If you need a coffee break, the recommended Drukarnia—on the right—is tops.) The **porches** extending out into the street, with access to cellars underneath, were a common feature in Gdańsk's golden age. For practical reasons, after the war, these were restored only on this street and a few others. Notice how the porches are bordered with fine stone relief panels and gargoyles attached to storm drains. If you get stuck there in a hard rainstorm, you'll understand why in Polish these are called "pukers." Enjoy a little amber comparison-shopping. As you stroll up to the towering brick St. Mary's Church, imagine the entire city like this cobbled lane of proud merchants' homes, with street music, delightful facades, and brick church towers high above.

Look up at the church tower viewpoint—filled with people who hiked 409 steps for the view. Our next stop is the church, which you'll enter on the far side under the tower. Walk around the left side of the church, appreciating the handmade 14th-century bricks on the right and the plain post-WWII facades on the left. (Reconstructing the Royal Way was better funded. Here, the priority was simply getting people housed again.) In the distance is the fancy facade of the armory (where you'll head after visiting the church).

• *But first, go inside...*

❾ St. Mary's Church (Kościół Mariacki)

Of Gdańsk's 13 medieval red-brick churches, St. Mary's (rated ▲▲) is the one you must visit. It's the largest brick church in the world—with a footprint bigger than a football field (350 feet long and 210 feet wide), it can accommodate 20,000 standing worshippers.

Cost and Hours: Church entry—likely free for now, tower climb—16 zł, Mon-Sat 8:00-17:30, Sun from 13:00, until 18:30 in July-Aug, tower typically open later in summer but generally closed in winter.

❷ **Self-Guided Tour:** Inside, sit directly under the fine carved and painted 17th-century

Protestant pulpit, two-thirds of the way down the nave (on the left side), to get oriented.

Overview: Built from 1343 to 1502 by the Teutonic Knights (who wanted a suitable centerpiece for their newly captured main city), St. Mary's remains an important symbol of Gdańsk. The church started out Catholic, became Lutheran in the mid-1500s, and then became Catholic again after World War II. (Remember, Gdańsk was a Germanic city before World War II and part of the big postwar demographic shove, when Germans were sent west and Poles from the east relocated here. Desperate, cold, and homeless, the new Polish residents moved into what was left of the German homes.) While the church was originally frescoed from top to bottom, the Lutherans whitewashed the entire place. Today, some of the 16th-century whitewash has been peeled back (behind the high altar—we'll see this area soon), revealing a bit of the original frescoes. The floor is paved with 500 gravestones of merchant families. Many of these were cracked when bombing sent the brick roof crashing down in 1945.

Most Gothic churches are built of stone in the basilica style—with a high nave in the middle, shorter aisles on the side, and flying buttresses to support the weight. (Think of Paris' Notre-Dame.) But with no handy source of stone available locally, northern Polish churches are built of brick, which won't work with the basilica design. So, like all Gdańsk churches, St. Mary's is a "hall church"—with three naves the same height and no exterior buttresses.

Also like other Gdańsk churches, St. Mary's gave refuge to the Polish people after the communist government declared martial law in 1981. When a riot broke out and violence seemed imminent, people flooded into churches, knowing that the ZOMO riot police wouldn't dare follow them inside.

Most of the church decorations are original. A few days before the Soviets arrived to "liberate" the city in 1945, locals—knowing what was in store—hid precious items in the countryside. Take some time now to see a few of the highlights.

• *From this spot, you can see most of what we'll visit in the church: As you face the altar, the astronomical clock is at 10 o'clock, the Ferber family medallion is at 1 o'clock, the Priests' Chapel is at 3 o'clock (under a tall, colorful window), and the magnificent 17th-century organ is directly behind you (it's played at each Mass and during free concerts on Fri in summer).*

Pulpit: For Protestants, the pulpit is important. Designed as an impressive place from which to share the Word of God in the people's language, it's located mid-nave so all can hear.

• *Opposite the pulpit is the moving...*

Priests' Chapel: The 1965 statue of Christ weeping commemorates 2,779 Polish chaplains executed by the Nazis. See the grainy black-and-white photo of one about to be shot, above on the right.

• *Head up the nave to the...*

High Altar: The main altarpiece, beautifully carved in 1517, is a triptych showing the coronation of Mary. She is surrounded by the Trinity: flanked by God and Jesus, with the dove representing the Holy Spirit overhead. The church's medieval stained glass was destroyed in 1945. Poland's biggest stained-glass window, behind the altar, is from 1980.

• *Directly to the right of the altar, high on a pillar, find the big, opulent family marker.*

Ferber Family Medallion: The falling baby (under the crown) is Constantine Ferber. As a precocious child, li'l Constantine leaned out his window on the Royal Way to see the king's processional come through town. He slipped and fell but landed in a salesman's barrel of fish. Constantine grew up to become the mayor of Gdańsk.

• *Now circle around behind the altar, on the right side. Search high above you, on the walls to your right, to spot those restored pre-Reformation frescoes. Behind the altar, look for a...*

Glass Case: This case was designed to hold Hans Memling's *Last Judgment* painting, which used to be in this church but is currently being held hostage by the National Museum (described later, under "Sights in Gdańsk"). To counter the museum's claim that the church wasn't a good environment for such a precious work, the priest had this display case built—but that still wasn't enough to convince the museum to give the painting back. (You'll see a smaller replica of the painting elsewhere in the church.) For years, the case was simply empty; more recently, finally taking the hint, the local priest has begun to display a few vestments and ecclesiastical gear here.

• *Now circle back the way you came to the area in front of the main altar and turn right into the transept. High on the wall to your right, look for the...*

Astronomical Clock: This 42-foot-tall clock is supposedly the biggest wooden clock in the world. Below it is an elaborate circular calendar that, like a medieval computer, calculates on which day each saint's festival day falls in different years (see the little guy on the left, with the pointer). Above are zodiac signs and the time (back then, the big hand was all you needed). Way up on top, Adam and Eve are naked and ready to ring the bell. Adam's been swinging his clapper at the top of the hour since 1473; these days, you'll hear the clock clang on the quarter-hour, with a big show each day at 11:55.

• *A few steps in front of the clock is a modern chapel with the...*

Memorial to the Polish Victims of the 2010 Smoleńsk Plane

Crash: The gold-shrouded Black Madonna honors the 96 victims of an air disaster that killed much of Poland's government—including the president and first lady—during a terrible storm over Russia. The main tomb is for Maciej Płażyński, from Gdańsk, who was leader of the parliament. On the left, the jagged statue has bits of the wreckage and lists each victim by name.

• *Head a few steps back toward the entrance, then look back at one of the nearby pillars to find a large painting (facing the back of the church).*

Replica of *Last Judgment* Altarpiece: This is a smaller, mustier replica of the exquisite, priceless altarpiece housed in the National Museum. If you're not planning to go see it at the National Museum, you could read the description on page 287 now.

• *In the back-left corner of the church are stairs—lots and lots of stairs—leading to the...*

Church Tower: You can climb 409 steps to burn off some pierogi and *pączki*, and to earn a grand city view. It's a long hike (and you'll know it—every 10th step is numbered). But because the viewpoint is surrounded by a roof, the views are distant and may not be worth the effort. The first third is up a tight, medieval spiral staircase. Then you'll walk through the eerie, cavernous area between the roof and the ceiling before huffing up steep concrete steps that surround the square tower (as you spiral up, up, up around the bells). Finally, you'll climb a little metal ladder and pop out at the viewpoint.

• *Leaving the church, angle left and continue straight up atmospheric* **Ulica Piwna** *("Beer Street")—a lovely lane lined with bars, cafés, and restaurants—toward the sprightly facade of the armory.*

❿ The Gdańsk Armory (Zbrojownia)

The 1605 armory, which we saw from a distance at the start of this walk, is one of the best examples of Dutch Renaissance architecture in Europe. Athena, the goddess of war and wisdom, stands in the center, amid motifs of war and ornamental pukers.

• *If you want to make your walk a loop, you're just a block away from where we started (to the left). Or, to continue through the Old Town to the European Solidarity Center's fine museum, follow the second part of this walk.*

PART 2: THROUGH THE OLD TOWN TO THE SHIPYARDS

The second part of this walk works its way out of the Main Town and heads into the Old Town, toward Solidarity Square and the shipyards. We'll walk along this street (which changes names a couple of times) nearly all the way. The walk ends at the European Solidarity Center's fine museum. You'll want plenty of time to tour the museum and linger over its exhibits, so if you're already pooped or it's getting late in the day, consider finishing this walk another time.

• *Facing the armory, turn right and head up Kołodziejska, which quickly becomes Węglarska. After two blocks (that is, one block before the big market hall), detour to the right down Świętojańska and use the side door to enter the brick church.*

⓫ St. Nicholas Church (Kościół Św. Mikołaja)

Near the end of World War II, when the Soviet army reached Gdańsk on its march westward, they were given the order to burn all the churches. Only this one survived—because it happened to be dedicated to Russia's patron saint. As the best-preserved church in town, it has a more dazzling interior than the others, with lavish black-and-gold Baroque altars.

• *Backtrack out to the main street and continue along it, passing a row of seniors selling their grown and foraged edibles. Immediately after the church is Gdańsk's...*

⓬ Market Hall

Built in 1896 and renovated in 2005, Gdańsk's market hall is fun to explore. Step inside (closed Sun) and appreciate the delicate steel-and-glass canopy overhead. Browse the market stalls; the meat is downstairs, and the veggies are outside on the adjacent square. As this was once the center of a monastic community, the basement has the graves of medieval Dominican monks, which were exposed when the building was refurbished: Peer over the glass railing and you'll see some of those scant remains.

Across the street from the Market Hall, a round, red-brick **tower,** part of the city's protective wall back in 1400, marks the end of the Main Town and the beginning of the Old Town.

• *Carry on. For an ice cream break, watch on the right (after crossing the street) for the recommended Paolo Gelateria. Another block up the street, on the right, is the huge...*

⓭ St. Catherine's Church (Kościół Św. Katarzyny)

"Katy," as locals call it, is the oldest church in Gdańsk, proud of its carillon (there's a small Clock Tower Museum in the tower, and you can hear carillon concerts on Fridays at 11:00; see www.carillongdansk.pl). In May of 2006, a carelessly discarded cigarette caused the church roof to burst into flames. Local people ran into the church and pulled everything outside, so nothing valuable was damaged; even the carillon bells were saved. However, the roof and wooden frame were totally destroyed. The people of Gdańsk were determined to rebuild this important symbol of the city. Within days of the fire, fundraising concerts were held to scrape together most of the money needed to raise the roof once more. Step inside.

The austere interior is evocative, with still-bare-brick walls that almost seem intentional—as if they're trying for an industrial-mod look.

• *The church hiding a block behind Katy—named for Catherine's daughter Bridget—has important ties to Solidarity and is worth a visit. Go around the right side of Katy and skirt the parking lot to find the entrance, on the side of the church near the far end.*

⓮ St. Bridget's Church (Kościół Św. Brygidy)

This was the home church of Lech Wałęsa during the tense days of the 1980s. The church and its priest, Henryk Jankowski, were particularly aggressive in supporting the ideals of Solidarity. Jankowski became a vocal advocate for the movement. In gratitude for the church's support, Wałęsa named his youngest daughter Brygida. Rated ▲, it's the city's second-most worthwhile church to enter, after St. Mary's.

Cost and Hours: 5 zł, Mon-Sat 10:00-18:30, Sun from 13:30.

Visiting the Church: Head inside. For your visit, start at the high altar, then circle clockwise back to the entry.

The enormous, unfinished **high altar** is made entirely of amber—more than a thousand square feet of it. Features that are already in place include the Black Madonna of Częstochowa, a royal Polish eagle, and the Solidarity symbol (tucked below the Black Madonna). The structure, like a scaffold, holds pieces as they are completed and added to the ensemble; as it grows,  it also spreads to adjacent walls, as if a slow-moving fungus. The giant bronze statues below the altar depict Cardinal Stefan Wyszyński (on the left, the head of the Polish Catholic Church through much of the communist period) and St. John Paul II (on the right).

The wrought-iron gate of the adjacent **Chapel of Fatima** (right of main altar) recalls great battles and events in Polish history from 966 to 1939, with important dates boldly sparkling in gold. Some say the Polish Church is too political. Others argue that it was only through a politically engaged Church that this culture survived the Partitions of Poland over a century and a half, plus the brutal antireligious policies of the communist period. The national soul of the Polish people—whether religious or not, and for better or for worse—is tied up in the Catholic faith.

Henryk Jankowski's tomb—a white marble box with dark-red trim—is along the same wall, but closer to the back of the church. Jankowski was a key figure during Solidarity times; the tomb proclaims him *Kapelan Solidarności* ("Solidarity Chaplain"). But his public standing took a nosedive near the end of his life—thanks to ego-driven projects like his amber altar, as well as accusations of anti-Semitism and corruption. Forced to retire in 2007, Jankowski died in 2010.

In the rear corner, where a figure lies lifeless on the floor under a wall full of wooden crosses, is the tomb of Solidarity martyr **Jerzy Popiełuszko.** A courageous and famously outspoken Warsaw priest, in 1984 Popiełuszko was kidnapped, beaten, and murdered by the communist secret police. Notice that the figure's hands and feet are bound—as his body was found. The crosses on the wall above are historic—each one was carried at various strikes against the communist regime. The communists believed they could break the spirit of the Poles with brutality—like the murder of Popiełuszko. But it only made the rebels stronger and more resolved to ultimately win their freedom.

Under the choir loft, step into the evocative chapel with **memorials** to other 20th-century Polish martyrs.

Near the exit, on a monitor, a fascinating 12-minute **video** shows great moments of this church, with commentary by Lech Wałęsa himself.

• *Return to the main street, turn right, and continue on. The big brick building ahead on the left, with the many windows in its roof, is the Great Mill. Walk just beyond the building and look down at the canal that once powered it.*

⓭ The Great Mill and Heweliusz Park

This huge brick building dates from the 14th century. Look at the waterfalls and imagine standing here in 1400—with the mill's 18 wheels spinning 24/7, powering grindstones that produced 20 tons of flour a day. Like so much else here, the mill survived until 1945. Today this building houses the **Amber Museum**—a starkly modern exhibit filling this old shell with countless examples of those precious deposits (described later).

Heweliusz Park, just beyond the mill, is worth a look. Just steps into the family-friendly park is a **fountain** that brings shrieks of joy to children on hot summer days. On the adjacent corner, notice a branch of the popular **Pellowski bakery**—a handy place to pick up a *pączek* (jelly doughnut) to enjoy at one of the benches.

Venturing farther into the park, in the distance is the **Old City Town Hall** (Dutch Renaissance style, from 1595). The monument near the top of the park honors the 17th-century astronomer **Jan Heweliusz.** He's looking up at a giant, rust-colored wall with a map of the heavens. Heweliusz built the biggest telescopes of his era to better appreciate and understand the cosmos. Behind the mill stands the **miller's home**—its opulence indicates that, back in the Middle Ages, there was a lot of money in grinding.

• *To get to the* **shipyards,** *keep heading straight up Rajska. You'll pass the modern Madison shopping mall. After another long block, jog right, passing to the right of the big, ugly, and green 1970s-era skyscraper. On your right, marked by the famous red logo on the roof, is today's* **Solidarity headquarters** *(which remains the strongest trade union in Poland, with 700,000 members, and is also active in many other countries). On the corner in front of the Solidarity building, look for two big chunks of* **wall:** *a piece of the Berlin Wall, and a stretch of the shipyard wall that Lech Wałęsa scaled to get inside and lead the strike. The message: What happened behind one wall eventually led to the fall of the other Wall.*

From here, hike on (about 200 yards) toward the huge, rust-colored building in the distance, angling left at the roundabout to reach the trio of tall, skinny crosses in front of it.

⑯ Solidarity Square and the Shipyards

Three tall crosses mark Solidarity Square and the rust-colored European Solidarity Center (with an excellent museum). For the exciting story of how Polish shipbuilders set in motion events that led to the end of the USSR, turn to page 270.

Sights in Gdańsk

MAIN TOWN (GŁÓWNE MIASTO) AND OLD TOWN (STARE MIASTO)

The following sights are listed roughly in the order you'll see them on the self-guided walk.

Museum of Gdańsk

The Museum of Gdańsk has four excellent branches—the Uphagen House, Main Town Hall, Artus Court, and Amber Museum—and a few lesser ones. Along with St. Mary's Church (described earlier), these are the four most important interiors in the Main Town. They are covered by separate tickets.

Cost: 22 zł each for Uphagen House, Main Town Hall, or Artus Court, 32 zł for Amber Museum. All are typically free on Mondays.

Hours: The **Uphagen House, Main Town Hall,** and **Artus Court** have the same hours, which are notoriously changeable but generally around June-Sept Tue-Sun 10:00-18:00, Mon from 12:00; Oct-May Wed-Mon 10:00-16:00, Thu until 18:00, closed Tue. The **Amber Museum** has different hours: July-Aug Mon 12:00-20:00, Tue-Sun 10:00-20:00; Sept-June Wed-Mon 10:00-18:00, closed Tue.

Information: The museums share a phone number and website (central +48 58 767 9100, www.muzeumgdansk.pl).

▲Uphagen House (Dom Uphagena)

This interesting place, at Ulica Długa 12, is your chance to glimpse what's behind the colorful facades lining this street. It's the only grand Gdańsk mansion rebuilt as it was before 1945, and it has the typical configuration of three parts: dolled-up visitors' rooms in front, a corridor along the courtyard, and private rooms in the back. The finely decorated salon was used to show off for guests. You'll see several examples of "Gdańsk-style furniture," characterized by three big, round feet along the front, lots of ornamentation, and usually a virtually impossible-to-find lock (sometimes hidden behind a movable decoration). Passing into the dining room, note the knee-high paintings of hunting and celebrations. Along the passage to the back, each room has a theme: butterflies in the smoking room, flowers in the next room, birds in the music room. In the private rooms at the back, the decor is simpler.

Back downstairs, you'll see the rustic working rooms: a humble bedroom, the kitchen, and the pantry. Step out into the courtyard to appreciate how it carves a little fresh air and sunshine out of a densely packed city. Back inside, look for the cross-section model showing the three parts of the house you just walked through. You'll exit through a room with photos of the house before the war, which were used to reconstruct what you see today.

▲▲Main Town Hall (Ratusz Głównego Miasta)

This landmark building contains remarkable decorations from Gdańsk's golden age. You can also climb 293 concrete steps to the top of the **tower** for commanding views (15 zł extra, closed Oct-April).

Visiting the Main Town Hall: Buy your ticket on the ground floor, which also houses a space for temporary exhibits. Then walk through the courtyard and up the stairs to the historic rooms. First you'll be directed to the room on your left, the **Great Weta Hall**—a meeting room with big portraits and big windows.

Then, returning to the room where you first entered, ogle the finely crafted spiral staircase. The ornately carved wooden **door** is all-original, from the 1600s. Above the door are two crosses under a crown. This seal of Gdańsk is being held—as it's often depicted—by a pair of lions. The felines are stubborn and independent, just like the citizens of Gdańsk. The surface of the door is carved with images of crops. Around the frame of the door are mermen, reminding us that this agricultural bounty, like so many of Poland's resources, is transported on the Vistula and out through Gdańsk.

Step through the ornate door into the **Red Hall,** where the Gdańsk city council met in the summertime. (The lavish fireplace, with another pair of lions holding the coat of arms of Gdańsk, was just for show. There's no chimney.) City council members would sit in the seats around the room, debating city policy. Marvel at the 17th-century inlaid wood panels (just overhead) showing slices of local life. Paintings on the wall above represent the seven virtues that the burghers meeting in this room should possess.

The exquisite ceiling—with 25 paintings in total—is all about theology. Including both Christian and pagan themes, the ceiling was meant to inspire the decision makers in this room to make good choices. Study the oval painting in the middle (from 1607)—the museum's highlight. It shows the special place Gdańsk occupies between God, Poland, and the rest of the world. In the foreground, the citizens of Gdańsk go about their daily lives. Above them, high atop the arch, God's hand reaches down (from within clouds of Hebrew characters) and grasps the Main Town Hall's steeple. The rainbow arching above also symbolizes God's connection to Gdańsk. Mirroring that is the Vistula River, which begins in the mountains of southern Poland (on the right), runs through the country, and exits at the sea in Gdańsk (on the left, where the rainbow ends).

Continue into the less impressive **Winter Hall,** with another fireplace (this one actually hooked up to a chimney) and another coat of arms held by lions. The desk behind glass belonged to Paweł Adamowicz, who served as the president (mayor) of Gdańsk during the tumultuous transitional period from 1998 through 2019—when he was, shockingly, stabbed during a charity event and died at age 53. You can see a photo of this beloved local politician on the wall behind.

From here, head up another flight of stairs to a series of rooms with **temporary exhibits.** Then, up yet another flight, is a fascinating exhibit about Gdańsk's time as a **"free city"** *(wolne miasto)* between the World Wars—when, because of its delicate ethnic mix of Poles and Germans, it was too precarious to assign it to either country. You'll see border checkpoints, uniforms, signs in German (the predominant language of "Danzig"), and reconstructed rooms (homes and shops) from the era.

Near the end of this section, you have the option to climb up to the top of the **tower.** Otherwise, head back down and out the way you came.

▲▲Artus Court (Dwór Artusa)

In the Middle Ages, Gdańsk was home to many brotherhoods and guilds (like businessmen's clubs). For their meetings, the city provided this elaborately decorated hall, named for King Arthur—a medieval symbol for prestige and power. Just as in King Arthur's Court, this was a place where powerful and important people came together. Of many such halls in Baltic Europe, this is the only original one that survives (in the tall, white, triple-

arched building behind Neptune statue at Długi Targ 43; enter through the door to the left of the big arches).

Visiting the Artus Court: In the grand hall, various **cupboards** line the walls. Each organization that met here had a place to keep its important documents and office supplies. Suspended from the ceiling are seven giant, elaborate **model ships** that depict Baltic vessels, symbolic of the city's connection to the sea.

In the far-back corner is the museum's highlight: a gigantic **stove** decorated with 520 colorful tiles featuring the faces of kings, queens, nobles, mayors, and burghers—a mix of Protestants and Catholics, as a reminder of Gdańsk's religious tolerance. Almost all the tiles are original, having survived WWII bombs.

Notice the huge **paintings** on the walls above, with 3-D animals emerging from flat frames. Hunting is a popular theme in local artwork. Like minting coins, hunting was a privilege usually reserved for royalty, but it was extended in special circumstances to the burghers of special towns...like Gdańsk. These "paintings" are new, digitally generated reproductions of the originals, which were damaged in World War II.

The next room—actually in the next building—is a typical **front room** of the burghers' homes lining Ulica Długa. Ogle the gorgeously carved wooden staircase, the Gdańsk-style cupboards, and three more model ships. A series of rooms with more artifacts leads to the exit.

▲Amber Museum (Muzeum Bursztynu)

This collection is displayed in a sleek, glossy, state-of-the-art space inside the very creaky and historic Great Mill, a short walk from the Main Town (and on the way to the Solidarity Sights, at Wielkie Młyny 16). The museum tells the story of the precious yellow

All About Amber

Poland's Baltic seaside is known as the Amber Coast. You can see amber *(bursztyn)* in Gdańsk's Amber Museum, in the collection at Malbork Castle (see the Pomerania chapter), and in shop windows everywhere.

This fossilized tree resin originated here on the north coast of Poland 40 million years ago. Scientists debate exactly what caused this sudden proliferation of sap—it may have been caused by shifting weather conditions, or in response to a new parasite or disease. Later—starting around 2.5 million years ago—Ice Age glaciers spread amber even further around the Baltic region. Then came human beings, who have been drawn to amber since the Stone Age. Archaeologists have found Roman citizens (and their coins) buried with crosses made of amber.

Almost 75 percent of the world's amber comes from northern Poland. It can be foraged, mined by digging deep holes, "fished" using nets, or accessed using hydraulic technology. And occasionally, it simply washes up on the beaches after a winter storm.

While we think of amber as simply yellow, it comes in some 300 distinct shades, from yellowish white to yellowish black, from opaque to transparent. Darker-colored amber is generally mixed with ash and sand—making it more fragile, and generally less desirable. Lighter amber is mixed with gasses and air bubbles. Some of the elaborate amber sculptures you'll see are joined with "amber glue"—melted-down amber mixed with an adhesive agent. More recently, amber craftsmen are combining amber with silver to create artwork—a method dubbed the "Polish School."

Dating back at least to the 16th century, some people believe that amber—specifically, the succinic acid found in white amber—has medicinal properties. A traditional cure for arthritis pain is to pour strong vodka over amber, let it set, and then rub it on sore joints. Other remedies call for mixing amber dust with honey or rose oil. It sounds superstitious, but users claim that it works.

deposits that the Baltic Sea is known for. But while the items displayed here are dazzling, the place is a bit light on actual information—this collection is all about ogling amber.

Visiting the Museum: From ye olde Gdańsk, you'll step through the creaky doors into a different world: glassy black surfaces that reflect the yellows, oranges, and browns of the amber everywhere you look. Buy your ticket and head up to tour the exhibit, which fills two floors upstairs.

Floor 1 covers the geology and history of amber. Timelines date back eons, and case after case of jagged chunks of raw amber illustrate the wide range of colors. One case shows smooth-polished amber with inclusions trapped inside (like those dino-DNA mosquitoes in *Jurassic Park*). You'll also learn about the various methods for finding amber (including special nets) and about its importance to golden-age Gdańsk. Touchscreens strain to explain the story of amber, but the information is pretty thin.

Floor 2 ("Amber in Culture") is simply a showcase of objects created from amber, including altars, chests, necklaces, brooches, chess sets, tankards, candelabras, miniatures, a bowl of fruit, pipes, clocks, an entire table, contemporary jewelry, and a working guitar—all beautifully lit, and all made or decorated with amber.

Back downstairs, the exit is through the extremely well-stocked gift shop (of course); there's also a handy café.

Other Museums in the Main Town

With so many worthwhile sights in town, you'll have your hands full with the biggies. But if you have a special interest, these museums are also worth considering for a visit:

The **Historical Zone of the Free City of Gdańsk** (Strefa Historyczna Wolne Miasto Gdańsk), tucked just off the main drag near the Green Gate, is the best place to learn about the fascinating period between World Wars I and II, when Gdańsk was not part of Germany or Poland but the self-governing Free City of Danzig. This modest museum earnestly shows off artifacts from the time—photos, stamps, currency (the Gulden), maps, flags, promotional tourist leaflets, and other Danzig artifacts (closed Mon, down the little alley just in front of the Green Gate at Warzywnicza 10A, +48 58 320 2828, www.strefahistorycznawmg.pl).

The **Archaeological Museum** (Muzeum Archeologiczne) is worth a quick peek: distinctive urns with cute faces (which date from the Hallstatt Period and were discovered in slate graves around Gdańsk), Bronze and Iron Age tools, before-and-after photos of WWII Gdańsk, and a reconstructed 12th-century Viking-like Slavonic longboat. You can also climb the building's tower, with good views up Mariacka street toward St. Mary's Church (closed Mon, Ulica Mariacka 25, +48 58 322 2100, www.archeologia.pl).

The **National Maritime Museum** (Narodowe Muzeum

Morskie) is an eclectic collection spread among several buildings on either side of the river. The main point of interest is the medieval Crane that dominates Gdańsk's historic waterfront; this recently reopened after a restoration. Next door is the skippable Maritime Cultural Center—of interest only to nautical nuts. Across the river, more exhibits fill the three rebuilt old granaries, and you can also crawl through the holds and scramble across the deck of a decommissioned steamship called the *Sołdek*—the first postwar vessel built at the Gdańsk shipyard (closed Mon, Ulica Ołowianka 9, +48 58 301 8611, www.nmm.pl).

Theater lovers may enjoy seeing the **Gdańsk Shakespeare Theater** (Teatr Szekspirowski), at the southern edge of the Main Town. As early as the 17th century, theater troupes from England would come to this cosmopolitan trading city to perform. In 1993, local actors revived the tradition with an annual Gdańsk Shakespeare Festival. In 2014, the city built the state-of-the-art Gdańsk Shakespeare Theater to honor its connection to the Bard. The architecture is minimalist, blocky, black brick (with a few symbolic faux buttresses to echo the gables of the surrounding buildings). The main theater can be modified to create three different types of performance spaces (proscenium, thrust stage, and theater-in-the-round)—and even has a retractable roof to wash the actors with direct sunlight. The theater hosts a wide variety of performances and festivals, and still does some Shakespeare in English during the annual Shakespeare Festival in summer. Call or check their website for details on tours and upcoming performances (Bogusławskiego 1, +48 58 351 0101, www.teatrszekspirowski.pl).

▲Fishmarket Square (Targ Rybny)

If out for a stroll, make your way just five minutes along the embankment past the Crane and swing bridge to this square, where a kid-friendly carousel spins next to a big Hilton hotel. It's no longer an actual fish market, and there's not much sightseeing here. But this vantage point offers great views up and down the river: Across the way, on Lead Island (Ołowianka), is the stately home of the Baltic Philharmonic, with its sail-like adornment, along with a giant Ferris wheel and a photo-op *GDAŃSK* sign. Downriver (to the left) you can see how the city is growing in that direction, with modern residential and commercial developments sprawling up the riverbank. Farther downstream (not visible from here) is Westerplatte, the point where World War II began. And upriver (to the right), you can see the three reconstructed old granaries and giant ship of the Maritime Museum, and beyond that, the swing bridge and Gdańsk's slick new city-center Granary Island development. This is a fine spot to find a bench and enjoy the buzz of a proud historic city on the rise.

SOLIDARITY AND THE GDAŃSK SHIPYARD

Gdańsk's single most memorable experience is exploring the shipyard (Stocznia Gdańska) that witnessed the beginning of the end of communism's stranglehold on Central and Eastern Europe. Taken together, the sights in this area are worth ▲▲▲. Here in the former industrial wasteland that Lech Wałęsa called the "cradle of freedom," this evocative site tells the story of the brave Polish shipyard workers who took on—and ultimately defeated—an Evil Empire. A visit to the Solidarity (Solidarność) sights has two main parts: Solidarity Square (with the memorial and gate in front of the shipyard), and the outstanding museum inside the European Solidarity Center.

Getting to the Shipyard: These sights cluster around Solidarity Square (Plac Solidarności), at the north end of the Old Town, about a 20-minute walk from the Royal Way. For the most interesting approach, follow Part 2 of my self-guided walk (earlier), which ends here. Or take tram #7 or #8 from the Brama Wyżynna stop (near the Upland Gate) or the train station to the Plac Solidarności stop.

Background: After the communists took over Central and Eastern Europe at the end of World War II, oppressed peoples throughout the Soviet Bloc rose up in different ways. The most dramatic uprisings—Hungary's 1956 Uprising and Czechoslovakia's 1968 "Prague Spring"—were brutally crushed under the treads of Soviet tanks. The formula for freedom that finally succeeded was a patient, nearly decade-long series of strikes and protests spearheaded by Lech Wałęsa and his trade union, called Solidarność— "Solidarity." (The movement also benefited from good timing, as it coincided with the *perestroika* and *glasnost* policies of Soviet premier Mikhail Gorbachev.) While politicians tussled from their plush offices, imagine the courage it took for Wałęsa and his fellow workers to fight communism on the front lines—armed with nothing more than guts.

▲▲▲Solidarity Square (Plac Solidarności) and the Monument of the Fallen Shipyard Workers

The seeds of August 1980 were sown a decade before. Since becoming part of the Soviet Bloc, the Poles staged frequent strikes, protests, and uprisings to secure their rights, all of which were put down by the regime. But the bloodiest of these took place in December of 1970—a tragic event memorialized by the **three-crosses monument** that towers over what's now called Solidarity Square.

The 1970 strike was prompted by price hikes. The communist government set the prices for all products. As Poland endured drastic food shortages in the 1960s and 1970s, the regime frequently announced what it called "regulation of prices." Invariably, this

meant an increase in the cost of essential foodstuffs. (To be able to claim
"regulation" rather than "increase," the
regime would symbolically lower prices
for a few select items—but these were
always nonessential luxuries, such as
elevators and TV sets, which nobody
could afford anyway.) The regime was
usually smart enough to raise prices on
January 1, when the people were fat and
happy after Christmas, and too hung-
over to complain. But on December
12, 1970, bolstered by an ego-stoking
visit by West German chancellor Willy

Brandt, Polish premier Władysław Gomułka increased prices. The
people of Poland—who cared more about the price of Christmas
dinner than relations with Germany—struck back.

A wave of strikes and sit-ins spread along the heavily industri-
alized north coast of Poland, most notably in Gdańsk, Gdynia, and
Szczecin. Thousands of angry demonstrators poured through the
gate of this shipyard, marched into town, and set fire to the Communist Party Committee building. In an attempt to quell the riots,
the government-run radio implored the people to go back to work.
On the morning of December 17, workers showed up at shipyard
gates across northern Poland, and were greeted by the army and
police. Without provocation, the Polish army opened fire on the
workers. While the official death toll for the massacre stands at 44,
others say the true number is much higher. The monument, with
a trio of 140-foot-tall crosses, honors those lost to the regime that
December.

Go to the middle of the **wall** behind the crosses, to the monument of the worker wearing a flimsy plastic work helmet, attempting to shield himself from bullets. Behind him is a list—pockmarked with symbolic bullet holes—of workers murdered on that
day. *Lat* means "years old"—many teenagers were among the dead.
The quote at the top of the wall is from St. John Paul II, who was
elected pope eight years after this tragedy. The pope was known for
his clever way with words, and this very carefully phrased quote—
which served as an inspiration to the Poles during their darkest
hours—skewers the regime in a way subtle enough to still be toler-
ated: "Let thy spirit descend, and renew the face of the earth—of
this earth" (that is, Poland).

Stretching to the left of this center wall are plaques representing labor unions from around Poland—and around the world
(look for the Chinese characters)—expressing solidarity with these
workers. To the right is an enormous Bible verse: "May the Lord

GDAŃSK & THE TRI-CITY

Lech Wałęsa

In 1980, the world was turned on its ear by a walrus-mustachioed shipyard electrician. Within three years, this seemingly run-of-the-mill Pole had precipitated the collapse of communism, led a massive 10 million-member trade union with enormous political impact, been named *Time* magazine's Man of the Year, and won a Nobel Peace Prize.

Lech Wałęsa was born in Popowo, Poland, in 1943. After working as a car mechanic and serving two years in the army, he became an electrician at the Gdańsk Shipyard in 1967. Like many Poles, Wałęsa felt stifled by the communist government and was infuriated that a system that was supposed to be for the workers clearly wasn't serving them.

When the shipyard massacre took place in December of 1970 (see page 270), Wałęsa was at the forefront of the protests. He was marked as a dissident, and in 1976, he was fired. Wałęsa hopped from job to job and was occasionally unemployed—under communism, a rock-bottom status reserved for only the most despicable derelicts. But he soldiered on, fighting for the creation of a trade union and building up quite a file with the secret police.

In August 1980, Wałęsa heard news of the beginnings of the Gdańsk strike and raced to the shipyard. In an act that has since become the stuff of legend, Wałęsa scaled the shipyard wall to get inside.

Before long, Wałęsa's dynamic personality won him the unofficial role of the workers' leader and spokesman. He negotiated with the regime to hash out the August Agreements, becoming a rock-star-type hero during the so-called "16 Months of Hope"... until martial law came crashing down in December 1981. Wałęsa was arrested and interned for 11 months in a country house. After

give strength to his people. May the Lord bless his people with the gift of peace" (Psalms 29:11).

Inspired by the brave sacrifice of their true comrades, shipyard workers rose up here in August 1980, formulating the **"21 Points"** of a new union called Solidarity. Their demands included the right to strike and form unions, the freeing of political prisoners, and an increase in wages. The 21 Points are listed in Polish on the panel at the far end of the right wall, marked *21 X TAK* ("21 times yes"). An unwritten precondition to any agreement was the right for the workers of 1980 to build a memorial to their comrades slain in 1970. The government agreed, marking the first time a communist being released, he continued to struggle underground, becoming a symbol of anticommunist sentiment.

Finally, the dedication of Wałęsa and Solidarity paid off, and Polish communism dissolved—with Wałęsa rising from the ashes as the country's first postcommunist president. But the skills that made Wałęsa a rousing success at leading an uprising didn't translate well to the president's office. Wałęsa proved to be a stubborn, headstrong politician, frequently clashing with the parliament. He squabbled with his own party, declaring a "war at the top" of Solidarity and rotating higher-ups to prevent corruption and keep the party fresh. He also didn't choose his advisors well, enlisting old friends as staffers who wound up immersed in scandal. His overconfidence was his Achilles' heel, and his governing style verged on authoritarian.

Unrefined and none too interested in scripted speeches, Wałęsa was a simple man who preferred playing Ping-Pong with his buddies to attending formal state functions. Though lacking a formal education, Wałęsa had unsurpassed drive and charisma... but that's not enough to lead a country—especially during an impossibly complicated, fast-changing time.

Wałęsa was defeated at the polls, by the Poles, in 1995, and when he ran again in 2000, he received a humiliating 1 percent of the vote. Since leaving office, Wałęsa has kept a lower profile but still delivers speeches worldwide. Many poor Poles grumble that Lech, who started life simple like them, has forgotten the little people. But his fans point out that he gives much of his income to charity. And on his lapel, he still always wears a pin featuring the Black Madonna of Częstochowa—the most important symbol of Polish Catholicism.

Poles say there are at least two Lech Wałęsas: the young, bombastic, working-class idealist Lech, at the forefront of the Solidarity strikes, who will always have a special place in their hearts; and the failed President Wałęsa, who got in over his head and tarnished his legacy.

regime ever allowed a monument to be built to honor its own victims. Wałęsa called it a harpoon in the heart of the communists. The towering monument, with three crucified anchors on top, was designed, engineered, and built by shipyard workers. The monument was finished just four months after the historic agreement was signed.

• *Now continue to the gate and peer through into...*

Gdańsk Shipyard (Stocznia Gdańska) Gate #2

When a Pole named Karol Wojtyła was elected pope in 1978—then visited his homeland in 1979—he inspired 40 million fellow citizens to believe that impossible dreams can come true. Prices continued to go up, and the workers continued to rise up. By the summer of 1980, it was clear that the dam was about to break.

In August, crane operator Anna Walentynowicz was fired unceremoniously just short of her retirement. (For more on Walentynowicz, see the sidebar.) This sparked a strike in the Gdańsk Shipyard (then called the Lenin Shipyard) on August 14, 1980. An electrician named Lech Wałęsa had been fired as an agitator years before. But on hearing news of the strike, Wałęsa went to the shipyard and climbed over the wall to get inside, soon taking over leadership for the strike.

These were not soldiers, nor were they idealistic flower children. The strike participants were gritty, salt-of-the-earth manual laborers: forklift operators, welders, electricians, machinists. Imagine being one of the 16,000 workers who stayed here for 18 days during the strike—hungry, cold, sleeping on sheets of Styrofoam, inspired by the new Polish pope, excited about finally standing up to the regime...and terrified that at any moment you might be gunned down, like your friends had been a decade before.

Workers, afraid to leave the shipyard, communicated with the outside world through this gate—spouses and siblings showed up here and asked for a loved one, and those inside spread the word until the striker came forward. Occasionally, a truck pulled up inside the gate, with Lech Wałęsa standing atop its cab with a megaphone. Facing the thousands of people assembled outside the gate, Wałęsa gave progress reports on the negotiations and pleaded for supplies. The people of Gdańsk responded, bringing armfuls of bread and other food to keep the workers going. Solidarity.

During the strike, two items hung on the fence. One of them (which still hangs there today) was a picture of Pope John Paul II—a reminder to believe in your dreams and have faith in God (for more on the Pope and his role in Solidarity, see page 66). The other item was a makeshift list of the strikers' 21 Points—demands scrawled in red paint and black pencil on pieces of plywood. (A replica now hangs above and on the right; the original is in the museum.)

• *Walk through the passage at the right end of the gate and enter the former shipyard.*

There's not much to see today, but during its peak from 1948 to 1990, the **shipyard** churned out over a thousand ships and employed 16,000 workers. About 60 percent of these ships were ex-

The Women of Solidarity

Anna Walentynowicz (1929-2010) worked as a welder and a crane operator at the Lenin Shipyard. While she began her ca-

reer as an exemplary socialist worker, the 1970 massacre of workers soured her on the communist regime. She joined an illegal trade union, distributed a workers' newsletter to agitate for change, and spoke up when a supervisor stole money from a workers' fund.

In the summer of 1980, at age 60, Walentynowicz was fired just a few months shy of her planned retirement. As the earliest strikes that would grow into Solidarity gained momentum, the rehiring of Walentynowicz was one of the strikers' 21 Points. Before Wałęsa became "the face of Solidarity," that face belonged to Walentynowicz. (Ultimately, Walentynowicz was reinstated and retired with her full pension.)

Another influential founder of Solidarity was shipyard nurse **Alina Pienkowska** (1952-2002). As the strike began, authorities cut off all phone lines—except the one to the clinic, which Pienkowska used to reach out to like-minded colleagues around Poland.

Just a few days into the strike, the authorities agreed to some of the workers' lesser demands; Lech Wałęsa, among others, chalked this up as a success and began to wind down the protests. Many of the strikers began to leave the shipyard and head for home.

But Pienkowska was aware that what had begun here in Gdańsk was already spreading across Poland. On a loudspeaker, she implored her fellow workers to stick to their strike, alongside other trade unions across Poland that had already begun to join their cause. In fact, so determined were Pienkowska and Walentynowicz to fully live the idea of "solidarity" that they locked the shipyard gates to prevent more workers from leaving. Because of these brave and principled women, many of the strikers decided to stay, and even many of those who left returned the next day (reportedly at the urging of their wives) to carry on—transforming what could have ended as a historical footnote into a world-changing event.

Tragically, both women met untimely deaths. Pienkowska died of cancer in 2002, at age 50. And Walentynowicz was aboard the plane filled with Polish politicians and other influential figures that crashed in Smoleńsk, Russia, on April 10, 2010. But their legacy lives on. While Lech Wałęsa became the movement's public face, Walentynowicz and Pienkowska are considered the conscience, heart, and soul of Solidarity. Both were ultimately awarded the Order of the White Eagle—Poland's highest honor.

ported to the USSR—and so, when the Soviet Bloc broke apart in the 1990s, they lost a huge market. Today, the facilities employ closer to 1,200 workers...who now make windmills.

Before entering the museum, take a look around. This part of the shipyard, long abandoned, is being redeveloped into a **"Young City"** (Młode Miasto), with shopping, restaurants, offices, and homes. Rusting shipbuilding equipment is being torn down, and old brick buildings are being converted into gentrified flats. Farther east, the harborfront is also being rejuvenated, creating a glitzy marina and extending the city's delightful waterfront people zone farther and farther to the north.

• *The massive, rust-colored European Solidarity Center, which faces Solidarity Square, houses the museum where we'll learn the rest of the story.*

▲▲▲European Solidarity Center (Europejskie Centrum Solidarności)

Europe's single best sight about the end of communism is made even more powerful by its location: in the very heart of the place where those events occurred.  Filling just one small corner of a huge, purpose-built educational facility, the permanent exhibition uses larger-than-life photographs, archival footage, actual artifacts, interactive touchscreens, and a state-of-the-art audioguide to eloquently tell the story of the end of Eastern European communism.

Cost and Hours: 30 zł, includes audioguide; Mon–Fri 10:00–19:00, Sat–Sun until 20:00; Oct–April Wed–Mon 10:00–17:00, Sat–Sun until 18:00, closed Tue; last entry one hour before closing, Plac Solidarności 1, +48 58 772 4000, www.ecs.gda.pl.

❯ **Self-Guided Tour:** First, appreciate the architecture of the **building** itself. From the outside, it's designed to resemble the rusted hull of a giant ship—seemingly gloomy and depressing. But step inside to find an interior flooded with light, which cultivates a surprising variety of life—in the form of lush gardens that make the place feel like a very expensive greenhouse. You can interpret this symbolism a number of ways: Something that seems dull and dreary from the outside (the Soviet Bloc, the shipyards themselves, what have you) can be full of brightness, life, and optimism inside.

In the lobby, buy your ticket for the permanent exhibit and pick up the essential, included audioguide. The exhibit has much to see, and some of it is arranged in a conceptual way that can be tricky to understand without a full grasp of the history. I've outlined the basics in this self-guided tour, but the audioguide can illuminate more details—including translations of films and eye-witness testimony from participants in the history.

Notice that the center also hosts temporary exhibits (filling a ground-floor space beneath the escalators), a "Play Department" area for kids, a simple **$ café**, and, back near the entrance, the more upscale **$$ AmberSide** restaurant. (For more eating options nearby, see page 298.)

• *The permanent exhibit fills seven lettered rooms—each with its own theme—on two floors upstairs. From the lush lobby, head up the escalator and into...*

The Birth of Solidarity (Room A): This room picks up right in the middle of the dynamic story we just learned out on the square. It's August 1980, and the shipyard workers are rising up. You step straight into a busy shipyard: punch clocks, workers' lockers, and—up on the ceiling—hundreds of plastic helmets. A big **map** in the middle of the room shows the extent of the shipyard in 1980. Nearby stands a small **truck;** Lech Wałęsa would stand on top of the cab of a truck like this one to address the nervous locals who had amassed outside the shipyard gate, awaiting further news.

In the middle of the room, carefully protected under glass, are those original **plywood panels** onto which the strikers scrawled their 21 demands and then lashed to the gate. Just beyond that, a giant video screen and a map illustrate how the strikes that began here spread like a virus across Poland. At the far end of the room, behind the partition, stand **two tables** that were used during the talks to end the strikes (each one with several actual items from that era, under glass).

After 18 days of protests (notice the dates marked on the floor), the communist authorities finally agreed to negotiate. On the afternoon of August 31, 1980, the Governmental Commission and the Inter-Factory Strike Committee (MKS) came together and signed the August Agreements, which legalized Solidarity—the first time any communist government had permitted a workers' union. As Lech Wałęsa sat at a big table and signed the agreement, other union reps tape-recorded the proceedings and played them later at their own factories to prove that the unthinkable had happened. Take a moment to linger over the rousing **film** that plays on the far wall, which begins with the strike, carries through with the tense negotiations that a brash young Lech Wałęsa held with the authorities, and ends with the triumphant acceptance of the strikers' demands. Lech Wałęsa rides on the shoulders of well-wishers out to the gate to spread the good news. The gate opens, the strikers file out, and the crowd cheers: "Leszek! Leszek!" (Lech-y! Lech-y!) The shipyard gate opens, and—finally!—the strikers get to return to the outside world.

• *Back by the original 21 demands, enter the next exhibit…*

The Power of the Powerless (Room B): This section traces the roots of the 1980 strikes, which were preceded by several far-less successful protests. It all begins with a kiss: a giant photograph of Russian premier Leonid Brezhnev mouth-kissing the Polish premier Edward Gierek, with the caption **"Brotherly Friendship."** Soviet premiers and their satellite leaders really did greet each other "in the French manner," as a symbolic gesture of their communist brotherhood.

Working your way through the exhibit, you'll see the door to a **prison cell**—a reminder of the intimidation tactics used by the Soviets in the 1940s and 1950s to deal with their opponents as they exerted their rule over the lands they had liberated from the Nazis.

The typical **communist-era apartment** is painfully humble. After the war, much of Poland had been destroyed, and population shifts led to housing shortages. People had to make do with tiny spaces and ramshackle furnishings. Communist propaganda blares from both the radio and the TV.

A map shows **"red Europe"** (the USSR plus the satellites of Poland, Czechoslovakia, Hungary, and East Germany), and a **timeline** traces some of the smaller Soviet Bloc protests that led up to Solidarity: in East Germany in 1953, in Budapest and Poznań in 1956, the "Prague Spring" of 1968, and other 1968 protests in Poland.

In the wake of these uprisings, the communist authorities cracked down even harder. Peek into the **interrogation room,** with a wall of file cabinets and a lowly stool illuminated by a bright spotlight. (Notice that the white Polish eagle on the seal above the desk is missing its golden crown—during communism, the Poles were allowed to keep the eagle, but its crown was removed.)

The next exhibit presents a day-by-day rundown of the **1970 strikes,** from December 14 to 22, which resulted in the massacre of the workers who are honored by the monument in front of this building. In the glass case, the leather jacket with bullet holes was worn by a 20-year-old worker who was killed that day. A wall of mug shots gives way to exhibits chronicling the steady rise of dissent groups through the 1970s, culminating in the June 1976 protests in the city of Radom (prompted, like so many other uprisings, by unilateral price hikes). On your way out of this section, you pass through a mock-up of a grocery store from the period…with empty shelves.

• *Loop back through Room A and proceed straight ahead into…*

Solidarity and Hope (Room C): While the government didn't take the August Agreements very seriously, the Poles did…and before long, 10 million of them—one out of every four, or effectively half the nation's workforce—joined Solidarity. So began what's often called the **"16 Months of Hope."** Newly legal, Solidarity continued to stage strikes and make its opposition known. Slick Solidarity posters and children's art convey the childlike enthusiasm with which the Poles seized their hard-won kernels of freedom. The communist authorities' hold on the Polish people began to slip. Support and aid from the outside world poured in, but the rest of the Soviet Bloc looked on nervously, and the Warsaw Pact army assembled at the Polish border and glared at the uprisers. The threat of invasion hung heavy in the air.

• *Exiting this room, head up the staircase and into...*

At War with Society (Room D): In this black room, you're greeted by a wall of TV screens delivering a stern message. On Sunday morning, December 13, 1981, the Polish head of state, **General Wojciech Jaruzelski**—wearing his trademark dark glasses—appeared on national TV and announced the introduction of **martial law.** Solidarity was outlawed, and its leaders were arrested. Frightened Poles heard the announcement and looked out their windows to see Polish Army tanks rumbling through the snowy streets. (On the opposite wall, see footage of tanks and heavily armed soldiers intimidating their countrymen into compliance.) Those who were children at the time recall turning on their televisions for a beloved Sunday-morning cartoon show, *Teleranek,* and instead seeing this chilling message. Jaruzelski claimed that he imposed martial law to prevent the Soviets from invading. Today, many historians question whether martial law was really necessary, though Jaruzelski remained unremorseful through his death in 2014.

Continuing deeper into the exhibit, you come to a **prisoner transport.** Climb up inside to watch chilling scenes of riots, demonstrations, and crackdowns by the ZOMO riot police. In one gruesome scene, a demonstrator is quite intentionally run over by a truck. From here, pass through a gauntlet of *milicja* riot-gear shields to see the truck crashing through a gate. Overhead are the uniforms of nine striking miners from the **Wujek mine** who were massacred on December 16, 1981 (their names are projected on the pile of coal below). The regime called this event "pacification."

Martial law was a tragic, terrifying, and bleak time for the Polish people. It did not, however, kill the Solidarity movement, which continued its fight after going underground. Passing prison cells, you'll see a wall plastered with handmade, underground posters and graffiti. Notice how in this era, **Solidarity propaganda** is much more primitive; circle around the other side of the wall to see several presses that were actually used in clandestine Solidarity print shops during this time. The outside world sent messages of support as well as supplies—represented by the big wall of cardboard boxes. This approval also came in the form of a Nobel Peace Prize for Lech Wałęsa in 1983; you'll see video clips of his wife

GDAŃSK & THE TRI-CITY

accepting the award on his behalf (Wałęsa feared that if he traveled abroad to claim it, he would not be allowed back into the country). On the other side of the room is an exhibit about Pope John Paul II's visit in the very tense days of 1983.

• *But even in these darkest days, there were glimmers of hope. Enter...*

The Road to Democracy (Room E): By the time the pope visited his homeland again in 1987, martial law had finally been lifted, and Solidarity—still technically illegal—was gaining momentum, gradually pecking away at the communists. Step into the small inner room with footage of the **pope's third pilgrimage** to his homeland in 1987, by which time (thanks in no small part to his inspirational role in the ongoing revolution) the tide was turning.

Step into the room with the big, white **roundtable.** With the moral support of the pope and the entire Western world, the brave Poles were the first European country to throw off the shackles of communism when, in the spring of 1989, the "Roundtable Talks" led to the opening up of elections. The government arrogantly called for parliamentary elections, reserving 65 percent of seats for themselves.

In the next room, you can see Solidarity's strategy in those **elections:** On the right wall are posters showing Lech Wałęsa with each candidate. Another popular "get out the vote" measure was the huge poster of Gary Cooper—an icon of America, which the Poles deeply respect and viewed as their friendly cousin across the Atlantic—except that, instead of a pistol, he's packing a ballot. Rousing reminders like this inspired huge voter turnout. The communists' plan backfired, as virtually every open seat went to Solidarity. It was the first time ever that opposition candidates had taken office in the Soviet Bloc. On the wall straight ahead, flashing a V-for-*wiktoria* sign, is a huge photo of Tadeusz Mazowiecki—an early leader of Solidarity, who became prime minister on June 4, 1989.

• *For the glorious aftermath, head into the final room.*

The Triumph of Freedom (Room F): This room is dominated by a gigantic **map of Central and Eastern Europe.** A countdown clock on the right ticks off the departure of each country from communist clutches, as the Soviet Bloc "decomposes." You'll see how the success of Solidarity in Poland—and the ragtag determination of a scruffy band of shipyard workers right here in Gdańsk—inspired people all over Central and Eastern Europe. By the winter of 1989, the Hungarians had opened their borders, the Berlin Wall had crumbled, and the Czechs and Slovaks had staged their Velvet Revolution. (Small viewing stations that circle the room reveal the detailed story for each country's own road to freedom.) Lech Wałęsa—the shipyard electrician who started it all by jumping over a wall—became the first president of postcommunist Poland. And a year later, in Poland's first true elections since World War II, 29 different parties won seats in the parliament. It was a free-election free-for-all.

In the middle of the room stands a white wall with **inspirational quotes** from St. John Paul II and Václav Havel—the Czech poet-turned-protester-turned-prisoner-turned-president—which are repeated in several languages. On the huge wall, the **Solidarity "graffiti"** is actually made up of thousands of little notes left behind by visitors to the museum. Feel free to grab a piece of paper and a pen and record your own reflections.

• *Finally, head downstairs into a peaceful space.*

Culture of Peaceful Change (Room G): Many visitors find that touring this museum—with vivid reminders of a dramatic and pivotal moment in history that took place in their own lifetimes and was brought about not by armies or presidents but by everyday people—puts them in an emotional state of mind. Designed for silent reflection, this room overlooks the monument to those workers who were gunned down in 1970. It shows footage of Pope John Paul II; Lech Wałęsa; Martin Luther King, Jr.; and others who dedicated their lives to peaceful change.

• *For an epilogue, continue deeper into the former shipyard to see one more important landmark from 1980. Exit the building the way you came in and turn left. The path leads to a low-profile, red-brick building about 80 yards ahead, the...*

Sala BHP

This is the building where the communists sat down across the table from Lech Wałęsa and his team and worked out a compromise (as seen in the videos inside the European Solidarity Center). Entering, turn left into the Small Hall to see shipyard photos, banners, office equipment, and other memorabilia from the time. The other side of the building (right from the entrance) is the actual, larger hall where those fateful meetings took place, with a long table set up on the stage. You'll see a model of the shipyard, circa 1980, and models of the various ships that were built here.

Cost and Hours: Free, daily 10:00-18:00, Oct-April until 16:00, www.salabhp.pl.

NORTH OF THE MAIN TOWN
▲▲Museum of the Second World War
(Muzeum II Wojny Światowej)

In 2017, Poland's definitive WWII museum opened in a state-of-the-art, purpose-built facility a 10-minute walk north of Gdańsk's Main Town. It uses artifacts, creative design, insightful storytelling, and ample archival footage to tell the story of the war that began right at Gdańsk's doorstep—focusing on the Polish experience, but also expanding its focus to other aspects of the conflict. At more than 50,000 square feet, it's one of the biggest historical exhibits in the world. (Pace yourself.) While those with a limited appetite for history may find it overwhelming, even those with a casual interest will be glad they invested two or three hours touring its exhibits.

As impressive as the museum is, it could have been that much better. The original design presented an ambitiously global, yet personal, perspective on the war—carefully calibrated to be evenhanded and international in its outlook. But as it neared completion, ruling politicians from the nationalistic Law and Justice Party deemed it too paci-fistic and "not Polish enough"— it needed to be more bombastic and emotional. They replaced

the museum director and his staff, and hired a new director who changed several exhibits to be more singularly patriotic—playing up the "martyrdom" aspect of Poland's role in the war. In the end, it's sad to think that this museum could have been Europe's best WWII museum—if only trained historians had been allowed to control it, rather than politicians. For that reason, I rate it ▲▲ rather than ▲▲▲.

Cost and Hours: 29 zł, free on Tue, essential audioguide-12 zł; Tue 10:00-16:00, Wed-Sun 10:00-18:00 (until 20:00 in July-Aug), closed Mon year-round, last entry one hour before closing; Plac Władysława Bartoszewskiego 1, +48 58 760 0960, www.muzeum1939.pl.

Getting There: It's a short walk north of the historical center. The most appealing approach is to walk north along the riverfront promenade all the way to its end; you'll see the giant, rust-red, glassy tower on your left.

Visiting the Museum: As you approach, appreciate the symbolic architecture of the site. The ground level—nicely landscaped, with inviting slingback chairs in the summer—represents the present. The museum's exhibit space is entirely underground—representing the past. And the tower rising above represents the future. All of the buildings are clad in rusted steel—the material of choice in this shipbuilding city.

Head down the stairs at the base of the tower, go inside, and take the elevator down to level -3. This area has ticket desks, a cloakroom, WCs, a $ bistro, a shop, a cinema, temporary exhibits, and the entrance to the permanent exhibition. For a more serious meal, you can ride the elevator up to floor 4 to find an affordable, bright **$** restaurant with views over the city.

When you buy your ticket, spring for the **audioguide,** which helpfully navigates the highlights of the sprawling exhibits and translates some of the films. It's geo-tagged, so it knows where you are and informs you accordingly.

Ticket and audioguide in hand, head through the turnstile. A long **corridor** stretches to your right; 18 clearly numbered exhibition halls weave in and out of this corridor, chronologically telling the story. As you crisscross through the corridor, take a moment to ponder its exhibits about everyday life in wartime, covering such topics as food and cooking, fashion and style, the black market, travel, and music.

Before heading into the main exhibition, consider turning left, into the **Time Travel** exhibit. Designed for Polish kids, it follows two children and their everyday life, before, during, and after the war—with the same apartment re-created for each time period.

The first part of the exhibit is straight ahead from the entrance turnstile: A movie that sets the stage by recapping the events of World War I and the interwar period.

Now proceed down the corridor and work your way chronologically through the numbered exhibits. Section **01**—spread across three smaller rooms—traces the rise of communism in the Soviet Union (the quern stone was used for grinding grain by ethnic Poles in Ukraine, many of whom perished under Stalin's policies), fascism in Italy (the Fiat embodies the populism—a car in every driveway—that drove Mussolini's propaganda), and Nazism in Germany (with a bust and posters of Hitler, some hateful anti-Semitic propaganda, a Hitler Youth uniform, and a clip from Leni Riefenstahl's *Triumph of the Will*).

Section **02** is a reconstructed Polish street from the interwar period. (Remember this.) The next hallway outlines the rise of imperialism in Japan, Franco's ascent in Spain, and Germany's dismantling of the Versailles system that ended the conflict of World War I. Gdańsk—then called Danzig—held a unique position: It was a free city, with Germany on one side and Poland on the

other. As Hitler rose, Western Europeans already knew that Danzig would be a bulwark against his aggression (see the stone border marker)—giving rise to the slogan "Die for Danzig." On the wall in the next room—wallpapered with giant swastikas and hammer-

and-sickles—find a replica of the secret Molotov-Ribbentrop Pact between the USSR and Nazi Germany, agreeing to divide Poland down the middle...and clearing the way for invasion.

In section **03,** you'll learn how that invasion took place on September 1, 1939, when Hitler invaded Poland (en route to Danzig) and quickly overran the country—the first use of his relentless Blitzkrieg ("Lightning War") strategy. One exhibit explains the first volley of that war, in which 200 Poles defended the military transit depot Westerplatte against 3,000 Nazi troops for seven days. You'll learn about the brutal Nazi atrocities from that first invasion, including photos of bombed-out cities. One of the museum's highlights is the film *Siege,* shot and narrated by American correspondent Julien Bryan, who was in Warsaw during the invasion and witnessed the Nazis bombarding a church during Mass, the bombing of a maternity ward, and a village of peasants machine-gunned from the air while digging up potatoes. You'll learn how soon, the Soviet Union also invaded, per their secret agreement—meeting the Nazis in the middle and splitting Poland in half (see the huge map on the wall).

Across the main corridor, section **04** outlines Soviet conquests in other parts of Europe (Finland, the Baltic states, Romania). Section **05** (with a JU-87 dive bomber suspended from the wall) explains how this was a new kind of war, relying heavily on air warfare (Hitler's Luftwaffe).

Back across the corridor, section **06** documents the ruthlessness of the Nazis, including their starvation of Soviet POWs (the "Hunger Plan" that killed more than three million captured troops), the 871-day Siege of Leningrad (today's St. Petersburg, where one million civilians starved to death), and air raids that killed another one million civilians.

Across the corridor, section **07** considers how totalitarian regimes recruited collaborators in the countries they occupied—employing methods from propaganda to intimidation. You'll see a replica of a "Red Corner"—a wood-paneled workers' meeting hall, draped in communist propaganda, that you'd find in any workplace or institution. A film on Soviet propaganda methods explains Stalin's philosophy of "national in form, Soviet in content"—appropriating locally beloved symbols but infusing them with a communist agenda.

Crossing the hall, giant letters spell out *TERROR.* Here, first bear left into section **08,** which explains how totalitarian regimes rounded up and executed elites (such as the USSR's

Katyń Massacre of Polish intelligentsia, close to the heart of every Pole). The room with a vast map on the floor illustrates forced resettlement; the doors lining the walls have exhibits explaining specific examples. You'll learn how heavily the occupying forces relied on forced labor—essentially exploiting 20 million slaves—including workers here in Gdańsk (the metal plates in revolving cases were used to keep track of workers). This section also has a powerful exhibit on daily life in Nazi concentration camps, with many powerful objects: striped uniforms and wooden clogs, a homemade nativity scene and tiny figures carved from a toothbrush by prisoners, a violin, and a baby's christening gown. You'll also see a wheelchair from a psychiatric hospital near Gdańsk. All of its inmates were executed.

As you circle back to the giant *TERROR* letters, section **09** explores the methodical implementation of the Holocaust, includ-

ing a train car used to transport prisoners. A wall of suitcases is a reminder of how prisoners were stripped of belongings on arrival. Nearby, a controversial exhibit touts the Poles who risked their lives to save their Jewish neighbors—with no mention of the Poles who looked the other way, or even collaborated with the Nazi occupiers. With this in mind, you'll walk through a room displaying photographs of hundreds of Jewish Holocaust victims. Section **10** considers other instances of ethnic cleansing during World War II, including Serbs killed in the Nazi puppet state of Croatia and Poles killed in Ukraine.

Section **11**—with the giant letters *OPÓR* ("Resistance")—explains the various ways that occupied peoples rose up. Poland maintained a government in exile, and a military that participated in Allied offensives (Poles were the first to reach the top of Monte Cassino in Italy)—essentially a continuation of prewar statehood, despite occupation. You'll learn about both civilian resistance movements and partisan fighting forces on the battlefields (such as Tito's Partisans in Yugoslavia). This section also honors various uprisings against totalitarian regimes.

Section **12** features the clandestine front—spies, espionage, and the battle over secrets. In a room with an actual Enigma machine, you'll learn how it was Polish mathematicians who first broke the Nazis' secret code...then furnished that breakthrough to the British. Today, Alan Turing and the other codebreakers at Britain's Bletchley Park get virtually all of the credit for the tens of thousands of lives that were saved. (Many Poles believe that the breaking of the Enigma code was Poland's single most important contribution to winning the war.)

Section **13** considers the ways that countries mobilize—economically and societally—in times of war. Wartime brought about such innovations as the jet engine, the computer, and the nuclear bomb. While the Nazis relied on slave labor to build armaments, the Allies mobilized female citizens...and outproduced their enemies three-to-one. In this section, you'll see a Sherman Firefly tank (built in the UK).

The very brief section **14** explains how the tide of war turned toward the Allies, while section **15** considers the postwar reality—which was cooked up even before Hitler was dead, when Churchill, FDR, and Stalin met in Yalta, agreeing to divvy up Europe after their victory. (Many Poles still consider this a betrayal: After their suffering and valiant contributions, they were effectively left to the whim of the USSR.) The postwar period was bittersweet: victory parades celebrating the defeat of evil, but also a Poland left in ruins, the rise of a ruthless Soviet empire in Eastern Europe, and a series of forced population resettlements (to match the new borders) that uprooted millions. The bright-white room commemorates the first-ever use of nuclear weapons: the bombing of Hiroshima (see the shards of pottery, symbolizing the devastation).

Section **16** shows the same city street we saw earlier—but now in ruins, presided over by a Soviet tank. Giant panels (added later) emphasize how Poland lost more lives per capita than any other nation in this conflict. Next, a map in the floor illustrates postwar forced population shifts, and a mockup of a courtroom considers both the triumphs and the failings of the postwar justice system: Yes, high-profile war criminals were prosecuted.  But the overflowing file cabinet on the dark side of the room is a reminder of the many lower-level war criminals who were never brought to justice.

Cross the destroyed street to section **17,** with photos of cities that were left in ruins at war's end; and section **18,** divided by a symbolic "Iron Curtain"—a reminder that World War II was only the beginning of a painful chapter for Poland and all of Central and Eastern Europe.

Just before you exit, playing overhead is a cheaply produced, rabble-rousing, hyperbolic, nakedly patriotic **movie** called *The Unconquered*...a sad reminder of the way a wonderful museum was mucked up by politics. (Before the right-wing government fired the museum director, this film was very different—ending the exhibit on a pensive note, with as many questions as answers. Now, it sends Polish visitors out into the world entirely assured of their own righteousness.)

Despite its shortcomings, the Museum of the Second World War is a powerful and comprehensive look at the most devastating conflict in human history, from the perspective of the country that was perhaps the most devastated by it.

Nearby: A short walk over a canal (across the Więcierze Bridge) from the museum is the **Polish Post Office of Danzig** (on Plac Obrońców Poczty Polskiej). History buffs recognize this landmark as part of the initial Nazi attacks on September 1, 1939, which began World War II. The post office—which was a nerve center for local Polish intelligence officers—was attacked by Nazi forces and defended by Polish officers. After 15 hours of fighting, everyone inside was dead or had fled; those who escaped were later executed. This event was immortalized in the 1959 Günter Grass historical novel *The Tin Drum*. The stately brick building is now a museum, and in the plaza out front is the giant and dramatic **Monument to the Defenders of the Polish Post Office** (from 1979): An angel hands a rifle down to a fallen fighter to continue the struggle; overhead, stylized birds flutter their wings dramatically into the sky.

SOUTH OF THE MAIN TOWN

A 10-minute walk south of the Main Town, this sight rounds out the Gdańsk experience for those with a special interest in art.

National Museum in Gdańsk
(Muzeum Narodowe w Gdańsku)

This art collection, housed in what was a 15th-century Franciscan monastery, is worth ▲▲ to art lovers for one reason: Hans Memling's glorious *Last Judgment* triptych altarpiece, one of the two most important pieces of art to be seen in Poland (the other is Leonardo da Vinci's *Lady with an Ermine,* in Kraków's Czartoryski Museum). If you're not a purist, you can settle for seeing the much smaller replica in St. Mary's Church. But if medieval art is your bag, it's worth a visit.

Cost and Hours: 15 zł, free on Fri; open Tue-Sun 11:00-18:00, closed Mon, last entry 45 minutes before closing; walk 10 minutes due south from Ulica Długa's Golden Gate, after passing the Shakespeare Theater take the pedestrian underpass beneath the big cross street, then continue down the busy street until you see signs for the museum; Ulica Toruńska 1, +48 58 301 6804, www.mng.gda.pl.

Visiting the Museum: Find the **altarpiece by Hans Memling** (c. 1440-1494)—from where you enter, it's usually at the top of the stairs and to the right. The history of the painting is as interesting as the work itself. It was commissioned in the mid-15th century by the Medicis' banker in Florence, Angelo di Jacopo Tani. The ship delivering the painting from Belgium to Florence was hijacked by a Gdańsk pirate, who brought the altarpiece to his hometown to be displayed in St. Mary's Church. For centuries, kings, emperors, and czars admired it from afar, until Napoleon seized it in the early 19th century and took it to Paris to hang in the Louvre. Gdańsk finally got the painting back, only to have it exiled again—this time into St. Petersburg's Hermitage Museum—after World War II. On its return to Gdańsk in 1956, this museum claimed it—though St. Mary's wants it back.

Have a close look at Memling's well-traveled work. It's the end of the world, and Christ rides in on a rainbow to judge humankind. Angels blow reveille, waking the dead, who rise from their graves. The winged archangel Michael—dressed for battle and wielding the cross like a weapon—weighs the grace in each person, sending them either to the fires of hell (right panel) or up the sparkling-crystal stairway to heaven (left).

It takes all 70 square feet of paneling to contain this awesome scene. Jam-packed with dozens of bodies and a Bible's worth of symbolism, and executed with astonishing detail, the painting can keep even a non-art lover occupied. Notice the serene, happy expressions of the righteous, as they're greeted by St. Peter (with his giant key) and clothed by angels. And pity the condemned, their faces filled with terror and sorrow as they're tortured by grotesque devils more horrifying than anything Hollywood could devise.

Tune in to the exquisite details: the angels' robes, the devils' genetic-mutant features, the portrait of the man in the scale (a Medici banker), Michael's peacock wings. Get as close as you can to the globe at Christ's feet and Michael's shining breastplate: You can just make out the whole scene in mirror reflection. Then back up and take it all in—three panels connected by a necklace of bodies that curves downward through hell, crosses the earth, then rises up to the towers of the New Jerusalem. On the back side of the triptych are reverent portraits of the painting's patron, Angelo Tani, and his new bride, Catarina.

Beyond the Memling, the remainder of the collection isn't too thrilling. The rest of the upstairs has more Flemish and Dutch art, as well as paintings from Gdańsk's golden age and various works by Polish artists. The ground floor features a cavernous, all-white cloister filled with Gothic altarpiece sculptures, gold and silver wares, and Gdańsk-style furniture.

OUTER GDAŃSK

These two sights—worthwhile only to those with a particular interest—are each within the city limits of Gdańsk, but they take some serious time to see round-trip.

Oliwa Cathedral (Katedra Oliwska)

The suburb of Oliwa, at the northern edge of Gdańsk, is home to this visually striking church. The quirky, elongated facade hides a surprisingly long and skinny nave. The ornately decorated 18th-century organ over the main entrance features angels and stars that move around when the organ is played. While locals are proud of this place, it takes some effort to reach—worthwhile only if you can make it to a concert.

Concerts: The animated organ performs its 20-minute show frequently, especially in summer (in high season, concerts at the top of most hours—confirm schedule online or at Gdańsk TI before making the trip, www.archikatedraoliwa.pl). Note that on Sundays and holidays, there are no concerts before 15:00.

Getting There: Oliwa is about six miles northwest of central Gdańsk, on the way to Sopot and Gdynia. To reach Oliwa from Gdańsk's main train station, you have two options: Ride **tram #6** or **#12**, get off at the Oliwa stop, and walk a few minutes through the park to the church (about 30 minutes total); or take an **SKM commuter train** to the Gdańsk Oliwa stop (15 minutes), then walk 15 minutes (or take a taxi) to Oliwski Park and the cathedral.

Westerplatte

World War II began on September 1, 1939, when Adolf Hitler sent the warship *Schleswig-Holstein* to attack this Polish munitions depot, which was guarding Gdańsk's harbor. Though it gives serious WWII history buffs goosebumps, casual visitors will find little to see here aside from a modest museum, a towering monument, and some old bunkers. For many, the reason to "go to Westerplatte" isn't for the destination, but for the chance to get there on a little cruise down the river...perhaps on a "pirate ship."

Getting There: The most enjoyable option is to ride a replica **17th-century galleon,** either the *Galeon Lew* ("Lion Galleon") or the *Czarna Perła* ("Black Pearl"). These over-the-top-touristy boats depart hourly from the embankment in the heart of Gdańsk (you can't miss them) for a lazy 1.5-hour round-trip cruise to Westerplatte and back. Alternatively, you can choose to get off at Westerplatte and return on a later boat. You'll see more industry than scenery, but it's a fun excuse to set sail (80 zł round-trip, 60 zł one-way, the two boats take turns departing at the top of each hour in season, +48 601 629 191, https://perlalew.pl). Two duller alternatives leave from nearby: big, modern **Żegluga Gdańska** boats (www.zegluga.pl); or cheaper but less frequent city-run **ZTM**

"**ferry trams**" *(tramwaj wodny)*, which depart from the embankment on the south side of the bridge (3-4/day). Another option is to take **bus** #106 or #138 from the main train station (about 30 minutes to Westerplatte).

Shopping in Gdańsk

The big story in Gdańsk is **amber** *(bursztyn)*, a fossil resin available in all shades, shapes, and sizes (see the "All About Amber" sidebar, earlier). The best place to browse and buy amber is along the atmospheric Ulica Mariacka (between the Motława River and St. Mary's Church). This pretty street, with old-fashioned balconies and dozens of display cases, is fun to wander even if you're not a shopper.

To avoid rip-offs—such as amber that's been melted and reshaped—always buy it from a shop, not from someone standing on the street. (But note that most shops also have a display case and salesperson out front, which are perfectly legit.) Prices everywhere are about the same, so instead of seeking out a specific place, just window shop until you see what you want. Styles range from gaudy necklaces with huge globs of amber, to tasteful smaller pendants in silver settings, to cheap trinkets. All shades of amber—from near-white to dark brown—cost about the same, but you'll pay more for inclusions (bugs or other objects stuck in the amber).

Gdańsk also has several modern shopping malls, most of them in the Old Town or near the main train station. The most impressive is the Forum, across the street from the Upland Gate; the Madison shopping center is between the Main Town and the Solidarity shipyard.

Entertainment in Gdańsk

Strolling the Embankments: This city feels made to order for simply strolling. Before or after dinner, you'll find yourself doing laps up and down both sides of the embankment and along the Royal Way. You'll pass plenty of tempting spots for a dessert or a drink (for ideas, see below).

Live Music: Check the schedule for the **Polish Baltic Philharmonic,** officially named for Fryderyk Chopin, which performs in the red-brick hall across the embankment from Fishmarket Square (near the drawbridge; www.filharmonia.gda.pl).

Drinks: As a lively town with lots of both tourists and students, Gdańsk has plenty of rowdy bars that fill up on weekends. But it also has some more refined watering holes that enjoy showing off special local liquors. Better restaurants are likely to have two hard drinks that are distinctly Gdańsk: **Goldwasser** is a sweet, faintly anisey liqueur flecked with actual gold (similar to Gold-schläger). **Machandel,** a juniper-based liquor, is served chilled in a shot glass with a dried plum on a toothpick. According to local superstition, for good luck, you're supposed to drink the shot, chase it with the dried plum, then break the toothpick.

While those are quite traditional, Gdańsk also has a new generation of producers creating all manner of distillates that go beyond the stereotypical "Polish vodka." **Podole Wielkie i Przy-jaciele** is an inviting, educational, and fun place to sample some locally made options. They specialize in *okowita*—a.k.a. aqua vita, "water of life"—usually based on wheat, barley, rye, or potato and infused with various flavors. They grow everything on their own farm, about 50 miles outside the city. They've also got a unique line of liquor distilled from various beers. The *i przyjaciele* in their name means "and friends," and they also carry some different drinks made by other local producers—ranging from gin and whiskey to more traditional vodka. You can stop in to do a tasting (priced per shot)—they enjoy guiding visitors through their options. The well-stocked shop has bottles generally in the 160-300-zł range (Mon-Sat until 21:00, Sun until 20:00, Chlebnicka 37/38, +48 730 850 066, www.podolewielkie.pl).

Sleeping in Gdańsk

The high season is generally May through September; at all of these places, you'll pay a bit less off-season. Many hotels are booked up (mostly with German and Scandinavian tourists) in peak season—reserve ahead.

IN THE MAIN TOWN

The Main Town is convenient for sightseeing, but some places come with nighttime noise—particularly in summer, when loud bars and discos keep things lively. Request a quiet room...and pack earplugs.

$$ Gotyk House is a small hotel that's comfortable while still respecting the sanctity of Gdańsk's oldest house (and suppos-edly the residence of Copernicus' longtime lover). You can't get more central in this city; the chimes from St. Mary's Church, next door, provide a pleasant soundtrack. The original, historic build-ing has five rooms (air-con only on top floor); a modern annex out back holds six additional rooms with air-conditioning and more refined touches. Neither building has an elevator, so be ready for stairs (Ulica Mariacka 1, +48 58 301 8567, www.gotykhouse.eu, reservation@gotykhouse.eu).

$ Hotel Admirał is simply practical: a big, solidly built, busi-ness-class place with 44 comfortable rooms tucked in a peaceful residential alley at the north end of the embankment, just a few

GDAŃSK & THE TRI-CITY

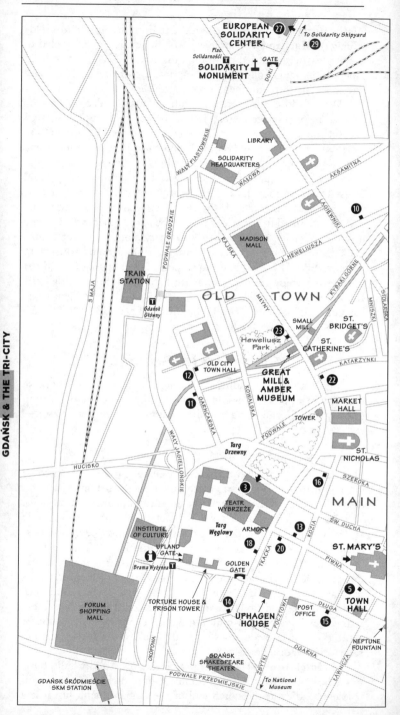

Gdańsk Hotels & Restaurants

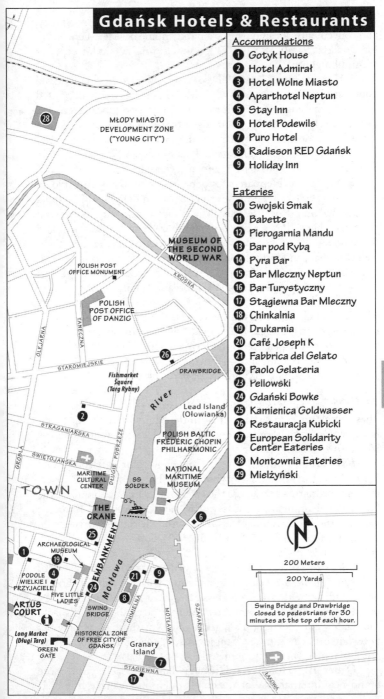

Accommodations

1. Gotyk House
2. Hotel Admirał
3. Hotel Wolne Miasto
4. Aparthotel Neptun
5. Stay Inn
6. Hotel Podewils
7. Puro Hotel
8. Radisson RED Gdańsk
9. Holiday Inn

Eateries

10. Swojski Smak
11. Babette
12. Pierogarnia Mandu
13. Bar pod Rybą
14. Pyra Bar
15. Bar Mleczny Neptun
16. Bar Turystyczny
17. Stągiewna Bar Mleczny
18. Chinkalnia
19. Drukarnia
20. Café Joseph K
21. Fabbrica del Gelato
22. Paolo Gelateria
23. Pellowski
24. Gdański Bowke
25. Kamienica Goldwasser
26. Restauracja Kubicki
27. European Solidarity Center Eateries
28. Montownia Eateries
29. Mielżyński

GDAŃSK & THE TRI-CITY

MŁODY MIASTO DEVELOPMENT ZONE ("YOUNG CITY")

MUSEUM OF THE SECOND WORLD WAR

POLISH POST OFFICE MONUMENT

POLISH POST OFFICE OF DANZIG

KROSNA

STAROMIEJSKIE

OLEJARNA

TANECZNA

DRAWBRIDGE

Fishmarket Square (Targ Rybny)

River

Lead Island (Ołowianka)

POLISH BALTIC FRÉDÉRIC CHOPIN PHILHARMONIC

STRAGANIARSKA

ŚWIETOJAŃSKA

GROBLA

DŁUGIE POBRZEŻE

MARITIME CULTURAL CENTER

SS SOŁDEK

NATIONAL MARITIME MUSEUM

TOWN

THE CRANE

ARCHAEOLOGICAL MUSEUM

EMBANKMENT

Motława

PODOLE WIELKIE I PRZYJACIELE

FIVE LITTLE LADIES

ARTUS COURT

SWING BRIDGE

Long Market (Długi Targ)

GREEN GATE

HISTORICAL ZONE OF FREE CITY OF GDAŃSK

Granary Island

STĄGIEWNA

CHMIELNA

MOTŁAWSKA

SZAFARNIA

ŁĄKOWA

200 Meters

200 Yards

Swing Bridge and Drawbridge closed to pedestrians for 30 minutes at the top of each hour.

steps off Fishmarket Square. Reliably comfortable, if not fancy, and conveniently located, this is a handy home base (air-con, elevator, Tobiasza 9, +48 58 320 0320, www.admiralhotel.pl, recepcja@ admiralhotel.pl).

$ Hotel Wolne Miasto ("Free City") offers lush, wood-carved public spaces with photos of old Gdańsk and 68 richly decorated rooms on the edge of the Main Town, just two blocks from the main drag. It's above a popular disco that gets noisy on weekends (Thu-Sat nights), so it's especially important to request a quieter room when you reserve (elevator, Ulica Świętego Ducha 2, +48 58 305 2255, www.hotelwm.pl, rezerwacja@hotelwm.pl).

$ Aparthotel Neptun lacks personality but owns a great location—on a slightly dreary side street between delightful Mariacka and the bustling Royal Way. While it's just a few steps to most of the town's big sights, it's just far enough away to avoid crowds and weekend noise. The 39 rooms and apartments are modern, efficient, well equipped, and forgettable...but well priced for the central location (air-con on top floor only, elevator, spa, Grzaska 1, +48 604 466 466, www.apartneptun.com, info@apartneptun.com).

$ Stay Inn couldn't be more central—facing the side of St. Mary's Church, right in the heart of the Main Town. Although the street it's on is quieter than most, a downstairs pub can be noisy on weekends. The place feels modern, and the 45 rooms are stylish and colorful (air-con, elevator, Piwna 28, +48 58 354 1543, www. stayinngdansk.com, booking@stayinngdansk.com).

ACROSS THE RIVER

These hotels are across the river from the Main Town, in the thriving new Granary Island area—still a short and easy walk to the Main Town sights.

$$$ Hotel Podewils is the top choice for a friendly, Old World splurge. Filling a storybook-cute house from 1728, overlooking the marina and across the river from a fine panorama of the Gdańsk embankment, it's classy. The public spaces and 10 rooms have all the modern amenities, but with plush, almost Baroque, decor (air-con, Szafarnia 2, +48 58 300 9560, www.podewils.pl, gdansk@podewils.pl).

$$ Puro Hotel, in the middle of Granary Island, is part of a Norwegian chain. It's big (eight floors), splashy, and fills brand-new buildings with towering glass atriums, a big restaurant, and a top-floor bar. The 211 rooms are modern, practical, and stylish; for the quality and location, it's a great value for those wanting a big hotel (air-con, elevator, spa, Stągiewna 26, +48 58 563 5000, www. purohotel.pl, gdansk@purohotel.pl).

Other Big Hotels on Granary Island: Each year, more brand-new international chain hotels open on Granary Island. If you're looking for big-hotel predictability (with air-con, elevators, etc.), consider two places filling sleek new buildings right along the embankment facing the Main Town: the smaller **$$ Radisson RED Gdańsk** (30 rooms, Chmielna 2, +48 58 600 2810, www.radissonhotels.com) and the gigantic **$ Holiday Inn** (240 rooms, Chmielna 1, +48 58 733 4000, www.ihg.com).

Eating in Gdańsk

With its heritage as a wealthy trading city, Gdańsk has its own distinct cuisine. While much of Poland—with its roots in poverty—dines on hearty, rustic countryside dishes, the Hanseatic merchants here preferred to flaunt their wealth with rich foods, lots of butter, and lively imported spices. For example, they favored deer (hunted—a pastime of the rich) over beef or pork (farm raised—a duty of the poor). This is perhaps best demonstrated by the local Goldwasser liqueur, with flecks of actual gold—see "Entertainment in Gdańsk," earlier. And, of course, you'll also find excellent Baltic seafood here on the north coast: Herring *(śledź)* is popular, as is cod *(dorsz)*.

IN THE MAIN TOWN AND OLD TOWN

My recommendations are scattered around the city center, all within about a 15-minute walk of each other and all near the main sightseeing zones. I've covered the scenic options along the embankment in a separate section.

$$ Swojski Smak ("Taste of Home"), tucked away from the touristy town center on a nondescript residential street partway to the Solidarity shipyards, is an intriguing combination of new and old. The menu is classic Polish fare, just like Babcia used to make: pierogi, hearty soups, potato pancakes, and a long list of nostalgic "dishes from childhood." But the setting is modern, industrial, and funky, with raw brick and a youthful, trendy vibe. They also pride themselves on their extensive selection of vodkas and good cakes (daily, Heweliusza 25/27, +48 58 320 1912, www.swojskismak.pl).

$ Babette is a delightful lunch or early dinner spot that feels both traditional and modern...trendy yet accessible. They serve a range of soups, stews, sides, and spreads, all with fresh-baked bread. Order at the counter, then find a table in the cozy contemporary café setting and dig in. It's an ideal spot for a hearty, quick, delicious meal (daily until 19:00, Garncarska 4/6, +48 535 717 766, www.pracowniababette.pl).

$ Pierogarnia Mandu, a few steps away from Babette, serves a wide variety of pierogi—all handmade (see them working through the window), with modern flourishes. Hiding in a nondescript residential zone between the train station and the main tourist area, it's worth seeking out for pierogi, plus a variety of other international dumplings. Book ahead to avoid waiting in line at the door. Don't come here in a hurry—it can take some time for your dumplings to be made to order (daily, Elżbietańska 4, +48 58 300 0000, www. pierogarnia-mandu.pl).

Potatoes!: Two places—each just a block off the main drag (in opposite directions)—offer tasty, hearty, affordable potato dishes. **$ Bar pod Rybą** ("Under the Fish") is nirvana for fans of baked potatoes *(pieczony ziemniak)*. They offer more than 20 varieties, piled high with a wide variety of toppings and sauces, from Mexican beef to herring to Polish cheeses. They also serve fish dishes with salad and potatoes, making this a cheap place to sample local seafood. The interior has big, comfy couches, and the outdoor seating fills a big stone balcony on atmospheric Piwna street (daily, Piwna 61, +48 58 305 1307, www.barpodryba.pl). **$ Pyra Bar** is another potato-based eatery; in addition to baked potatoes, they also have individual-sized casseroles (similar to a gratin) and potato pancakes—all available with a wide range of toppings. I'd skip the dull interior; eat here only if you can enjoy the lovely outdoor seating on a characteristic corner. Pick a table, then go inside to order at the bar (daily, Garbary 6/7, +48 58 301 9282, www.pyrabar.pl).

Milk Bars: Gdańsk has several classic, basic, fill-the-tank milk bars that are handy for grabbing a quick meal. **$ Bar Mleczny Neptun** owns a prime location, right on the main drag facing the Main Town Hall (daily until 19:00, Ulica Długa 33, +48 58 301 4988). **$ Bar Turystyczny** ("Tourist") is misnamed—it's beloved by locals and always jammed (daily until 18:00, on the way between the Main Town and the Solidarity sights at Szeroka 8, +48 58 301 6013). **$ Stągiewna Bar Mleczny,** in the middle of Granary Island across the river, is a classy, updated, modern milk bar with appealing outdoor seating (daily until 18:00, Stągiewna 15, +48 570 112 222). For more on milk bars, see page 26.

Georgian: **$$ Chinkalnia,** part of a Ukrainian chain that's now opening up locations around Poland, is an excellent place to sample Georgian food in a central setting, a half-block off the Royal Way. Choose between the cozy Georgian-village interior, or outdoor tables on a characteristic street. The photographic menu offers a user-friendly introduction to this delicious cuisine; for starters, the namesake *chinkali* are handheld dumplings (daily, Tkacka 6, +48 573 189 707). For a quick primer on Georgian food, see page 30.

Coffee: **$ Drukarnia** ("Printer") is the best spot in town for gourmet coffee in a modern, trendy setting that still melds well with the tradition all around it. The industrial-mod interior fills two floors, and the outdoor seating occupies a stone balcony at a prime location along Gdańsk's loveliest street, Mariacka. In addition to coffee and creative tea drinks, they have craft beers, breakfast, and other light bites—sandwiches and cakes (daily, Mariacka 36, +48 510 087 064).

Hipster Bar/Café: Café Joseph K, on charming Piwna street, is a popular hangout for coffee, craft beer, and creative cocktails. Similar to Drukarnia (but edgier and less coffee focused), they have a modern interior and stay-awhile outdoor tables. Locals marvel at how this place attracts revelers both young and old, with a mix of light communist-era kitsch and a trendy currency (long hours daily, Piwna 1, +48 572 161 510).

Ice Cream: The people of Gdańsk—and its many visitors—seem obsessed with ice cream *(lody)*. There are two good options offering better quality: **Fabbrica del Gelato,** tucked between giant hotels on a back street of Granary Island, is run by mother-and-son team Natalja and Boris, who trained with Italian experts and now enjoy creating their own delicious, often creative flavors (daily, Chmielna 3/4, +48 530 181 917). **Paolo Gelateria** is another good choice, also with some interesting flavors (the chocolate and mushroom is strangely delicious), on the way between the Main Town and the Solidarity sights (daily, across from the Great Mill/Amber Museum at Podwale Staromiejskie 96, +48 504 222 651).

Pączki **and Other Pastries: Pellowski,** with multiple locations, is a small chain that locals swear by for pastries, especially *pączki* (jelly doughnuts). There's a handy one at the Heweliusz Park next to the Amber Museum.

On the Riverfront Embankment

Perhaps the most appealing dining zone in Gdańsk stretches along the riverfront embankment near the Crane. On a balmy summer evening, the outdoor tables here are enticing. This area is popular—consider scouting a table during your sightseeing, and reserve your choice for dinner later that night. These places are slightly pricier than other options in town, but worth considering for the views and ambience—especially if

it's nice enough to sit outside. While these choices line up along the Main Town side of the river, you'll find plenty more options—generally trendier and more international—across the river.

$$ Gdański Bowke is rollicking and ye olde, with model ships hanging from the rafters and a lively energy. The menu of classic local dishes looks like a big, vintage newspaper. They brew their own beer, and often have live music out on the embankment (daily, Długie Pobrzeże 11, +48 58 380 1111).

$$$ Kamienica Goldwasser is a classy choice, offering more elevated Polish and international cuisine in a posh European setting. Choose between cozy, romantic indoor seating on several levels, or scenic outdoor seating (daily, occasional live music, Długie Pobrzeże 22, +48 58 301 8878).

$$ Restauracja Kubicki, along the water just past the Hilton, has a long history (since 1918), but a recent remodel has kept the atmosphere—and its food—feeling fresh. This is a good choice for high-quality Polish and international cuisine in a fun, sophisticated interior that's a clever mix of old and new (daily, Wartka 5, +48 58 301 0050).

NEAR THE SOLIDARITY SHIPYARD

This zone is still being developed, but some interesting dining options are opening up for those visiting the monuments and museum.

The **European Solidarity Center** itself has both a basic $ café and a nicer sit-down $$ restaurant.

A thriving new food hall, **Montownia,** may be open by the time you visit. This former industrial complex has been completely rejuvenated as a super-trendy commercial hub with more than 20 eateries (www.montowniafoodhall.pl; about a five-minute walk straight ahead, as you exit the European Solidarity Center).

And then there's a completely unexpected, hidden gem of a wine bar in the middle of industrial blight. If you leave the European Solidarity Center to the left, pass the Sala BHP, cross the wide street, and angle left through the parking lot to the run-down-looking, red-brick building, you'll discover **$$ Mielżyński**—a posh, upscale, inviting wine shop with an industrial-hip wine bar upstairs. They serve both Polish and international wines in a sophisticated setting, paired with thoughtfully crafted dishes. This is a classy oasis for in-the-know wine lovers willing to go looking for it (daily, Ulica Doki 1, +48 500 019 898, www.mielzynski.pl).

Gdańsk Connections

BY TRAIN

Gdańsk is well connected to the Tri-City via commuter SKM trains (explained later, under "Getting Around the Tri-City"). It's also connected to Warsaw and Kraków by the high-speed EIC line (which requires reservations). Given the distance between Gdańsk and other Polish destinations, also consider domestic flights: LOT has easy flights between Gdańsk and Kraków for not much more than a train ticket.

From Gdańsk by Train to: Malbork (2/hour, about half are express EIC trains that take 30 minutes, the rest are slower regional trains that take around 45 minutes), **Toruń** (4/day direct, 2.5 hours; more with a change in Bydgoszcz or Iława, 3 hours), **Warsaw** (hourly, 3 hours on express EIC train), **Kraków** (6/day direct, 5.5 hours, plus 9-hour night train), **Berlin** (1/day direct, 6 hours; 3/day, 7.5 hours, change in Poznań).

BY BOAT

Boats depart from Gdańsk's embankment to nearby destinations, including **Westerplatte** (the monument marking where World War II started—see page 289) and **Hel** (the beachy peninsula, described later; most boats take about 2 hours and are operated by Żegluga Gdańska, www.zegluga.pl). Some boats go only in the summertime (July-Aug), while others continue into the shoulder season; if connections from Gdańsk are limited, you may find more options from Gdynia. Boats generally don't run in winter (Nov-March). As schedules are changeable, confirm your plans carefully at the TI.

BY CRUISE SHIP

A few cruise ships (under 800 passengers) dock in **Gdańsk,** near the Westerplatte monument (described earlier; connected to the center by 45-minute pleasure-boat trip or 30-minute ride on bus #106 or #138 to the Brama Wyżynna stop at the start of my self-guided walk; some cruise lines also offer a direct shuttle into town).

Many cruises advertising a stop in "Gdańsk" actually dock in the nearby town of **Gdynia** (described later in this chapter).

The Tri-City (Trójmiasto)

Gdańsk is the anchor of the three-part metropolitan region known as the Tri-City (Trójmiasto). The other two parts are as different as night and day: Sopot, a swanky resort town, and Gdynia, a practical, nose-to-the-grindstone business center. The Tri-City as a whole is home to bustling industry and a sprawling university, with several campuses and plenty of well-dressed, English-speaking students. Beyond the Tri-City, the long, skinny Hel Peninsula—a sparsely populated strip of fishing villages and fun-loving beaches—arches dramatically into the Baltic Sea.

Sopot—boasting sandy beaches, tons of tourists, and a certain elegance—is the most appealing day-trip option. Gdynia is less romantic, but comes with an excellent Emigration Museum

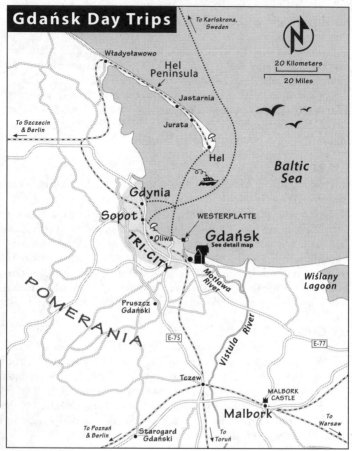

and offers a glimpse into workaday Poland. Hel, which requires the better part of a day to visit, is worthwhile only if you've got perfect summer weather and a desire to lie on the beach.

GETTING AROUND THE TRI-CITY

Gdańsk, Sopot, and Gdynia are connected by two different types of trains, both of which use Gdańsk's main train station: regional commuter trains (*kolejka*, operated by SKM) and trains operated by Poland's national railway (PKP). The SKM trains are cheaper, a bit slower, and more frequent than long-distance PKP trains. Trains to Hel are always operated by PKP.

Buying Tickets: Confusingly, SKM trains and PKP trains are covered by different tickets, which cost about the same (figure around 4-6 zł one-way between Gdańsk and Gdynia). Check posted schedules or look online to figure out which train works for you. For an SKM train, you can just hop on board, then pay the attendant in the first car (credit cards OK). For PKP trains, buy your ticket at a machine or ticket window before you board. Note that some special PKP trains require reservations, which cost extra.

Using the Right Stop: Each city has multiple stops. Remember, in Gdańsk, use either Gdańsk Główny (the main station for SKM and PKP) or Gdańsk Śródmieście (SKM only). For Sopot, use the stop called simply Sopot. For Gdynia, it's Gdynia Główna (the main station).

Boat Alternative: For a more romantic—and much slower— approach, consider a boat (see "Gdańsk Connections," earlier).

Sopot

Sopot (SOH-poht), dubbed the "Nice of the North," was a celebrated haunt of beautiful people during the 1920s and 1930s, and it remains a popular beach getaway to this day.

Sopot was created in the early 19th century by Napoleon's doctor, Jean Georges Haffner, who believed Baltic Sea water to be therapeutic. By the 1890s, it had become a fashionable seaside resort. This gambling center boasted enough high-roller casinos to garner comparisons to Monte Carlo.

The casinos are gone, but the health resorts remain, and you'll still see more well-dressed people here per capita than just about anywhere else in the country. While it's not quite Cannes, Sopot feels relatively high class. But even so, a childlike spirit of summer-vacation fun pervades this St-Tropez-on-the-Baltic, making it an all-around enjoyable place.

You can get the gist of Sopot in just a couple of hours. Zip in on the train, follow the main drag to the sea, wander the pier, get your feet wet at the beach, then head back to Gdańsk. Why not come here in the late afternoon, enjoy those last few rays of sunshine, stay for dinner, and then take a twilight stroll on the pier?

Orientation to Sopot

The main pedestrian drag, Monte Cassino Heroes street (Ulica Bohaterów Monte Cassino), leads to the Molo, the longest pleasure pier in Europe. From the Molo, a broad, sandy beach stretches in each direction. Running parallel to the surf is a tree-lined, people-filled path made for strolling.

Tourist Information: The TI is in front of the train station at Dworcowa 4 (daily 9:00-17:00, +48 501 590 773, www.sopot.pl). A second branch is near the base of the Molo at Plac Zdrojowy 2 (closed Sat-Sun).

Arrival in Sopot: From the SKM station, exit to the left and walk down the street. After a block, you'll see the PKP train station on your left. Continue on to the can't-miss-it main drag, Ulica Bohaterów Monte Cassino (marked by the big red-brick church steeple). Follow it to the right, down to the seaside.

Sights in Sopot

▲Monte Cassino Heroes Street
(Ulicà Bohaterów Monte Cassino)

Nicknamed "Monciak" (MOHN-chak) by locals, this in-love-with-life promenade may well be Poland's most manicured street (and is named in honor of the Polish soldiers who helped the Allies pry Italy's Monte Cassino monastery from Nazi forces during World War II). The street is lined with happy tourists, trendy cafés, al fresco restaurants, movie theaters, and late 19th-century facades (known for their wooden balconies). The most popular building along here (on the left, about halfway down) is the so-called **Crooked House** (Krzywy Domek), a trippy, Gaudí-inspired building that looks like it's melting. Hard-partying Poles prefer to call it the "Drunken House," and say that when it looks straight, it's time to stop drinking.

Molo (Pier)

At more than 1,600 feet long, this is Europe's longest wooden entertainment pier. While you won't find any amusement-park rides, you will be surrounded by vendors, artists, and Poles having the time of their lives. Buy a *gofry* (Belgian waffle topped with whipped cream and fruit) or an oversized cloud of *wata cukrowa* (cotton candy), grab your partner's hand, and stroll with gusto (small entry fee, open long hours daily, www.molo.sopot.pl).

Climb to the top of the Art Nouveau lighthouse for a waterfront panorama. Scan the horizon for sailboats and tankers. Any pirate ships? For a jarring reality check, look over to Gdańsk. Barely visible from the Molo are two of the most important sites in 20th-century history: the towering monument at Westerplatte, where World War II started; and the cranes rising up from the Gdańsk Shipyard, where Solidarity was born and European communism began its long goodbye.

In spring and fall, the Molo is a favorite venue for pole vaulting—or is that Pole vaulting?

The Beach

Yes, Poland has beaches. Nice ones. When I heard Sopot compared to places like Nice, I'll admit that I scoffed. But when I saw those stretches of inviting sand as far as the eye can see, I wished I'd packed my swim trunks. (You could walk from Gdańsk all the way to Gdynia on beaches like this.) The sand is finer than anything I've seen in Croatia...though the water's not exactly crystal-clear. Most of the beach is public, except for a small private stretch in front of the Grand Hotel Sopot. Year-round, it's crammed with locals. At these northern latitudes, the season for bathing is brief and crowded.

Overlooking the beach next to the Molo is the **Grand Hotel Sopot.** It was renovated to top-class status just recently, but its history goes way back. They could charge admission for a multiroom suite that has hosted the likes of Adolf Hitler, Marlene Dietrich, and Fidel Castro (but not all at the same time). With all the trappings of Sopot's belle époque—dark wood, plush upholstery, antique furniture—this room had me imagining Hitler sitting at the desk, looking out to sea, and plotting the course of World War II.

Gdynia

Compared to its flashier sister cities, straightforward Gdynia (guh-DIN-yah) is all business. Gdynia is less historic than Gdańsk or Sopot, as it was built almost entirely in the 1920s to be Poland's main harbor after "Danzig" became a free city. Called "The Gateway to Poland," the city's waterfront is built on large concrete piers (a communist-style fountain in the middle of the park marks the original coastline). Although nowhere near as attractive as Gdańsk or Sopot, Gdynia has an upscale, modern feel and a lovely waterfront promenade (www.gdynia.pl).

Gdynia is a major business center and—thanks to its youthful, progressive city government—has edged ahead of the rest of Poland economically. It enjoys one of the highest income levels in the country. The fine Modernist architecture of the downtown has been renovated, and Gdynia is becoming known for its top-tier shopping—all the big designers have boutiques here. If a Pole has been shopping on Świętojańska street in Gdynia, it means that he or she has some serious złoty.

Because Gdańsk's port is relatively shallow, the biggest cruise ships must put in at Gdynia...leaving confused tourists to poke around town looking for some medieval quaintness before coming to their senses and heading for Gdańsk. Gdynia is also home to a major military harbor and an important NATO base.

To get a taste of Gdynia, take the train to the Gdynia Główna station, follow signs to *wyjście do miasta*, cross the busy street, and walk 15 minutes down Starowiejska. When you come to the intersection with the broad Świętojańska street, turn right (in the direction the big statue is looking) and walk two blocks to the tree-lined park on the left. Head through the park to the Southern Pier (Molo Południowe). This concrete slab—not nearly as charming as Sopot's wooden-boardwalk version—features a modern shopping mall and a smattering of sights, including an aquarium and a pair of permanently moored museum boats.

The big sightseeing draw in Gdynia is at the fairly distant Nabrzeże Francuskie (French Quay, where cruise ships arrive—handy for cruisers but a taxi or Uber ride away for tourists coming on the train). Here you'll find the excellent Emigration Museum, telling the story of Poles who left through Gdynia to find a better life in the New World.

GDAŃSK & THE TRI-CITY

Sights in Gdynia

▲▲Emigration Museum (Muzeum Emigracji)

This museum, right next to Gdynia's cruise terminal, fills the former Marine Station building at the address Polska 1. This building opened in 1933, becoming the main port of departure for Polish American Lines passenger steamers to New York City and Quebec. For a time, vast numbers of Poles emigrated to the New World through right here. (Before that time, they mostly went through Hamburg or Bremen.) After World War II, the

Iron Curtain slammed shut, the line was severed, and the Marine Station remained bombed out for decades. Now it has been renovated and hosts a high-tech, engaging museum that tells the story of the 3.5 million Poles who left their homeland in search of a better life between the mid-19th century and World War II. Concise yet informative, engaging, and all in English, the exhibit is a delight for anyone, and worth ▲▲▲ for Polish Americans.

Cost and Hours: 18 zł, free on Wed; open Tue 12:00-20:00,

Wed-Sun 10:00-18:00, closed Mon; good 10-zł audioguide, www.polska1.pl.

Getting There: It's a 25-minute, dreary walk from Gdynia's main train station. The taxis waiting out front overcharge; you'll get a more reasonable price if you order an Uber or call for a taxi (try Hallo Express, +48 602 119 190). Or you can take a bus: #119 and #133 go from near the station to the Dworzec Morski/Muzeum Emigracji stop.

Visiting the Museum: Buy your ticket on the main floor, where you'll also find WCs, a café, and a museum shop. Then head upstairs, through the middle of the cavernous building, to find the exhibit entrance. Inside, the permanent exhibition tells the story of Polish emigration. You'll see photos of famous Poles who left (from Kościuszko to Chopin), and learn about the various waves of emigration throughout Polish history and what sparked each one: the Partitions in the late 18th century, failed uprisings in 1830 and 1864, and the potato famine (Poland suffered like Ireland did—the wall of potatoes symbolizes how important this staple was to peasant life). The Industrial Revolution sparked a different kind of (internal) emigration, as rural farming families moved into the cities for work.

The exhibit introduces the Sikora family and follows their emigration from Chmielnik to Chicago, by way of the port of Bremen. You'll learn how the "emigration industry" operated: Steamer lines conducted a medical examination of each passenger before they left Europe—because if they were rejected upon examination once they arrived in the New World, the company had to pay to ship them back. Exhibits include a mock-up of a train station, the deck of an Atlantic steamship, a cross-section of life below decks, and a peek into a tight sleeping quarters, crammed with bunks where the poorest passengers would spend 10 days on turbulent seas. Finally, you arrive in New York City. Imagine seeing a wall of skyscrapers after a long journey from a thatched village. The train car is a reminder that from New York, new arrivals spread out across North America. Chicago is famous for its huge Polish émigré population, but you'll learn that many Poles also went to Brazil ("Brazilian Fever").

You'll learn about the history of Gdynia (a purpose-built port, created entirely after World War I) and see a giant replica of the MS *Stefan Bathory*—a passenger steamer that was built here. (Sadly, when transatlantic travel

ended after World War II, ships like this one were scrapped.) In the World War II section, trees cut down to their stumps represent the forced displacement of populations during and after the war. You'll learn about the "Polish diaspora" around the world (Chicago, Rio, Britain, Australia). At the end of World War II, Polish officers who had fought alongside the Western Allies were warned not to return to Poland—where they'd be executed as potential rabble-rousers against the Soviet regime. So they stayed where they were, creating a new wave of "emigration." The exhibit ends with a kitschy look at Poland under communism (and Solidarity).

Exiting the exhibit, step out onto the long terrace that looks out over the cruise port. While it serves tourists today, this port evokes the millions of brave Poles who left behind everything they knew, set sail across a dangerous ocean, and had the courage to seek a new life in a New World.

ARRIVING BY CRUISE IN GDYNIA

Many Northern European cruises include a stop at "Gdańsk"; most of these actually put in at Gdynia's sprawling port. And, while Gydnia's town center is relatively manicured and pleasant, its port area is the opposite. Cruise ships are shuffled among hardworking industrial piers with few amenities. Port information: www.port. gdynia.pl.

Each of the port's many piers is named for a country or region. Most cruise ships use **French Quay** (Nabrzeże Francuskie), which is also home to Gdynia's best sight, the **Emigration Museum**. This deserves at least an hour of your time—or more, if you have Polish ancestry—and is a good place to spend any remaining time before "all aboard."

To get from your cruise ship to Gdańsk, the best option is a **shuttle bus-plus-train connection.** The shuttle drops you off at Skwer Kociuski, in downtown Gdynia (5-10-minute trip). From here, it's about a 15-minute walk to the train station (Dworzec Główna), then a 30-to-40-minute ride into Gdańsk (for details on various train options, see "Getting Around the Tri-City," earlier). If you're taking an SKM train that uses the Gdańsk Śródmieście stop, get off there for a quicker walk into the town center; otherwise, use the main Gdańsk Główny stop. Returning to Gdynia on the train, you want the Gdynia Główna stop.

Some cruise lines may offer a **direct shuttle bus** all the way to Gdańsk, which can be worth paying for, in the interest of efficiency.

Taxi drivers line up to meet arriving cruise ships. Cabbies here are usually unofficial (and therefore can set their own, inflated rates). It's worth ordering an Uber or calling for a taxi to get legitimate rates. Taxi drivers generally take euros, though their off-the-cuff exchange rate may not be favorable.

For more details on Gdynia's port—and several others on the Baltic, North Sea, and beyond—pick up the *Rick Steves Scandinavian and Northern European Cruise Ports* guidebook.

Hel Peninsula (Mierzeja Helska)

Out on the edge of things, this slender peninsula juts 20 miles into the ocean, providing a sunny retreat from the big cities—even as it shelters them from Baltic winds. Trees line the peninsula, and the northern edge is one long, sandy, ever-shifting beach.

On hot summer days, Hel is a great place to frolic in the sun with Poles. Sunbathing and windsurfing are practically religions here. Small resort villages line Hel Peninsula: Władysławowo (at the base), Chałupy, Kuźnica, Jastarnia, Jurata, and—at the tip—a town also called Hel. Beaches right near the towns can be crowded in peak season, but you're never more than a short walk away from your own stretch of sand. There are few permanent residents, and the waterfront is shared by budget campgrounds, hotels hosting middle-class families, and mansions of Poland's rich and famous (former president Aleksander Kwaśniewski has a summer home here).

The easiest way to go to Hel—aside from coveting thy neighbor's wife—is by boat (see "Gdańsk Connections," earlier). Most trains and buses to Hel depart from Gdynia, so you'll likely need to transfer there if coming from Gdańsk. On sunny summer days—when Hel is notorious for its hellish traffic jams—overland transit is crowded and slow. The bus that connects Władysławowo to the outlying towns and beaches of Hel is—no joke!—bus #666.

POMERANIA

Malbork Castle • Toruń

The northwestern part of Poland—known as Pomerania (Pomorze, as in "along the sea")—is red-brick fairy tale country. While the region has nothing to do with excitable little dogs, it does offer two of Poland's top attractions outside of the big cities: Malbork, the biggest Gothic castle in Europe, is one of the best castles in Central Europe. And farther south, the Gothic town of Toruń—the birthplace of Copernicus—holds hundreds of beautiful buildings...and, it seems, even more varieties of tasty gingerbread. The story of this region—which was part of the German world for much of its history—is tied inexorably to the Teutonic Knights, who ruled over this northern swath of present-day Poland and fortified their holdings with elegant red brick...still the hallmark of Pomerania.

Be prepared for a higher language barrier here; unlike Kraków and Warsaw, English is not the default. While they do get foreign visitors, most are Germans or Scandinavians—Americans make up a tiny percentage of the mix.

PLANNING YOUR TIME

Malbork works well as a side trip from Gdańsk (frequent trains, 30-45 minutes each way), and it's also on the main train line from Gdańsk to Warsaw. And Toruń is well worth a stroll or an overnight if you want to sample a smaller Polish city. Unfortunately, Toruń is on a different train line than Malbork—visiting both in one day makes for a very long day. Consider doing Malbork as a side trip from Gdańsk, then visit Toruń on the way to or from Warsaw. If opting for this plan, Toruń is also a delightful place to settle in for the night.

Malbork Castle

Malbork Castle is soaked in history. The biggest brick castle in the world, the largest castle of the Gothic period, and one of Europe's most imposing fortresses, it sprawls on a marshy plain at the edge of the town of Malbork, 35 miles southeast of Gdańsk. This was the headquarters of the Teutonic Knights, the Germanic band of ex-Crusaders who dominated northern Poland in the Middle Ages. It's worth ▲▲▲ for castle lovers, or ▲▲ for anyone.

Touring the massive castle, you'll see good exhibits on amber and armor, walk through vast halls with graceful Gothic arches and fan vaulting, learn a bit about the Teutonic Knights, and see enough red brick to last a lifetime. Visiting the whole place is a bit exhausting, but this chapter's self-guided tour helps you focus on the highlights.

GETTING THERE

Malbork is conveniently located right on the express train line between Gdańsk and Warsaw. Coming by train from Gdańsk, be ready for grand views of the castle on your right as you cross the Nogat River. Bag storage is available at the station's lockers (next to the exit doors).

Figure around 20 zł for a **taxi** or **Uber** to the castle. Or it's an easy, 15-minute, mostly downhill **walk:** Leave the station to the right, walk straight past the bus stops, and go through the pedestrian underpass beneath the busy road (by the red staircase). Ascending the stairs on the other side, turn right and follow the busy road (noticing peek-a-boo views on your right of the castle's main tower). Take the first right and head down Kościuszki, the main shopping street (partway down on the right, a fancy peach-colored building houses the TI). Near the bottom of Kościuszki, at the fountain and the McDonald's, jog right, then—at the roundabout—turn left to cross the moat. The castle ticket office will be on your right.

If you want to avoid the uphill walk back to the station, ask the info desk clerk in the castle ticket office to call a (fairly priced) taxi for you.

ORIENTATION TO MALBORK CASTLE

Cost: The main "historical route" costs 80 zł and includes an audioguide. On Mondays, and after hours on other days—when the interiors are closed—you can pay 40 zł for a "green route" that includes only the exteriors.

Hours: The main "historical route" is open Tue-Sun 9:00-19:00 (Oct-April until 15:00), last entry two hours before closing. If you come on Mon, or after the last entry time Tue-Sun (17:00-18:30 in season and 13:00-14:30 off-season), you can get into the exteriors-only "green route." The grounds stay open one hour later (until 20:00 in season, 16:00 off-season).

Information: +48 55 647 0978, www.zamek.malbork.pl.

Crowd-Beating Tips: The castle is busiest at midday, when there can be a line for tickets. If you anticipate crowds—or arrive to see a line—you can use your phone to buy a ticket on their website.

Tours: You're required to visit either with a guided tour or with an audioguide. Effectively, most visitors simply borrow an included audioguide—then either use it, or ignore it and follow my self-guided tour. You can ask about the availability of an English tour, but these are relatively rare.

Eating: At the castle courtyard, **$ Restauracja Piwniczka** has stick-to-your-ribs, beer-hall fare served in atmospheric cellars or at outdoor tables. Several cheap **$ food stands** cluster outside the castle (by the river). To escape the crowds, after your castle visit you can take the footbridge across the river, then turn right along the opposite riverbank and go through the long parking lot to reach **$ Bistro na Fali,** perched on a small hill looking back over the castle (daily, Wałowa 10, +48 534 610 670, www. bistronafali.pl).

Best Views: The views of massive Malbork are stunning—especially at sunset, when its red brick glows. Be sure to walk out across the footbridge over the Nogat River. The most scenic part of the castle is the twin-turreted, riverside Bridge Gate, which used to be connected by a bridge to the opposite bank.

BACKGROUND

When the Teutonic Knights were invited to Polish lands in the 13th century to convert neighboring pagans, they found the perfect site for their new capital here, on the bank of the Nogat River.

Construction began in 1274. After the Teutonic Knights conquered Gdańsk in 1308, the order moved its official headquarters from Venice to northern Poland, where they remained for nearly 150 years. They called their main castle Marienburg, the "Castle of Mary," in honor of the order's patron saint. Poles call it "Malbork."

At its peak in the early 1400s, Malbork was both the imposing home of a seemingly unstoppable army and Europe's final bastion of chivalric ideals. Surrounded by swamplands, with only one gate in need of defense, it was a tough nut to crack. Malbork Castle was never taken by force in the Middle Ages, though it had to withstand various sieges by the Poles during the Thirteen Years' War (1454-1466)—including a campaign that lasted more than three years. Finally, in 1457, the Polish king gained control of Malbork by buying off Czech mercenaries guarding the castle. Malbork became a Polish royal residence for 300 years. But when Poland was partitioned in the late 18th century, this region went back into German hands. The castle became a barracks, windows were sealed up, delicate vaulting was damaged, bricks were quarried for new buildings, and Malbork deteriorated.

In the late 19th century, Romantic German artists and poets rediscovered the place. An architect named Konrad Steinbrecht devoted 40 years of his life to Malbork, painstakingly resurrecting the palace's medieval splendor. A half-century later, the Nazis used the castle to house POWs. Hitler—who, like many Germans, had a soft spot for Malbork's history—gave the order to defend it to the last man. About half of the castle was destroyed by the Soviet army, who saw it as a symbol of long-standing German domination. But it was restored once again, and today Malbork has been returned to its Teutonic glory.

❷ SELF-GUIDED TOUR

The official "historical tour" of Malbork lasts about three hours; my tour of the highlights takes about half that long, unless you linger. Use the map in this section to navigate. The castle complex is a bit of a maze, with multiple entrances and exits for each room, often behind closed (but unlocked) doors. Don't be shy about grabbing a medieval doorknob and letting yourself in. If you're here on a Monday or after hours, on a "green route" ticket, you won't have access to many of the indoor areas described on this tour.

Entering the Castle Complex

From the ticket office, exit straight ahead and belly up to the brick wall by the bronze model for a panoramic view of the giant complex. Slowly pan across one of Europe's most intimidating fortresses—home to the Grand Master, monks, and knights of the Teutonic Order. The High Castle (where the monks lived) is on

POMERANIA

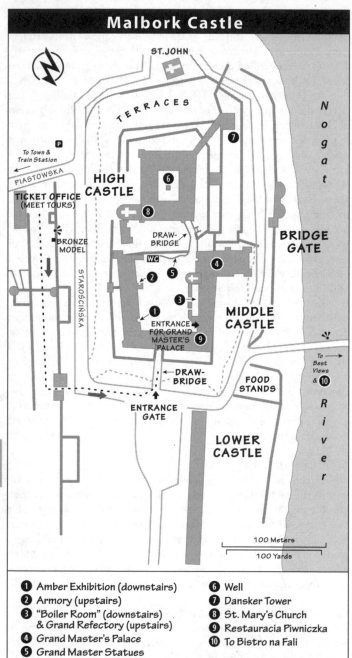

Malbork Castle

ST. JOHN

TERRACES

Nogat

To Town &
Train Station

PIASTOWSKA

HIGH
CASTLE

6 Well

TICKET OFFICE
(MEET TOURS)

BRONZE
MODEL

STAROŚCIŃSKA

BRIDGE
GATE

DRAW-
BRIDGE

WC

8 St. Mary's Church

2
5
4

1

3

MIDDLE
CASTLE

ENTRANCE
FOR GRAND
MASTER'S
PALACE

9

To
Best
Views
& **10**

DRAW-
BRIDGE

FOOD
STANDS

ENTRANCE
GATE

LOWER
CASTLE

River

100 Meters

100 Yards

POMERANIA

1 Amber Exhibition (downstairs)

2 Armory (upstairs)

3 "Boiler Room" (downstairs)
   & Grand Refectory (upstairs)

4 Grand Master's Palace

5 Grand Master Statues

6 Well

7 Dansker Tower

8 St. Mary's Church

9 Restauracia Piwniczka

10 To Bistro na Fali

the left, marked by the 30-foot-tall statue of Mary at the end of St. Mary's Church. To the right is the Middle Castle, where the knights lived. We'll loop around the right end (Middle Castle), working our way inside and ending at the High Castle.

The bronze **model** shows the realm of the Teutonic Knights at their peak—stretching from Gdańsk in the north to Toruń to the south, and, waaaay up on the northeast, the city of Kłajpeda, today part of Lithuania. For more than a century (1308-1410), the Teutonic Knights were a formidable presence. For more on this history, see the sidebar later in this chapter.

• *Now turn right and cross the drawbridge under the brick tower. Keep going alongside the moat, turning left to cross another drawbridge into the castle ward. Ahead and to the right, the long, low-lying building was the Lower Castle, where servants and support staff lived. Just before that, on the left, is yet another drawbridge. Show your ticket here and cross partway over the bridge—pausing just outside the brick gate.*

Entrance Gate

Above the door to the brick gate is a sculpture of the Virgin Mary with Baby Jesus, next to a shield and helmet. The message is two-fold: This castle is protected by Mary, and the Teutonic Knights are here to convert pagans—by force, if necessary.

From the drawbridge, look right to observe the formidable fortifications. The Teutonic Knights connected nearby lakes to create a system of canals, forming a moat around the castle that could be crossed only by drawbridge. The rooster-capped corner tower (which contains a toilet) is connected by a sky bridge to the fancy Gothic 14th-century facade of the brick infirmary—kept at a distance for disease control.

Continue farther, until you're inside the gate structure itself. Imagine the gate behind you slamming shut. Look up to see wooden chutes where archers are preparing to rain arrows down on you. Your last thought: Maybe we should have left the Teutonic Knights alone after all.

Before you're pierced by arrows, read the castle's history in its walls: The foundation is made of huge stones—rare in these marshy lands—brought from Sweden. But most of the castle, like so many other buildings in northern Poland, was built with handmade red brick. Throughout the castle, the darker-colored, rougher brick is original, and the lighter-colored, smoother brick was used during later restorations (in the 19th century, and again after World War II). Marvel at the ironclad doors and the heavy portcullis.

Venture through two more enclosed spaces, watching for the holes in the wall (for more guards and soldiers). Ponder the fact that you must pass through five separate, well-defended gates to reach the...

Middle Castle (Zamek Średni)

This part of Malbork, built at an uphill incline to make it even more imposing, was designed to impress. Knights and monks lived here.

Let's get oriented: To your left is the east wing, where visiting monks would sleep. Today, this houses the Amber Exhibition (ground floor) and the armory (upstairs). To the right (west) as you enter the main courtyard is the Grand Refectory (closer to the entrance) and the Grand Master's Palace (the taller, squarer building at the far end).

• *Enter the ground floor of the building on the left (go through the small door and take a few steps down). Here you'll tour the...*

Amber Exhibition

Amber, precious petrified tree sap, is found here in Poland; for a primer, read the "All About Amber" sidebar on page 267. You'll start 42 million years ago and follow the story of amber, then walk down the dimly lit corridor, checking out huge chunks of raw amber and illuminated displays of inclusions (bugs and other organic objects stuck in the amber, à la *Jurassic Park*). Some of the ancient amber artifacts displayed here are up to 3,000 years old, found in graves.

At the end of the corridor, U-turn and work your way back up a parallel hall, lined with all manner of exquisite amber creations: boxes, brooches, necklaces, chess sets, pipes, miniature ships, wine glasses, and belts for skinny-waisted, fashion-conscious women. Many of the finely decorated jewelry boxes and chests have ivory, silver, or shell inlays—better for contrast than gold. The portable religious shrines and altars allowed travelers to remain reverent on the road and still pack light. Notice the wide range of amber colors—from opaque white to transparent yellow to virtually black.

• *Exit at the far end. As you emerge into the Middle Castle courtyard, go up the wooden staircase on your right, go inside, turn left and walk to the end of the long hall, and go up the stairs. Here you'll find the...*

Armory

This enjoyable, well-displayed collection includes an impressive array of swords, armor, and other armaments. Look for the 600-year-old "hand-and-a-half" swords—too big to be held in one hand. Tucked behind the cannons is a giant shield. A row of these shields could be lined up to form a portable wall—called a phalanx—to protect the knights. In the big room with the decoratively

POMERANIA

hilted swords, look for the terrifying "flame-bladed sword." You'll also see pikes, maces, crossbows, rifles, and horse armor. And in the room with the body armor, the centerpiece is a suit of armor from the hussars—Polish horse-back knights. Equipped with wings, it created a terrifying sound when the horses were galloping.

• *At the end of the armory, head down the modern stairs and back outside (a handy WC is straight ahead). Cross the main courtyard, angling downhill, and enter the smaller courtyard through the passage next to the stubby, dark-wood-topped tower. Find the (unlabeled and sometimes closed) door to a dark, steep flight of stairs that leads down into the...*

"Boiler Room"

The Teutonic Knights had a surprisingly sophisticated method for heating this huge complex. You see a furnace down below and a holding area for hot rocks above. The radiant heat given off by the rocks spread through the vents without also filling them with smoke (illustrated by a chart on the wall). This is one of 11 such "boiler rooms" in the castle complex. As you tour the rest of the castle, keep an eye out for saucer-sized heating vents in the floor.

• *Climb back up the stairs, take an immediate left through a tiny arch, and then go left again, up through the second door (not down through the first door, which takes you out of the castle). This leads into the...*

Grand Master's Palace

This was one of the grandest royal residences in medieval Europe, used in later times by Polish kings and German kaisers. (Today, it's sometimes used for special exhibitions.)

• *From the kitchen—with its huge chimney (wow!)—turn left into the big and bright...*

Grand Refectory: With remarkable palm vaulting and grand frescoes, this dining hall hosted feasts for up to 400 people to celebrate a military victory or to impress visiting dignitaries. In the floor, notice the 36 heating vents—which are directly above the boiler room you just visited—designed to keep the VIPs warm.

• *At the far end of the refectory, climb the stairs into the...*

Private Rooms of the Grand Master:

POMERANIA

Though the Teutonic Order dictated that the monks sleep in dormitories, the Grand Master made an exception for himself—with this suite of private rooms. This area is a bit of a maze, so stick with me (or just wander around looking for each of these rooms): From the hall where you enter, bear left into another hall, with show-off decor—including some 15th-century original frescoes of wine leaves and grapes.

Go through the door to the left of the fireplace into the Grand Master's **bedroom,** decorated with (now very faint) frescoes of four virgins—female martyrs. Beyond that is the green-walled **study** of the Grand Master.

Continue through the study and you'll step into the Top Knight's dining room, the **Winter Refectory,** with fewer windows (better insulation) and more of the little heating vents in the floor. The walls are draped with tapestries, which also helped warm things up a bit.

For a dramatic contrast, continue into the next room—the **Summer Refectory.** With big stained-glass windows and deli-

cate vaulting supported by a single central pillar, this room was clearly not designed with defense in mind. In fact, medieval Polish armies focused their attacks on this room. On one legendary occasion, the attackers—tipped off by a spy—knew that an important meeting was going on here and fired a cannonball into the room. It just missed the pillar. (You can see where the cannonball hit the wall, just above the fireplace.) The ceiling eventually did collapse during World War II.

Continue through the Summer Refectory, stepping out into a hallway. Turn right, noticing the washbasin and trough along the corridor. Anyone wanting an audience with the Grand Master had to wash both his hands and his feet. Farther along, find the stairs down (on your left).

• Take those stairs back out in the courtyard. On your right are four...

Grand Master Statues

Though this was a religious order, these powerful guys look more like kings than monks. From left to right, shake hands with Hermann von Salza (who was Grand Master when the Teutonic Knights came to Poland), Siegfried von Feuchtwangen (who actually moved the T. K. capital from Venice to Malbork, and who conquered Gdańsk for the knights—oops, can't shake his hand, which was supposedly chopped off by Soviet troops), Winrich von

The Teutonic Knights

The Order of the Teutonic Knights began in the Holy Land in 1191, during the Third Crusade. These militarized German monks built hospitals and cared for injured knights. When the Crusades ended in the 12th century, the knights returned to Europe and reorganized as a chivalric order of Christian mercenaries—pagan-killers for hire.

In 1226, a northern Polish duke called in the Teutonic Knights to subdue a tribe of pagans who had been attacking his lands. Clad in their white cloaks with skinny black crosses,

the Teutonic Knights spent 60 years "saving" the pagans by turning them into serfs or massacring them.

Job done, the Teutonic Knights decided to stick around. With the support of the pope and the Holy Roman Emperor (who were swayed by the knights' religious zeal), the knights built one of Europe's biggest and most imposing fortresses: Malbork. In 1308, they seized large parts of northern Poland (including Gdańsk), cutting off Polish access to the Baltic Sea. The knights grew rich from Hanseatic trade, specializing in amber, grain, and timber. By the late 14th century, the Teutonic Knights had grown to become Europe's largest-ever monastic state and were threatening to overtake Lithuania.

Inspired by a mutual desire to oust the Teutonic Knights, the Poles and the Lithuanians teamed up. In 1386, Polish princess Jadwiga married Lithuanian prince Władysław Jagiełło, kick-starting a grand new dynasty: the Jagiellonians.

Every Pole knows the date July 15, 1410: the Battle of Grunwald. King Władysław Jagiełło and Lithuanian grand duke Vytautas the Great led a ragtag army of some 40,000 soldiers—Lithuanians, Poles, other Slavs, and even speedy Tatar horsemen—against 27,000 Teutonic Knights. At the end of the day, some 18,000 Poles and Lithuanians were dead—but so were half of the Teutonic Knights, and the other half had been captured. Poland and Lithuania were victorious.

The Battle of Grunwald marked the beginning of the end for the Teutonic Knights, who were conclusively defeated during the Thirteen Years' War (1454-1466). The order officially dissolved in 1575, when they converted to Protestantism and much of their land was folded into Prussia. Later, 19th-century Polish Romantics reimagined the Teutonic Knights as an early symbol of Germanic oppression—poignant among Poles, who suffered through a new round of German abuse in World War II. Some conspiracy theorists believe the Teutonic Knights are still very much active...but that's another story.

POMERANIA

Kniprode (who oversaw Malbork's golden age and turned it into a castle fit for a king), and Markgraf Albrecht von Hohenzollern (the last Grand Master before the order dissolved and converted to Protestantism).

• *We're heading into the final section of the castle. Before we do, it's a good time for a break—WCs and eateries are in this courtyard. When you're ready, continue into the High Castle. To the right of the Grand Masters, cross over the...*

Drawbridge

As you cross, notice the extensive system of fortifications and moats protecting the innermost part of the castle just ahead. Once inside the gate, on your left is a door leading to a green zone that runs around the High Castle. Here you'll see a collection of stone catapult balls that were actually fired at this castle when it was under siege. (Look high above to see the dents such stones can make.) This is a fun area to explore on your way back out of the castle...if you're not castled out by that point.

Continue straight ahead from the drawbridge, into a passage that's lined with holes to the sides (for surveillance) and with chutes up above (to pour scalding water or pitch on unwanted visitors). It's not quite straight—so a cannon fired here would hit the side wall of the passage, rather than enter the High Castle and its central courtyard...which is what you're about to do now.

High Castle (Zamek Wysoki)

This is the heart of the castle and its oldest section. From this spot, the Teutonic Knights governed their vast realm—the largest monk-ruled territory in European history. As much a monastery as a fortress, the High Castle was off-limits to all but 60 monks of the Teutonic Order and their servants. (The knights stayed in the Middle Castle.) Here you'll find the monks' dormitories, chapels, church, and refectory. As this was the nerve center of the Teutonic Knights, it was also their last line of defense. They stored enormous amounts of food here in case of a siege.

In the middle of the High Castle courtyard is a **well**—an essential part of any inner castle, especially one as prone to sieges as Malbork. At the top is a sculpture of a pelican. Because this noble bird was believed to kill itself to feed its young (notice that it's piercing its own chest with its beak), it was often used in the Middle Ages as a symbol for the self-sacrifice of Jesus.

• *Take some time to explore the...*

POMERANIA

Ground Floor

Immediately to your left is a door leading to the **prison,** with small "solitary confinement" cells near the entrance. Diagonally across the courtyard, hiding in the far corner, is an exhibit on **stained-glass windows** from the castle church.

Back near where you entered the courtyard, step into the **kitchen.** This exhibit—with a long table piled with typical ingredients from that time—gives you a feel for medieval monastery life. The monks who lived here ate three meals a day and drank lots of beer (made here) and wine (imported from France, Italy, and Hungary). A cellar under the kitchen was used as a simple refrigerator—big chunks of ice were cut from the frozen river in winter, stored in the basement, and used to keep food cool in summer. Behind the long table, see the big dumbwaiter (with shelves for hot dishes), which connects this kitchen with the refectory upstairs. Step into the giant stove and peer up into the biggest chimney in the castle.

• *Now go back out into the courtyard and climb up the stairs near where you first entered.*

Middle Floor

• *From the top of the stairs, the first door on the left (with the colorfully painted arch) leads to the most important room of the High Castle, the...*

Chapter Room: Monks gathered here after Mass, and it was also the site for meetings of Teutonic Knights from throughout the realm. If a Grand Master was killed in battle, the new one would be elected here. Carvings above each chair indicated the status of the man who sat there. The big chair belonged to the Grand Master. Notice the little windows high on the wall above his chair, connecting this room to the church next door. Ecclesiastical music would filter in through these windows; imagine the voices of 60 monks bouncing around with these acoustics.

While monks are usually thought to pursue simple lives, the elegant vaulting in this room is anything but plain. The 14th-century frescoes (restored in the 19th century) depict Grand Masters. In the floor are more vents for the central heating.

• *Leave the Chapter Room and walk straight ahead, imagining the monk-filled corridors of Teutonic times. The first door on the right is the...*

Treasury: As you explore the five rooms of the tax collector and the house administrator, notice the wide variety of safes and other lock boxes. Documents, amber, and coins were kept behind heavily armored and well-locked doors.

• *Continue around the cloister. At the end of the corridor, spot the little devil (see photo next page) at the bottom of the vaulting (on the right, just above your head). He's pulling his beard and crossing his legs—pointing you down the long corridor leading about 100 yards away from the cloister to the...*

Dansker Tower: From the devil's grimace, you might have guessed that this tower houses the latrine. Four wooden toilet stalls filled this big room. Where one is missing, you can look down to see how the "toilets" simply dropped the waste into the moat. For obvious sanitary (and olfactory) reasons, this potty tower is set apart from the main part of the castle. The bins above the toilets were filled with cabbage leaves, to be used by the T. K. as TP (and as an organic form of Preparation H). This tower could also serve as a final measure of defense—it's easier to defend than the entire castle. Food was stored above, just in case. More info on this grand castle WC is on the wall.

• *Return down the long corridor. Before the end, on the right-hand side of the long passage, a door leads into the...*

Church Exhibition: Once dormitories for the monks, these three rooms now display a wide range of relics from the church. In the last room, on the far wall, is the artistic highlight of the castle: a finely carved and gilded three-panel altarpiece from 1504 featuring the coronation of Mary. Mary's face is mesmerizing. Characteristic of the late Gothic period, the robes seem to fly unrealistically (as if they were bent metal).

• *Back out in the main cloister, turn right and continue to the end, arriving at the...*

POMERANIA

Golden Gate: This elaborate doorway—covered in protective glass—marks the entrance to St. Mary's Church. Before entering, examine this rare original **door.**

Ringed with detailed carvings from the New Testament and symbolic messages about how monks of the Teutonic Order should live their lives, it's a marvelous example of late 13th-century art. At the bottom-left end of the arch, find the five wise virgins who, having filled their lamps with oil and conserved it wisely, are headed to heaven. On the right, the five foolish virgins who overslept and used up all their oil are damned, much to their dismay.

Step inside **St. Mary's Church** to appreciate a glorious Gothic interior—recently reopened after a lengthy restoration. Straight

ahead from where you entered, look for the 14th-century cross, which was partly burned when the castle was destroyed. Throughout the space, notice how the restorers intentionally used different materials to distinguish repairs from different eras: the brighter plaster dates from the recent work, while the darker plaster (closer to the area where you entered) is from the 19th century.

• *Back outside, go through the narrow door next to the Golden Gate and hike up the tight spiral staircase to the final set of exhibits.*

Top Floor

Walk through a space with temporary exhibits. At the end, descend into the **monks' common room** (left, at the bottom of the stairs). Over the fireplace is a relief depicting the Teutonic Knights fighting the pagans. To the left and above (see the stone windows) is a balcony where musicians entertained the monks after a meal.

The next, very long room, with seven pillars, is the **refectory,** where the monks ate in silence. Along the right-hand wall are

lockable storage boxes for tableware. At the end of this room, just beyond another ornate fireplace, notice the grated hole in the wall. This is where the dumbwaiter comes up from the kitchen (which we saw below). Beyond this room is an exhibit about the architectural renovation of the castle.

• *Your Malbork tour ends here. You leave the way you came. En route, you can walk around terraces lining the inner moat, between the castle walls (stairs lead down off the drawbridge, by the catapult balls). It's hardly a must-see, but it's pleasant enough, with the Grand Master's garden, a cemetery for monks, and the remains of the small St. Anne's Chapel (with Grand Master tombs).*

MALBORK CONNECTIONS

From Malbork by Train to: Gdańsk (2/hour, 30 minutes on express EIC train, 45 minutes on slower regional train), **Toruń** (about every 2 hours, 2.5 hours, change in Iława), **Warsaw** (hourly, 2.5 hours on express EIC train).

Toruń

Toruń (TOH-roon) is a living fairy tale that feels like Poland's best-kept secret...and one of Europe's, too. This pretty, lazy Goth-

ic town, conveniently located about halfway between Warsaw and Gdańsk, is well worth a few hours to stroll the lively streets, ogle the huge red-brick buildings, and savor the flavor of perhaps Poland's most livable city. You won't regret spending the night...but when it's time to leave, you may regret spending just one.

With about 210,000 residents and 30,000 students (at Copernicus University), Toruń is a thriving burg. Like Kraków (and unlike most other Polish cities), Toruń escaped destruction during World War II and remains well preserved today. Locals brag that their city is a "mini Kraków." But that sells both cities short. Toruń lacks Kraków's over-the-top romanticism, and its sights are quickly exhausted. On the other hand, Toruń may well be Poland's most user-friendly city: tidy streets with a sensible grid plan, wide pedestrian boulevards crammed with locals who greet each other like they're long-lost friends, and an easygoing ambience that seems to say, "Hey—relax." It's jammed with Polish school groups and families, and some in-the-know Germans...but few Americans.

Toruń clings fiercely to its two claims to fame: It's the proud birthplace of the astronomer Copernicus (Mikołaj Kopernik), and home to a dizzying variety of gingerbread treats (*piernika;* pyer-NEE-kah).

Orientation to Toruń

Everything in Toruń worth seeing is in the walled Old Town, climbing up a gentle hill from the Vistula River. The broad, traffic-free main drag, Ulica Szeroka (called Różana at the entrance of town), bisects the Old Town, running parallel to the river. You can walk from one end of the town center to the other in about 15 minutes.

The helpful **TI** is right where the main square meets the main walking street, Ulica Szeroka (daily 10:00-17:00, closed Sun in winter, Ulica Szeroka 43, +48 56 621 0930, www.visittorun.com).

POMERANIA

ARRIVAL IN TORUŃ

Toruń's main train station (Toruń Główny) is across the river from the Old Town, about a mile away. The tidy main hall sits between tracks 1 and 2. Lockers are between the food hall and track 2.

To reach the Old Town, you can take a **taxi**—they wait out the door from the main hall (figure 20-25 zł or less to Plac Rapackiego, the start of my Toruń Walk, or most recommended hotels). To go by **bus,** first buy a single ticket from the Relay kiosk inside the station (about 4 zł), then use the escalators, stairs, or elevator to descend to the pedestrian underpass and exit toward *Ul. Kujawska* (past platform 4). You'll surface near an old steam locomotive; nearby is the stop for bus #27 to Plac Rapackiego, the first stop after the long bridge. (Buses #11 and #14 also make this trip.) To return to the station, catch the bus across the busy road from where you got off. Note: Public transit is free for anyone over age 65 (just show your passport if asked).

Alternate Train Station: Some (but not all) trains also stop at **Toruń Miasto** station, which is a bit closer to the Old Town (about a 15-minute walk along the river). Check schedules carefully to see if your train stops here; those overnighting in town may find it more convenient.

Toruń Walk

This lazy, low-impact self-guided walk takes you through the heart of Toruń—showing you pretty much everything you'd want to see on a brief visit. With no stops, you could do it all in about 45 minutes.

• *Coming from the train station, the bus stop is at...*

Plac Rapackiego

The park that rings Toruń—once the site of the medieval city wall—is an inviting people zone. From the bus stop, walk straight ahead through the park, toward town. You'll pass a borrow-a-bike station and a futuristic sculpture, labeled *Solimnia Regit,* honoring hometown boy Copernicus' heliocentric theory...more on him later. The big, historic, ornately gabled building on your left is the Collegium Maximum, the historic headquarters of Toruń's prestigious university.

Carry on straight ahead, going below the narrow house marked *1936* and the adjoining local Solidarity headquarters. Under the tower, you'll find some remaining tram tracks, commemorating the line that ran along the city's main drag from 1936 until 1970. You'll pop out on the town's main drag.

• *Continue one block straight along the main street to reach the bustling...*

Accommodations

1. Hotel 1231 & Restaurant
2. Hotel Czarna Róża
3. Solaris Hotel
4. Hotel Karczma Spichrz & Restaurant

Eateries

5. Chleb i Wino
6. Maneken
7. Georgian Bakery
8. Serce Gruzji
9. Pod Modrym Fartuchem

10. Luizjana (2)
11. Jan Olbracht
12. Pierogarnia Stary Młyn
13. Tradycyjne Prawdziwe Pierniki Gingerbread Shop

Sights

14. Old Town Hall District Museum
15. Museum of the History of Toruń
16. Museum of Toruń Gingerbread
17. Gingerbread Museum

Old Town Market Square (Rynek Staromiejski)

This square is surrounded by huge brick buildings and outdoor restaurants buzzing with lively locals (for tips, see "Eating in Toruń," later).

The **Old Town Hall** (Ratusz Staromiejski) fills the middle of the square. Like the Cloth Hall in Kraków, this building began life as a general market. Toruń is, at its heart, a trading city, and benefitted tremendously from its membership in the Hanseatic League—a trade union of Northern European maritime cities. Toruń's prime position on the Vistula River, navigable by oceangoing vessels, put it on the map and allowed it to prosper. The Old Town Hall contains a fine, if dated, museum, and you can pay to climb its tower for a town view. To escape the square's bustle, you can step into this building's serene brick courtyard, with the ticket office and museum entrance (for details, see "Sights in Toruń," later).

The ornate, dark-red building with the pointy spires facing the Old Town Hall is the **Artus Court,** marking the location where the medieval town council and merchants' guilds met. While the town was founded in 1231, the current building is Neo-Gothic, dating from 1891; inside its dramatic, vertical, covered courtyard, you'll find a New Orleans-themed restaurant (seriously...see "Eating in Toruń," later). In the pavement directly in front of this building, plaques celebrate famous people who were born here or have ties to this town...sort of a Toruń walk of fame.

Toruń seems to specialize in statues that spin fanciful tales. The first of these is at the nearest corner of the Old Town Hall. Look for the fountain with the guy playing a violin. This is a **rafter** *(retman)*—one of the medieval lumberjacks who lashed tree trunks together and floated them down the Vistula to Gdańsk. This particular rafter came to Toruń when the town was infested with frogs. He wooed them with his violin and marched them out of town. (Hmm...sounds like a certain pied piper...)

Standing by the fountain, look in the direction the rafter's bow is pointing. Two doors to the right of the giant Artus Court, at the very top of the skinny greenish building, spy the silhouette of a **cat.** According to local legend, while prowling the rooftops in the 17th century, this cat saw an invading Swedish army. So, he began howling loudly, waking the town just in time to prepare for the battle.

Now walk along the front of the Old Town Hall. At the far corner, the bigger statue depicts **Mikołaj Kopernik,** known internationally as Nicolaus Copernicus (1473-1543). This Toruń-born son of aristocrats turned the world on its ear when he suggested that the sun, not the earth, is the center of the universe (the "heliocentric theory"). Toruń is seriously proud of this local boy done good—he's the town mascot, as well as the namesake of the local university. Among its fields of study, Copernicus U. has a healthy astronomy program. There's a planetarium in the Old Town (just past the far corner of the square) and a giant radio telescope on the outskirts. Despite all the local fuss over Copernicus, there's some dispute about his "nationality": He was born in Toruń, but at a time when it was the predominantly German town of "Thorn." So, is he Polish...or German? (For more on Copernicus, you can visit his birth house—now a museum—two blocks away; described later, under "Sights in Toruń.") Either way, this statue is the town's top selfie spot—you'll see Polish families lining up to snap the perfect photo.

Copernicus faces a shiny **donkey** at the corner of Szeroka and Żeglarska streets. Notice the sharp ridge on the donkey's back, which recalls a humiliating punishment. Centuries ago, delinquents and petty criminals needing to be set straight would be forced to straddle this donkey—after townspeople had tied heavy stones to their feet, weighing them down painfully.

• But you're on vacation—and, rather than humiliation, you get gingerbread. Follow your nose to the right, down Żeglarska street, which is lined with...

Gingerbread Shops

For Poles, Toruń is synonymous with gingerbread (piernika)—you'll smell its heavenly scent all over town. When Chopin visited, most of his impressions of Toruń revolved around gingerbread. Today, this Toruń treat can be topped with different kinds of jams or glazes, and/or dipped in chocolate. But historically, gingerbread was more straightforward—and a valuable commodity. The honey used in its dough and for glazing acted as a preservative, allowing gingerbread to be traded far and wide. And its spices aid digestion, so it served a medicinal purpose as well. Thanks to Hanseatic League connections, Toruń's bakers had access to exotic, imported spices such as white ginger, cinnamon, clove, anise, citrus skins, cardamom, and peppercorns (for which piernika is named). Traditionally, gingerbread dough was pressed into wooden molds, giving each cookie a distinctive shape.

While you'll spot a half-dozen options for buying gingerbread within a few steps of here, I like the one marked **Tradycyjne Prawdziwe Pierniki** (on the right, at #25). This shop has a fun system: All the varieties cost the same, so you can assemble just the mix you like by pointing. Róża is rose, malina is raspberry, czarna porzeczka is black currant, morela is apricot, and—of course—czekolada is chocolate.

• A few steps down and across the street is the...

Cathedral of Two Saint Johns (Katedra Św. Jana Chrzciciela i Jana Ewangelisty)

Dedicated in the 12th century to both John the Baptist and John the Evangelist, this is the parish church of the Old Town. Its massive bulk dominates the view of Toruń from across the river. From street level, appreciate the architectural heaviness: The marshy land lacked big stones, so instead of flying buttresses, medieval engineers employed an overbuilt brick structure so they could go big.

If it's open, step into the interior, with graceful Gothic austerity—delicate ribs and whitewashed walls. The gravestones of

big shots pave the floor. Each trade guild had its own chapel, with its own fancy altar. On the wall to the left of the main altar, notice the finely restored 13th-century *Last Judgment* fresco. As you leave, head to the back-right corner (opposite where you came in) and find the colorful baptismal font where, in 1473, Copernicus was baptized (free entry, tower climb extra, irregular hours).

• *Having satisfied your ginger tooth and seen the town's most important church, head back to the square and that painful donkey, turn right, and join the human stream down the appropriately named...*

Ulica Szeroka ("Wide Street")

This intoxicating-in-good-weather pedestrian promenade leads through the heart of town. Embedded in the paving bricks are the

coats of arms of Toruń's medieval trading partners. On each side of the street is an eclectic commotion of fun facades and intriguing shops. Stow your guidebook for a few minutes and just stroll and window-shop. I'll meet you just before you get to a clock tower in the middle of the street.

About 30 yards before the road forks at the stately, white Empik building, look down narrow **Przedzamcze street** to the right to see fragments of the town wall. This marks the border between the Old Town and the New Town (chartered only about 30 years later—both in the 13th century). While these areas are collectively known today as the unified "Old Town," they were quite different in the Middle Ages—each with its own market square and separated by a wall. Because the New Town lacked the easy access to the river, most of its residents were craftspeople who supplied the traders in the Old Town.

At the start of Przedzamcze street, on the left, notice the small, fenced stretch of stream that runs underground through town. Next to the stream is another legendary monument: a **dragon.** As the plaque explains, back in 1746, locals swore in official

POMERANIA

records that they saw a real-life, six-foot-long dragon right about here.

• *Across Szeroka street from Przedzamcze, Strumykowa street leads to the better of Toruń's two gingerbread museums (described later).*

Let's take a quick spin through the New Town. Bear left at the clock tower to head up Królowej Jadwigi street. At the first street on the left, look for the green statue of the **gingerbread seller** *(piernikarka)—with lots of goodies in her basket.*

Another block straight ahead, you pop out at...

New Town Market Square (Rynek Nowomiejski)

This sleepy, inviting square is nearly as appealing as its Old Town counterpart. Its centerpiece is an angular and austere **Evangelical Church**—a reminder that this northern part of Poland, with its Prussian roots, isn't just for Catholics.

At the near end of the church, look for yet another fairy-tale statue—this time, one that may be more familiar: the **Goose That Laid the Golden Egg.**

Do a slow spin around the square, surveying options for a meal (either now or later—for recommendations, see "Eating in Toruń," later). In addition to a historic pub, the far corner of the square has a surprising concentration of Georgian restaurants, from the republic in the Caucasus. If you haven't tried this delicious cuisine before, now's a good chance. (For more on Georgian food, see page 30.)

• *When you're ready, we'll backtrack through town for our final stop—a look at the castle where Toruń began.*

Head out of the square the way you came, on Królowej Jadwigi, just two short blocks to the intersection at the clock tower. Bear right here, then turn left down Przedzamcze—passing the dragon and his stream that we saw earlier. We'll follow that (underground) stream down toward the river. When you reach the parking lot, bear left under the stubby, standalone brick gate. Emerging on the other side, you'll see an old mill straight ahead and a crenellated brick tower on your right. You're standing in the middle of what's left of...

Toruń Castle

This castle, built by the Teutonic Knights who were so influential in northern Poland in the Middle Ages (see page 317), was destroyed in the 15th century by the locals—who, aside from a heap of bricks, left only the tower that housed the Teutonic toilets. You can pay to enter the ruins nearby—basically just foundations—but there's little to see. However, what survives is one of the better toilet towers in Europe—which was connected to the castle by an elevated walkway and located far enough away to keep things hygienic. (Notice how it was positioned to drop into the dragon's stream—which you

POMERANIA

can see uncovered here again.) The old mill next to the toilet is now a recommended hotel and restaurant named 1231, for the date the Teutonic Order arrived here.

• *Our walk is over. You can backtrack the way you came and explore more of the city (including the sights listed next). Or you can take a quick riverside stroll: Go under the toilet tower and down to the Vistula River, turn right, and stroll along the castle and 14th-century city walls back to your starting point (and the bus stop back to the station). The road is called Bulwar Filadelfijski—for Toruń's sister city in Pennsylvania.*

Sights in Toruń

Toruń is more about strolling than it is about sightseeing—the town's museums are underwhelming. Aside from its half-dozen red-brick churches (any of which are worth dropping into), the following attractions are worth considering on a rainy day.

Hours: Almost all of these sights—everything except the second Gingerbread Museum—are operated by the city and have the same hours: Tue-Sun 10:00-18:00, Oct-April until 16:00, closed Mon year-round (www.muzeum.torun.pl).

City History Museums

Toruń operates two different history museums. Both show off intimate bits and pieces of history—from pewter tankards to old gingerbread molds—that show the richness of this traders' city. They're essentially redundant—pick one.

The **Old Town Hall District Museum,** inside the centerpiece building on the main square, has more impressive spaces—including Gothic corridors and royal meeting rooms upstairs. But the collection is dusty and challenging to appreciate. The highlight is the Gothic Gallery on the main floor—featuring medieval church art saved from the region's churches, with lots of Marys (the patron of the Teutonic Order), and a close-up look at some 14th-century stained glass. You can also pay to climb the 176 narrow wooden steps to the top of the **tower** for great views over the city center (36.50 zł combo-ticket covers museum and tower, 22.50 zł for one or the other, tower open until 20:00 in May-Sept).

A few blocks away, the **Museum of the History of Toruń** fills an old red-brick granary with four floors of well-explained artifacts, colorful exhibits, and English translations. While the space is less impressive, it's a more meaningful experience. Your ticket includes an informative, 13-minute 3-D movie (with English subtitles) about the town's history on the top floor (19.50 zł, Łazienna 16).

POMERANIA

Gingerbread Museums

Toruń has various gingerbread experiences (mainly oriented to Polish school groups and families) that enjoy teaching about this important local product. Buying and sampling gingerbread is the only "essential" Toruń experience, but these options round out your visit nicely. Unlike cookies, you should choose just one.

The **Museum of Toruń Gingerbread,** just off the main drag at the far end of town, is more of a traditional museum. It fills the historic red-brick Weese family gingerbread factory, established in 1885. (The company still makes gingerbread, in a modern plant on the outskirts.) After watching a brief film, you'll walk through three floors of quaint, modern exhibits that trace the history of gingerbread: artifacts (molds, ovens) in the cellar, a recreated late 19th-century street on the upper floor, and an interesting overview of the gingerbread-making process on the main floor. For a separate fee, they offer hands-on **gingerbread demonstrations**—predominantly in Polish, but if the guide speaks some English, they may add some extra commentary for you (36.50 zł combo-ticket includes museum and demo, 22.50 zł for one or the other, Strumykowa 4).

The **Gingerbread Museum** (Muzeum Piernika), between the main square and the river, is popular with kids and with anyone wanting an English demonstration rather than a traditional museum. Costumed medieval bakers spend about an hour walking you through the traditional process of rolling, cutting out, baking, and tasting your own batch of gingerbread cookies. After aging for 12 weeks to achieve the proper consistency, the dough bakes for only 12 minutes—or, according to medieval bakers, about 50 Hail Marys (34 zł, daily 10:00-18:00, Polish tours at the top of each hour, English tours about once daily—likely at 14:00 but confirm ahead, in peak times it's smart to reserve online in advance, Rabiańska 9, +48 56 663 6617, www.muzeumpiernika.pl).

Old Toruń Gingerbread (Piernikarnia Starotoruńska), a block above the main square, is similar to the Gingerbread Museum, with costumed bakers and a hands-on demonstration, but feels less crowded and less commercial. English demonstrations are sporadic; call or email ahead to see if one is scheduled (32 zł, daily 10:00-18:00, Franciszkańska 16, +48 56 621 1019, zwiedzajtorun@gmail.com).

Copernicus House (Dom Kopernika)

Filling a pair of gabled brick buildings between the main square and the river, this museum celebrates the hero of Toruń. As much about medieval Toruń as about the famous astronomer and sprawling over several floors, the exhibits loosely explain Nicolaus Copernicus' life and achievements, with several re-created Gothic rooms. However, it's not engaging and fails to do justice to this very important native son; ultimately, it's a big disappointment and skippable for casual visitors. If you do visit, I wouldn't bother paying the additional fee for the "4-D cinema"—while it provides a weighty introduction to astronomy and astrophysics, from the Big Bang to the plight of Pluto, it barely mentions Copernicus.

Cost and Hours: 22.50 zł, 4-D cinema-22.50 zł, Kopernika 15, +48 566 605 613.

Other Toruń Museums

Toruń is a popular destination for Polish families, and the TI loves to suggest attractions for those with more time. The **"Mill of Knowledge"** is a hands-on science museum designed for kids, with six floors of interactive exhibits. The **Travelers Museum** focuses on Toruń native Tony Halik, who hosted a travelogue TV show that was many Poles' gateway to the world. The **Toruń Fortress Museum,** just north of the Old Town, offers a glimpse inside the city's impressive red-brick fortifications. The city has two **open-air folk museums:** one just north of the Old Town, and a better one, called Olender, a few miles south of the river. And in the park ringing the Old Town, just a two-minute walk from the bus stop, is the **Fontanna Cosmopolis,** a dancing fountain that thrills kids with a little music-and-lights show each evening (generally runs May-Oct, get details at TI).

Sleeping in Toruń

$$ Hotel 1231 is trying to go high-class in this small town. It has 22 modern rooms filling a restored 13th-century mill at the bottom of town, next to the old toilet tower, with 20 additional sleek rooms in an annex. They also have a restaurant, bar, fitness center, sauna, "golf simulator," and other amenities—all run with a whiff of pretense (air-con, elevator, Przedzamcze 6, +48 56 619 0910, www.hotel1231.pl, recepcja@hotel1231.pl).

$ Hotel Czarna Róża ("Black Rose") feels fresh and modern, with 23 rooms on a back street. About half of the rooms are in the older building and cheaper, while the rest are pricier, as they have an elevator, air-con, and river views (Rabiańska 11, +48 56 19637, https://hotelczarnaroza.pl, hotel@hotelczarnaroza.pl).

$ Solaris Hotel, beautifully located just steps off the main square, has 23 conventional, cozy rooms tucked into a historic town house. It's quirky but central and friendly (air-con, elevator, Panny Marii 9, +48 56 471 3042, https://hotelsolaris.pl, recepcja@ hotelsolaris.pl).

$ Hotel Karczma Spichrz ("Granary") has 24 rooms in a renovated old granary, and 20 more in a newer annex. Rustic and creaky, it has huge wooden beams around every corner (low ceilings, thin floors and walls can be noisy, air-con, elevator, a block off the main drag toward the river at Ulica Mostowa 1, +48 56 657 1140, www.spichrz.pl, hotel@spichrz.pl).

Eating in Toruń

Toruń is a great place to eat, with lots of tempting options—including several non-Polish, international choices. In this gingerbread-crazy town, look for various drinks, dishes, and desserts with that distinctive flavor (including gingerbread beer).

Old Town Market Square: The square surrounding the Old Town Hall is ringed with stay-awhile al fresco tables, any of which is a good choice for a scenic meal; most are open long hours daily. Favorites include **$$ Chleb i Wino** ("Bread and Wine"), which feels a bit more upscale, with Polish and Mediterranean dishes; and **$ Maneken,** the original outpost of a popular chain, which serves savory crêpe dishes in a convivial, trendy-feeling interior.

New Town Market Square: This out-of-the-way square is especially sleepy at night. There are some great choices here, including three Georgian restaurants. The **$ Georgian bakery** at #26 is handy for picking up a quick and tasty meal. Of the sit-down places, **$ Serce Gruzji** is charming, tasty, and family run (closed Mon, at #1, +48 787 383 665). A few steps away, **$$ Pod Modrym Fartuchem** ("Blue Apron Inn") fills a charming gabled house with cozy tables, ye olde ambience, and traditional food—continuing a legacy that dates back to 1489 (daily, at #8, +48 533 331 985).

Cajun: Luizjana, named for the US state, serves Cajun cooking that's better than it has any right to be, and offers a nice break from traditional Polish fare. They have two locations (both open daily for lunch and dinner); I'd opt for the one that fills the (covered) courtyard of the Artus Court, facing the Old Town Hall. This beautiful space is a lovely spot for a meal, and the New Orleans soundtrack is lively...even if it feels a bit out of place (Ulica Rynek Staromiejski 6, +48 883 117 711). The other location is on a more humdrum side street, with indoor and outdoor tables (Mostowa 10, http://restauracjaluizjana.pl).

Brewery: $ Jan Olbracht, filling a characteristic old brick building a short walk off the main drag, is a glitzy microbrewery with five beers on tap (you can order a sampler) plus pub grub (daily, Szczytna 15, +48 797 903 333, www.browar-olbracht.pl). Roughly across the street is a classic milk bar, Pod Małgośka.

Traditional Restaurants in Hotels: The recommended **$$ Spichrz** and **$$$ 1231** hotels both have traditional restaurants in historic spaces, with tempting menus of stick-to-your-ribs traditional fare. Spichrz is a bit ye olde and more casual; 1231 feels more upscale (see contact information earlier).

Hearty Pierogi: Pierogarnia Stary Młyn ("Old Mill"), on a side street near the history museum, has an over-the-top-rustic interior (and some outdoor tables) and a long menu of pierogi—boiled, baked, pan-fried—with various fillings (daily, Łazienna 28, +48 566 210 309). This is a small chain, with a few other locations as well.

Toruń Connections

Toruń is a natural stopover on the way between Warsaw and Gdańsk. The connection to Warsaw or Gdańsk is quick and easy; to reach Malbork, you'll usually need to change.

From Toruń by Train to: Warsaw (every 2 hours direct, 3 hours on express IC train), **Gdańsk** (4/day direct, 2.5 hours; additional options with a change in Bydgoszcz or Iława, 3 hours), **Malbork** (about every 2 hours, 2.5 hours, change in Iława), **Kraków** (1/day direct, 6.5 hours; more options with a change in Warsaw: 7/day, 6 hours), **Berlin** (4/day, 6 hours, change in Poznań).

By Bus: If heading to **Gdańsk,** consider buses operated by Flixbus, which are cheaper than the train (www.flixbus.com).

POMERANIA

PRACTICALITIES

This section covers just the basics on traveling in Poland (for much more information, see *Rick Steves Central Europe*). You'll find free advice on specific topics at RickSteves.com/tips.

MONEY

Poland uses a currency called the złoty: 4 Polish złoty (zł) = about $1. To roughly convert Polish złoty into dollars, divide by four (40 zł = about $10, 100 zł = about $25, 200 zł = about $50). Check Oanda.com for the latest exchange rates.

To get cash, use a debit card to withdraw złoty from an ATM (known as a *bankomat* in Poland). When possible, use a bank-run ATM located just outside that bank.

Before departing, call your bank or credit-card company: Confirm that your card(s) will work overseas, ask about international transaction fees, and alert them that you'll be making withdrawals in Europe. Also ask for the PIN number for your credit card—it may be required for some purchases. (Allow time for your bank to mail your PIN to you.)

Contactless pay options are now standard in much of Europe. Check to see if you already have—or can get—a tap-to-pay version of your credit card (look on the card for the tap-to-pay symbol—four curvy lines) and consider setting up your smartphone for contactless payment. Both options are more secure than a physical credit card: Instead of recording your credit-card number, a one-time encrypted "token" enables the purchase and expires shortly afterward.

US credit cards may not work at some self-service payment machines (transit-ticket kiosks, parking kiosks, etc.). If your card won't work, look for a cashier who can process the transaction manually—or pay in cash.

Pickpockets target tourists, so keep your backup cash, credit cards, and passport secure in your money belt, and carry only a day's spending money and one card in your front pocket or wallet.

Always Choose to Pay in the Local Currency: When making a credit card transaction, the payment terminal will often ask whether you want to pay in US dollars or in the local currency. Always refuse the conversion and choose the local currency. While this "service"—called Dynamic Currency Conversion (DCC)—offers the illusion of convenience, it comes with a poor exchange rate and/or higher fees, and you'll wind up losing money.

STAYING CONNECTED

The simplest solution is to bring your own device—mobile phone, tablet, or laptop—and use it just as you would at home (following the money-saving tips below). For more on phoning, see RickSteves.com/phoning. For a one-hour talk covering tech issues for travelers, see RickSteves.com/mobile-travel-skills.

To Call from a US Phone: Phone numbers in this book are presented exactly as you would dial them from a US mobile phone. For international access, press and hold the 0 key until you get a + sign, then dial the country code (48 for Poland) and phone number. To dial from a US landline, replace + with 011 (US/Canada international access code).

From a European Landline: Replace + with 00 (Europe international access code), then dial the country code (48 for Poland) and phone number.

Within Poland: To place a domestic call (from a Polish landline or mobile), drop the +48 and dial the phone number.

Tips: If you bring your own mobile phone, consider signing up for an international plan; most providers offer a simple bundle that includes calling, messaging, and data.

Use Wi-Fi whenever possible. Most hotels and many cafés offer free Wi-Fi, and you may also find it at tourist information offices (TIs), major museums, public-transit hubs, and aboard trains and buses. With Wi-Fi you can use your device to make free or low-cost calls via a calling app such as Skype, WhatsApp, FaceTime, or Google Hangouts. When you need to get online but can't find Wi-Fi, turn on your cellular network (or turn off airplane mode) just long enough for the task at hand.

Most **hotels** charge a fee for placing calls from a room phone—ask for rates before you dial. You can use a prepaid international phone card (usually available at newsstands, tobacco shops, and train stations) to call out from your hotel.

Sleep Code

Hotels in this book are categorized according to the average price of a standard double room with breakfast in high season. 4 zł = about $1.

$$$$	**Splurge:**	Most rooms over 900 zł (€200)
$$$	**Pricier:**	700-900 zł (€150-200)
$$	**Moderate:**	500-700 zł (€100-150)
$	**Budget:**	250-500 zł (€50-100)
¢	**Backpacker:**	Under 250 zł (€50)
RS%	**Rick Steves discount**	

Unless otherwise noted, credit cards are accepted and hotel staff speak basic English. Comparison-shop by checking prices at several hotels (on each hotel's own website, on a booking site, or by email). For the best deal, *book directly with the hotel.* Ask for a discount if paying in cash; if the listing includes **RS%,** request a Rick Steves discount.

SLEEPING

I've categorized my recommended accommodations based on price, indicated with a dollar-sign rating (see sidebar). In Poland, you can choose from a variety of stylish and charming hotels and guesthouses. Many hotels fall in this book's lower price ranges (**$** and **$$**). This is a reflection not of quality but of the value of Poland compared to other destinations in Central Europe. Don't be put off by seemingly low prices: Even elegant choices don't break the bank here.

Book your accommodations as soon as your itinerary is set, especially if you want to stay at one of my top listings or if you'll be traveling during busy times. You can do this by checking hotel websites and booking sites such as Hotels.com or Booking.com.

After you've zeroed in on your choice, book directly with the hotel itself. This increases the chances that the hotelier will be able to accommodate special needs or requests (such as shifting your reservation). And when you book by phone or email, the owner avoids the commission paid to booking sites, giving them wiggle room to offer you a discount, a nicer room, or a free breakfast (if it's not already included).

For complicated requests, send an email with the following information: number and type of rooms; number of nights; arrival date; departure date; any special requests; and applicable discounts (such as a Rick Steves discount, cash discount, or promotional rate). Use the European style for writing dates: day/month/year.

Room prices can fluctuate significantly with demand and amenities (size, views, and so on), but relative price categories remain constant. City taxes, which can vary from place to place, are usually insignificant (a few dollars per person, per night). In

Restaurant Code

Eateries in this book are categorized according to the average cost of a typical main course. Drinks, desserts, and splurge items (steak and seafood) can raise the price considerably. 4 zł = about $1.

$$$$	**Splurge:** Most main courses over 90 zł (€20)
$$$	**Pricier:** 70-90 zł (€15-20)
$$	**Moderate:** 50-70 zł (€10-15)
$	**Budget:** Under 50 zł (€10)

In Poland, a milk bar or takeout spot is **$;** a basic sit-down eatery is **$$;** a casual but more upscale restaurant is **$$$;** and a swanky splurge is **$$$$.**

general, hotel prices can soften if you do any of the following: offer to pay cash, stay at least three nights, or travel off-season.

Websites such as Airbnb, FlipKey, Booking.com, and VRBO let you browse a wide range of properties. Alternatively, rental agencies such as Interhomeusa.com and Rentavilla.com can provide a more personalized service (their curated listings are also more expensive).

EATING

I've categorized my recommended eateries based on the average price of a typical main course, indicated with a dollar-sign rating (see sidebar). Poland offers good food for relatively little money. Polish cuisine has a reputation for being heavy and hearty, with lots of pork, potatoes, and cabbage...which is true. But the food here is also delicious, with more variety than you might expect. For all the details about Polish food, see page 27. International restaurants provide a welcome change of pace and are especially good in big cities such as Kraków and Warsaw. Seek out Italian, Indian, sushi, Mediterranean, and other alternatives (I've recommended several in this book).

Tipping: To pay, ask for the *rachunek* (rah-KHOO-nehk). Tip only at restaurants that have table service. If you order your food at a counter, don't tip. At restaurants that have a waitstaff, round up the bill 5-10 percent after a good meal. My rule of thumb is to estimate about 10 percent, then round slightly to reach a convenient total (for a 73 zł meal I pay 80 zł, just under 10 percent).

TRANSPORTATION

Public transportation is the best way to connect the cities in this book.

By Train: Poland has an extensive rail network; you can reach most towns and cities by train. Since point-to-point tickets are affordable, a rail pass won't likely save you money (but to review your options, visit RickSteves.com/rail). To research train schedules and

PRACTICALITIES

fares, visit the Polish rail site, Intercity.pl, or Germany's all-Europe timetable, Bahn.com. While most short-haul journeys don't require a seat reservation, you must reserve for some high-speed trains (such as the Warsaw-Kraków express). Schedules will indicate when a seat assignment is required on EuroCity or InterCity long-distance trains. It's also smart to reserve a sleeping berth if you're taking a night train. For more tips, see "Train Station Lingo" on page 14.

By Bus: The dominant outfit in Poland is the German-owned Flixbus (www.flixbus.com), which offers easy online booking and generally comfortable buses with air-conditioning and Wi-Fi. Other companies seem to come and go regularly, so search online to find the latest options (GetByBus.com is a good place to start).

By Car: It's cheaper to arrange most car rentals from the US. If you're planning a multicountry itinerary by car, be aware of often-astronomical international drop-off fees. For tips on your insurance options, see RickSteves.com/cdw. Bring your driver's license. You're also required to carry an International Driving Permit (IDP), available at your local AAA office ($20 plus two passport-type photos, www.aaa.com).

For route planning, the mapping app on your phone works fine for navigating Poland's roads. To save on data, most apps allow you to download maps for offline use (do this before you need them, when you have a strong Wi-Fi signal). Some apps—including Google Maps—provide offline route directions, but you'll need data access for current traffic.

Poland is building a network of new expressways, but they're not yet complete (you'll pay tolls to take completed segments—take a toll ticket as you enter the expressway, then pay when you get off, based on how far you've traveled). Locals travel long distances on two-lane country roads. Since each lane is about a lane and a half wide, passing is commonplace. Slower drivers should keep to the far-right of their lane, and not be surprised when faster cars zip past them. A car is an expensive headache in cities—park it safely (get tips from your hotel).

You're required to have your headlights on whenever you're driving (even in broad daylight), seat belts are mandatory, and hand-held mobile-phone use is forbidden. You're not allowed to turn right on a red light, unless a sign or signal specifically authorizes it, and on expressways it's illegal to pass drivers on the right. Ask your car-rental company about these rules, or check the "International Travel" section at Travel.State.gov (enter a country in the "Learn About Your Destination" box, then select "Travel and Transportation").

By Plane: Consider covering long distances on a budget flight, which can be cheaper (and much faster) than a train. Poland's national carrier, LOT Airlines (www.lot.com), generally charges reasonable fares for short-distance trips. Or try some no-frills carriers, such as Wizzair.com, Smartwings.com, EasyJet.com, and Ryanair.com. To compare several budget airlines, see Skyscanner.com.

HELPFUL HINTS

Book Ahead: You definitely want to book well in advance for Auschwitz-Birkenau and the Oskar Schindler Factory Museum in Kraków.

Travel Advisories: Before traveling, check updated health and safety conditions, including restrictions for your destination, at Travel.State.gov (US State Department travel pages) and CDC.gov (Centers for Disease Control and Prevention). The US embassy website for Poland is another good source of information (see below). While most countries no longer require proof of Covid-19 vaccination for entry, some sights or tours may still have vaccination requirements (check websites). Even if it's not required for your itinerary, it's smart to pack a copy of your vaccine record and/or store a photo of your Covid-19 vaccine card on your phone.

Emergency and Medical Help: For any emergency service—**ambulance, police,** or **fire**—call **112** (operators typically speak English). If you get sick, do as the locals do and go to a pharmacist for advice. Or ask at your hotel for help—they'll know the nearest medical and emergency services.

For **passport problems,** contact the **US Embassy** in Warsaw (+48 22 504 2000, Pl.USEmbassy.gov) or the **US Consulate** in Kraków (+48 12 424 5100, Pl.USEmbassy.gov/embassy-consulate/krakow); or the **Canadian Embassy** in Warsaw (+48 22 584 3100; Poland.gc.ca).

ETIAS Registration: You may need to register with the European Travel Information and Authorization System (ETIAS) before you travel (quick and easy process, check https://travel-europe.europa.eu/etias_en).

Theft or Loss: To replace a passport, you'll need to go in person to an embassy (see above). Cancel and replace your credit and debit cards by calling these 24-hour US numbers with a mobile phone: Visa (+1 303 967 1096), Mastercard (+1 636 722 7111), and American Express (+1 336 393 1111).

File a police report either on the spot or within a day or two; you'll need it to submit an insurance claim for lost or stolen items, and it can help with replacing your passport or credit and debit cards. For more information, see RickSteves.com/help.

Time: Poland uses the 24-hour clock. It's the same through 12:00 noon, then keep going: 13:00, 14:00, and so on. Poland, like most of continental Europe, is six/nine hours ahead of the East/West Coasts of the US.

Sightseeing: Many museums are closed or have reduced hours at least a few days a year; confirm the latest times with the

local TI or its website. To find your way around, the best naviga-
tion tool is on your phone. **Google Maps** (and similar apps) offer
turn-by-turn directions for walking and driving, as well as detailed
public transit instructions in most big cities.

Holidays and Festivals: Poland celebrates many holidays,
which can close sights and attract crowds (book hotel rooms
ahead). For more on holidays and festivals, check Poland's website:
www.poland.travel. For a simple list showing major—though not
all—events, see RickSteves.com/festivals.

Numbers and Stumblers: What Americans call the second
floor of a building is the first floor in Europe. Europeans write dates
as day/month, so Christmas is 25/12. Commas are decimal points
and vice versa—a dollar and a half is 1,50, and there are 5.280 feet in
a mile. Poland uses the metric system: A kilogram is 2.2 pounds; a
liter is about a quart; and a kilometer is six-tenths of a mile.

RESOURCES FROM RICK STEVES

This Snapshot guide, excerpted from the latest edition of *Rick
Steves Central Europe,* is one of many titles in my series of guidebooks on European travel. I also produce a public television series,
Rick Steves' Europe, and a public radio show, *Travel with Rick Steves.*
My free online video library, Rick Steves Classroom Europe, offers
a searchable database of short video clips on European history,
culture, and geography (Classroom.RickSteves.com). My website,
RickSteves.com, offers free travel information, a forum for travelers' comments, guidebook updates, my travel blog, an online travel
store, and information on European rail passes and our tours of
Europe. If you're bringing a mobile device, you can download my
free Rick Steves Audio Europe app that features dozens of self-
guided audio tours of the top sights in Europe and travel interviews
about Poland. For more information, see RickSteves.com/audioeu-
rope. You can also follow me on Facebook, Twitter, and Instagram.

ADDITIONAL RESOURCES

Tourist Information: Poland.travel
Passports and Red Tape: Travel.State.gov
Packing List: RickSteves.com/packing
Travel Insurance: RickSteves.com/insurance
Cheap Flights: Google Flights and Skyscanner
Airplane Carry-on Restrictions: TSA.gov
Updates for This Book: RickSteves.com/update

HOW WAS YOUR TRIP?

To share your tips, concerns, and discoveries after using this book,
please fill out the survey at RickSteves.com/feedback. Thanks in
advance—it helps a lot.

INDEX

Explore Europe

At ricksteves.com you can browse through thousands of articles, videos, photos and radio interviews, plus find a wealth of money-saving travel tips for planning your dream trip. And with our mobile-friendly website, you can easily access all this great travel information anywhere you go.

TV Shows

Preview the places you'll visit by watching entire half-hour episodes of *Rick Steves' Europe* (choose from all 100 shows) on-demand, for free.

ricksteves.com

your travel dreams into affordable reality

Radio Interviews

Enjoy ready access to Rick's vast library of radio interviews covering travel tips and cultural insights that relate specifically to your Europe travel plans.

Travel Forums

Learn, ask, share! Our online community of savvy travelers is a great resource for first-time travelers to Europe, as well as seasoned pros.

Travel News

Subscribe to our free Travel News e-newsletter, and get monthly updates from Rick on what's happening in Europe.

Classroom Europe®

Check out our free resource for educators with 500 short video clips from the *Rick Steves' Europe* TV show.

Audio Europe™

Rick's Free Travel App

Get your FREE **Rick Steves Audio Europe**™ app to enjoy...

- Dozens of self-guided tours of Europe's top museums, sights and historic walks
- Hundreds of tracks filled with cultural insights and sightseeing tips from Rick's radio interviews
- All organized into handy geographic playlists
- For Apple and Android

With Rick whispering in your ear, Europe gets even better.

Find out more at ricksteves.com

Pack Light and Right

Gear up for your next adventure at ricksteves.com

Light Luggage

Pack light and right with Rick Steves' affordable, custom-designed rolling carry-on bags, backpacks, day packs and shoulder bags.

Accessories

From packing cubes to moneybelts and beyond, Rick has personally selected the travel goodies that will help your trip go smoother.

Shop at ricksteves.com

Rick Steves has

Save time and energy

This guidebook is your independent-travel toolkit. But for all it delivers, it's still up to you to devote the time and energy it takes to manage the preparation and logistics that are essential for a happy trip. If that's a hassle, there's a solution.

Rick Steves Tours

A Rick Steves tour takes you to Europe's most interesting places with great

great tours, too!

with minimum stress

guides and small groups. We follow Rick's favorite itineraries, ride in comfy buses, stay in family-run hotels, and bring you intimately close to the Europe you've traveled so far to see. Most importantly, we take away the logistical headaches so you can focus on the fun.

Join the fun

This year we'll take thousands of free-spirited travelers—nearly half of them repeat customers—along with us on 50 different itineraries, from Athens to Istanbul. Is a Rick Steves tour the right fit for your travel dreams?

Find out at ricksteves.com, where you can also check seat availability and sign up. Europe is best experienced with happy travel partners. We hope you can join us.

A Guide for Every Trip

BEST OF GUIDES

Full-color guides in an easy-to-scan format. Focused on top sights and experiences in the most popular European destinations

Best of England
Best of Europe
Best of France
Best of Germany
Best of Ireland
Best of Italy
Best of Scotland
Best of Spain

COMPREHENSIVE GUIDES

City, country, and regional guides printed on Bible-thin paper. Packed with detailed coverage for a multi-week trip exploring iconic sights and venturing off the beaten path

Amsterdam & the Netherlands
Barcelona
Belgium: Bruges, Brussels, Antwerp & Ghent
Berlin
Budapest
Central Europe
Croatia & Slovenia
England
Florence & Tuscany
France
Germany
Great Britain
Greece: Athens & the Peloponnese
Iceland
Ireland
Istanbul
Italy
London
Paris
Portugal
Prague & the Czech Republic
Provence & the French Riviera
Rome
Scandinavia
Scotland
Sicily
Spain
Switzerland
Venice
Vienna, Salzburg & Tirol

HE BEST OF ROME

e, Italy's capital, is studded with
an remnants and floodlit-fountain
es. From the Vatican to the Colos-
with crazy traffic in between, Rome
derful, huge, and exhausting. The
, the heat, and the weighty history

of the Eternal City where Caesars walked
can make tourists wilt. Recharge by taking siestas, gelato breaks, and after-dark
walks, strolling from one atmospheric
square to another in the refreshing evening air.

Pantheon—which
dome until the
2,000 years old
over 1,500).
Athens in the Vat-
es the humanistic

diators fought
other, entertaining
Rome ristorante.

Rick Steves books are available from your favorite bookseller.
Many guides are available as ebooks.

POCKET GUIDES
Compact color guides for shorter trips

Amsterdam
Athens
Barcelona
Florence
Italy's Cinque Terre
London
Munich & Salzburg

Paris
Prague
Rome
Venice
Vienna

SNAPSHOT GUIDES
Focused single-destination coverage

Basque Country: Spain & France
Copenhagen & the Best of Denmark
Dublin
Dubrovnik
Edinburgh
Hill Towns of Central Italy
Krakow, Warsaw & Gdansk
Lisbon
Loire Valley
Madrid & Toledo
Milan & the Italian Lakes District
Naples & the Amalfi Coast
Nice & the French Riviera
Normandy
Northern Ireland
Norway
Reykjavík
Rothenburg & the Rhine
Sevilla, Granada & Southern Spain
St. Petersburg, Helsinki & Tallinn
Stockholm

CRUISE PORTS GUIDES
Reference for cruise ports of call

Mediterranean Cruise Ports
Scandinavian & Northern European
  Cruise Ports

Complete your library with...

TRAVEL SKILLS & CULTURE
Study up on travel skills and gain insight on history and culture

Europe 101
Europe Through the Back Door
Europe's Top 100 Masterpieces
European Christmas
European Easter
European Festivals
For the Love of Europe
Italy for Food Lovers
Travel as a Political Act

PHRASE BOOKS & DICTIONARIES
French
French, Italian & German
German
Italian
Portuguese
Spanish

PLANNING MAPS
Britain, Ireland & London
Europe
France & Paris
Germany, Austria & Switzerland
Iceland
Ireland
Italy
Scotland
Spain & Portugal

Photo Credits

Avalon Travel
Hachette Book Group
1700 Fourth Street
Berkeley, CA 94710

Text © 2024 by Rick Steves' Europe, Inc. All rights reserved.
Maps © 2024 by Rick Steves' Europe, Inc. All rights reserved.
Portions of this book originally appeared in *Rick Steves Central Europe*, 11th Edition.

Printed in Canada by Friesens.
Seventh Edition. First printing February 2024.

ISBN 978-1-64171-565-2

For the latest on Rick's talks, guidebooks, tours, public television series, and public
radio show, contact Rick Steves' Europe, 130 Fourth Avenue North, Edmonds, WA
98020, +1 425 771 8303, RickSteves.com, rick@ricksteves.com.

Rick Steves' Europe
Managing Editor: Jennifer Madison Davis
Editorial Group Manager: Cathy Lu
Editors: Glenn Eriksen, Julie Fanselow, Suzanne Kotz, Rosie Leutzinger, Matthew
Lombardi, Teresa Nemeth, Jessica Shaw, Carrie Shepherd, Chelsea Wing
Creative Director: Sandra Hundacker
Maps & Graphics: Orin Dubrow, David C. Hoerlein, Lauren Mills, Mary Rostad

Avalon Travel
Senior Editor & Series Manager: Madhu Prasher
Associate Managing Editors: Jamie Andrade, Sierra Machado
Copy Editor: Maggie Ryan
Proofreaders: Elizabeth Jang, Patrick Collins
Indexer: Stephen Callahan
Production: Christine DeLorenzo, Rue Flaherty, Jane Musser, Lisi Baldwin,
Ravina Schneider
Cover Design: Kimberly Glyder Design
Maps & Graphics: Kat Bennett

Let's Keep on Travelin'

Your trip doesn't need to end.

Follow Rick on social media!